street art
SANTIAGO
CHILE

street art
SANT

Lord K2

IAGO CHILE

Schiffer Publishing Ltd
4880 Lower Valley Road • Atglen, PA 19310

Other Schiffer Books on Related Subjects:

100 European Graffiti Artists, Frank "Steam 156" Malt, 978-0-7643-4658-3

Graffiti South Africa, Cale Waddacor, 978-0-7643-4657-6

Street Talking: International Graffiti Art, Mike Popso, 978-0-7643-4199-1

Library of Congress Control Number: 2015933026

Type set in Rockwell Rusted/Rockwell

ISBN: 978-0-7643-4927-0

Printed in China

Published by Schiffer Publishing, Ltd.
4880 Lower Valley Road
Atglen, PA 19310
Phone: (610) 593-1777; Fax: (610) 593-2002
E-mail: Info@schifferbooks.com

For our complete selection of fine books on this and related subjects, please visit our website at www.schifferbooks.com. You may also write for a free catalog.

This book may be purchased from the publisher. Please try your bookstore first.

We are always looking for people to write books on new and related subjects. If you have an idea for a book, please contact us at proposals@schifferbooks.com.

Schiffer Publishing's titles are available at special discounts for bulk purchases for sales promotions or premiums. Special editions, including personalized covers, corporate imprints, and excerpts can be created in large quantities for special needs. For more information, contact the publisher.

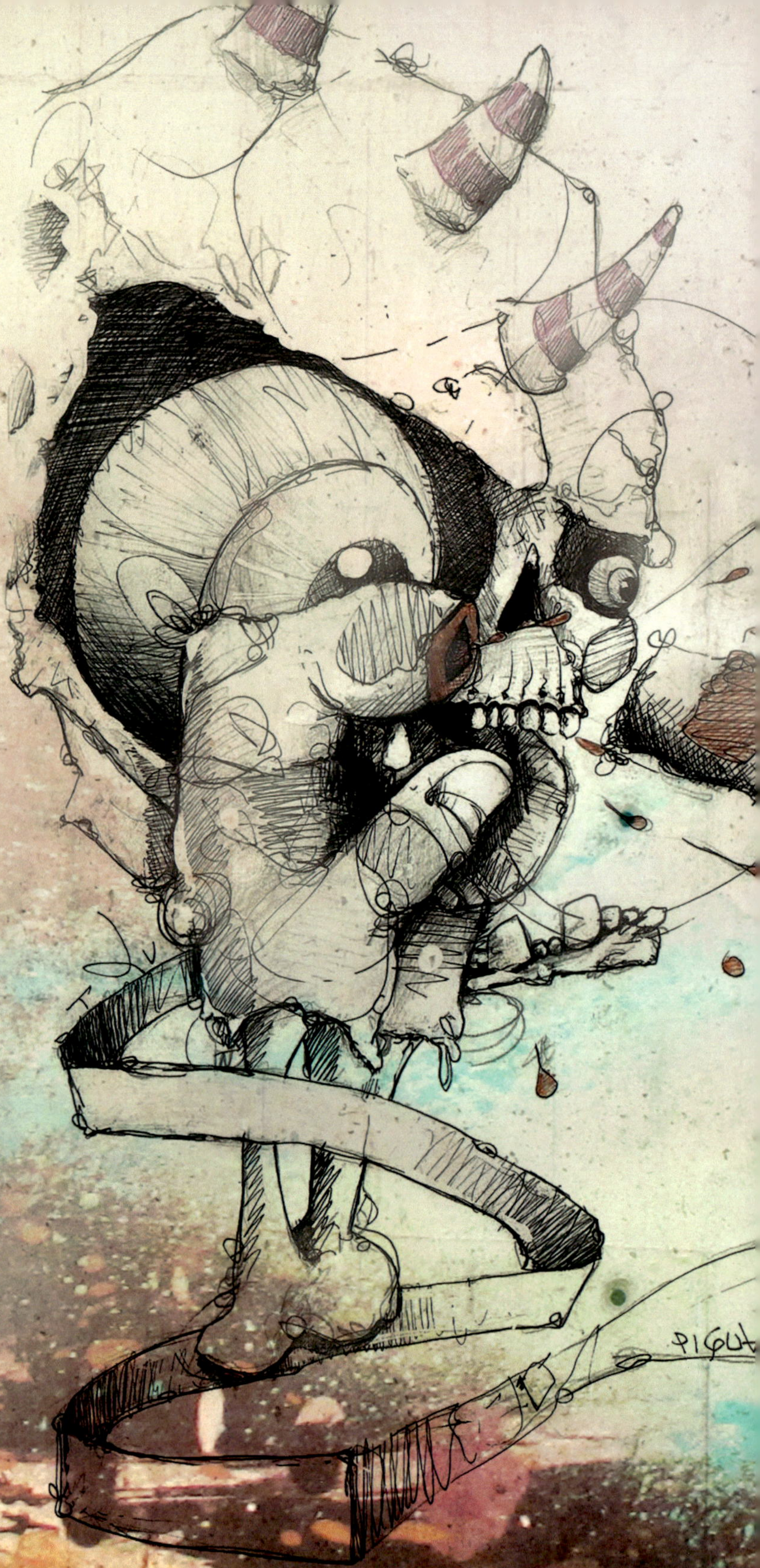

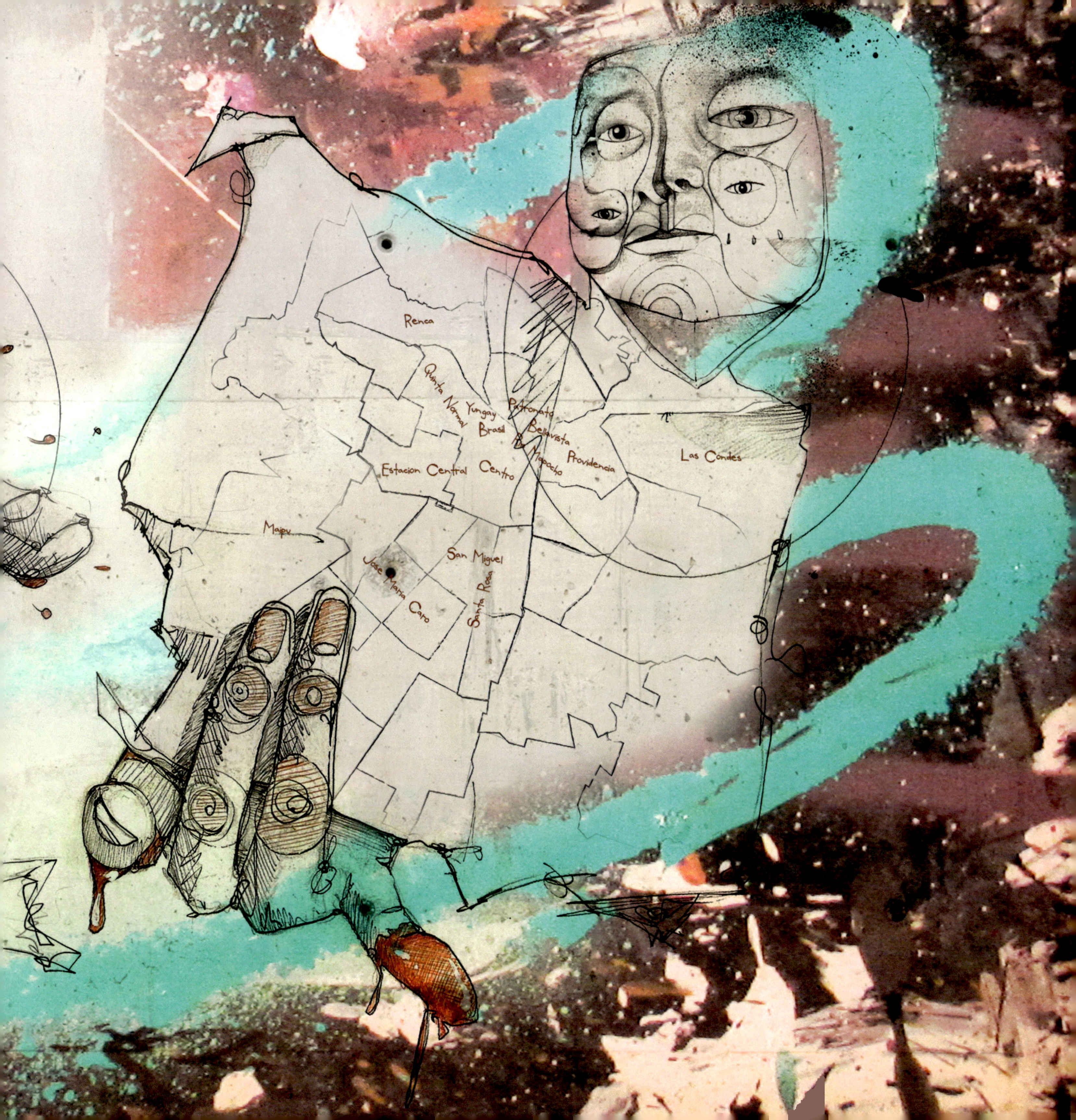
Renca
Quinta Normal
Yungay
Patronato
Brasil
Bellavista
Mapocho
Providencia
Las Condes
Estacion Central
Centro
Maipu
San Miguel
Jose Maria Caro
Santa Rosa

I set off, armed with backpack, some rudimentary street Spanish, and a camera. My passion for urban art—both my own and others'—had finally compelled me to explore and document stencil graffiti in Latin America.

Having lived and studied stencil graffiti in Buenos Aires, Argentina, I knew that city's thriving art scene first-hand. I also knew the art scenes in Brazil's Rio de Janeiro and São Paulo, as well as in Bogotá, Colombia—but nothing had prepared me for the progressive, vibrant street art of Santiago, Chile.

Tucked away in the Andes, the Chilean capital seems cut off from the rest of the world. I had expected it would be a short stay. But when I first walked the streets, I found a treasure trove of graffiti. I'd anticipated seeing stencil art, but was surprised to find plenty of free-hand graffiti. A lot of it was high-quality work. After a couple of days exploring, I met old skool graffiti artist Nebs Pereira, who's well acquainted with most of the graffiti artists in Chile. He gave me a long list of telephone numbers, but I quickly learned that with Santiago's street artists, numbers and introductions are hardly necessary. All I had to do was walk around.

I stumbled across new artists, one after the other. Their warm welcomes were often followed by invitations to stay and watch them paint. Most of these artists took the challenges of the work in stride, viewing my cameras only as an appendage of me. In no time I found myself falling into the clutches of this seductive underground scene.

As I discovered more and more unique works, I began to see the contours of a book. I envisioned a volume showcasing the art painted on this urban landscape, but I also wanted to give the artists a voice within the text.

Again and again I was struck by their eloquence when talking about their own works and their whole street art scene. Running through these commentaries was a common theme: this art wasn't just underground; it was almost totally hidden from the rest of the world. Though so much quality work was going on here, the media didn't pay much attention. That was when I set out with artists Piguan and Zaines, recording conversations with a wide range of graffiti practitioners. Through lots of interviews we gathered opinions, philosophies, narratives, and experiences. The result is more than a hundred pages of juicy information and ideas. We could've included a lot more, and condensing was a challenge, but ultimately our editing produced what we saw as the best of so many great voices. These artists' voices add context and depth to the art we've displayed here.

Rather than concentrating on just a few artists, I experienced the whole of Santiago's street art scene. This book passes through neighborhood by neighborhood, as I did. On this trip I learned how Santiago's graffiti transcends localities. Though most of these artists work in their own neighborhoods, their art connects, spreading across Santiago.

Once the book's content took shape, we faced the challenge of how to put it all together. Graphic designer Jorge Cordoba and I discussed our options. I wanted something innovative, a work that would set new standards for anything that followed. So we've gone beyond the wall, giving you this street culture's flavor by fusing the images and ideas of Santiago's street artists, combining sketchbooks, art, urban landscapes, and text. What stands out is the spirit of communion and the high standard of talent. Santiago's street artists share walls, ideas, arguments, and common ground as they paint, drink, and have barbecues. These people have fun!

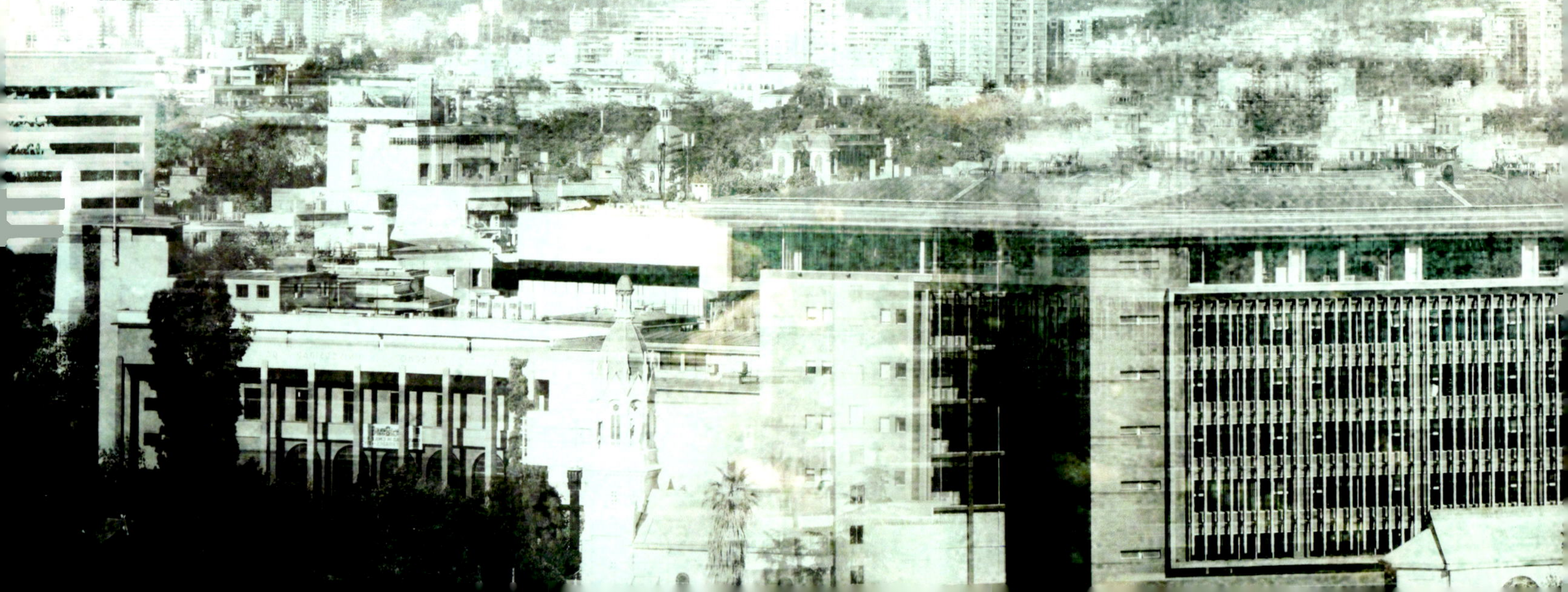

I will emphasize that none of the opinions expressed in the book are my own. All the text is raw and directly from the horses' mouths.

I wish this book to be a celebration of all that makes Santiago's unique street art scene.

"¡Al centro, adentro !" **LORD K2**

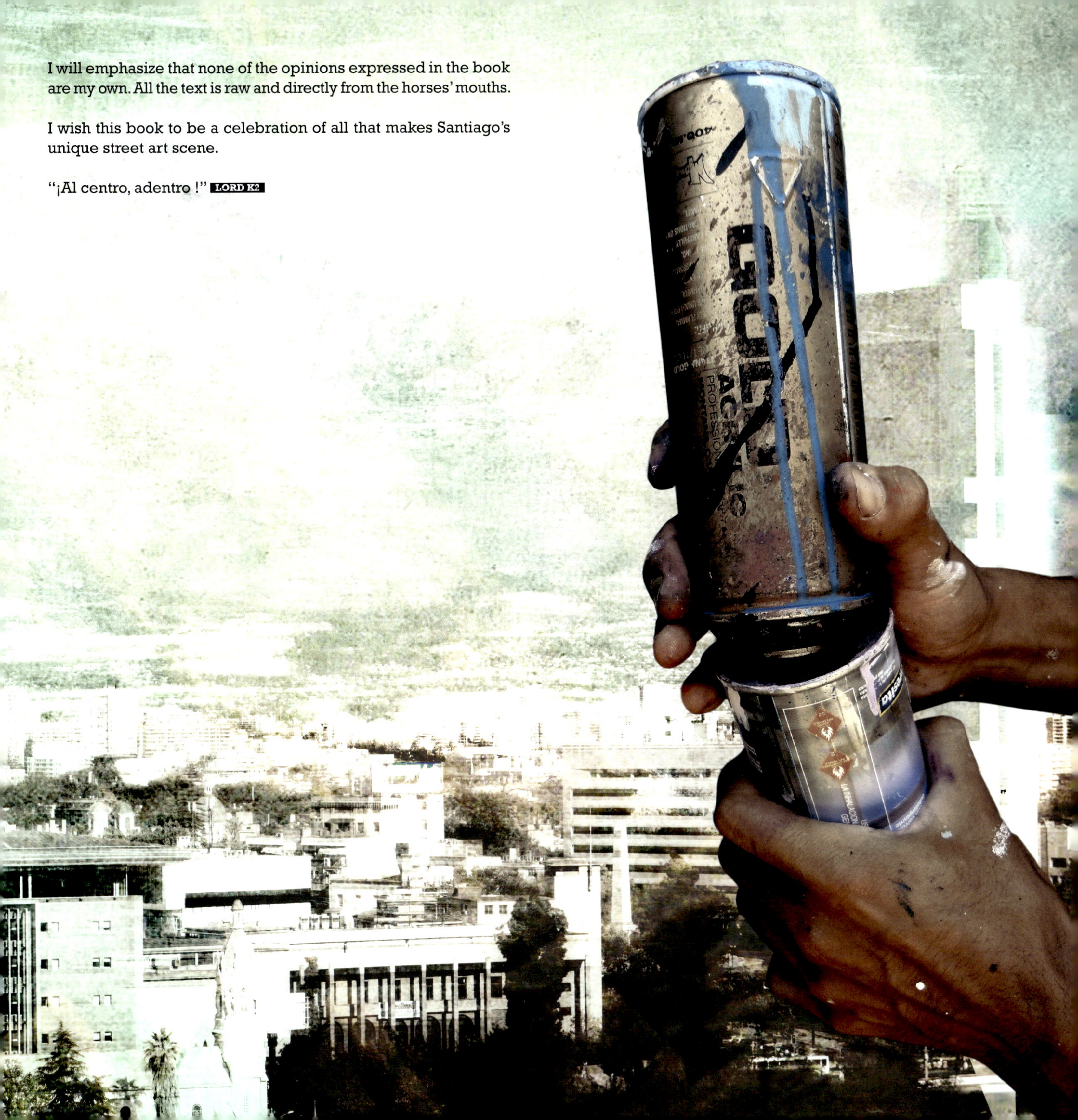

The Scene

What do we think of when we hear about graffiti or street art? Perhaps that street art has become one of the creative expressions with the most impact at a global level. It's even possible to say that it has become, among the youth of major cities, a global culture that transcends differences in location. While the styles, techniques, meanings, and motivations of graffiti artists are infinite, there is something that unites them: the systematic condition of being and working on the streets in front of a wall. There are some who do it illegally, in search of the adrenaline rush that comes from hiding from authorities. There are those who ask for permission, and others who seek to protest and denounce injustices. Some artists experiment and play with paints. Some paint in groups, while others paint alone. Paintings are sometimes based on a sketch, while sometimes they're improvised. However, all the artists share a common thread: being outside, feeling the pulse of the city, seeing people's faces, smelling paint, covering surfaces, and looking for walls. As commuters pass by hurriedly on their way to work or home, painters are right there, too, but seeing things from a different perspective and vibrating with another frequency. Street art and graffiti go beyond just painting the street; they are a way of life and a magic key that give the artist access to an unconventional dynamic and the opportunity to meet new people and even travel the world. Street art is a global game, and it is happening here, in Santiago, Chile.

History

We asked ourselves in the beginning, "What do we think of when we hear about graffiti or street art?" Perhaps cities like São Paulo, New York, Paris, or Berlin come to mind. But the truth is that Santiago, Chile, has one of the richest and most authentic graffiti and street art scenes in the world. Perhaps this is due to the city's simultaneous isolation from and connection with the rest of the world. We must recall that Chile was a battlefield during the Cold War, when it became, in 1970, the first Western country to elect a socialist president, Salvador Allende, in a democratic election. Many muralist brigades helped to expand the message of socialist idealism by painting images and symbols of power and the Popular Unity coalition on walls. A few years later, when General Augusto Pinochet's dictatorship began, muralism became a clandestine weapon of resistance of the lower classes of Santiago who were strongly repressed by military and intelligence organizations. Toward the end of the 1980s and the beginning of the 1990s, political and Latin American-themed muralism continued to be popular in the neighborhoods of the city that held a combative identity. At the same time, a certain discontent towards politics and political parties began to grow, mainly among young people.

With the return to democracy in 1990, Chile opened up to economic globalization and the cultural influence of Western epicenters, like North America and Europe. Mass media, such as television and film, played an important role in spreading new values and trends in popular culture to youth, such as hip hop, break dance, and graffiti. Chile, once characterized by strong ideological polarization and economic inequality, didn't hesitate to adopt and reinterpret rap as a form of counterculture resistance, especially among youth from low-income neighborhoods who continued to be discriminated against, sometimes solely on the basis of how they looked or where they lived.

At the same time, many political exiles began returning to the country, many bringing with them their children who had been born and raised in foreign lands. These children brought with them new practices, knowledge, and lifestyles, including graffiti. The influence of these kids at the beginning of Santiago's street art scene was crucial. From the beginning, street art in Chile didn't simply reflect what was happening in North America or Europe but instead displayed its own identity. For example, the extensive use of the paint brush and the paint roller derived from the use of these tools in the muralist brigades and also came about because of easy access to latex, toners, and tints. From an early stage, the Santiago scene was characterized by experimentation with different methods than those used in New York and Europe. Chile developed a strong bombing scene with a marked tendency to develop characters, influenced in part by early contact with another important global scene, that of São Paulo, Brazil. A few years after the rise of street art in Santiago, a conference on graffiti was organized and some of the best artists in the São Paulo scene were invited. This international exchange left an impression on many young Chilean artists who later became major influences on the following generations.

Identity

While there are diverse styles, techniques, characters, textures, and typographies in Santiago street art, many agree that this school rose and perfected itself with the use of latex, employed mainly because of its low cost and the difficulty of finding cans of professional aerosol paint and other specialized accessories. As Santiago's street scene began, it was also very difficult to get access to information; in those days before internet access, the only outside source of inspiration an artist might have was the occasional magazine brought over from another country by a friend, then photocopied and distributed between artists in the Mapocho Station or other meeting points.

This lack of contact with the external world marked the identity of the Santiago scene. It became known for its ingenuity and sensitivity in the face of poverty and deprivation. This is why there is an abundance of "figurative bombings": drawings made by a simple and swift trace with color limited to two shades, the background color and the color used for borders and details. Unlike in other countries, such as Argentina, painting on the street in Chile was a matter of life and death during the dictatorship, and then continued to be repressed by police in the '90s.

This is why some say that the Santiago scene came to perfection through stress. Painters had to develop their techniques and shape their artworks while seized by fear, always looking over their shoulders. By the end of the '90s and with the beginning of a new century, the political scene became calmer and graffiti was no longer forbidden or considered a grave crime. With the opening of the economy, the lower cost of supplies, and free access to imports, street artists had new tools available to them, such as paints, valves, and masks. As restrictions lifted, a new generation of painters and graffiti artists, still influenced by those who had come before them, began to multiply by the hundreds in Santiago.

Present

Today in Santiago, thanks to graffiti and street art, there are real open-air museums and galleries, such as in the Bellavista neighborhood and the San Miguel commune, in La Cisterna, along the Avenida Santa Rosa, in Pedro Aguirre Cerda, in Independencia, and in Recoleta.

Unfortunately, not everyone sees the value of this form of art. It is incredible how blind certain politicians and military leaders can be about the culture and education of Chile. In other Latin American countries, street art and muralism are publicly celebrated and even considered an attraction for tourists. But in Chile, there is a permanent tendency toward stigmatization and criminalization of the scene.

The relationship between street art and contemporary art has also been troubled, as the latter is still an elitist scene reserved for certain social classes. But graffiti and street art have great potential to affect change: they can bring a breath of fresh air and permanent inspiration to the world of visual arts and they can democratize artistic action, opening the experience to all citizens, regardless of social class or education. With the accessibility of graffiti and street art, the schism between the artist and the public is demolished. Anyone can paint on the street; there is no need for a conventional education in the fine arts.

The movement is becoming more and more organized with each passing day. Artists are forming collective groups and conducting expositions and conferences. Projects in which graffiti and street art unite with social work and various social movements are having a major impact. Today, urban art and other nonconventional movements targeting youth, such as hip hop, are starting to be seen as ways to learn that are parallel and complementary to the official educational system. For this reason, many of today's artists provide workshops and guidance to children and teenagers in places where the State and the market have not been able to do so.

To conclude, I would like to add a personal statement. Without a doubt, the graffiti scene and street art in Santiago reached maturity early on. By the end of the '90s, some of the artists who currently represent Chilean graffiti around the world were already painting on the streets. Many of these artists grew up as part of a post-dictatorship generation when individualism was prioritized, and consequently, many were lost in struggles over ego and fame. This is why I believe the graffiti and street art scene in Santiago has big potential for the future. The new generations, the new school, are in charge of taking the movement a step up—to take it to a level of organization, linked to education, with the acceptance of popular art in the heart of Chilean society, beyond egos and territorial disputes.

BRIAN GRAY

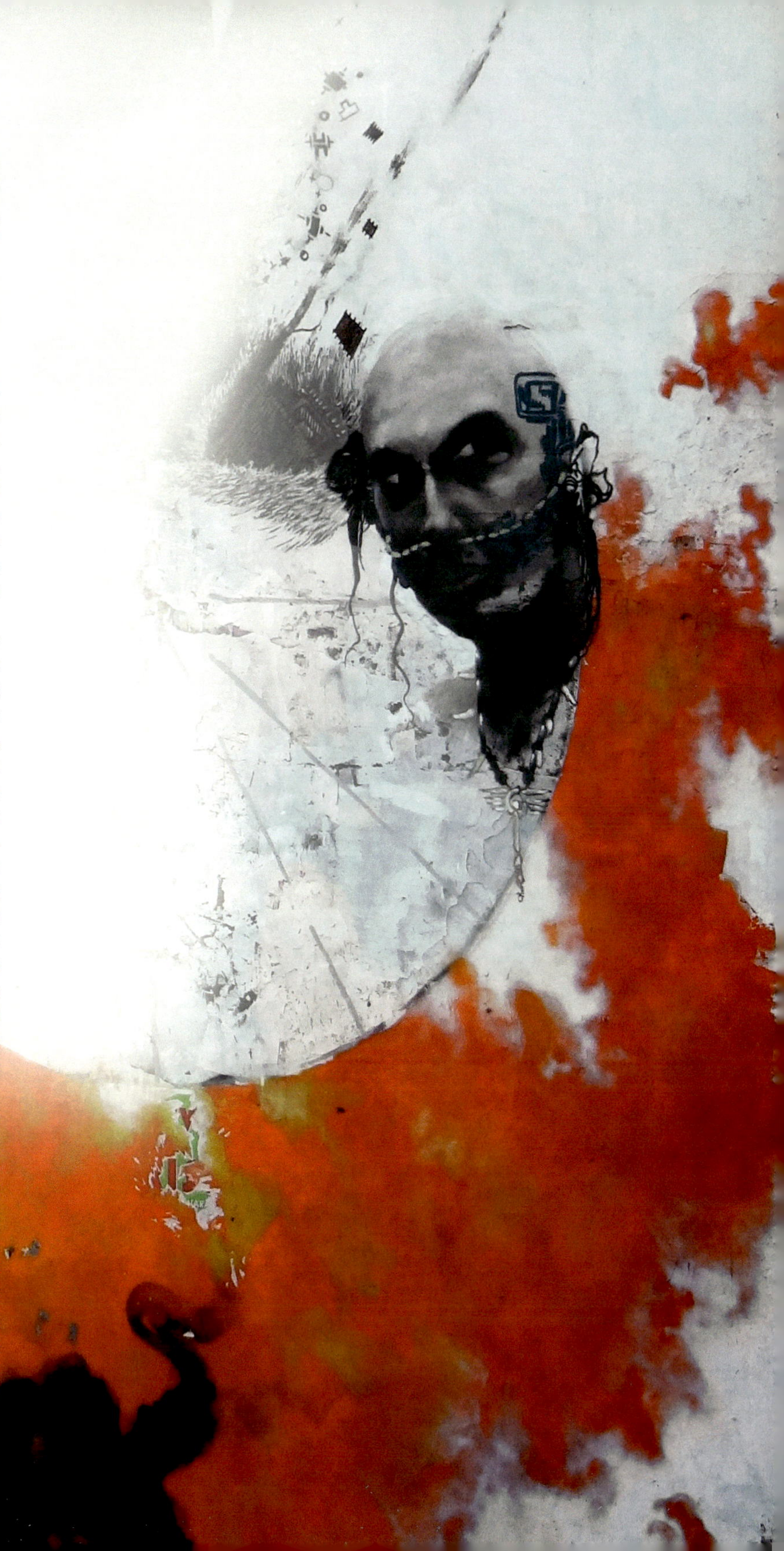

Bellavista

Area: 0.9 km^2
Population: 7000
Average annual income: n/a
Population below poverty line: n/a
Graffiti prevalence: 10/10

"I was born and raised in Bellavista, and I have been painting here for eight years. I was really lucky to grow up in this barrio and was always surrounded by murals and characters. There are many house façades and also many metal gate doors of commercial spaces, however, most are intervened. There are all sorts of urban art forms in this 'hood including stickers, throw ups, stencils, mosaics, and big murals. Many factors influence the time graffiti will last in this area. Murals and graffiti are always being renovated. Some last a year, others more, some less, but this is part of the evolution of the painter and also their lack of respect. There are always new murals in this barrio. The owners of a house may want you to change the mural painted on it because they are tired of it or if it has deteriorated, or the house or building will change owners and the new owners will erase the mural. Some erase previous works without discretion. Bellavista experiences a high turnover of residents, but I always feel relaxed here. Since I was a child I have walked these streets and have witnessed evolution, conflicts, the new, horrid constructions, and respect and lack of it. I have many friends in the barrio. I will never stop painting here, and I have never had a problem with the police while painting here." PIGUAN

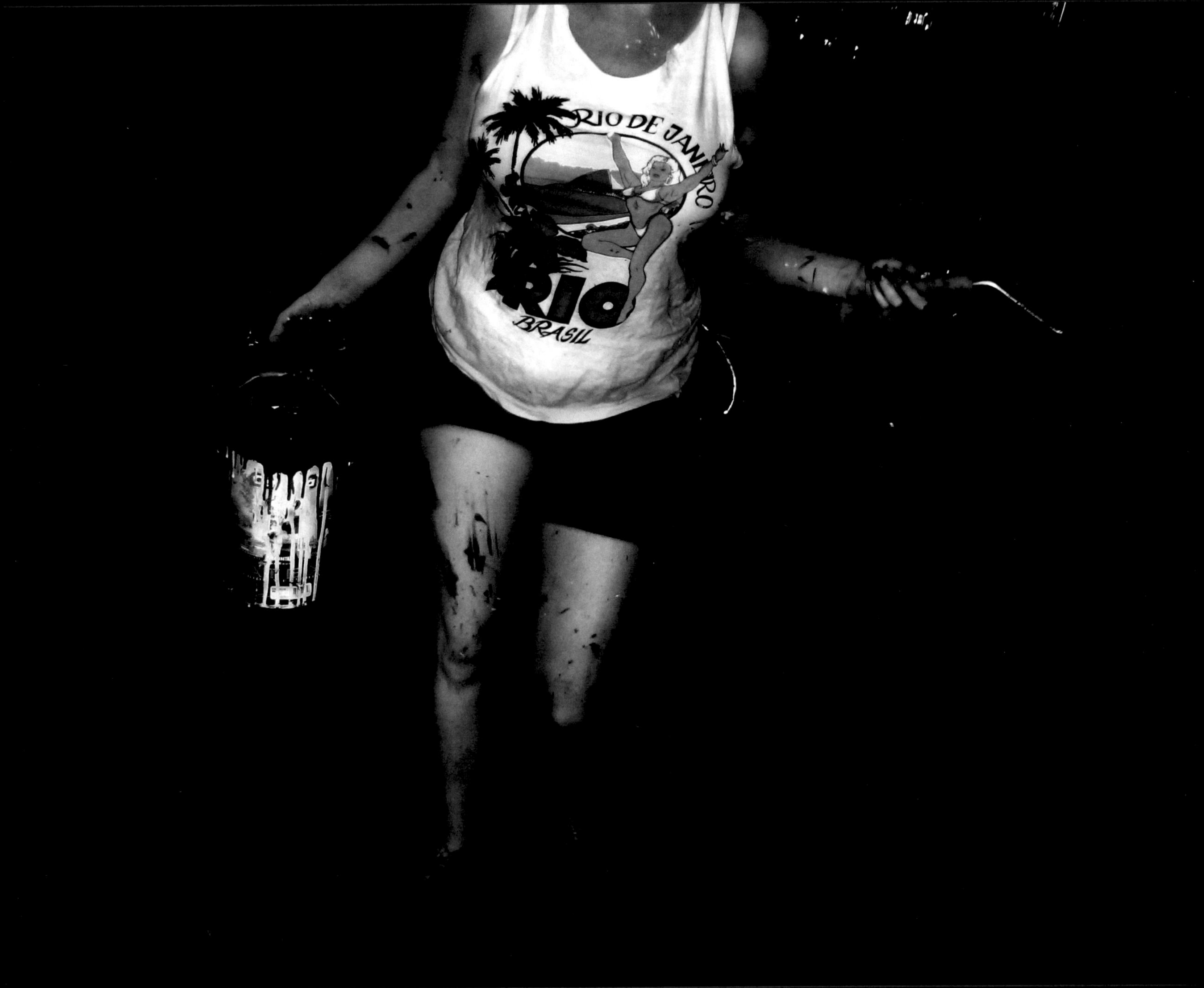
RIO DE
RIO
BRASIL

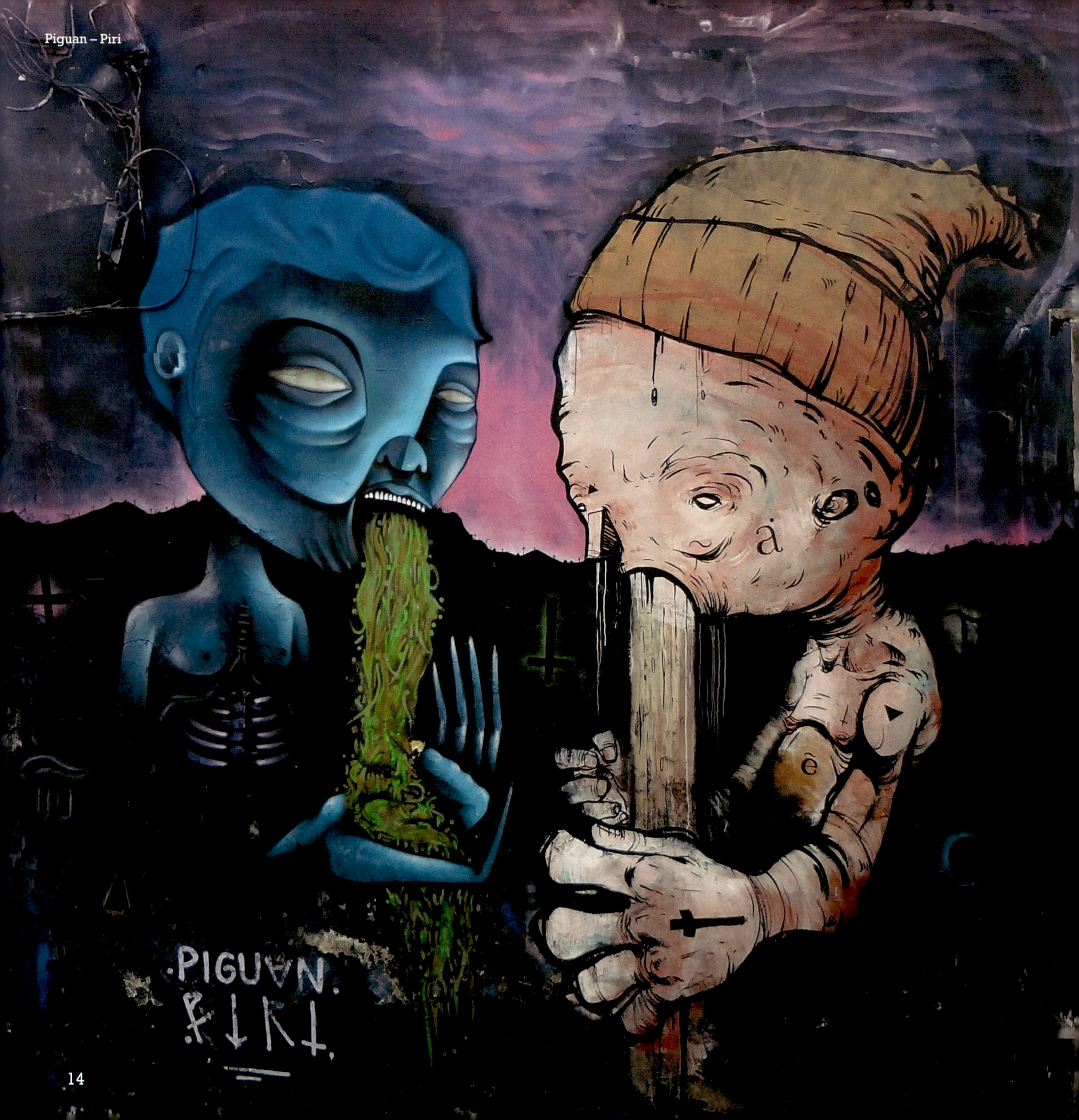
PIGUAN.

"Initially, my art was nothing more than vomiting, letting go of everything that I had in my head, things that bothered me, my problems and so on." PIGUAN

"Painting should always have a reason for being — not a fixed reason that is imposed upon us, but a personal reason by which the artist can develop his vision to approach society and himself." PIRI

"For me graffiti is like being an excellent comic book illustrator. A good illustrator can draw any style that is asked of him. You should be able to handle all styles and strokes." GUZTOK

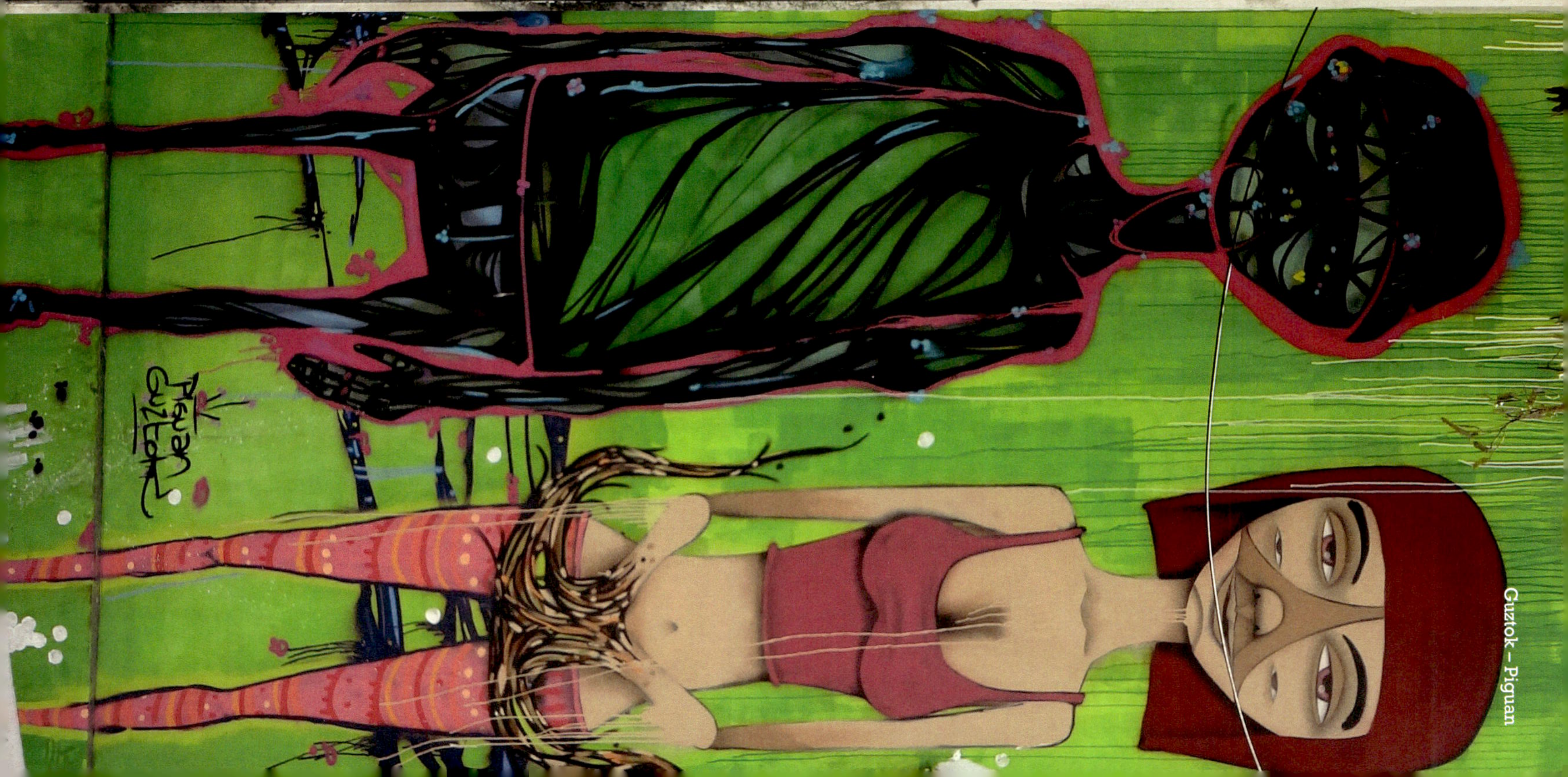

Guztok – Piguan

Piri

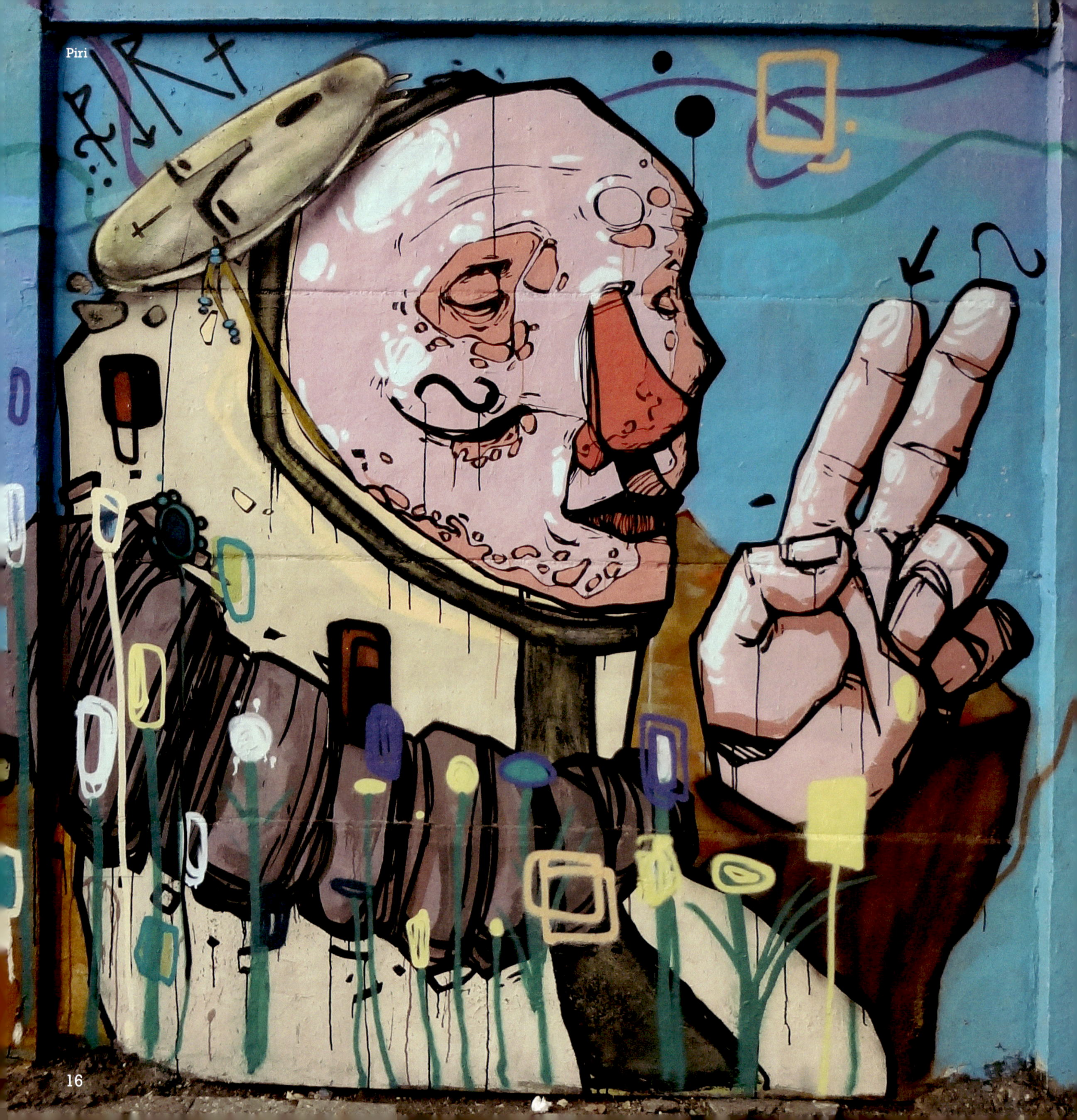

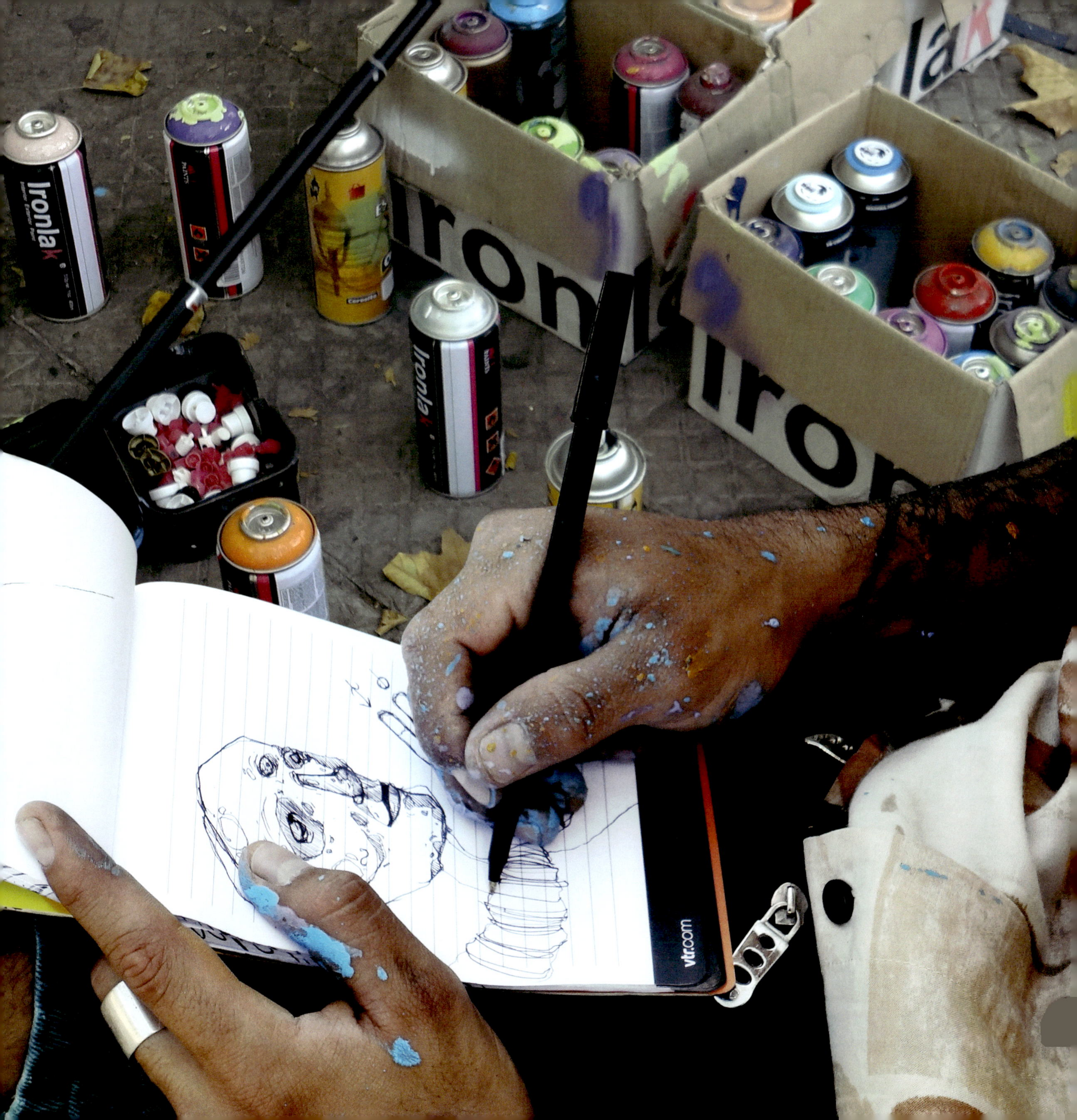
Ironlak
vtr.com

Faya

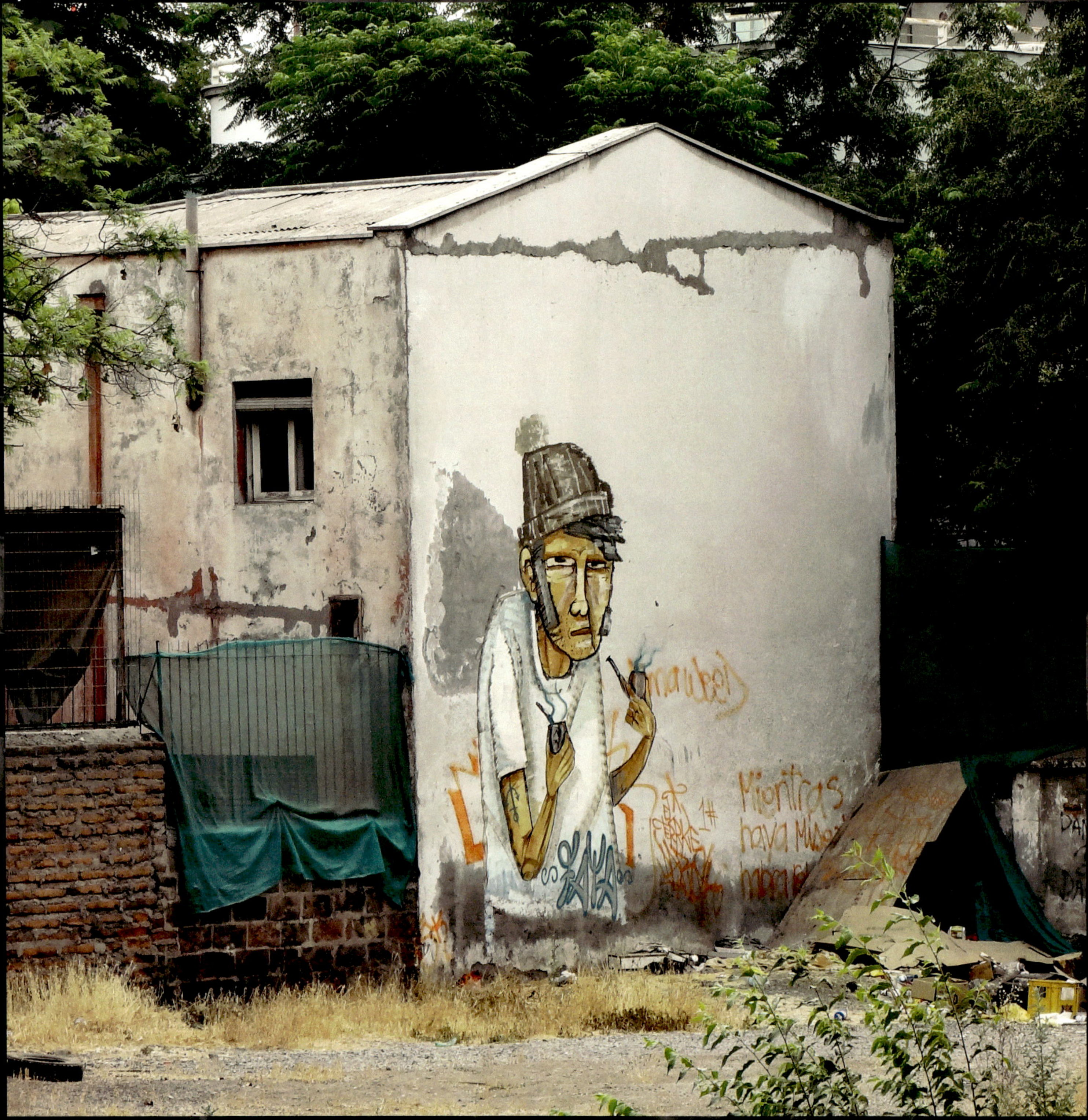

Piguan – Bus

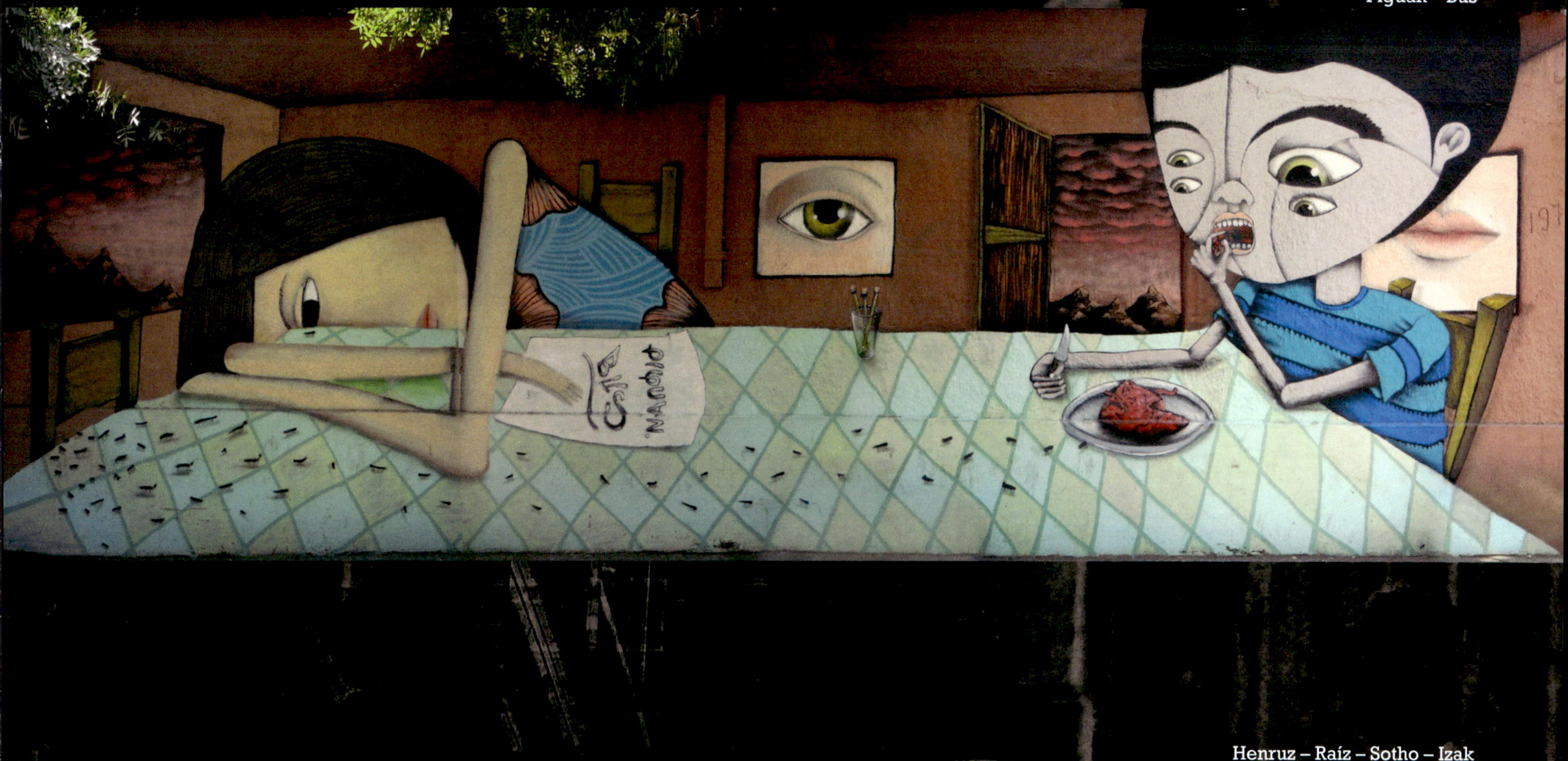

Henruz – Raíz – Sotho – Izak

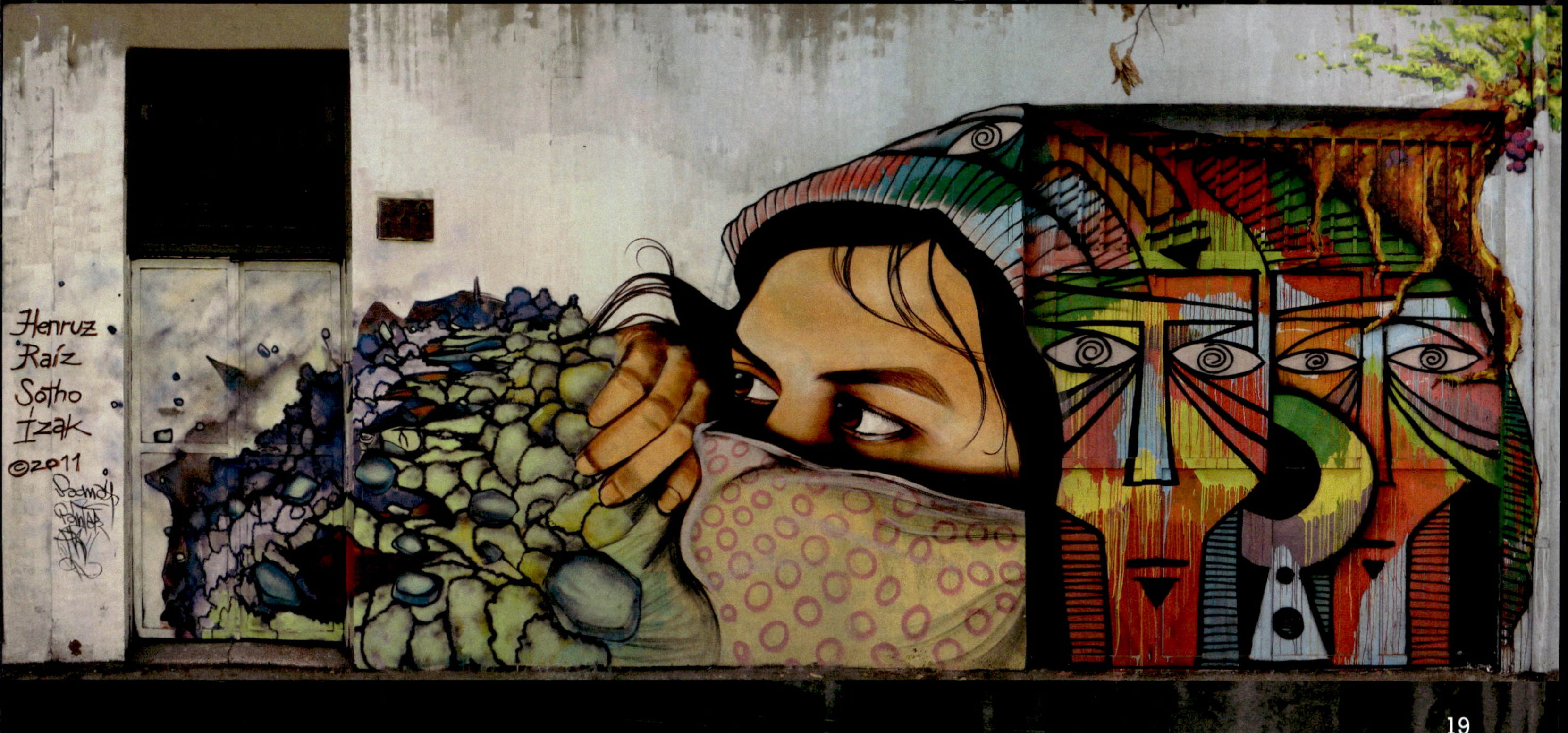

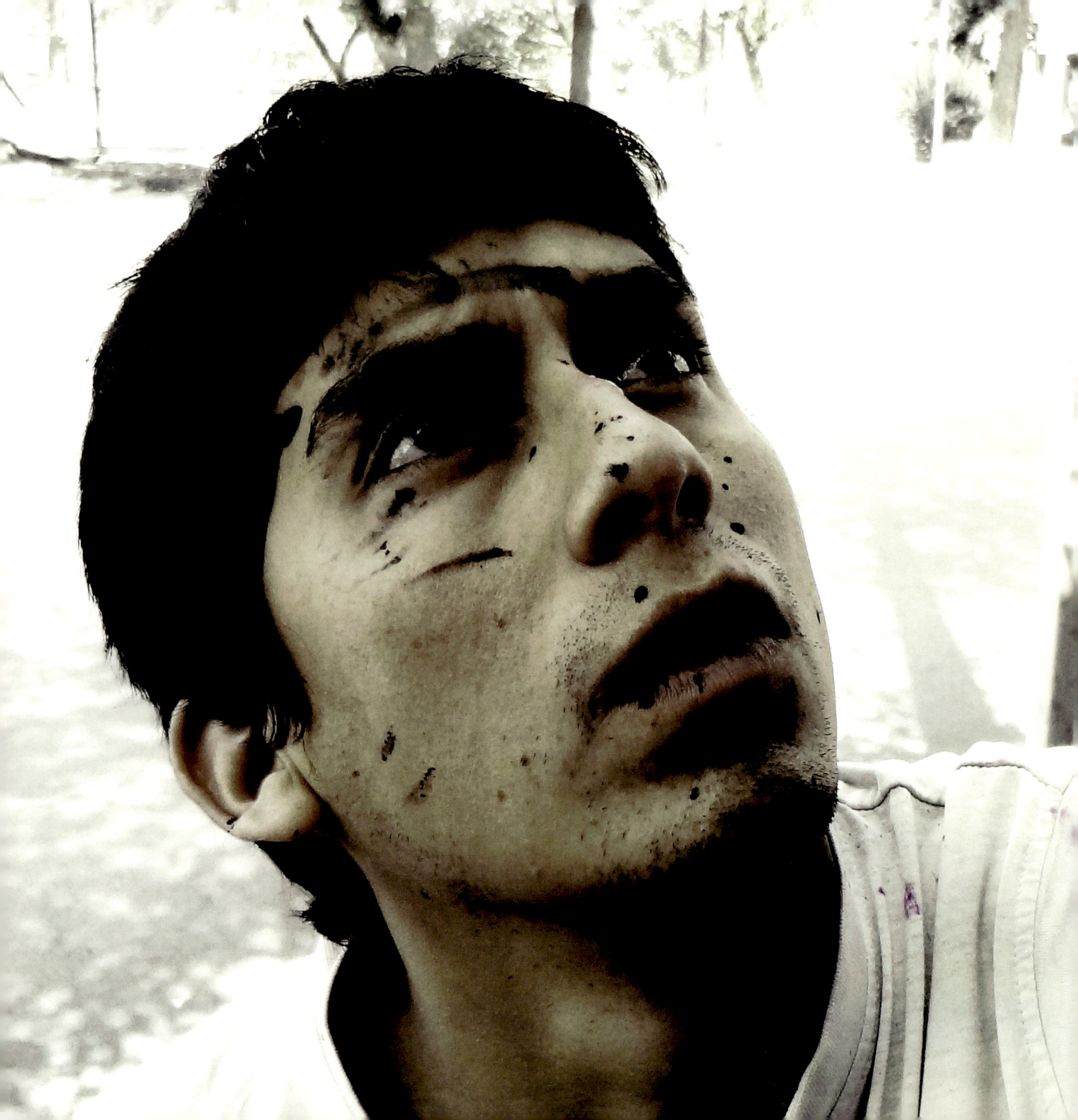

"Zero contribution to society? That's ridiculous. As graffiti artists, we are going to remind them a thousand times what bastards they are and write 'Fuck the police' everywhere."

"So many times, laypeople pass by graffiti works and fail to capture the differences between one and another and instead view them all as dirt, as if a vandal came along to defile and soil the wall. Yet, what they may view as a dirty wall is actually what an artist painted and designed.

"Each tag—the artist's unique symbols and styles—has a particular look. The lettering has a particular form, which is an aspect that all graffiti artists notice, but something that the average person doesn't always recognize. In each tag, I see flecks of color. At times there are walls that are completely marked up, yet the people who see them say, 'This wall is dirty, it's all scribbled on.' In contrast I see flecks of distinct colors that contribute to an abstract painting.

"I don't consider graffiti an art, because first off, the truth is that I don't know what art is. I don't know how to define it. I've never studied art, nor do I think it is necessary to study art to know what it is. There's no sense in discussing what art is. In the moment, anything can be art and even in discussing whether something is or isn't art, it already becomes meaningless.

"If all human activity was considered art, then maybe I would consider graffiti as art, but in reality I don't consider it real art. While it can have many colors, many forms, and many patterns that can be viewed with admiration, in truth what we really do is mark up the streets. If you're going around marking up the streets and the public buses, is that art? It's questionable. If it's going to be a tag with lettering, and all the world considers it better than a dirty wall, well it's not art, but it's graffiti. We flood the streets with symbols and colors, and let the people decide if they like them or not. If people want to appreciate what I do, or if they don't want me to do it, it makes no difference to me. If I receive more insults than applause for my graffiti in the streets, so be it. I'm going to continue doing it. I consider myself an anarchist, and therefore enjoy delivering an anarchistic message. I strongly question the prevailing social system and therefore graffiti has served as a great outlet for me to express my thoughts. I am from Santiago, Chile, where we paint the public buses. We do this because we like to distinguish them, and because the bus fare is so expensive that it's a robbery. The public transportation is a mafia in the sense that those who have money pay the fare, and those that don't unfortunately have to walk, or simply don't pay and are therefore subject to a fine.

"Everything that we question is seen in the work that we do. There are many times when we don't create for the sake of being artists, but rather for the act of transgression and of bypassing the law. This is what graffiti is, it's a mix of desires to overcome authority and laws, and when one questions whether something is or isn't graffiti, we simply continue painting and scribbling to make our point.

"Like many countries in Latin America, Chile experienced a dictatorship and those who currently govern the country are heirs to this matter and were those who imposed the dictatorship and the police that worked for them. In contrast, graffiti is for the people. It's popular expression. We express all that we carry within ourselves, and in this moment we have hatred and anger toward all our social inequalities. We have a hatred for all the injustices and will continue expressing our feelings toward society through our work.

"So fuck the police who are at the services of the rich and the businesses. Cheers to all my people, to all members of the population, to all the workers who day after day get up despite getting paid a shit salary. Strength to all those who fight for the revolution that we are going to create. Thanks to the graffiti that reminds us everyday that we are a marginalized people who will no longer remain compliant."

I asked Jony what his tag was, and he suggested that I meet him the following day on the corner of Bellavista and Purisima. On the next page, see his unusual tagging style.

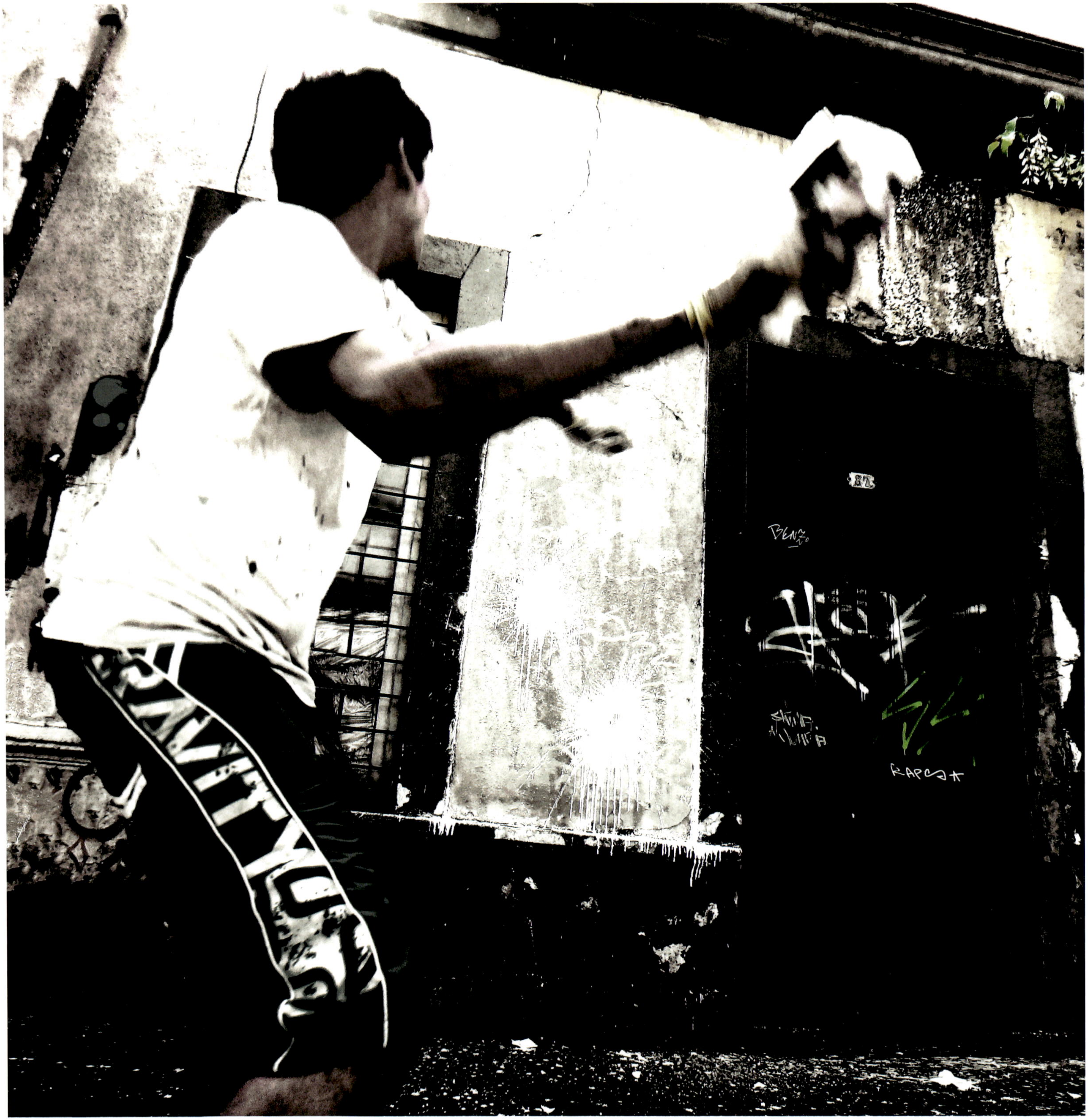

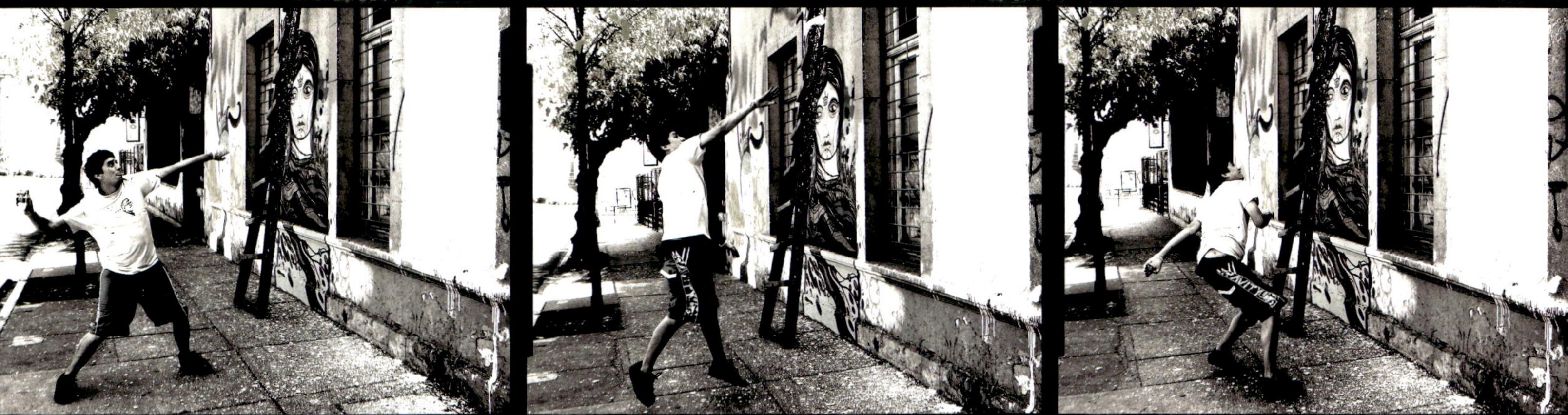

"I don't perceive it as vandalism or as a form of leaving an ideological mark, nor do I do it to break the law."

"My style of tagging is to throw three paint bombs. I fill up three glass bottles with paint, then I chuck them against a wall or a surface so that I am left with three bombs marked side by side. This method permits me to reach surfaces that are distant, so that I don't need to get up close to the wall with a can of paint. I can tag tall buildings, play around with the colors, and adjust the sizes of the bombs as needed. I chose this form of tagging as I was looking for a less traditional way of leaving my mark. It's quick, versatile, and effective. I like the fact that this process takes place on the streets, so that people can see it. When I walk by, I like to appreciate my own stains on the city." JONY

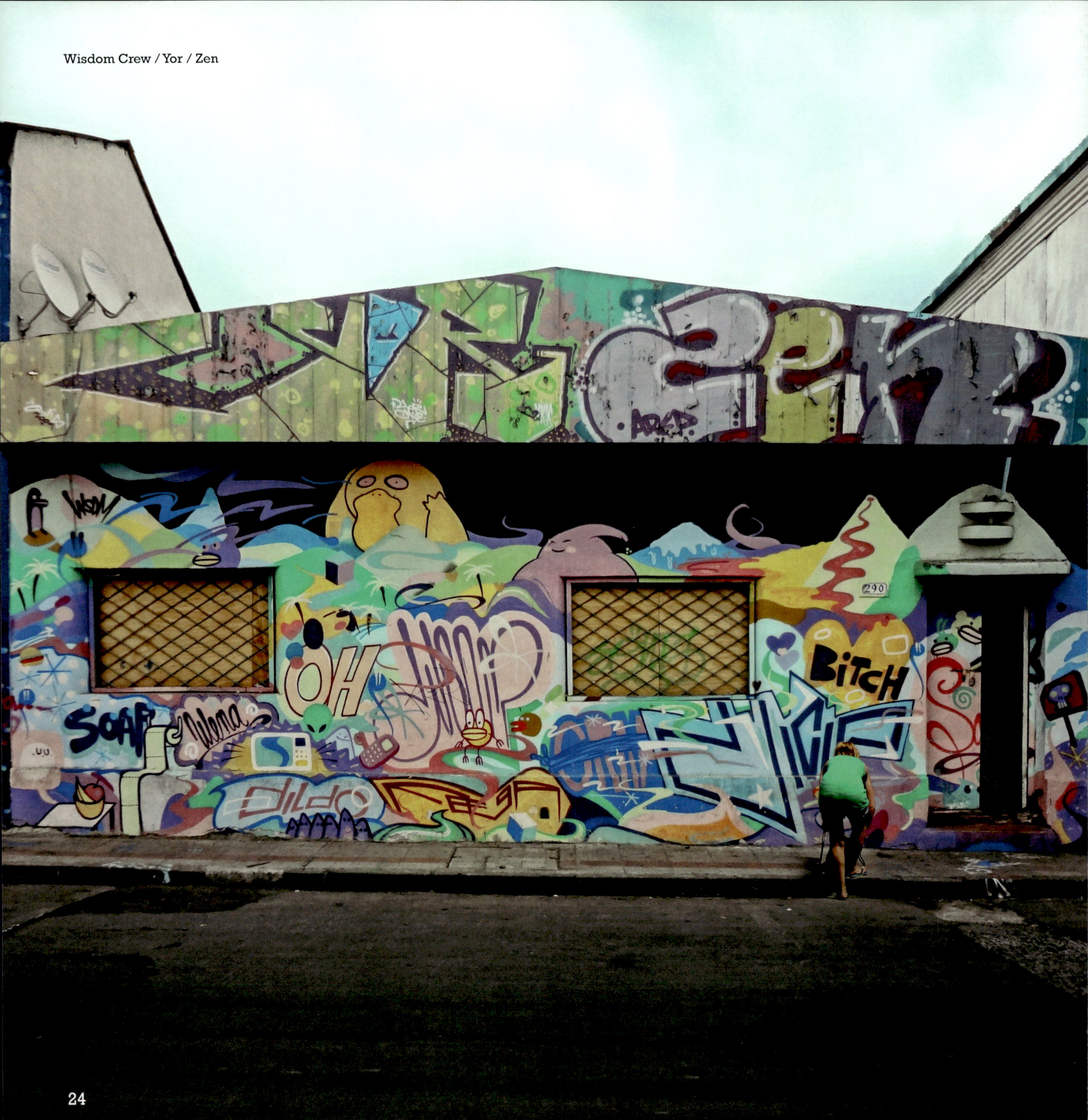

Wisdom Crew / Yor / Zen

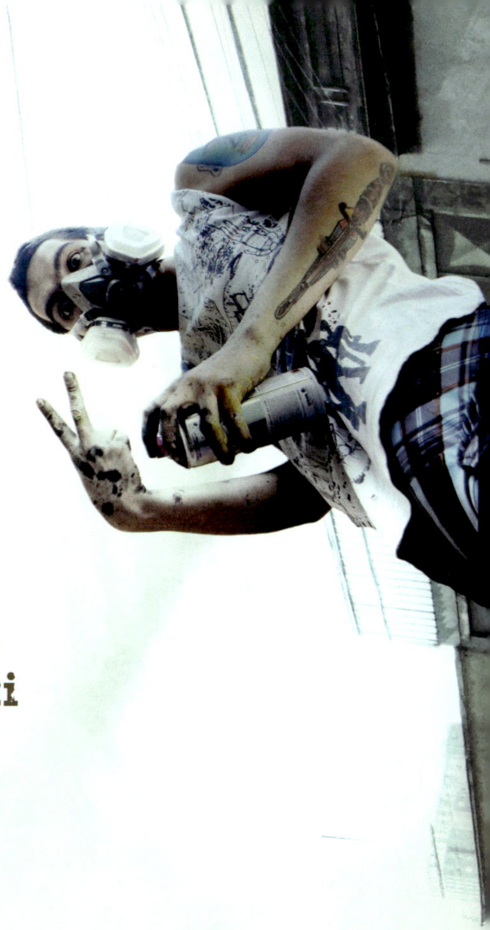

"My crew chose **this barrio** because it is **comfortable** to **paint** in, not so that everyone would see **our street art.**

"We don't **paint** our tags, we paint **random words,** mostly to **annoy** the other graffiti **artists** that tag their name **all the time.**

"**Everything** that could possibly happen **occurred** in this place: **happiness**, friendship, love, shame, violence, **and death. Everything** that makes that barrio **unique.**" WISDOM CREW

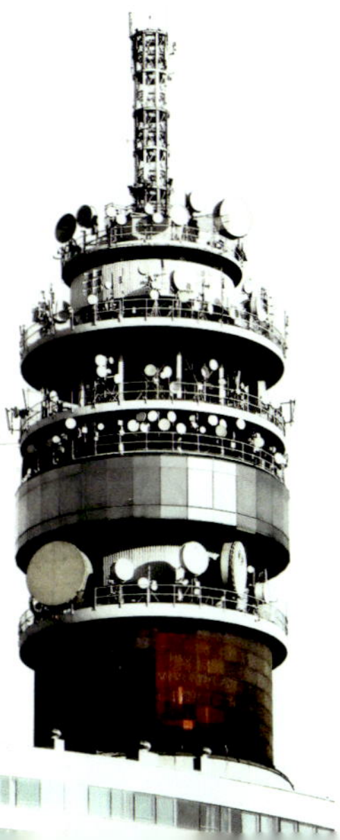

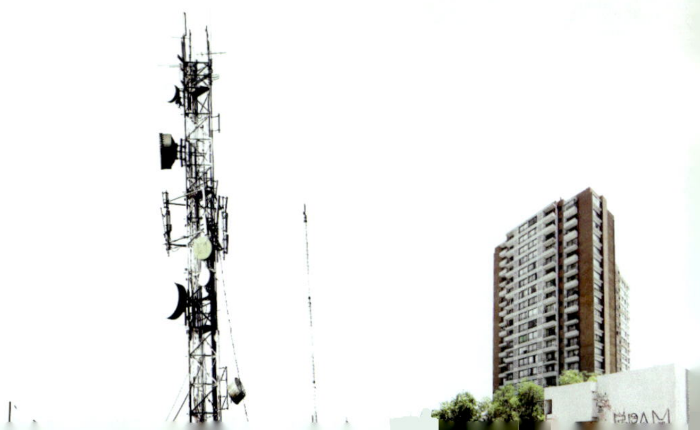

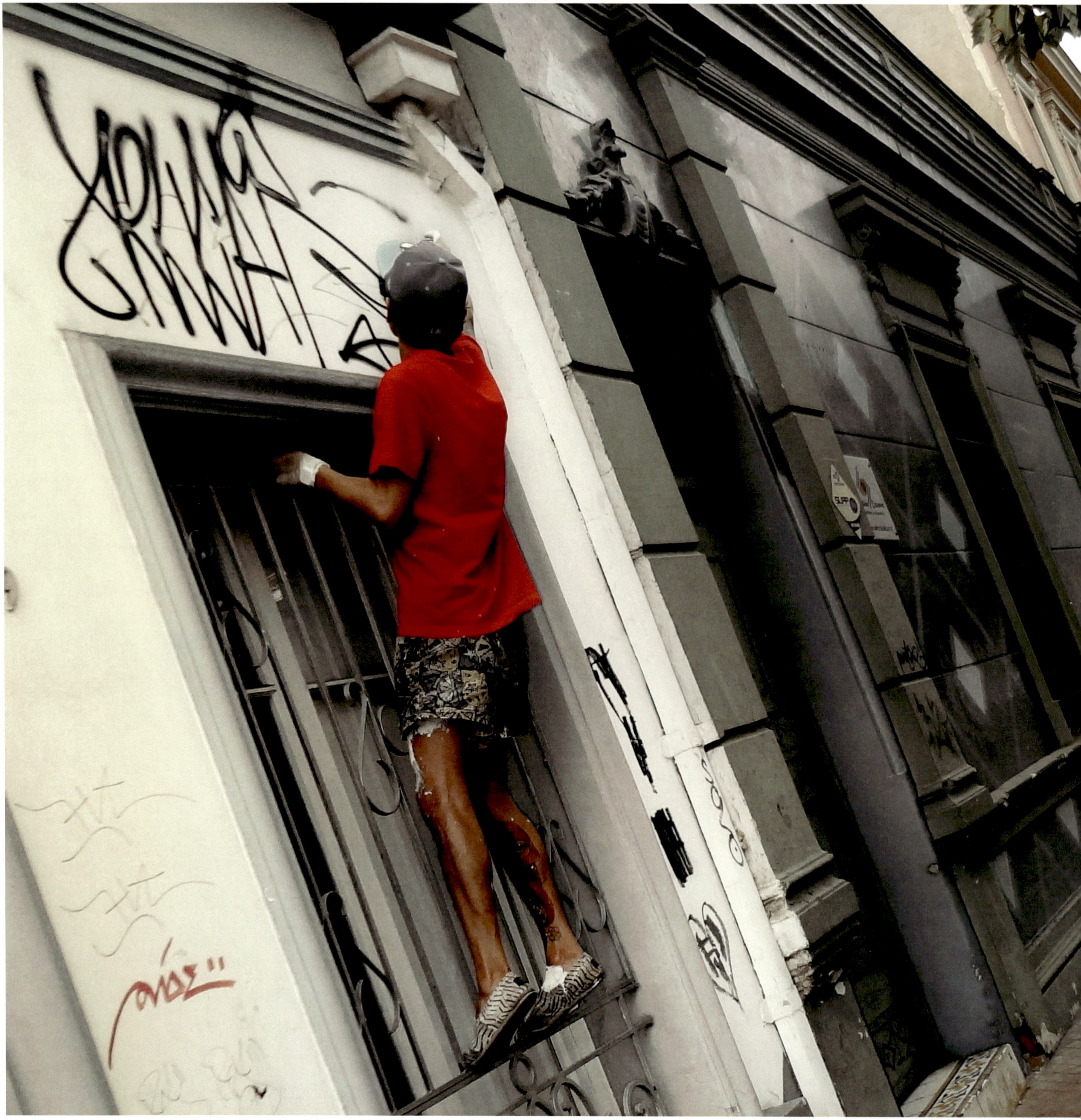

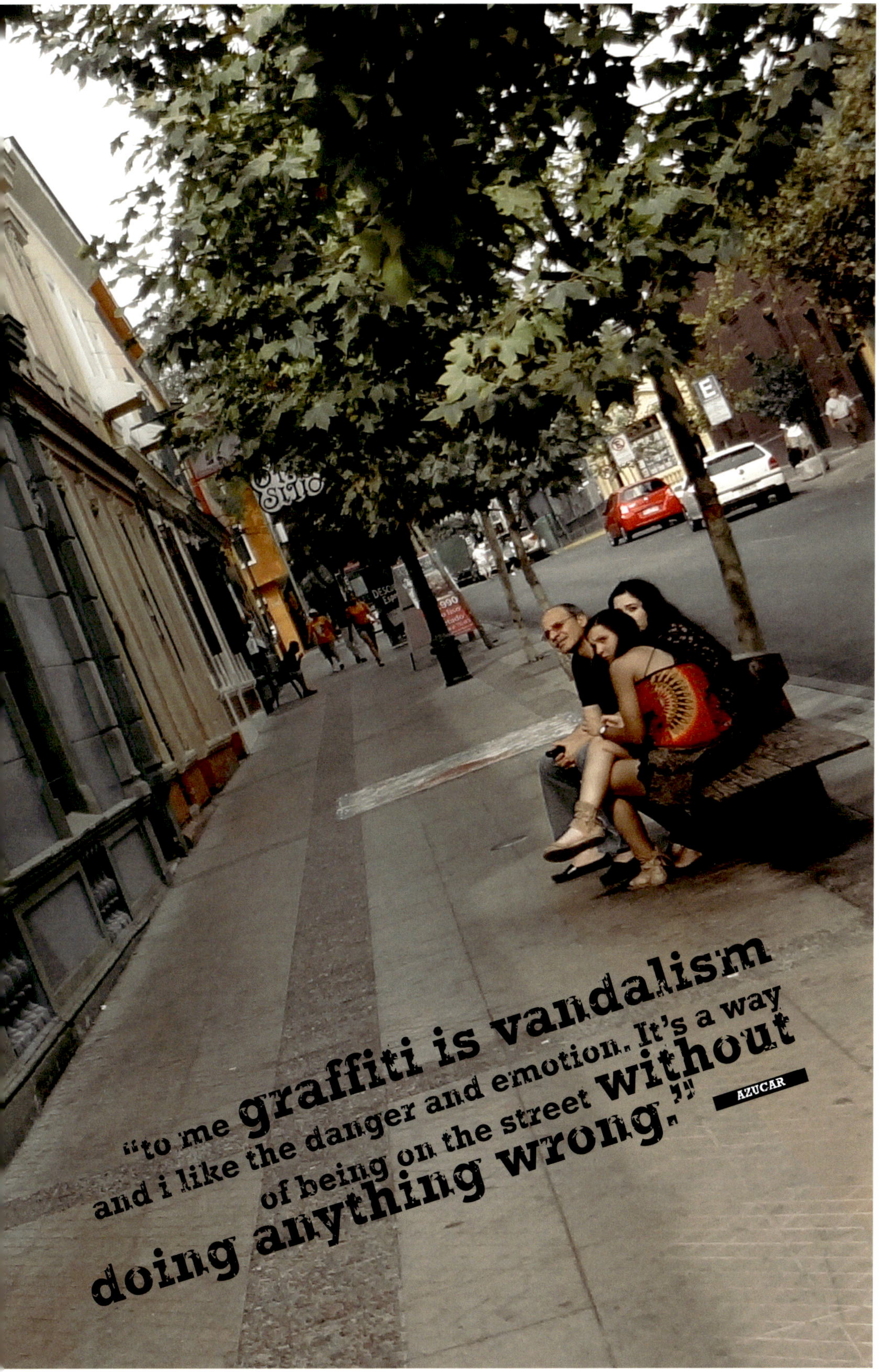

"to me **graffiti is vandalism** and i like the danger and emotion. It's a way of being on the street **without doing anything wrong.**"

AZUCAR

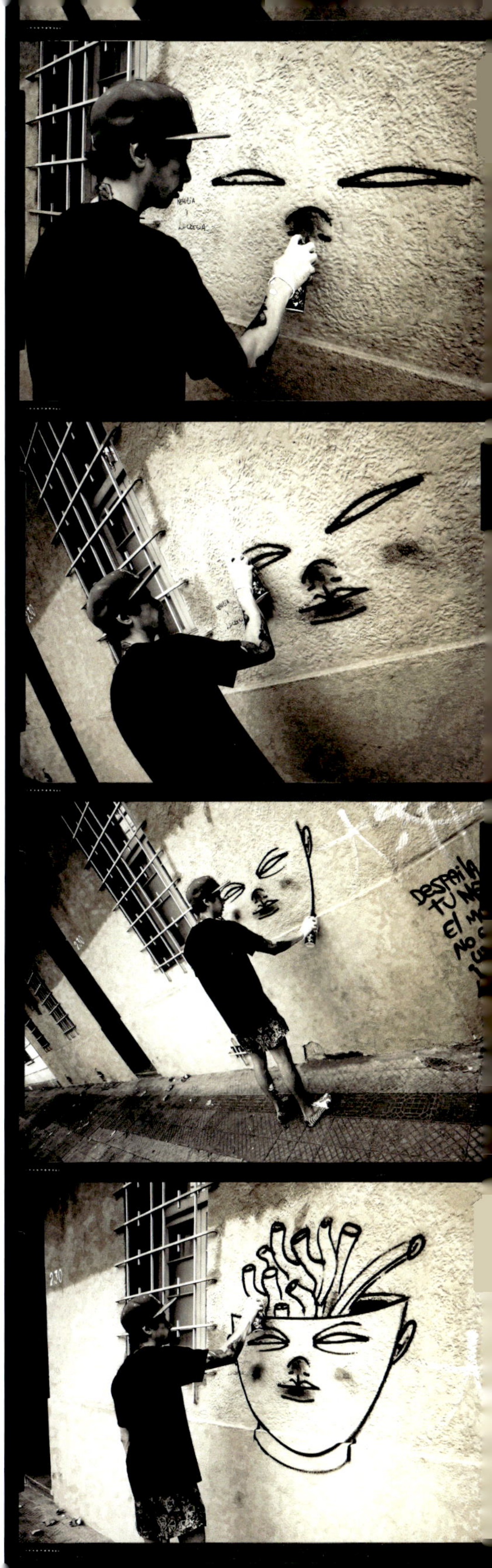

"The crew and I usually spend most of our time in Bellavista, the neighborhood that we come from. This neighborhood is a great place to display our works as many tourists visit this area. They see our work all over Bellavista and can then appreciate the art which Chile has to showcase. Since Chilean artists tend to use their roots as the subject for their work, this serves as an exhibit of our culture. The tourists tend to take many photos of our art and return home to show it to their friends and family. They can easily see the quality of our work that I believe measures up to what is being done in the rest of the world.

"I don't like graffiti that much. I don't like typography either as I feel that it is overcome by the ego. Wishing to tag my name all over the place so that everybody knows who I am doesn't encourage evolution and isn't experimental. However, when you draw characters and more artistic things, you create the possibility of evolving. It is beyond wanting to plonk your name on the streets. It's something that you can call your own. It allows you to leave a mark by doing something that you really want to express, without anticipating or expecting a reaction from anybody." FAYA

Santana – Naska

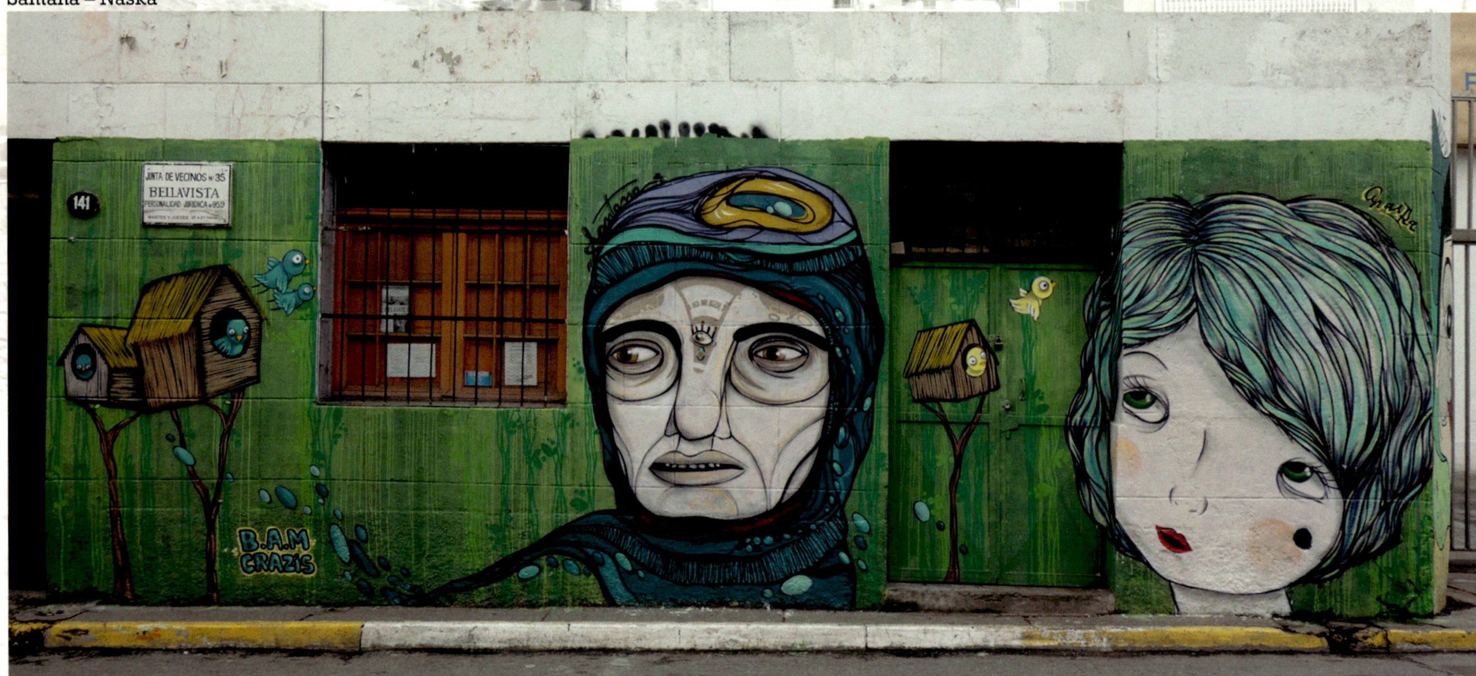

Faya

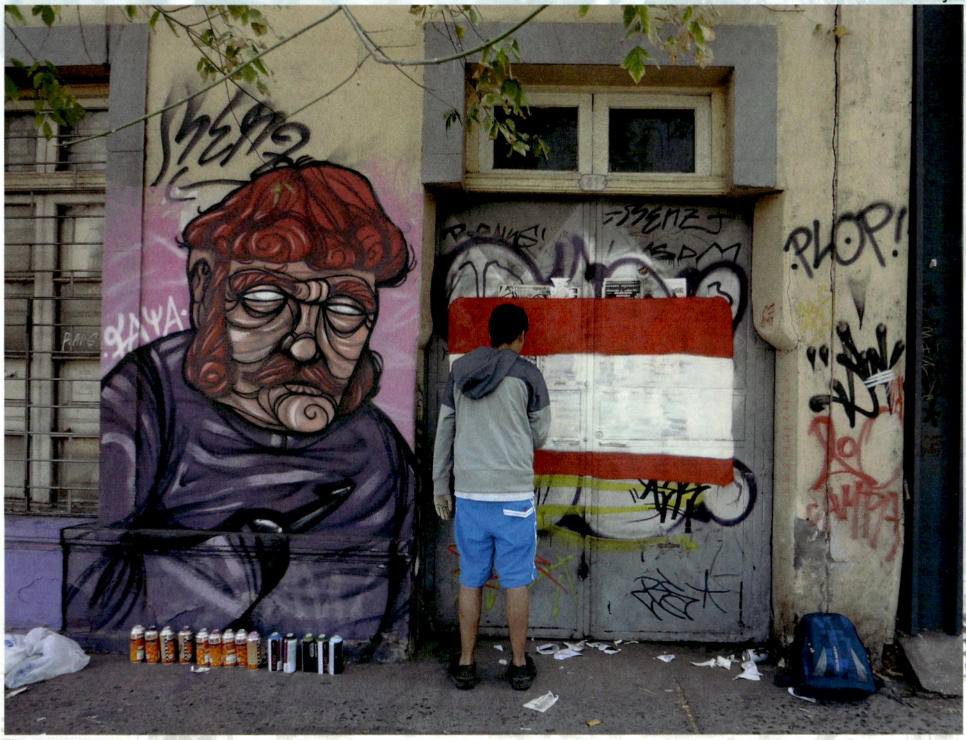

Santana

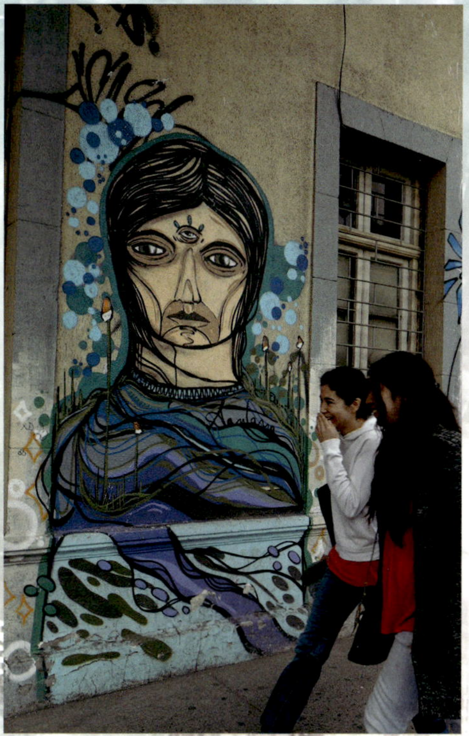

Santana – Faya

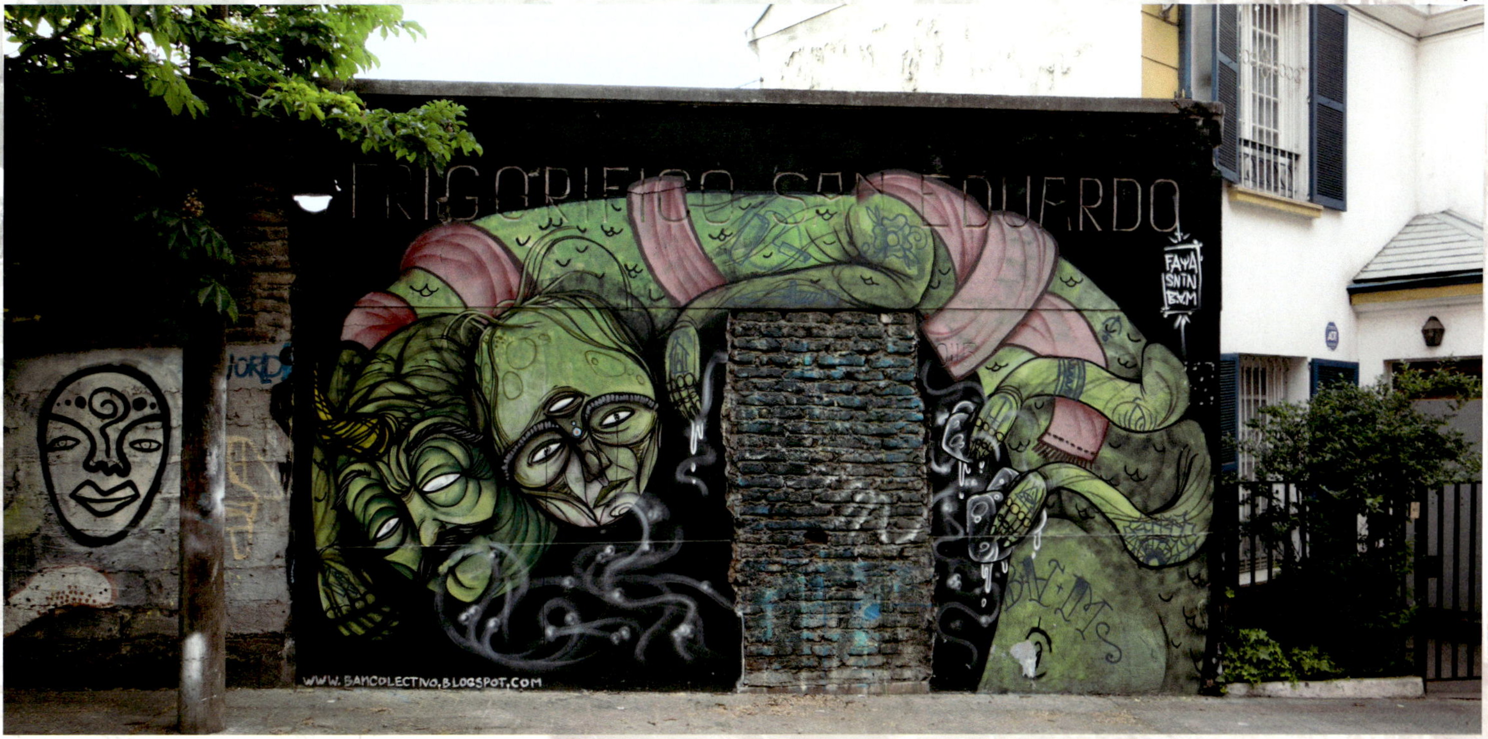

"The art in galleries is elitist, **it's designed** for those who go there to study **particular types** of works by 'The fools of art'! We prefer a beggar instead of a rich man to see our **works** on the street and **admire it.** That **is more fulfilling!**" ENGRUDOORS

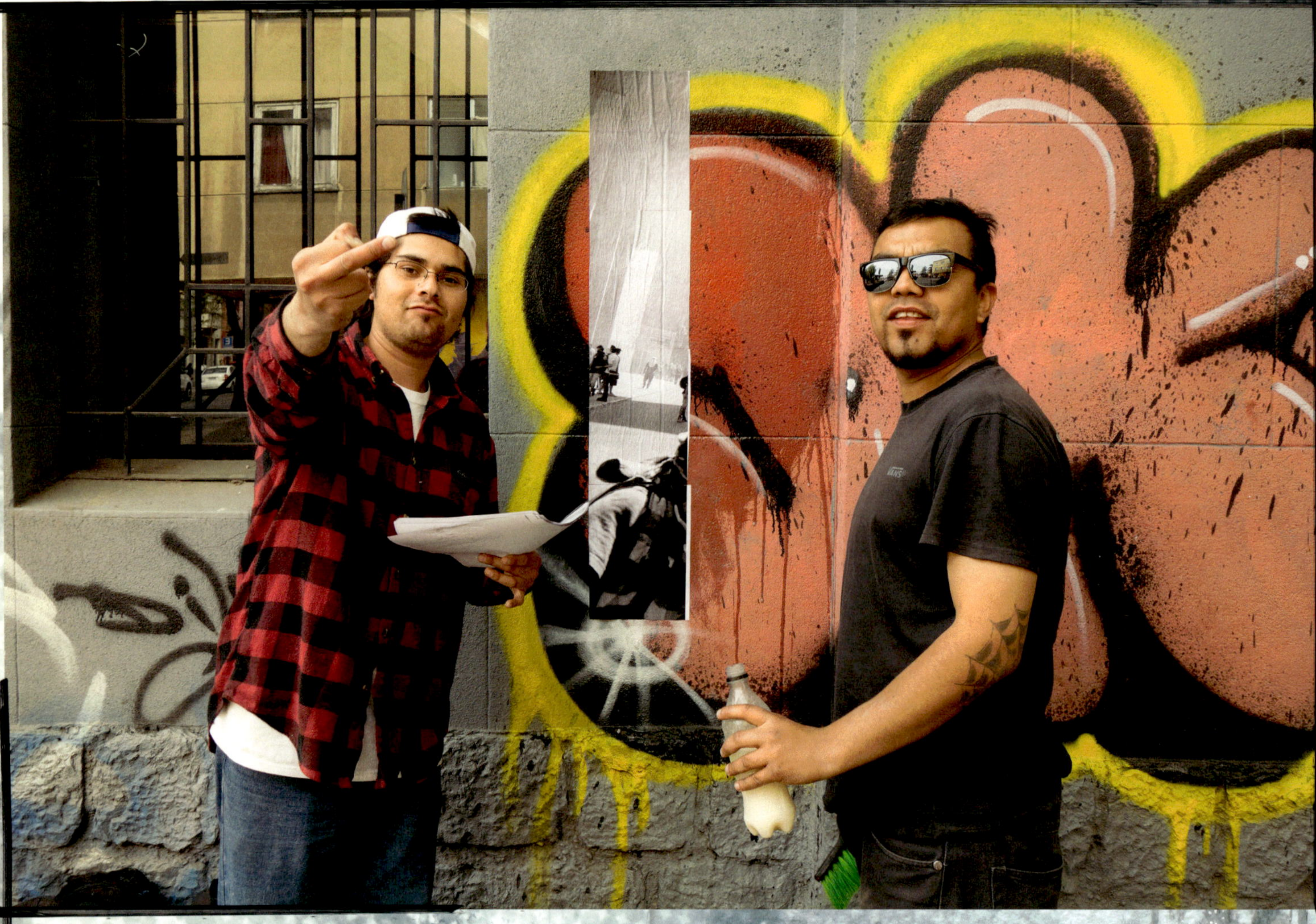

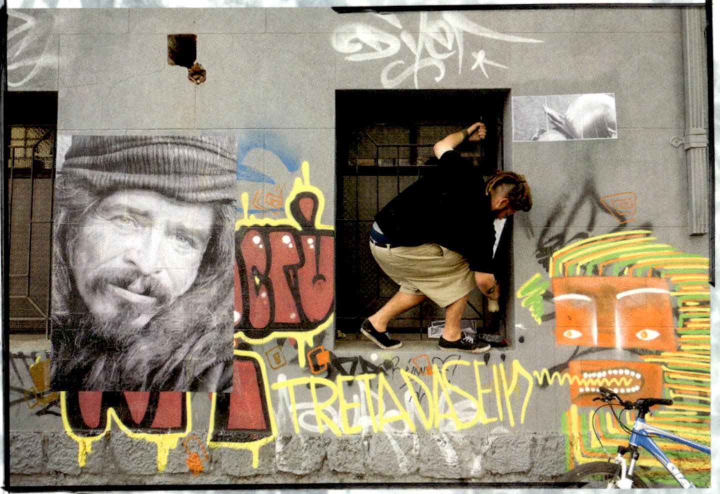

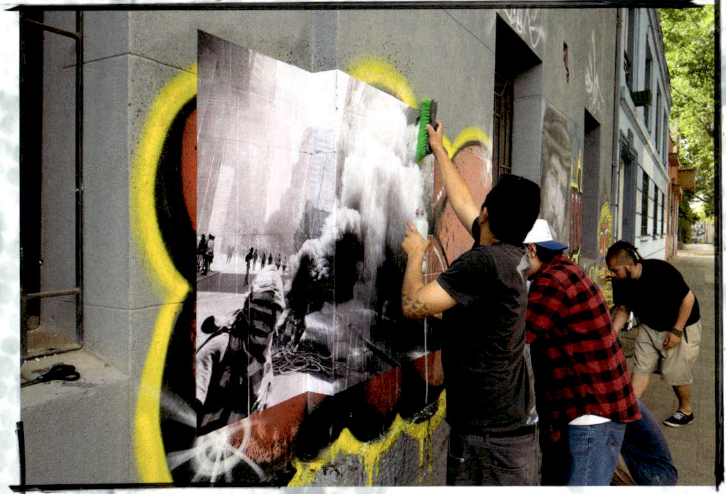

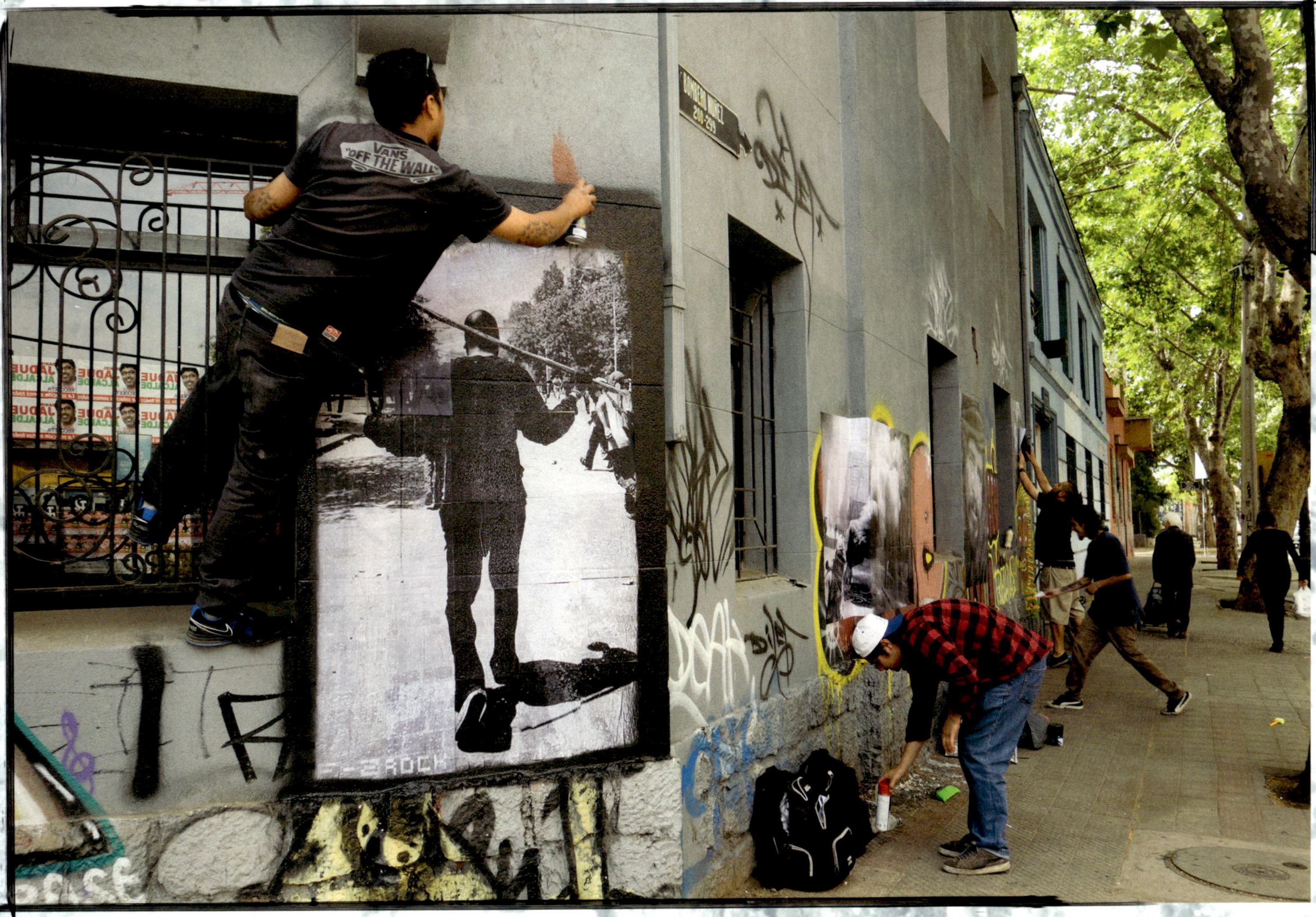
VANS
"OFF THE WALL"

Mars

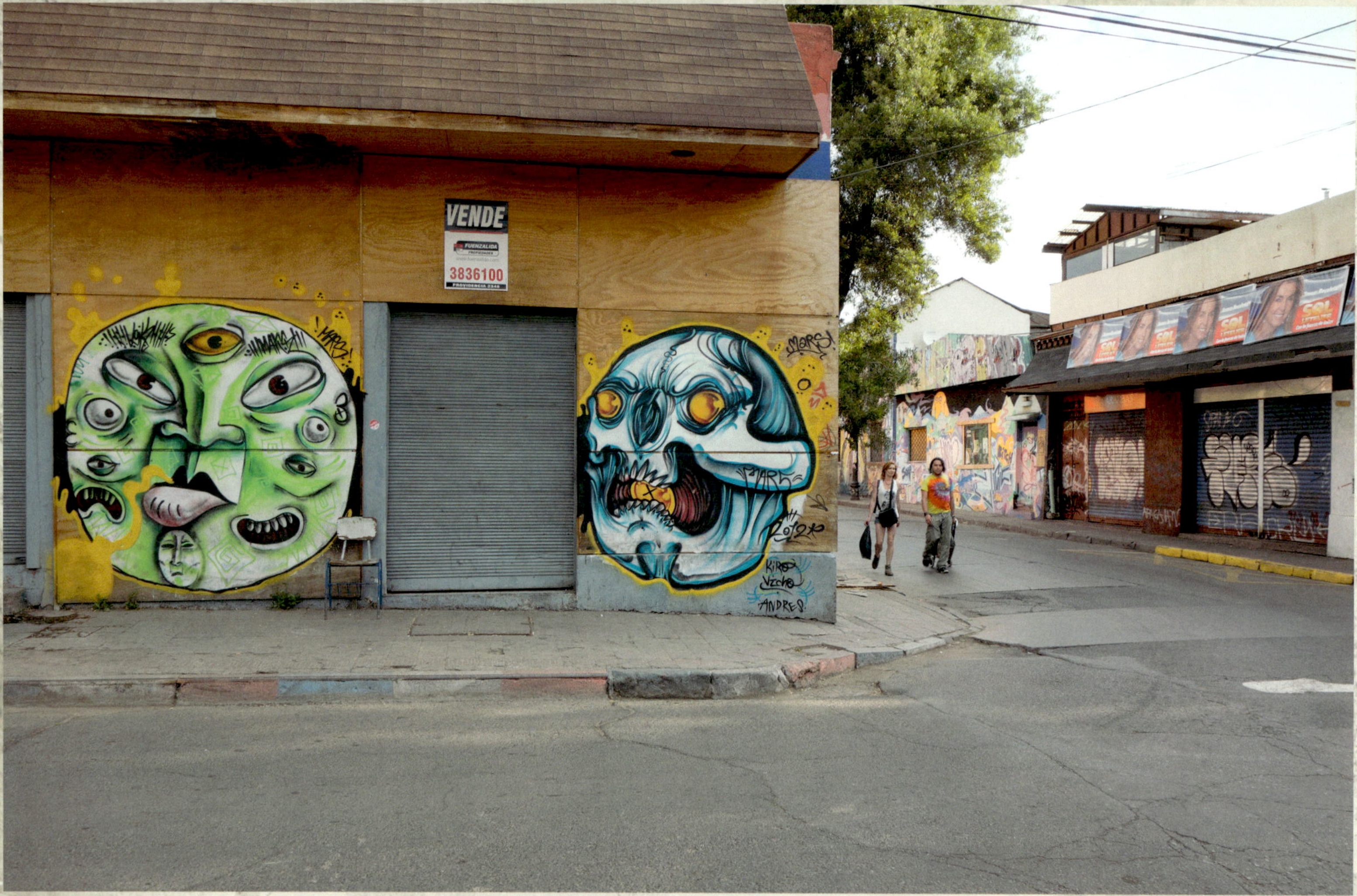

Niquito – Alterna

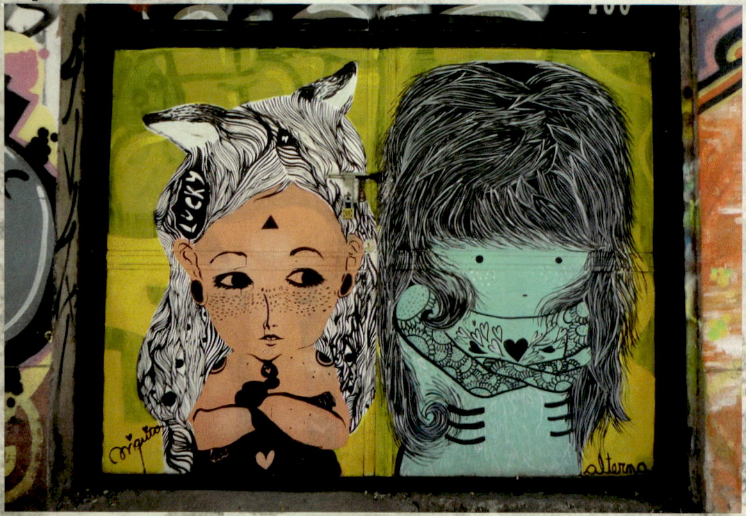

Niquito – Alterna

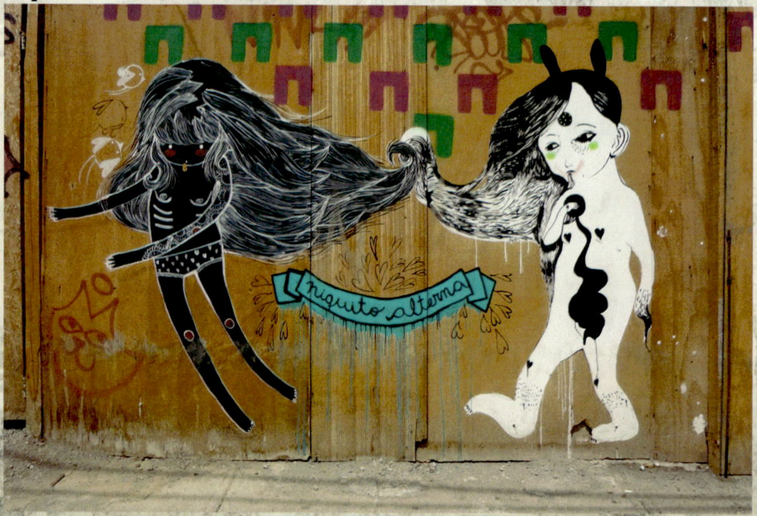

Naska

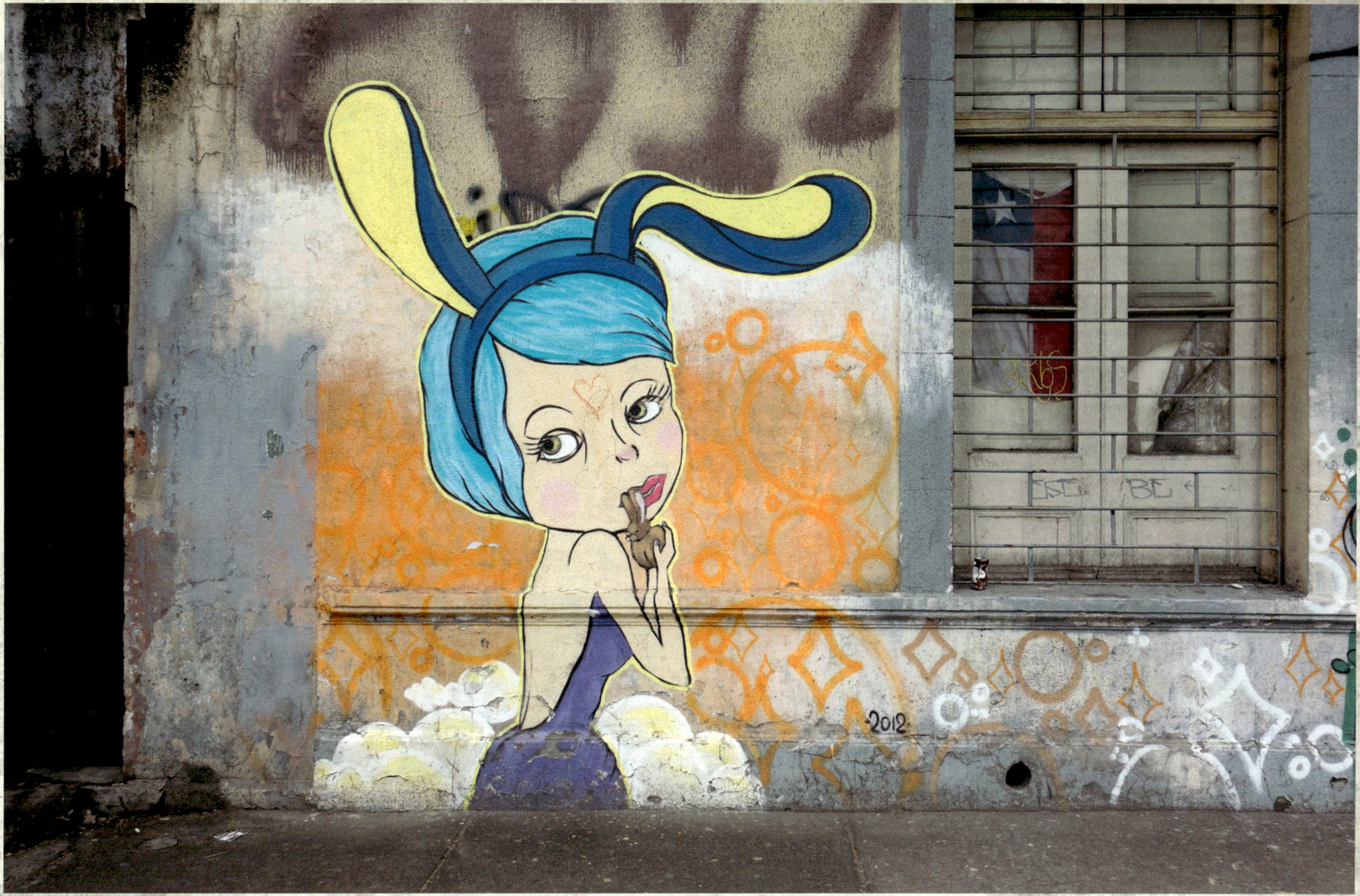

Drems

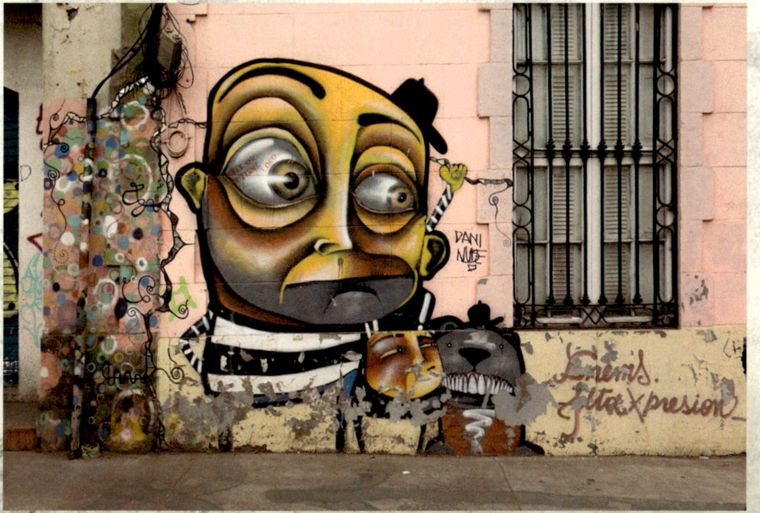

Coas

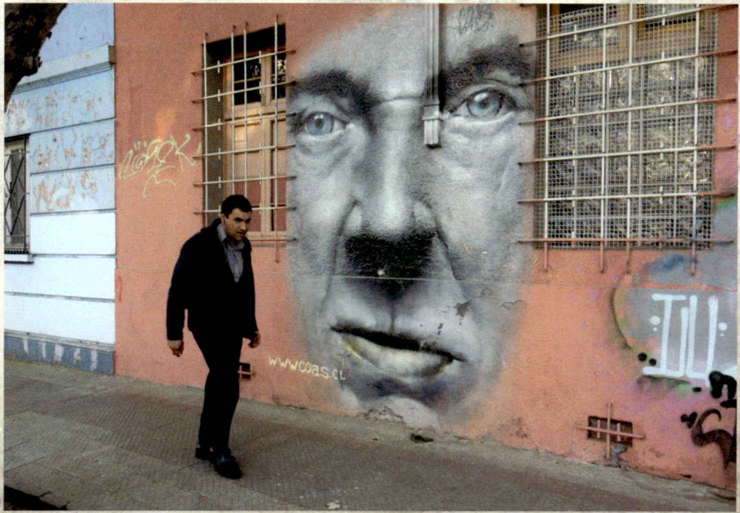

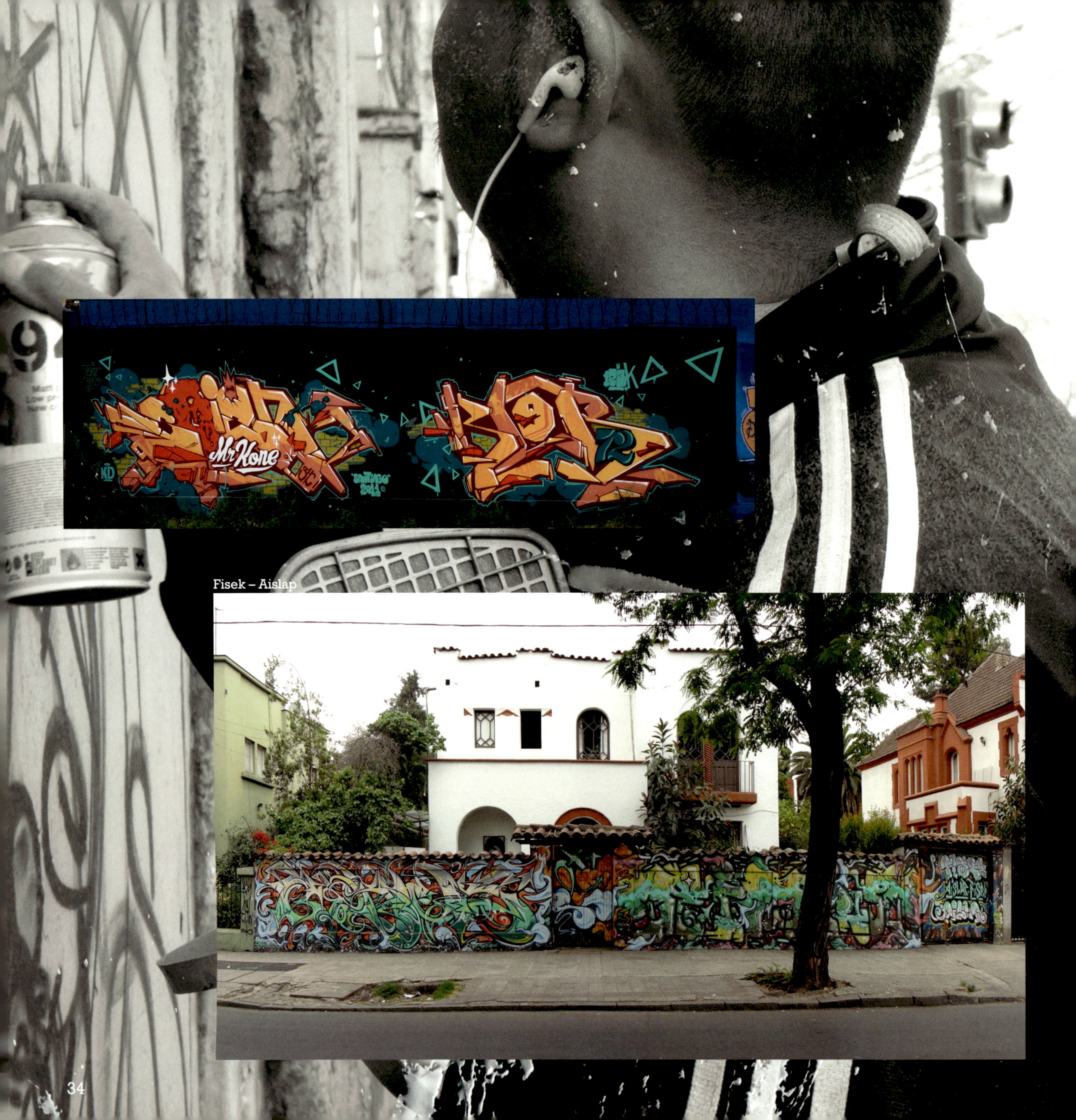

Fisek – Aislap

"Graffiti is letters. The cartoons, backgrounds, everything that comes up are parallel things, but in its essence, it is letters. For me, the concept of wildstyle is incredibly important. It has to do with crazy typography, with the direction of the arrows and with the personality of the letters. These have an abstract impact on people, but my main audience isn't the people, it's me. I do this first for me, so that I can contemplate my graffiti and focus on the details. Then there are other graffiti artists who understand my style and, finally, the general public. Graffiti is a fetish. Staring at a work that you completed and writing your name on it is narcissistic. The bigger the piece, the stronger the impact. Graffiti is about impact. Maybe you walked by so quickly that you couldn't read what it said, but judging from the style, you know Fisek painted it. Graffiti has a sense of liberty—nobody can restrain me, and if I wish to draw crazy typography it's all the same. This is why I occupy the street. For me graffiti also represents a side of me that I do not show in daily life. It's a form of vomiting and letting out repressed emotions. I say it or do it with my artistic expression, with something violent. It's the other me, the devil." **FISEK**

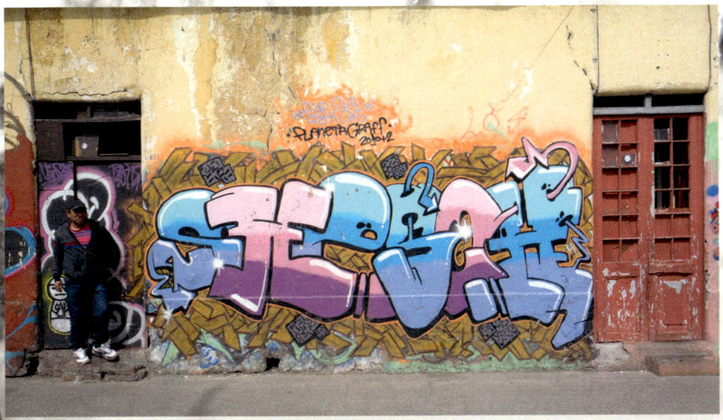

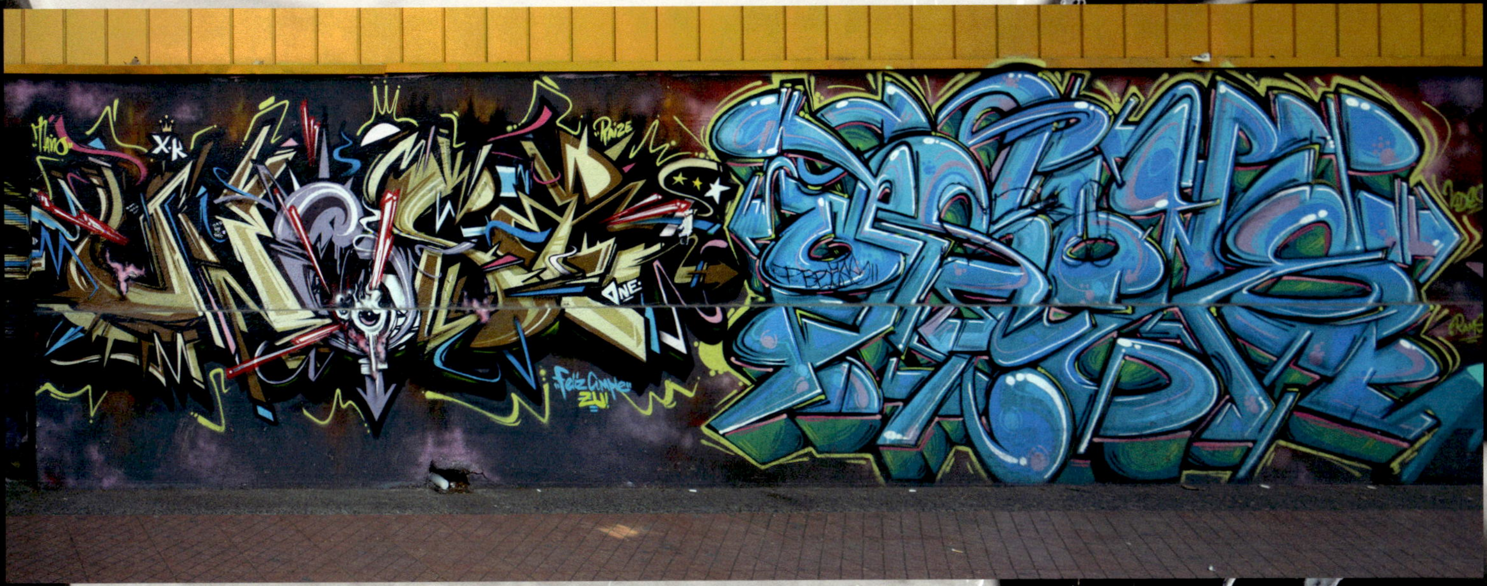

Barrio Brazil

Area: 0.58 KM^2
Population: n/a
Average annual income: n/a
Population below poverty line: n/a
Graffiti prevalence: 8/10

"I have a romantic relationship with this barrio. I love the architecture, the exquisite corners that make great canvases, the antique façades, the people, and the vibrancy. There are many abandoned parts that make a great location to paint or engage in street art. There is a diverse socio-economic mix in the barrio, from those in extreme poverty to the wealthy.

"Graffiti tends to last a long time, generally until the artist decides to renovate his own work. There is a dense amount of street art which includes, murals, stencils, and paste ups. The styles tend to vary a lot. I tend to appreciate all the different styles. When I began to paint the streets in the year 2000, there was hardly any graffiti. It was a forgotten neighborhood. There has been a street art evolution, and now there are many different murals from different artists, creating an open gallery of sorts without limits.

"There is a lot of new construction here, I feel that developers have very little respect for the identity of the neighborhood and are killing it off little by little, I find the avarice and capitalism of the construction companies to be disgusting. However, I still very much enjoy walking around Barrio Brazil. I go out to shop and I say, 'Hi,' to my neighbors, friends and bums. They taught me many things, and they remind me of the nostalgia of an old town, but one in constant evolution." YALUS

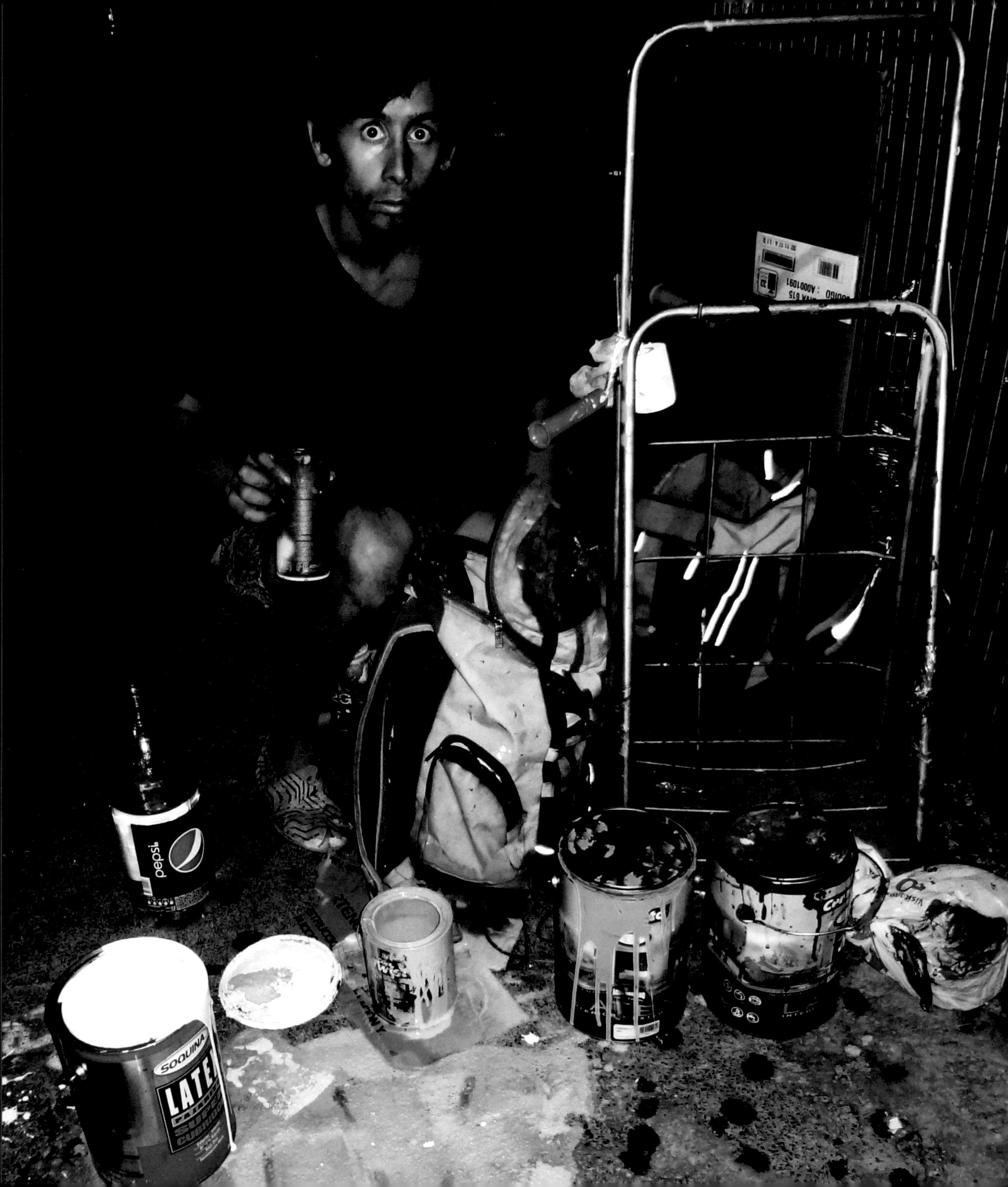
pepsi
SOQUINA

Cubdos – Pium – Azúcar

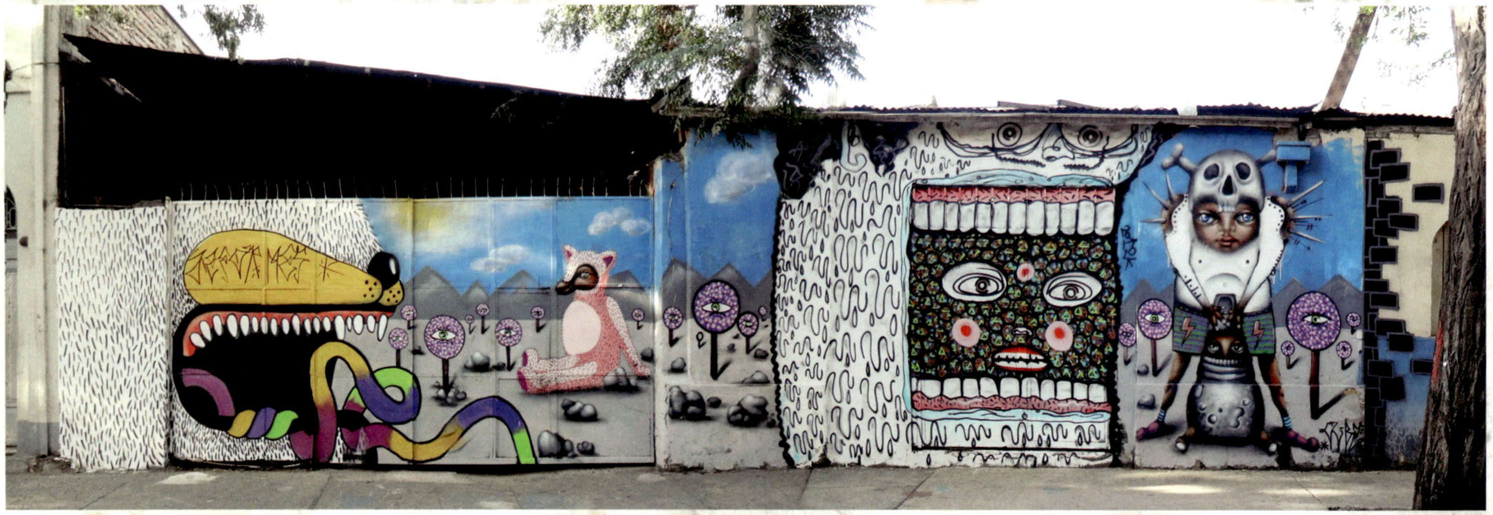

"Even though it may be unsightly to see idiots tagging on walls, many of them don't have any other way of expressing themselves. Maybe they are vandalizing, but they could be doing worse things. I was an introverted young person who didn't have many friends and who nobody knew. I began to hang out with other dudes who were also very quiet and we began to paint graffiti. Other guys liked what we did, and that drew attention to us. I offer my apologies to those whose houses I vandalized, but at least it served the purpose of helping me gain maturity. Most of graffiti artists don't paint to attack the system. They wish to be heard and let people know 'I was here.' There is nothing more pleasurable than doing something illegal like walking all night with a spray can in hand, painting graffiti. When you experience this you will realize what I'm talking about." **DEFOS**

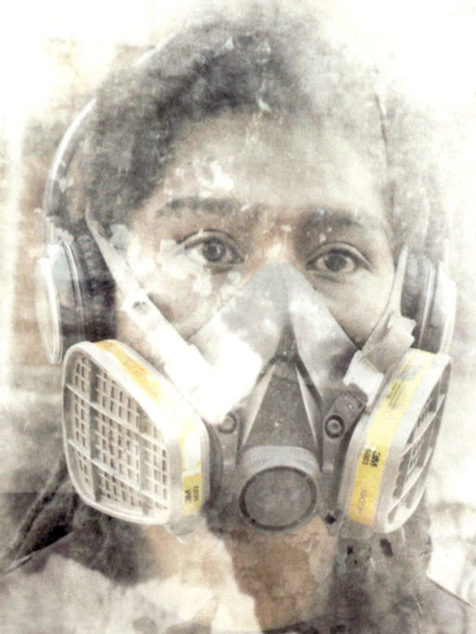

Pium – Azúcar

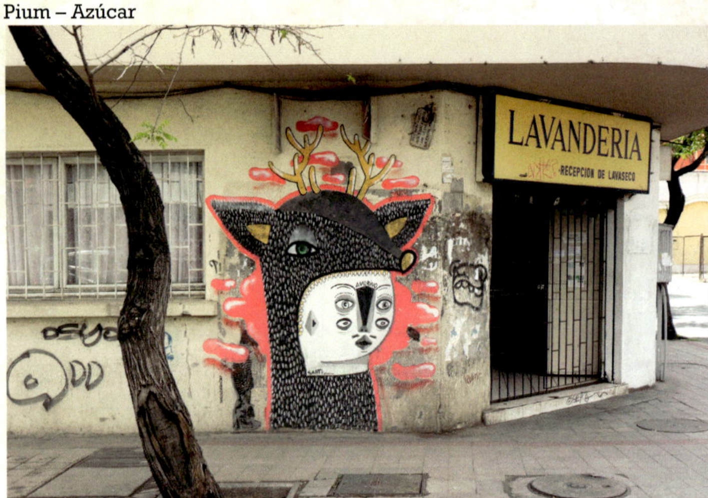

"Graffiti is having a major impact in cities. New spaces are becoming available, and there are projects to paint entire neighbourhoods." **MC PATO EGROSONE**

Henruz – Mara – Shampú – Nebs

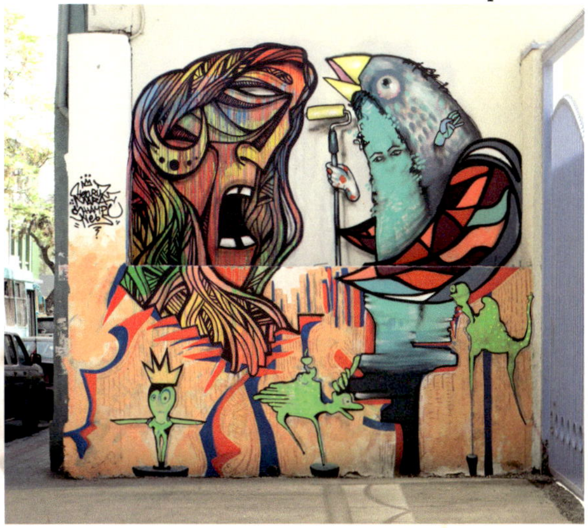

"We are interested in the city and its expansion. We want to take back the barrio and denounce this invasive and disrespectful expansion of the city, [like what is happening in] Brazil. They are amputating the barrio and turning it into nothing. While it is a barrio, it has historic value within Santiago. We believe that it is the people that make this barrio, so this is why we portray people in our murals as well as houses, architecture, and anything that shows that the painting is inserted within a context, independent of the point of view of the audience. It's always improvised. From the moment that we start to paint we always say, "Let's establish a horizon and from there on we begin to compose." We once painted a series of murals that symbolized the 'goodbye of the beautiful barrio,' in places where a construction company was installing itself. We painted houses that began to escape, symbolizing the barrio that begins to leave, like the populations of Brazil who begin to emigrate. If they leave, the barrio emigrates." **MUTAY**

Mokas

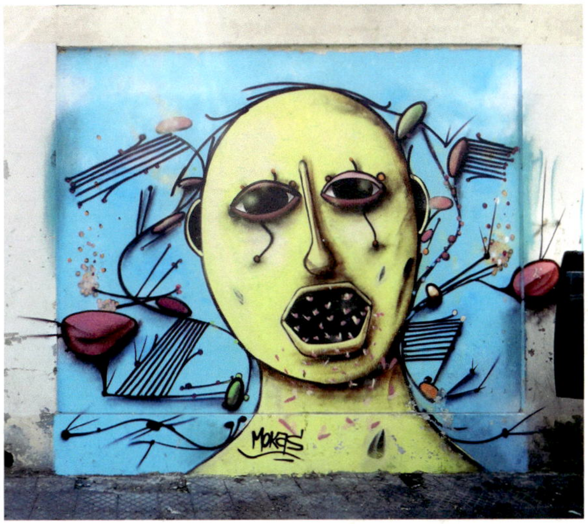

"During the student conflicts, I saw a great amount of graffiti with messages pertaining to that movement, and I think that's fine. The history of this movement has been silenced, and now there is an opportunity for graffiti artists to express themselves. Graffiti has been under an incredibly repressive vision that catalogs it as vandalism. It has taken time for it to be considered art.

"If you don't paint on the street, then you don't paint graffiti. If you don't do what you think, then it is only a thought. When you make graffiti a part of you, anything that you see reminds you of it. It's not just painting on a wall, but also feeling that graffiti makes you freer. It's like a canal by which you begin to filter many of the things that happen to you. It has nothing to do with sex; graffiti frees men and women alike, and all can take part in it." **WEND**

Unknown

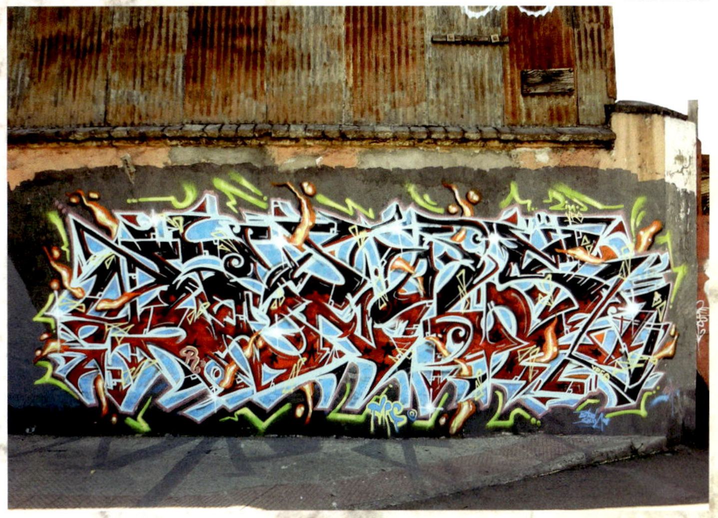

"I don't have a defined style; my style is to constantly change and not enclose myself. I like challenges, like finding a wall and searching for inspiration to paint. I am drawn to painting at night and working quickly. I used to love creating big productions, but now I've changed. I'm in another phase of my life. What most inspires me is the sensation of liberty. Today, I comprehend it, and it comes naturally to me, because I have done it all my life. Going out into the streets, taking cans and painting makes you free. Trashing and spewing in a space makes you free and a transgressor, which makes you a distinct type of human being. That's what I seek for myself: a life that doesn't transform into the life of a common person, but into something different, not because of egocentricity, but only so I can feel good." **KASINO**

"Muralism in Chile has a collective connotation of teamwork. Anyone who doesn't know how to paint can participate, in contrast to graffiti, which is more personal, and where graffiti artists work alone or in groups of three or two."

"My artwork comes from muralism and is inspired by occupying public space and communicating messages. My technique comes from style. We use paintbrushes: one would outline with black and others would be in charge of filling in the images. This began around 1970, which is when people began to occupy public space, such as the Chicanos in the United States with their graffiti. Without knowing that this was being done in other parts of the world, we were doing it here in Chile. Painting public space is a form of protest and the only means of communication that we had at the socio-economical level.

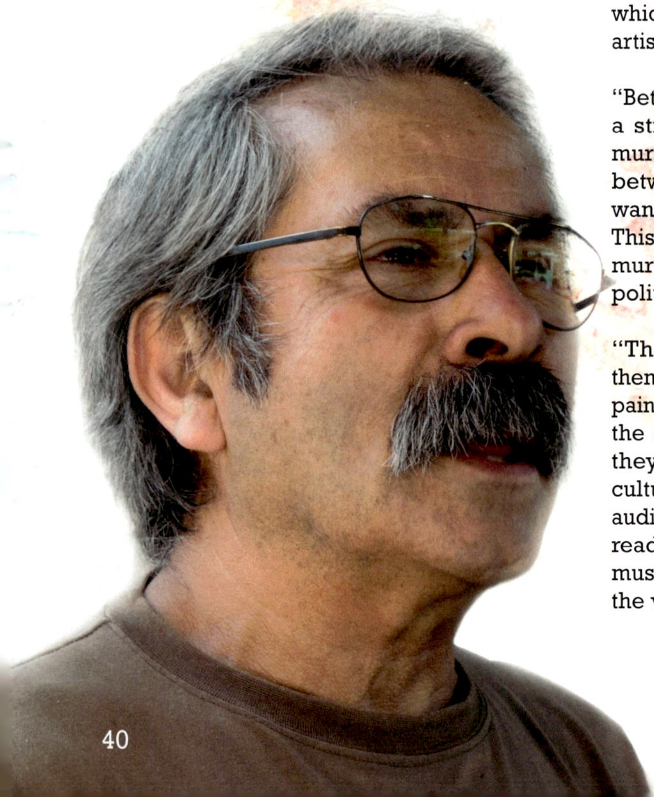

"During the dictatorship, muralism began to pop up in the lower class neighborhoods as a form of protest and as a means of expressing your existence, your being alive, and your desires or your support of the struggle of the lower classes against the dictatorship. This gave birth to a generation of youth during the 1980s and 1990s that began to use the language of graffiti. Today, this generation of youngsters are between twenty-seven and thirty years of age, approximately, and they are the eldest with the most style. Youth had the capacity to move swiftly, with agility and strength, so they grouped together and began the language of graffiti artists.

"Muralism in Chile has a collective connotation of teamwork. Anyone who doesn't know how to paint can participate, in contrast to graffiti, which is more personal and where graffiti artists work alone or in groups of three or two.

"Between the 1980s and the 1990s there was a strong definition of what qualified as muralism and graffiti. There was an abyss between the two techniques, and one didn't want to have anything to do with the other. This is because the dictatorship stigmatized muralism as a political channel for certain political parties.

"There is a need for youth to express themselves. Graffiti and other forms of public painting is their canvas of preference because the streets aren't private, they're free and they belong to everyone. Now, all these cultural expressions are directed toward an audience that is in transit; therefore, the visual read of a mural must be very quick and it must educate, orient, convince, and make the viewer want to participate.

"Our muralism has the social function of involving and making participants of the entire community or the passing spectators. It is not necessary to be an artist to occupy public space. When others get involved, there is a social liberation of the community and of art.

"What I do began forty years ago and is now coming back. I continue to work with this technique, but not with nostalgia. There is an identity, a seal, a characteristic that distinguishes paintings and is uniform despite the diversity of graffiti artists. The style of the Ramona Parra Brigade has become commonplace and is a language of its own, an inheritance. Maybe it had an individual origin, but today it is everyone's heritage, an identity and national style.

"Art is permanently alive. He who wants to paint graffiti and never wants his work to be erased doesn't know the rules of the game. I need to work hard to occupy the same space tomorrow. I recall that we would paint murals on the same wall of Plaza Italia during the rule of Allende. In the morning, we would paint beautiful murals only to erase them in the afternoon and paint another. It never pained me to paint another one, because I communicated one thing to the commuter in the morning and when he returned in the afternoon, the space would be changed and he would find another message on the same wall. This is when the city comes alive, and is a portfolio that is constantly being updated. It has something to do with performance art, with an artistic intervention of the streets. I would beware of paint brands, nowadays. They sponsor artists but their objectives are to sell clothes and shoes. That is their only interest in the youth." **MONO GONZÁLEZ**

"Muralism is concerned with **expressing** an idea, a political movement. Graffiti is a more **liberal and enjoyable** expression; it's more about having a **good time.**" ACCK

"Graffiti is **vandalism** and self-advertising, and muralism, particularly **the brigade** in Chile, is a **political action** with a political cause to spread a political **ideology.**" YISA

"The **problem** with muralism is that there isn't much **innovation.** I read a book about **muralism** in Mexico and many of the **works** that I saw in the book were **similar** to what is being painted **today.**" GUZTOK

"Graffiti is **like pricking** the system and **muralism** is like sending **a letter** to the **system.**" AGOTOK

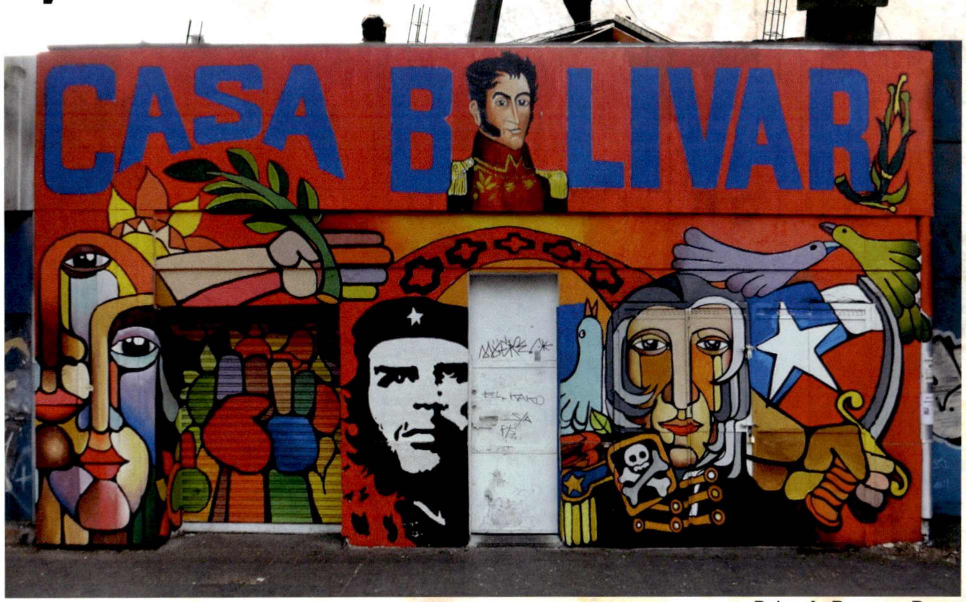

Brigada Ramona Parra

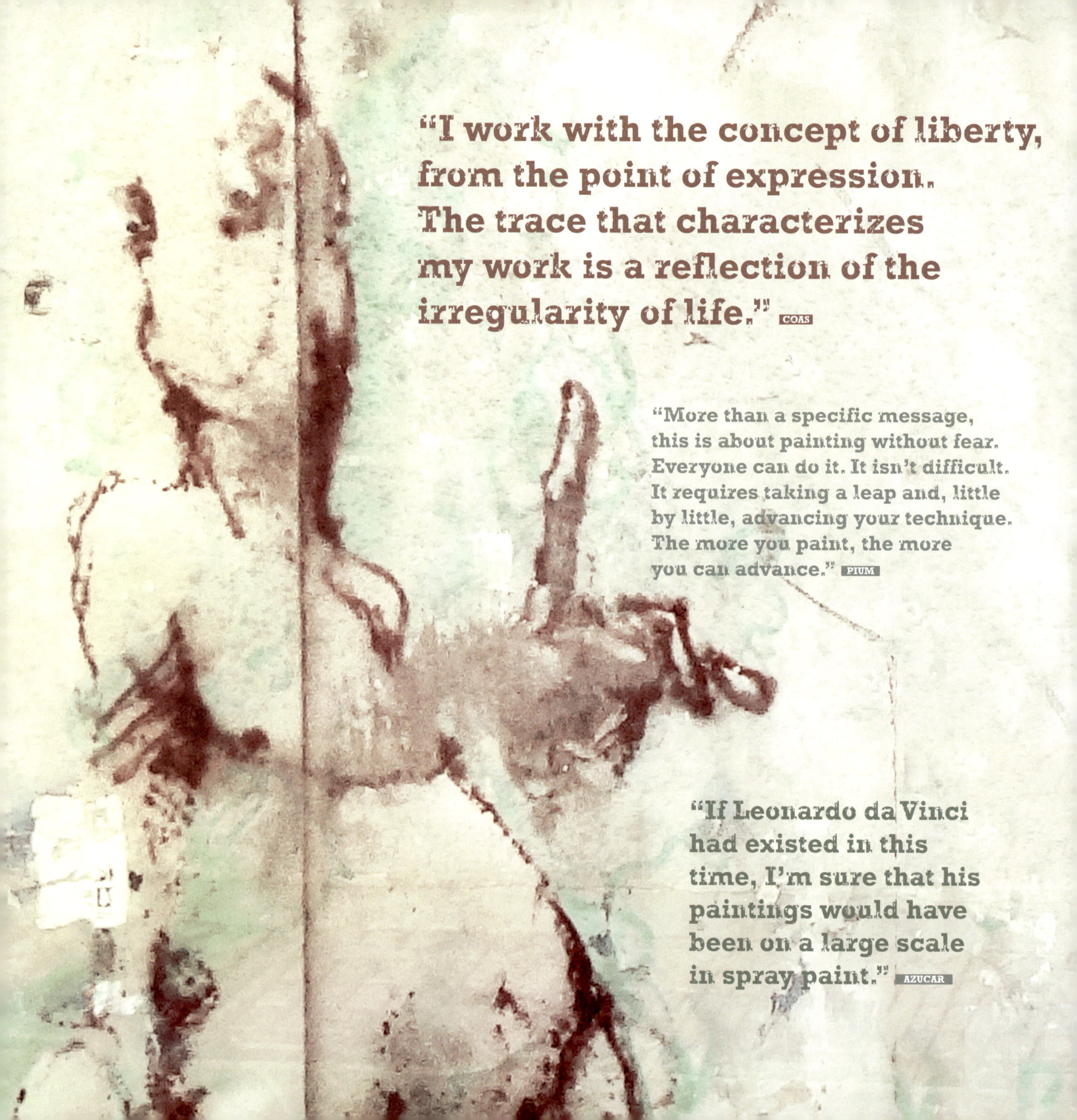

"I work with the concept of liberty, from the point of expression. The trace that characterizes my work is a reflection of the irregularity of life." COAS

"More than a specific message, this is about painting without fear. Everyone can do it. It isn't difficult. It requires taking a leap and, little by little, advancing your technique. The more you paint, the more you can advance." PIUM

"If Leonardo da Vinci had existed in this time, I'm sure that his paintings would have been on a large scale in spray paint." AZUCAR

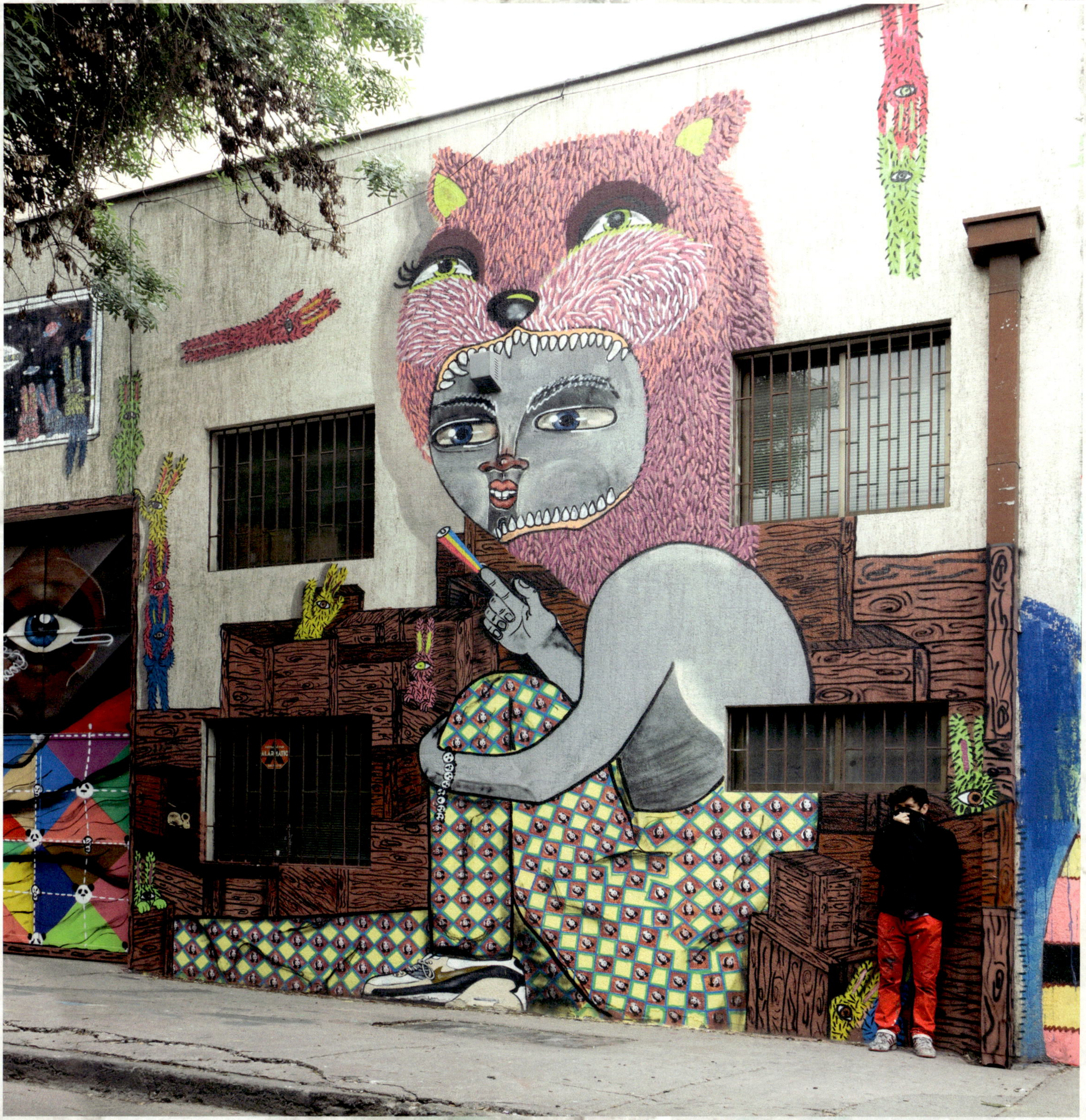

"Not **everyone** who paints the **street is** a graffiti **artist.** Only the ones who do it **illegally qualify.**

"If a worker were told **to spray-paint** an **image outside** a home... would that be considered **graffiti**, too? That doesn't **count for me.**" AZÚCAR

"**The way I work** is that if there are people **living in** the house, I will ask **permission** to paint on the wall. If the house is **abandoned,** and there is **no one** living there, then **I will paint.**

"Here in **the centre** of the city, **people** have very deteriorated **facades** and they don't mind that **you paint** them so that the **look** of their house is **freshened up.**" PIUM

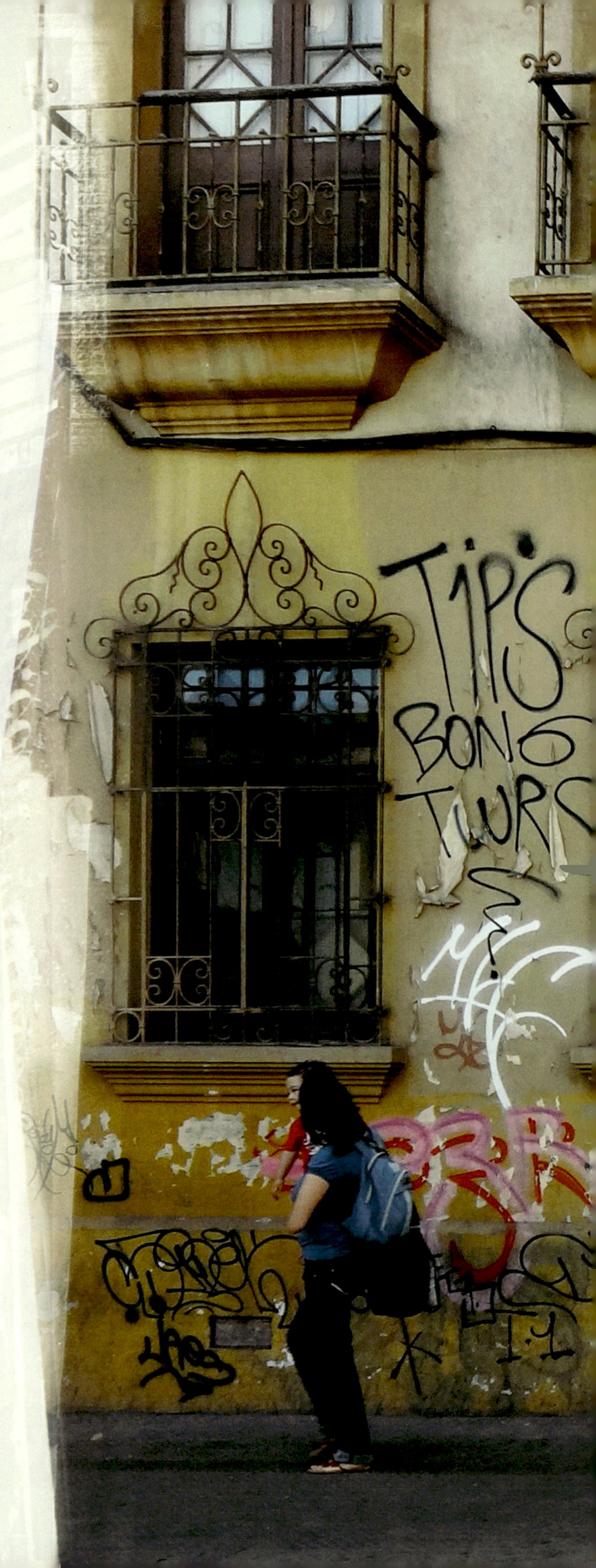

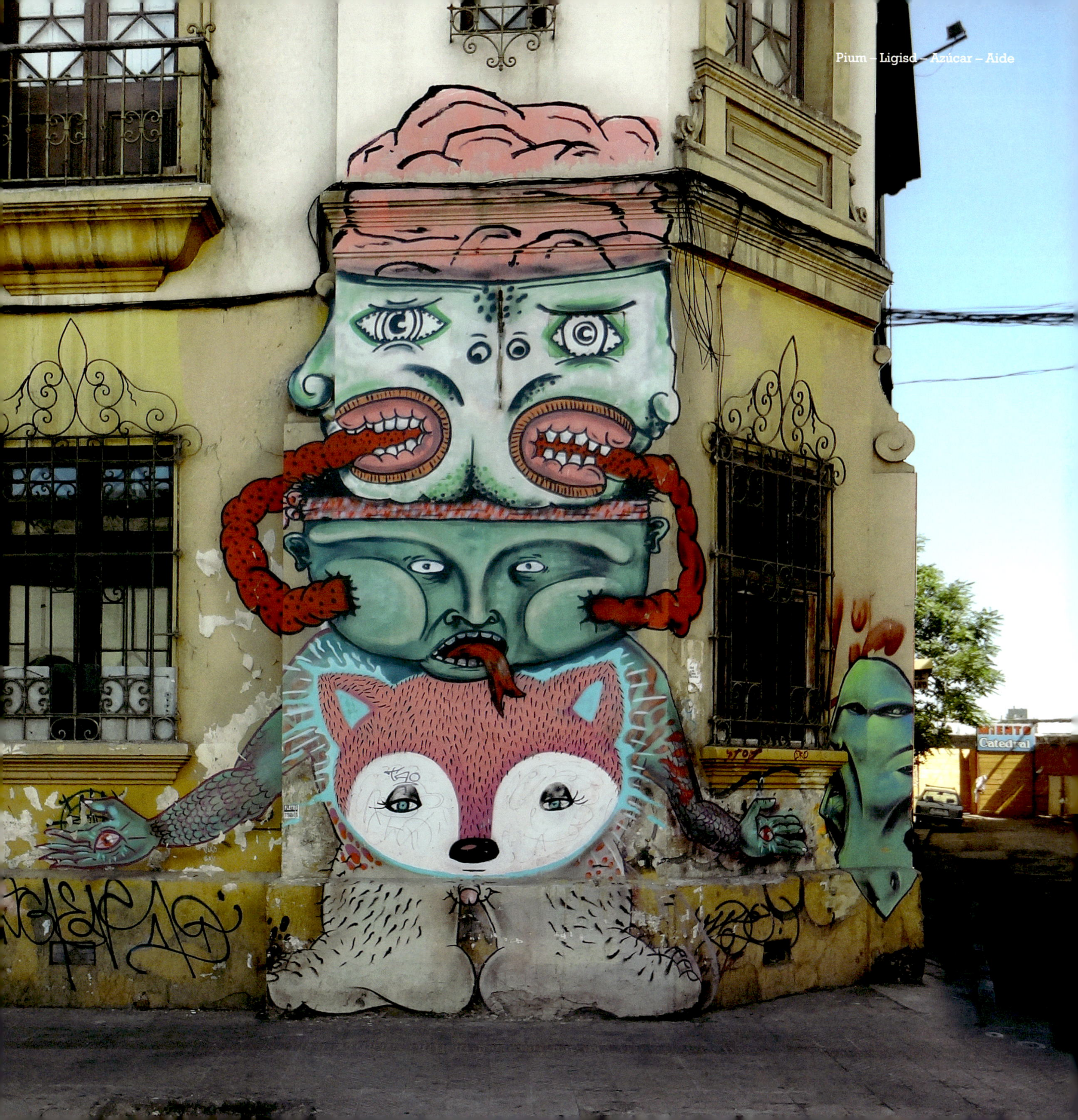

Pium – Ligisd – Azúcar – Aide

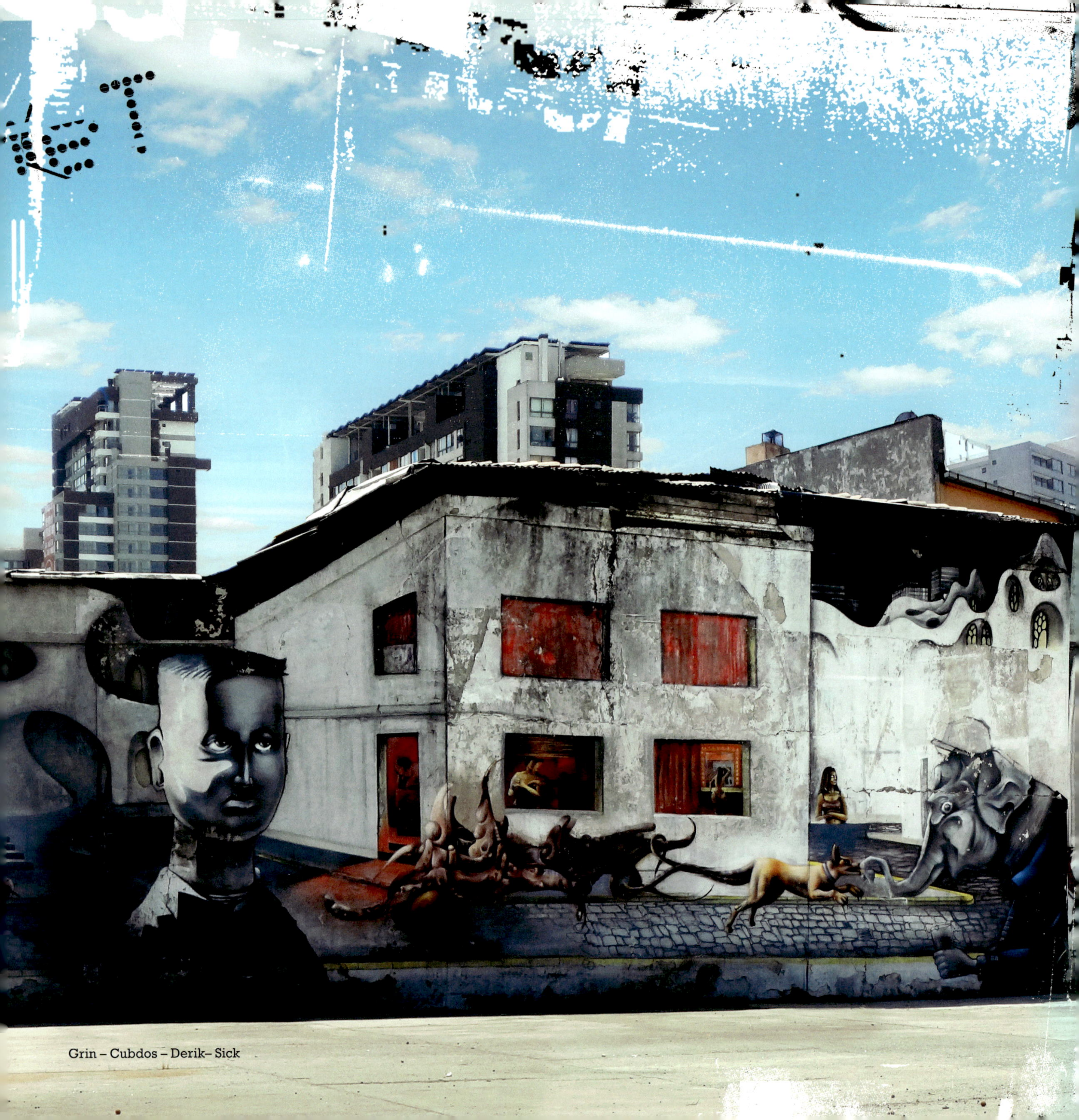

Grin – Cubdos – Derik– Sick

"Between the years 2000 and 2010 there was a really important crew that made history in the Santiago graffiti art scene. They are the DVE crew, comprised of Cekis, Grin, Derik, and Sick. They created a new school of graffiti art that motivated a lot of aspiring artists who now have their own unique styles." **CN6**

"I have been painting for several years, and you could say that I belong to the old school. At first, it was difficult to access information, magazines, valves, and specialized cans as there weren't any shops dedicated to selling graffiti merchandise. I recall that in those times we were all impressed by Cekis's tag, because we didn't have fat caps, so we couldn't figure out how he did it. We would go to the supermarket and steal deodorant to use the valves. We would cut them and modify them, but our tags wouldn't come out the same. We were also influenced by the visit of Os Gemeos. They came with the bombing technique and told us that we had to bomb Santiago. Today, everything is different, as there is internet access and many resources. Artists are able to develop their own style in less time.

"I believe that it is difficult to deliver a message through painting because the interpretations of the observers are very diverse and ambiguous. Paintings speak for themselves, beyond the painter. Obviously, there exists an intrinsic content that generates and is externalized, but that content is mainly internal. The textual idea that "I'm going to express this concept in a drawing" doesn't exist. What I do is in the form, the color, the volume of the painting itself. When I work, there are certain elements that I generally use, like the face, the human figure, and children. I try to center my work in a context that can manifest questions in the mind of the observer, but only through the image, not literally. I don't feel like I'm involved in anything, I just want to shock people. If I paint a child with a machine gun, that will shock people, but I don't mean to criticize or make a discourse about it. If I wanted to do that I would meet with a politician and tell him what's going on in the barrios with children. That's a social worker's job. If I'm asked, 'What does your painting express?', I don't feel like responding, because what I do is realism and from that human beings generate interpretations and their own responses." **CUB2**

"I arrived in Chile in 1993. I came with the skills that I learned in France, and I had five years of painting experience under my belt. Over here, nobody painted. A friend of mine introduced me to Nelson, because I wouldn't buddy up with just anyone. Cekis lived in Macul at the time. I began to go out with him, and we would scribble. We liked graffiti in the same way, and we were both addicted to painting. One day, he asks me, "Do you know anyone else that paints?" and I told him, "Six months ago, I met a guy from Pincoya who also paints decently." I was talking about Derik. We all came from different neighborhoods in Santiago, and we began to paint, to go out and see how we worked together. The three of us were inseparable and we became friends. Then, we said, "Let's form a group," and we named ourselves Of The Old School, because we were old school. Later on, Grin entered our group in '97 or '98. He befriended Cekis and then us. As DVE, we painted in Santa Rosa with Alameda and Plaza Italia. Those were the first big productions that we did.

"In 1997, there was a convention in El Bosque. In attendance were Gemeos, Vitche, and Herbert. There were many Brazilian artists, and this was the first big gathering where many artists from different countries came together. This is where I met Agotok; they had started painting a week before. This congregation was monumental, because it allowed people who had never met before, to do so.

"I have great memories of gatherings at Estacion Mapocho. The good thing was that all the different hip-hop inspired movements got together, especially the breakers [breakdancers]. Graffiti in Chile began due to the breakers, because they had seen Beat Street, and some began to paint Cool Style. They didn't have a defined style because the internet didn't exist and there were no magazines, only photocopies. All of them would gather at Estacion Mapocho from different communes to share photos, sketches, converse, have a good time, smoke weed, drink beer, and be together. Everyone would freestyle, leaf through magazines, and the breakers would dance. This happened every Sunday, from two in the afternoon until it dissolved, sometimes lasting until ten at night." **SICK**

"The first time I came to Chile, it was in 2003. At that time, I've been very excited by the quality and variety of street art in Santiago with my meeting with the DVE, Adep, Tpm, Qm, etc… Chile was for me with Brazil, the other Latin American street art place to be. Returning in 2011, I saw how graffiti and street art in Santiago had evolved and was developed in all areas of the city." **SETH**

Piguan – Naira

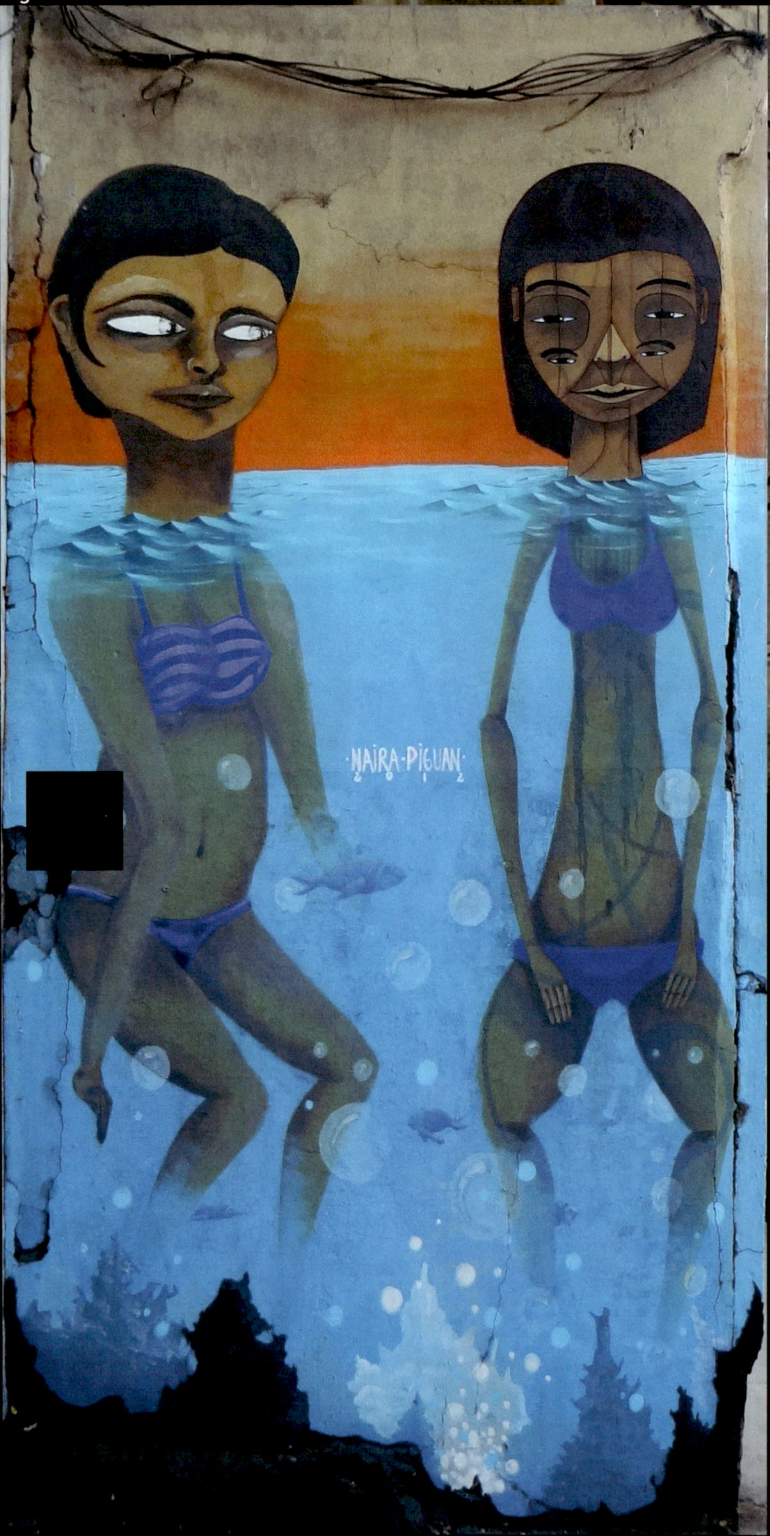

"Art implies a change, a before and an after, a process in which something takes value, or transforms into something admirable. A wall, an object or any material, such as fabric, acquires a certain quality given by the artist that satisfies the subject who views it and transforms the piece into art. Graffiti also responds to this necessity, the need to give value to a wall and, broadly speaking, to a city.

"In Santiago, graffiti is an open gallery, without filters or established rules. Each person or group finds a wall and paints what they wish, which causes heightened competition between artists and a need to be identified by a personal style. For this reason, many types of paintings can be found in Santiago, such as pieces with the themes of politics, football, abstracts, ethnicity, and realism, among many more.

"There is a need to communicate something to the audience. The wall succeeds in transmitting content, in conjunction with the artist's commitment to the skill and a search for enjoyment each time he or she takes on a project. The latter is the most important factor during the painting process as it's during this time that the message of the piece is created: Experiences, passersby, neighbors, the day itself, and the feeling are what is captured on the wall.

"Colleges still see this technique as something foreign to them, and muralism at the painting level, sculpting, engraving, and other techniques aren't taught in art school. However, including these subjects within a curriculum is being increasingly considered, as street art is taking an important role within the national culture and the quality of the city.

"Street art transcends social and academic barriers as it is primarily of an autodidactic nature. Schools have a similar disposition; old generations teach new ones, international knowledge mixes with national, and a great variety of styles are generated, all united by a common historic root. Colleges are still unsure of how to take on the subject, how to teach it despite its lack of classic structure. It is an art that evolves every day." NAIRA

"I went from the trestle to the wall. I actually didn't have a trestle, but painted in my room kneeling down, or on the ground, wherever I was. I was always painting on canvas, tablets, and cartons. I was suffering financially, so I would paint on any surface I could find. Sometimes, people would gift me canvasses for birthdays.

"I dedicate most of my works to exploring deformity. I like to paint characters with two heads, four legs, and six hands. Characters that are enormous with a small head. With time I have been evolving and adding more aesthetic to these creatures, making them more pleasing to the eye. I carry a lot of resentment with me and that always pops up in my work, as well." **PIGUAN**

Naira

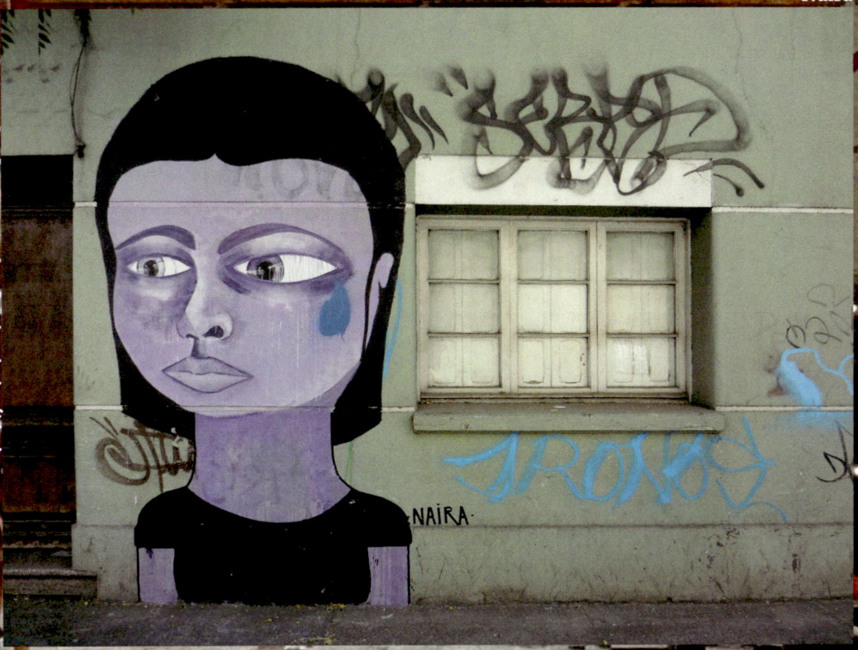

Piguan – Naira

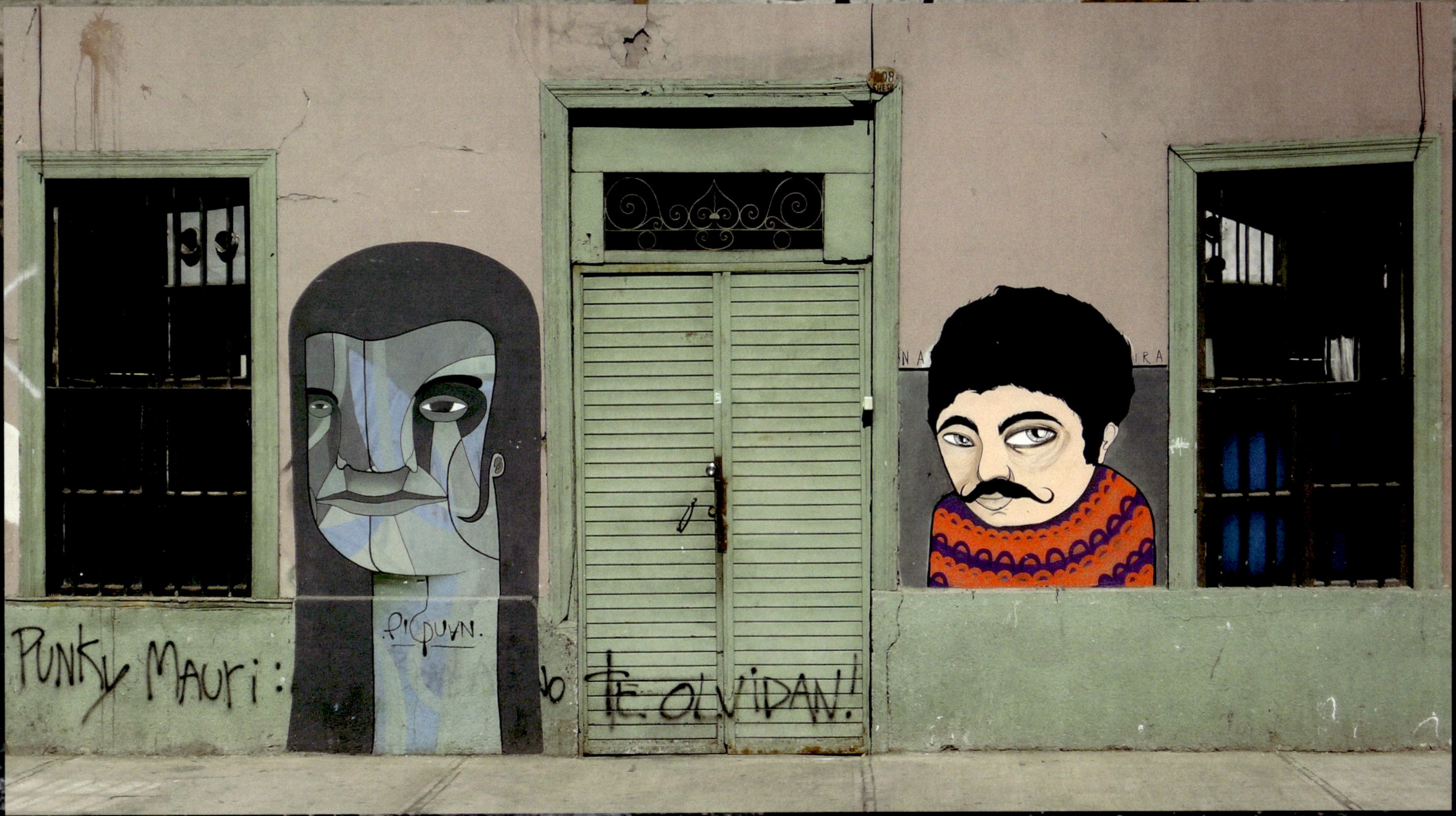

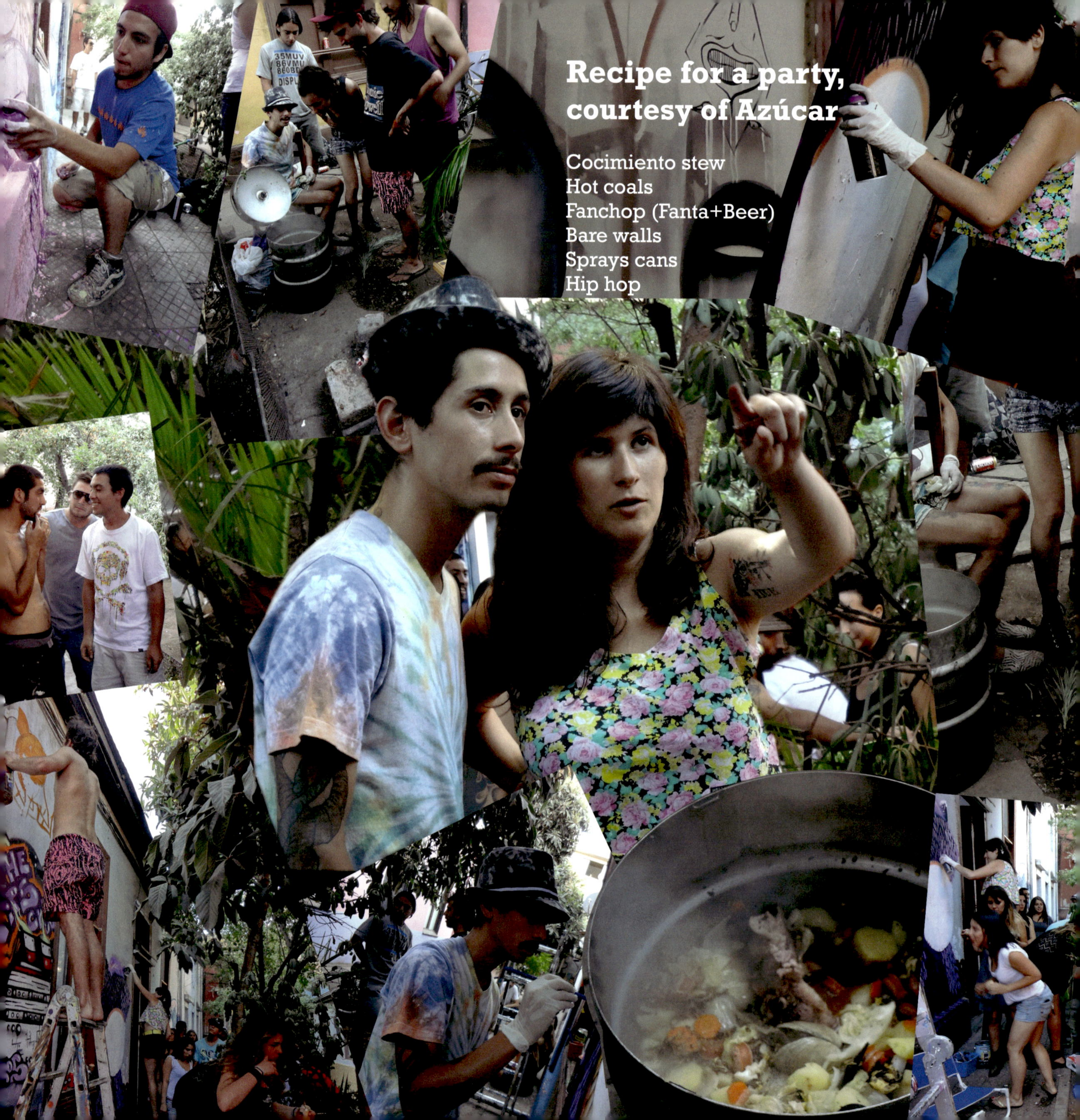

Recipe for a party, courtesy of Azúcar

Cocimiento stew
Hot coals
Fanchop (Fanta+Beer)
Bare walls
Sprays cans
Hip hop

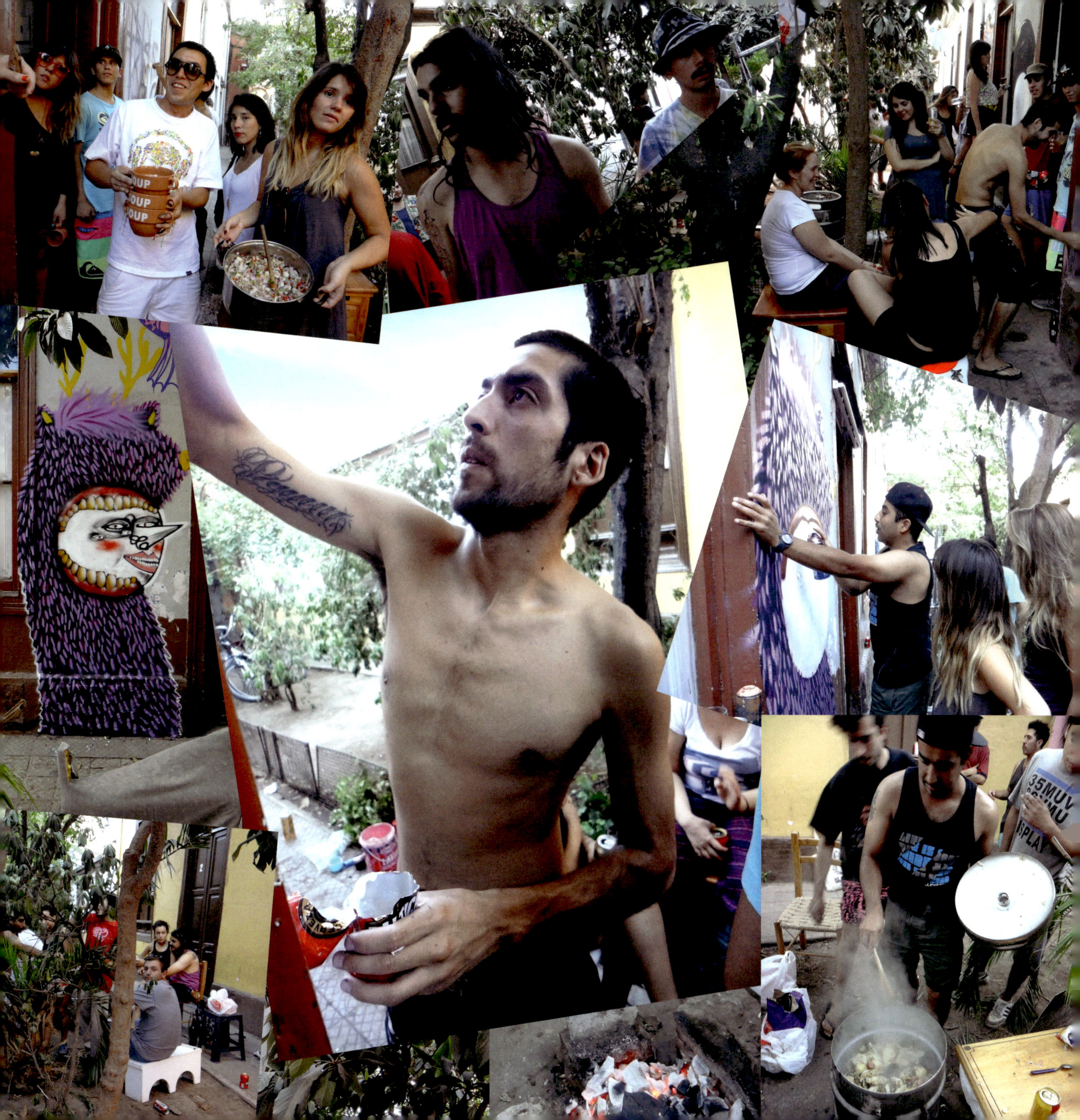

Centro

Area: 20.7 km^2
Population: 392,695
Average annual income: US $28,648
Population below poverty line: 7.3%
Graffiti prevalence: 7/10

"I have always lived in the center of the city; only recently did I move to Bellavista. The center of the city is characterized by an abundant amount of transit at any hour. For this reason, I've always preferred painting on the weekends, especially Sundays, as the rest of the week is chaos, and I like to paint calmly. During the week, many commuters circulate, and there is bountiful commerce causing two faces of Bellavista to share space: the residents who live here and the people that work here, and those that are just passing by.

"In general, nobody paints with color in Centro, unless he is painting a patrimonial building. Criteria must be applied. If you paint on a governmental or law enforcement building, you will be arrested. In general, I have never had problems. Very few times have I had to ask permission to paint. The reality is that there are very few walls in Centro, as most are building or business façades. In Paseo Bulnes, there are various available walls that are usually painted, but every so often, they are renewed. I used to paint often near Tucapel Jimenez street, because I lived there.

"Graffiti that is painted in Centro lasts a long time, approximately two years, before it is erased, unless it is a bomb. The Centro is full of bombs—that is what it has mostly, and they are always being erased only to appear again later. Each time that I pass by the streets of my old barrio, I feel nostalgic, like when you smell perfume that you used in previous years. Many memories of that time in my life come to mind, and, of course, I also feel the desire to renovate the walls that I had painted." NASKA

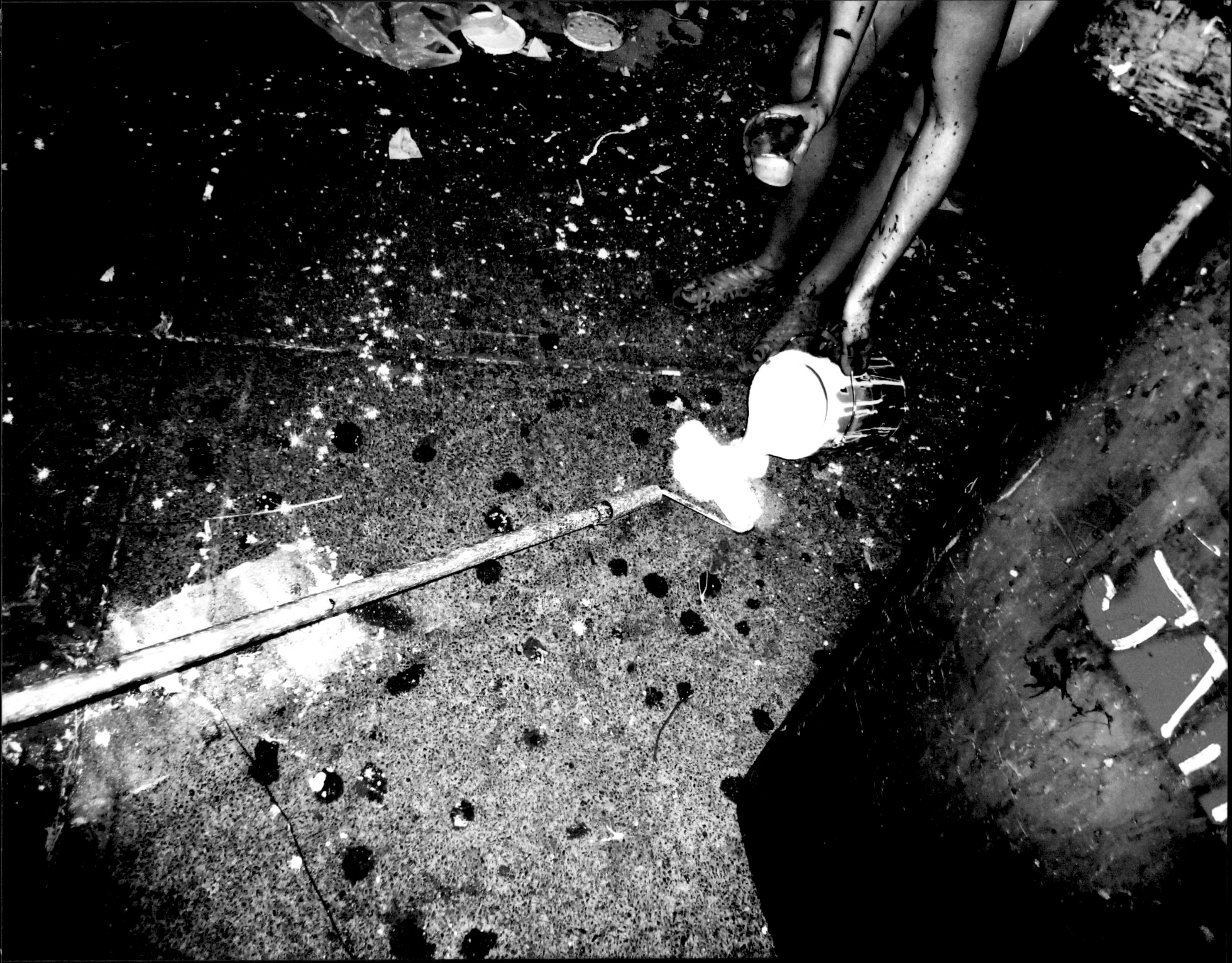

"I would **define** my style as simple, impregnating, **irregular**, and **raw**. It is a **true** reflection of my **personality**." COAS

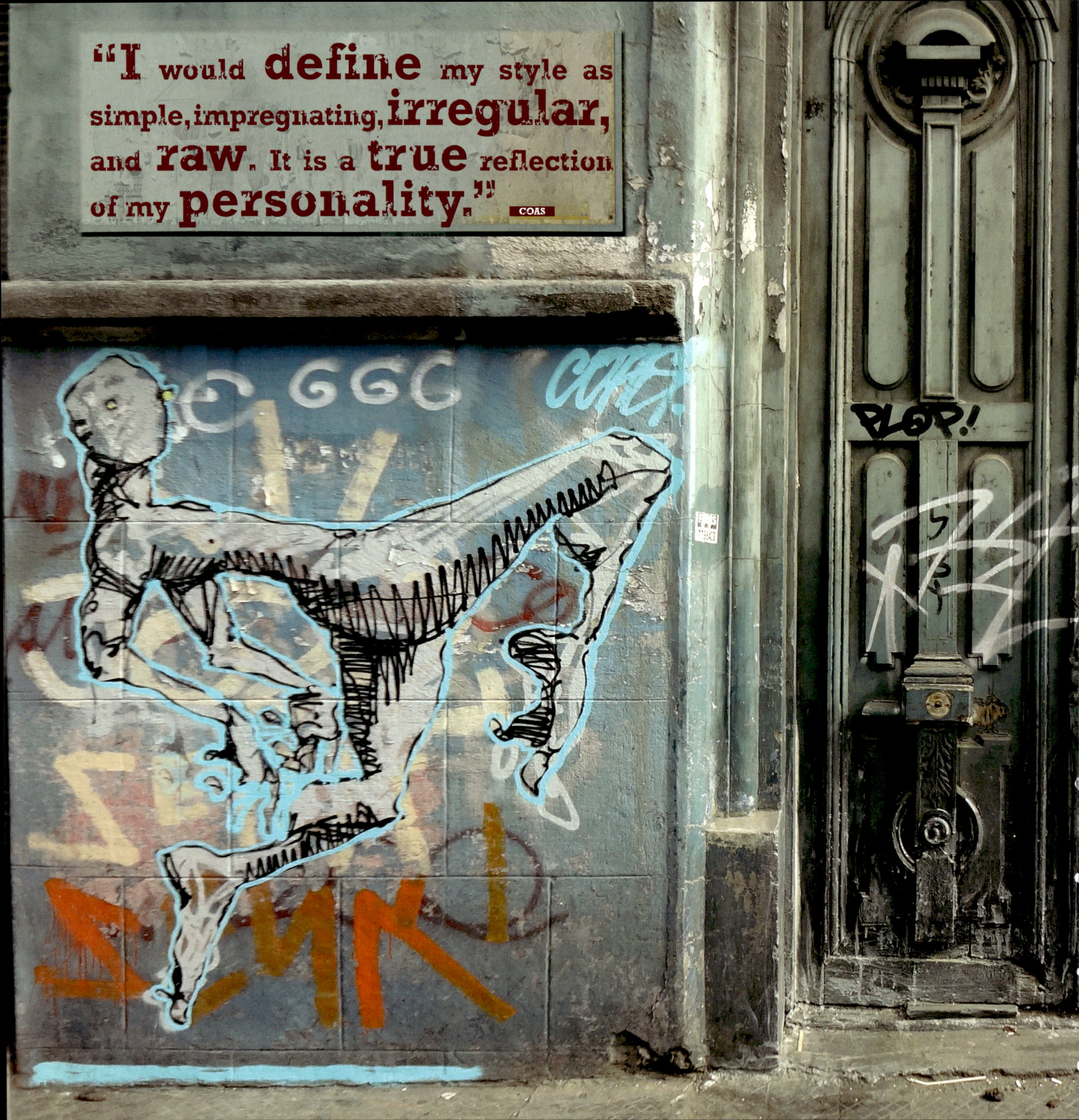

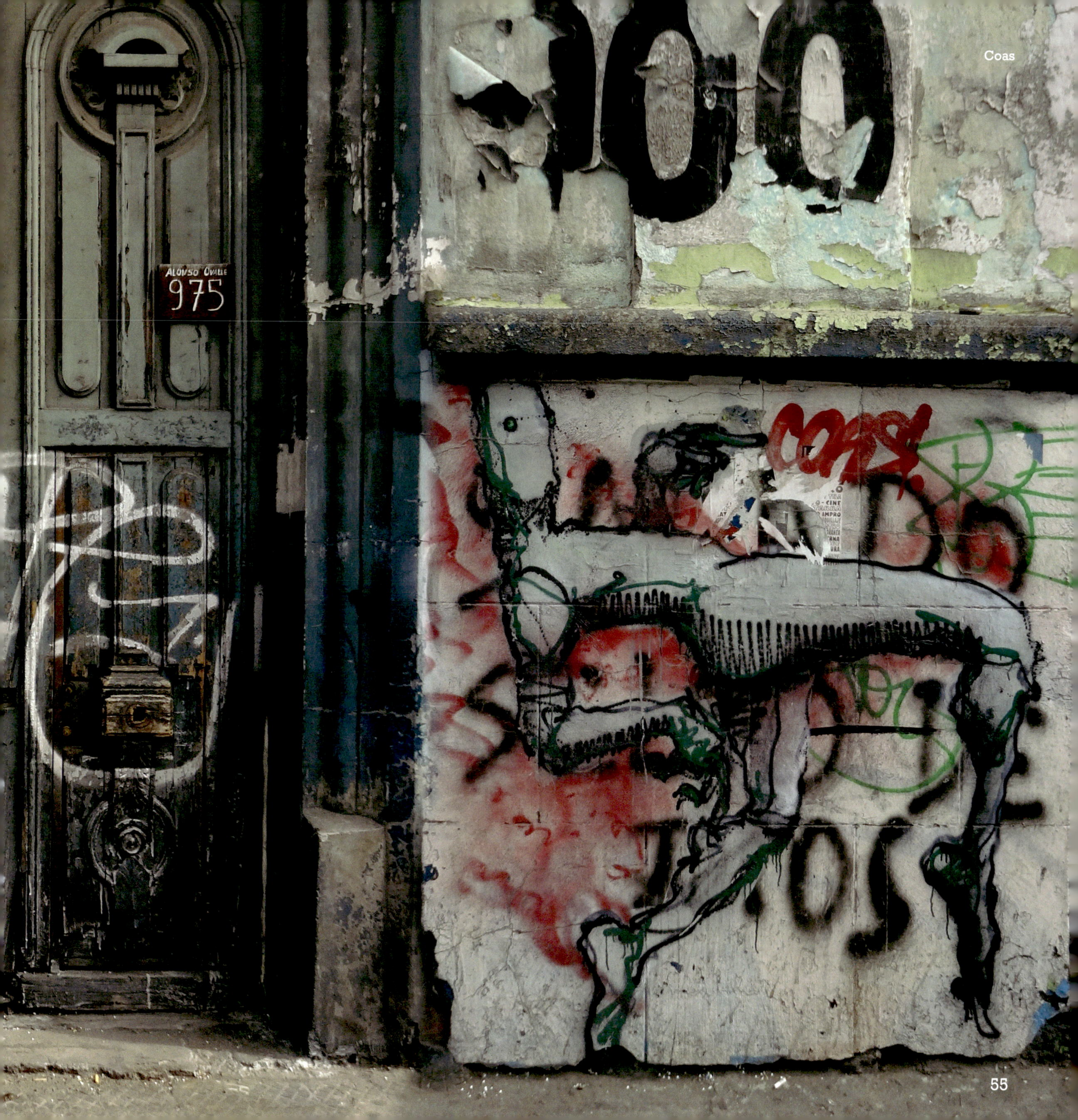
ALONSO OVALLE
975

"In my opinion, tattoos are a vehicle for telling your story and expressing who you are.

"In Chile, many graffiti artists have tattoos, including myself. There are many tattoo shops all around.

"Many graffiti artists choose to become tattoo artists as they can continue to draw and also make a living out of it.

"Graffiti and tattoos are both personal. You leave a part of yourself in it. They are like mirrors that reflect your personality." FAYA

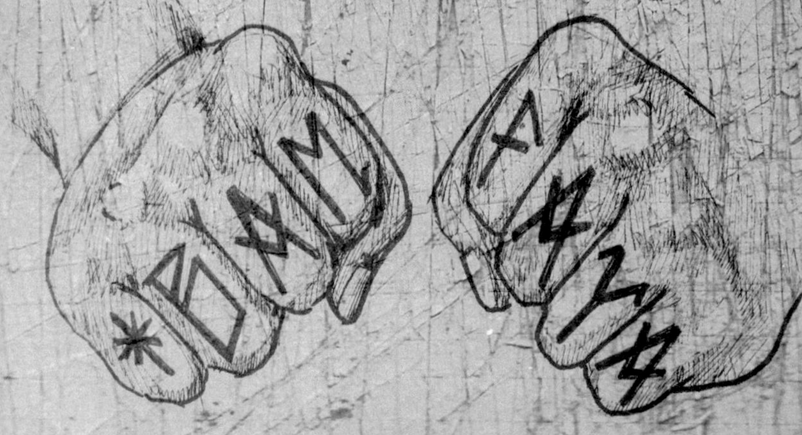

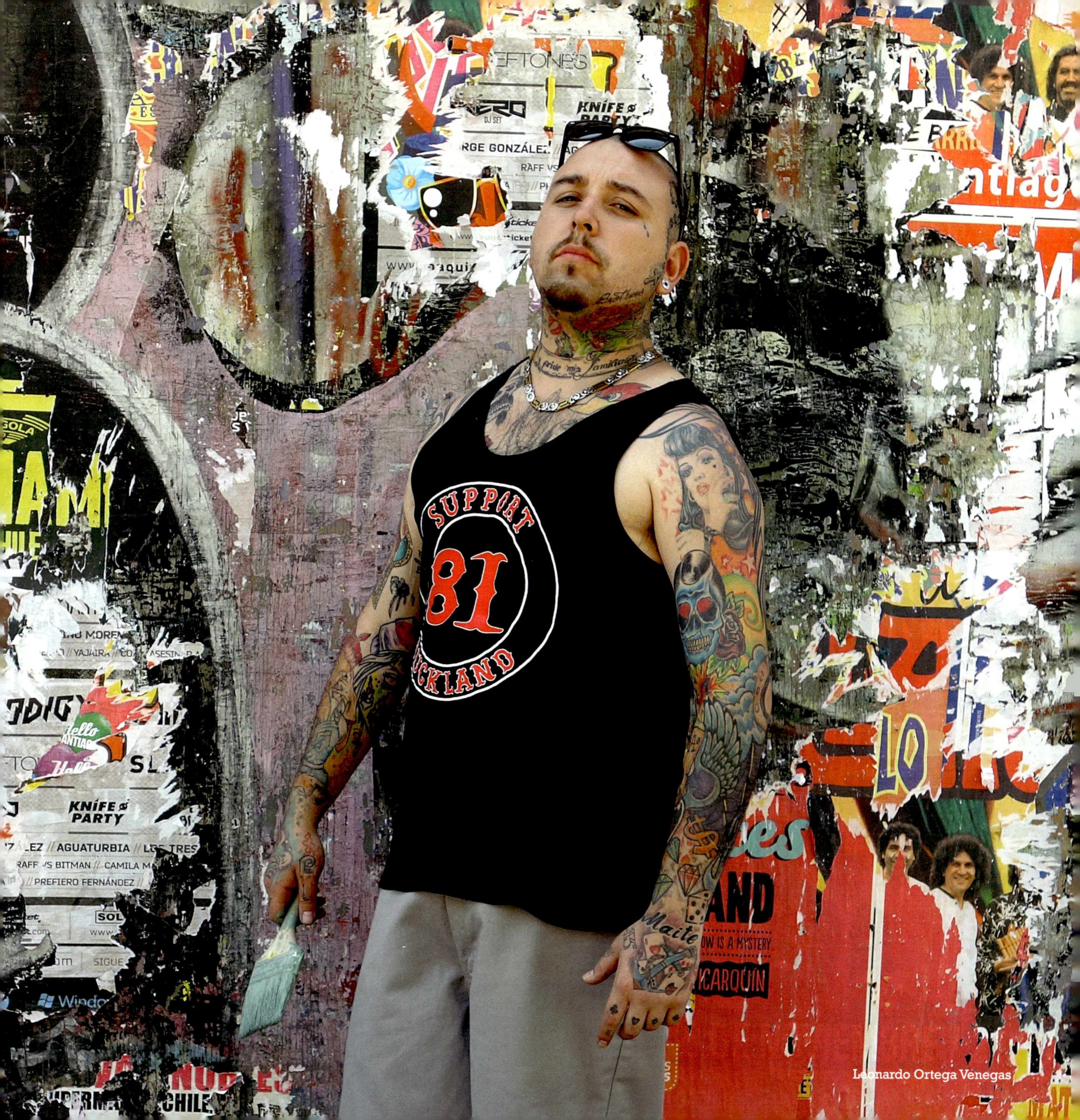

Leonardo Ortega Venegas

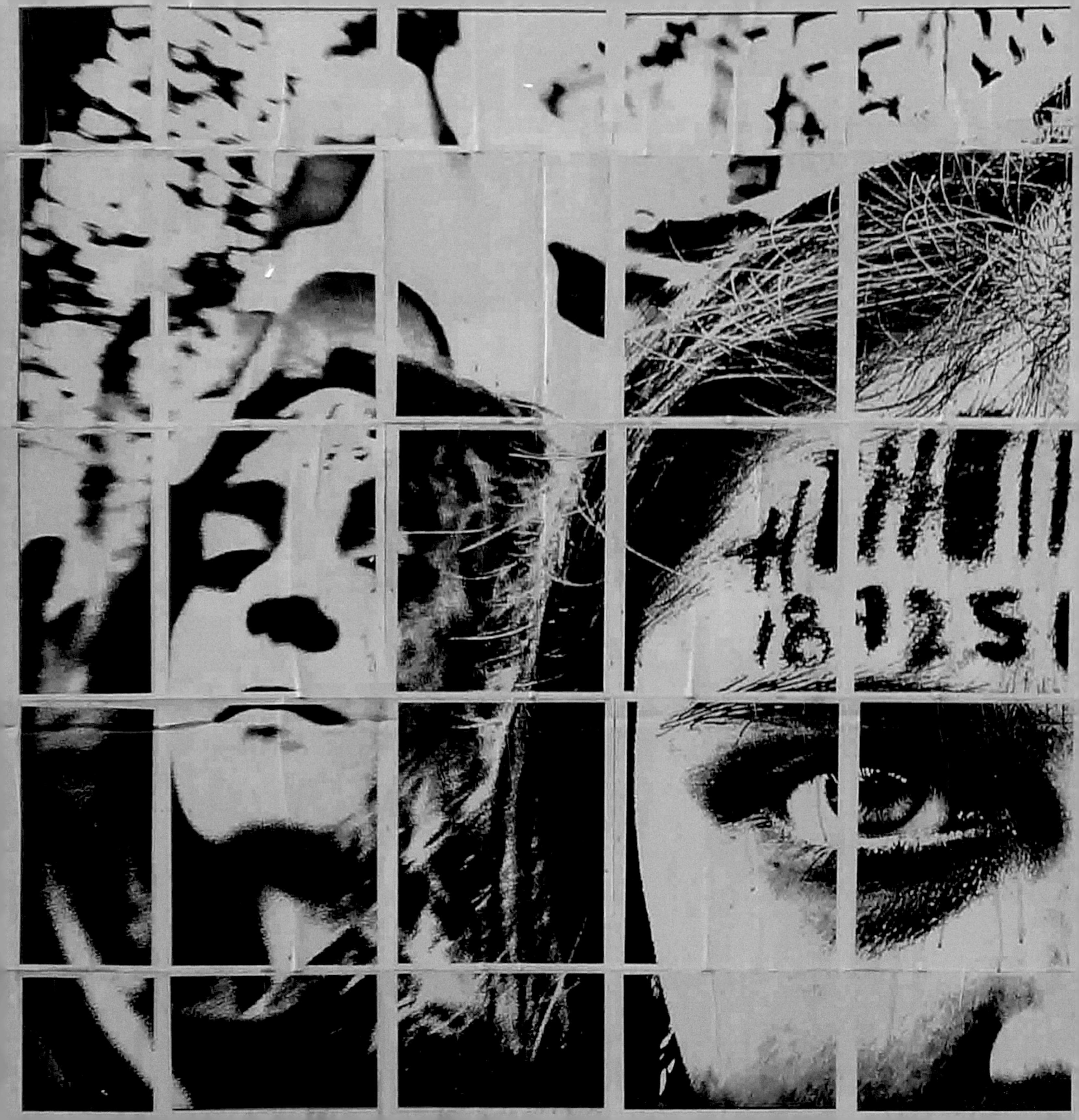

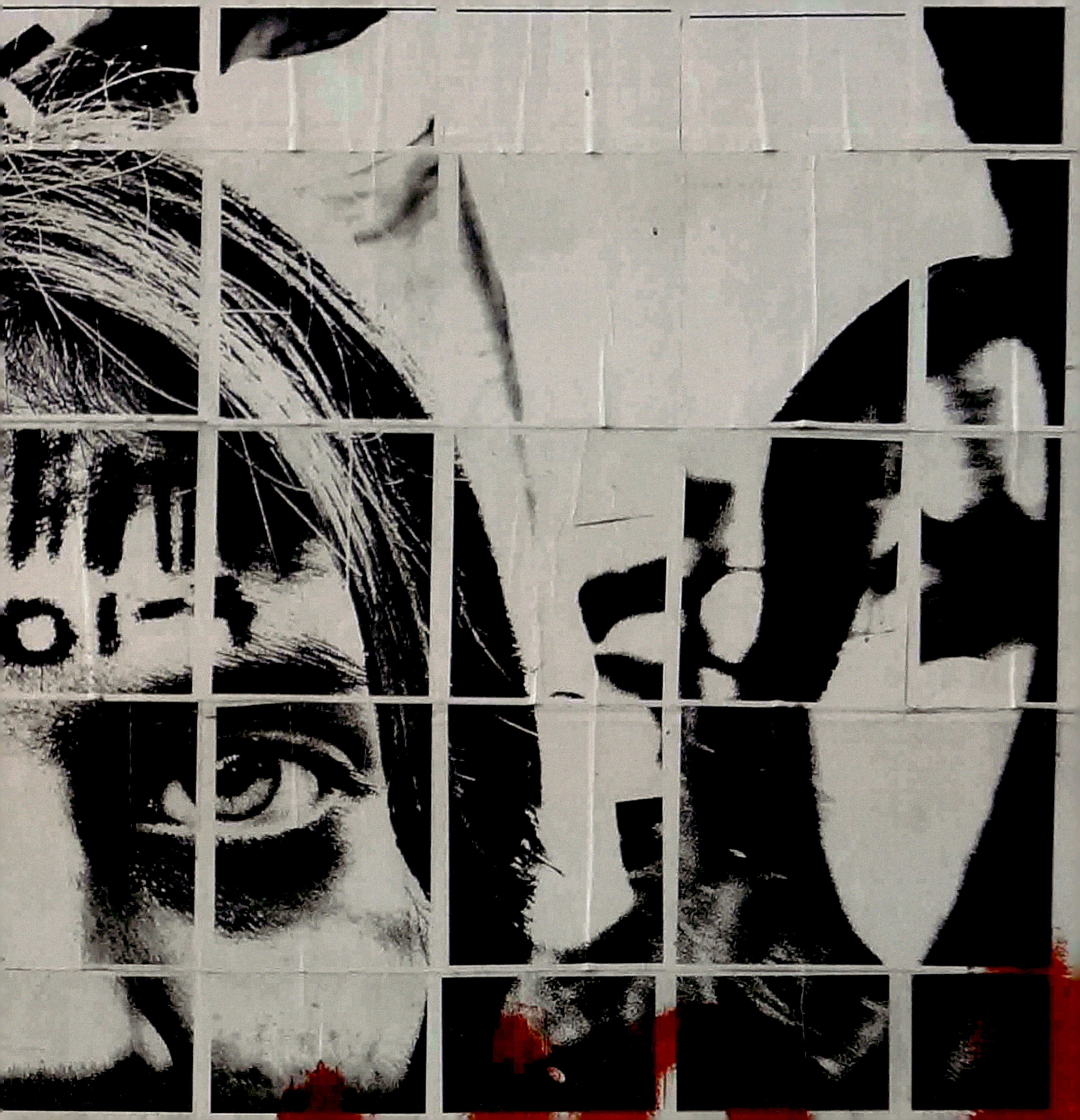

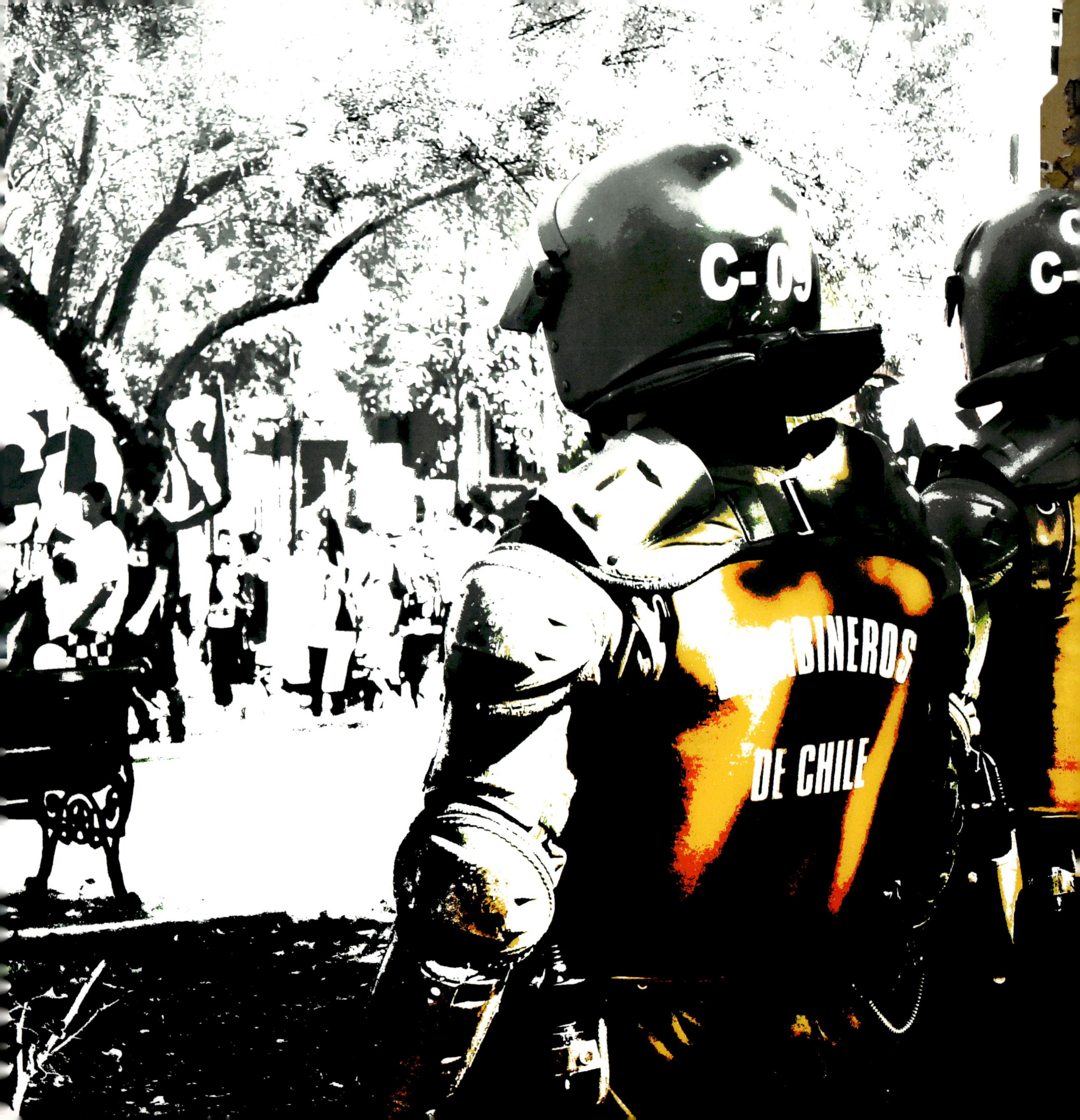
BINEROS
DE CHILE

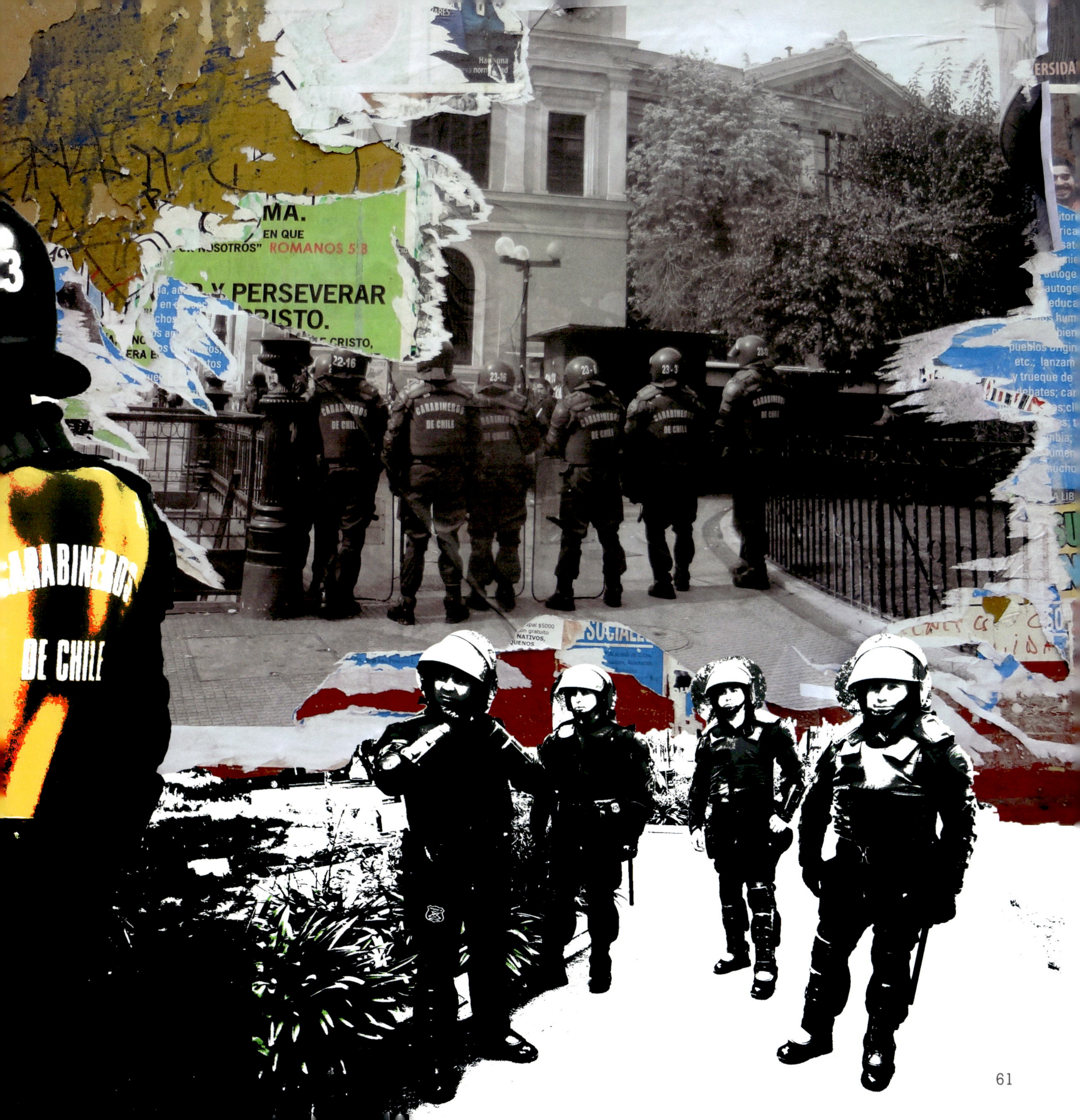
MA.
EN QUE
ROMANOS 5:8
PERSEVERAR
CRISTO.
CARABINEROS
DE CHILE
NATIVOS,
pueblos origin
etc.; lanzam
y trueque de
debates; car

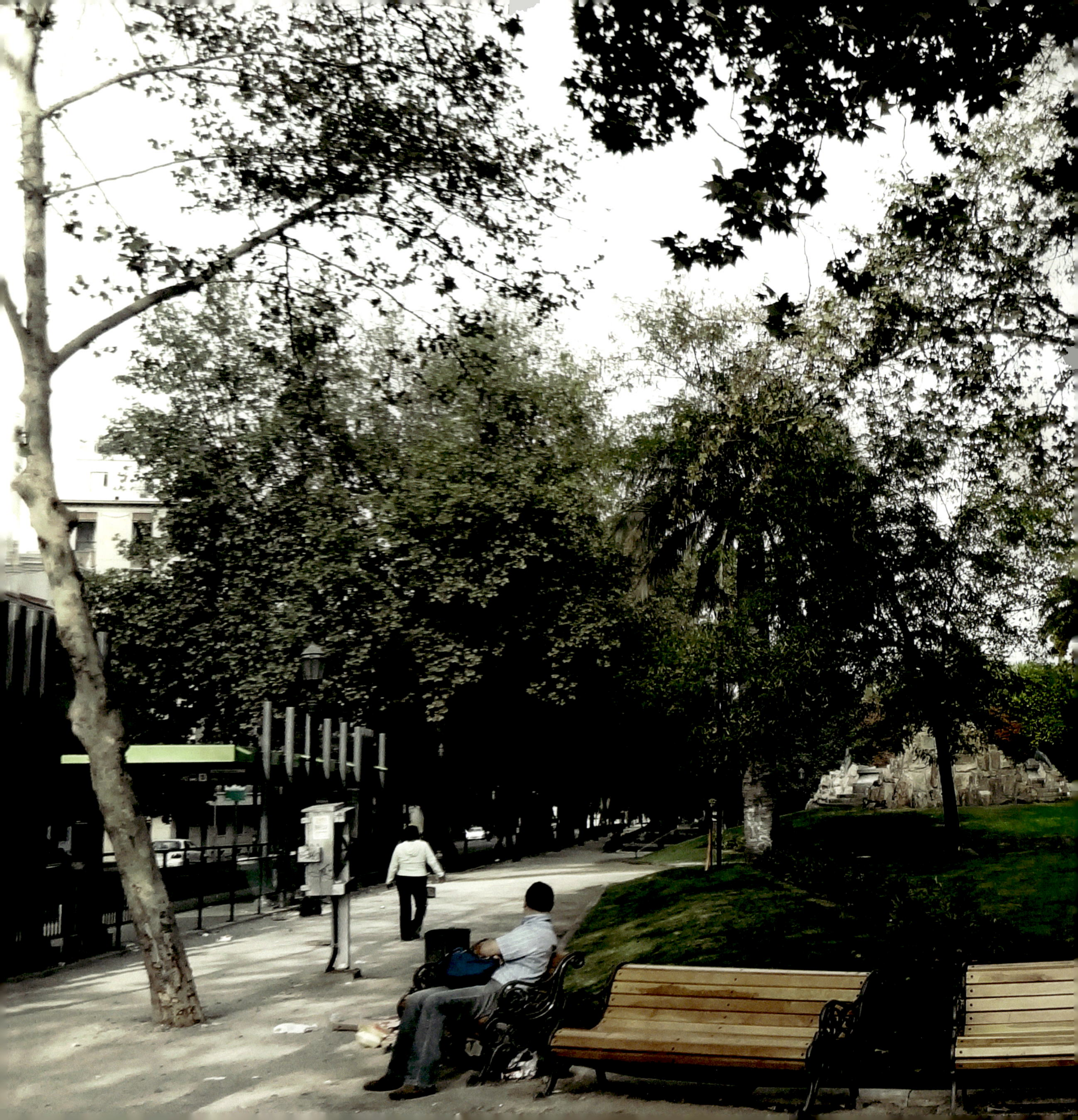

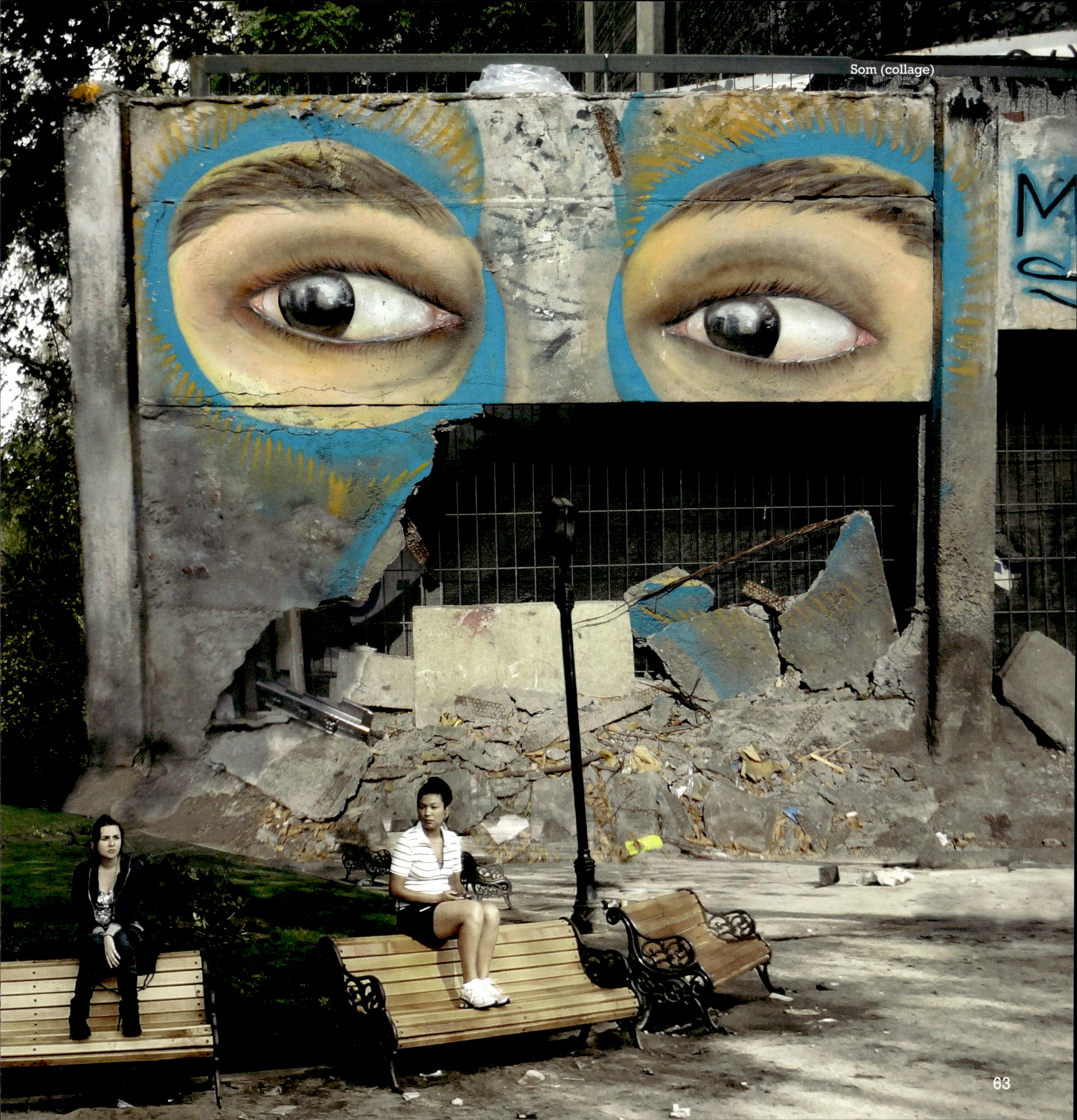

Som (collage)

"where everything is bathed with fabulosity, in the context of the ordinary"

"I describe the instance of intervention made to the habitat of commuters and people who transit through the streets of a city as an ephemeral act that exists to disappear, as the urban support is in permanent flow and movement. I refer to the interventions that can be found in the street. In Santiago's case there aren't many of these, but wall pastes are more attractive than tags. The power that intervention has is incredible, and it functions as a form of performance on the spatial level and extends a moment where everything is bathed with fabulosity, in the context of the ordinary. Interventions rarely demand a high level of investment, but the shock and the game that is created with the spectator breaks the structure of the everyday commute with something new that the commuter is not used to seeing." **ZAINES**

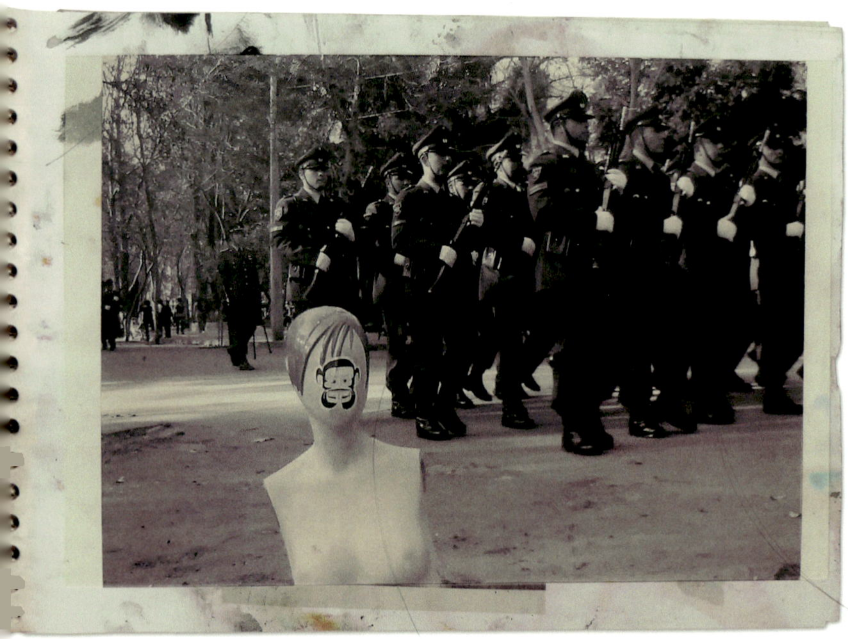

"I believe there are common denominators, although I can't speak for the others, but in my case, I am a person who walks frequently and that is anti-Transantiago [public transportation]. I only use it when it's necessary. I live within forty minutes walking distance from my studio and I walk, so I don't have to take the Transantiago. These kinds of walks help you reflect on your life and the street. Graffiti helps you understand what the street is, and what is really going on. In school they teach you about "weight contrast" and people associate this with symmetry, but then you stand in the middle of Alameda and see that the traffic jam exists only on one side. So, the street isn't organized in the way the academy teaches you. One of the works that I consider most important was an installation that I worked on in La Moneda, a floor mat made of raisins. I locked myself in my studio for many days, sewing together five thousand raisins. Raisins symbolise memory. I installed the mat made of raisins at the door of La Moneda. I went to install it with a film director friend of mine, and as I was placing it down, we were surrounded by police, special forces and palace guards. I was very lucky, because one of the palace guards told me that I had to ask permission at another address. I decided that I couldn't go ask permission empty-handed. I went on the Counsel of Culture's website, I jotted down a couple of names from the hierarchical scale, and said, "I come on behalf of this person." They let me pass, and I got to the presidential administrator, who gave me his email address and told me that the process needed to be carried out through writing. I told him that Chilean art depended on him and that I needed his permission. Then he told me, "All right, let's meet in my office so you can explain the concept to me." What I look for, I told him, is to recuperate the Chilean historical memory that will be reflected by the footprints that enter La Moneda. This was a lie! The real concept was the squishing of the memory by the guys whoenter La Moneda. Busy talking on their cell phones, they would step on the mat and fall in my trap." **NEBS PEREIRA**

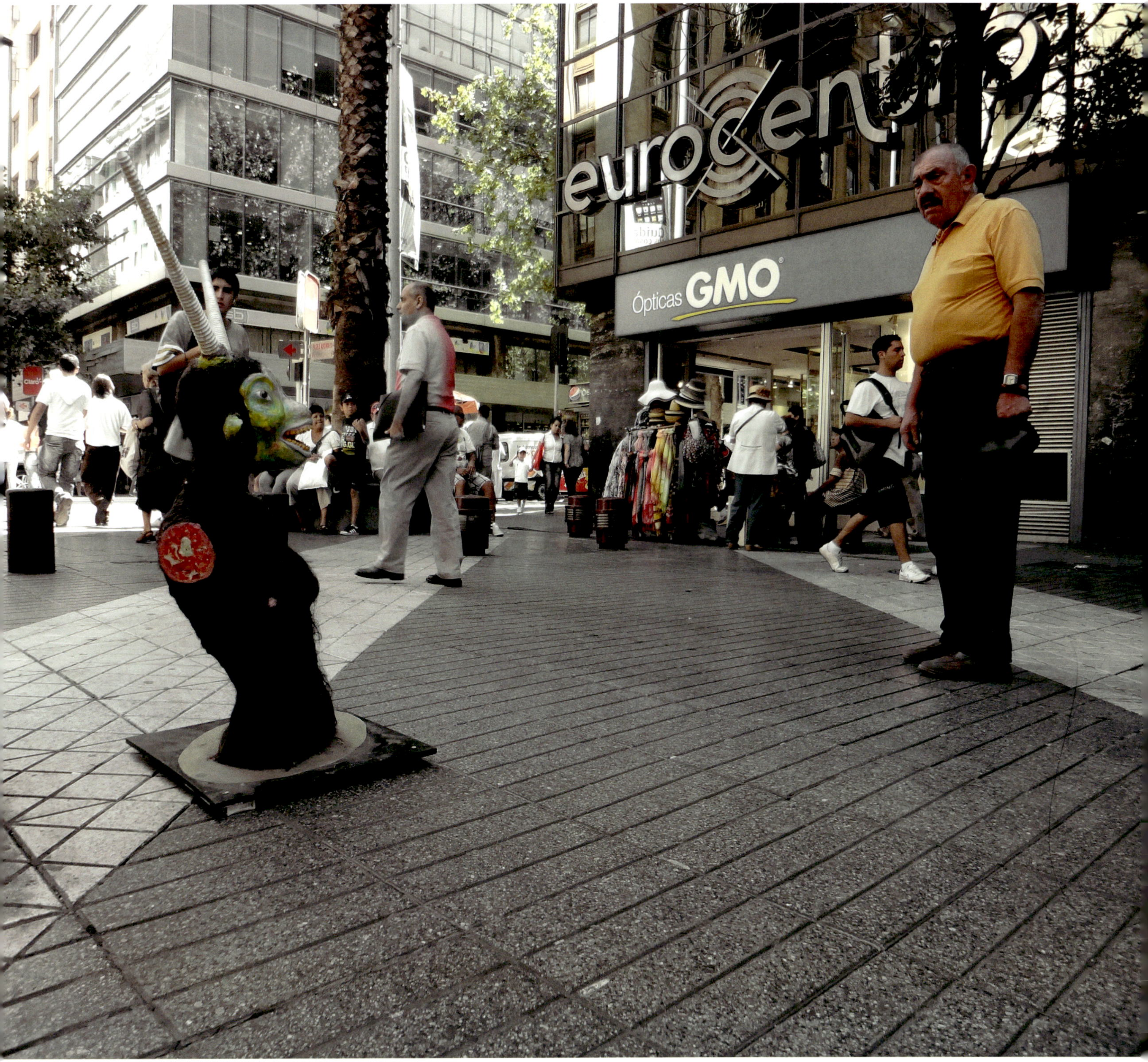
Ópticas GMO

Derik

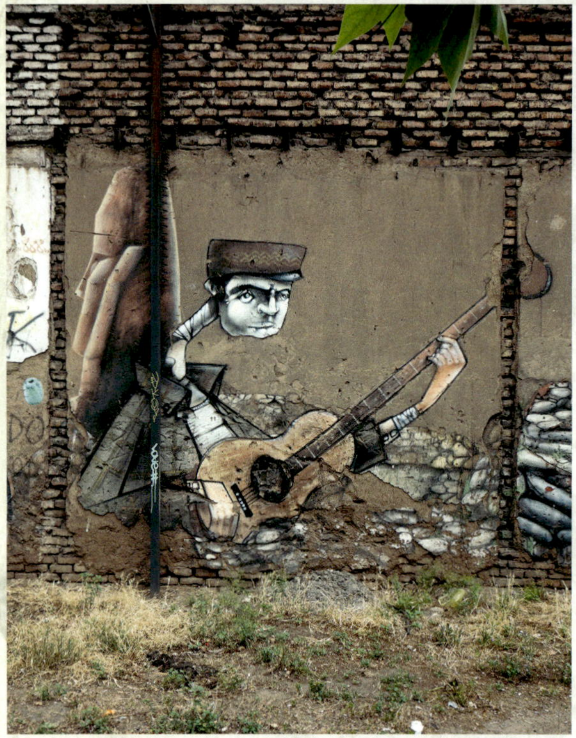

Nao – Degra

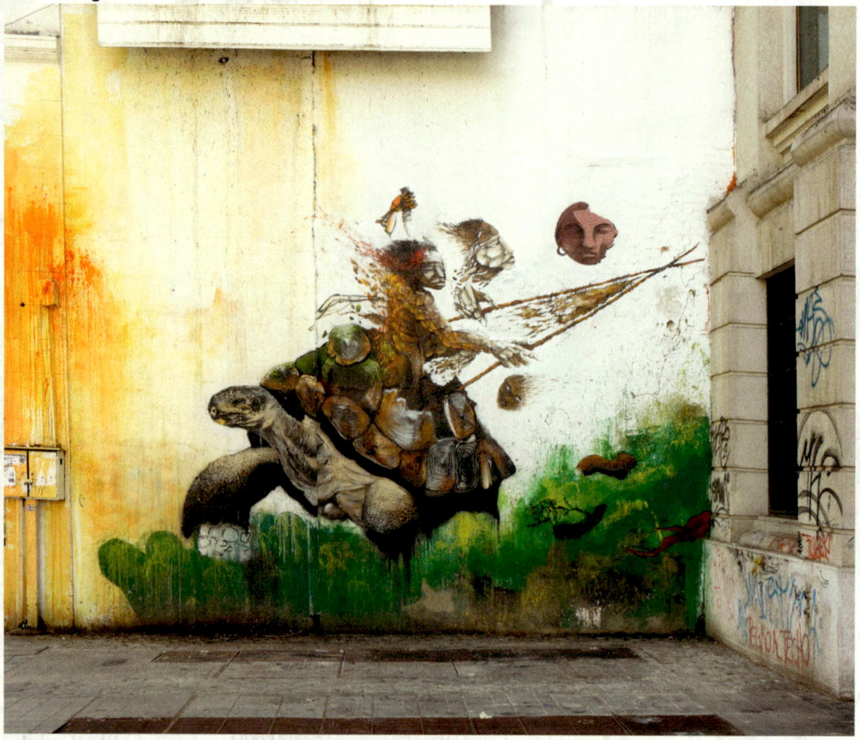

Tanck – Estoy

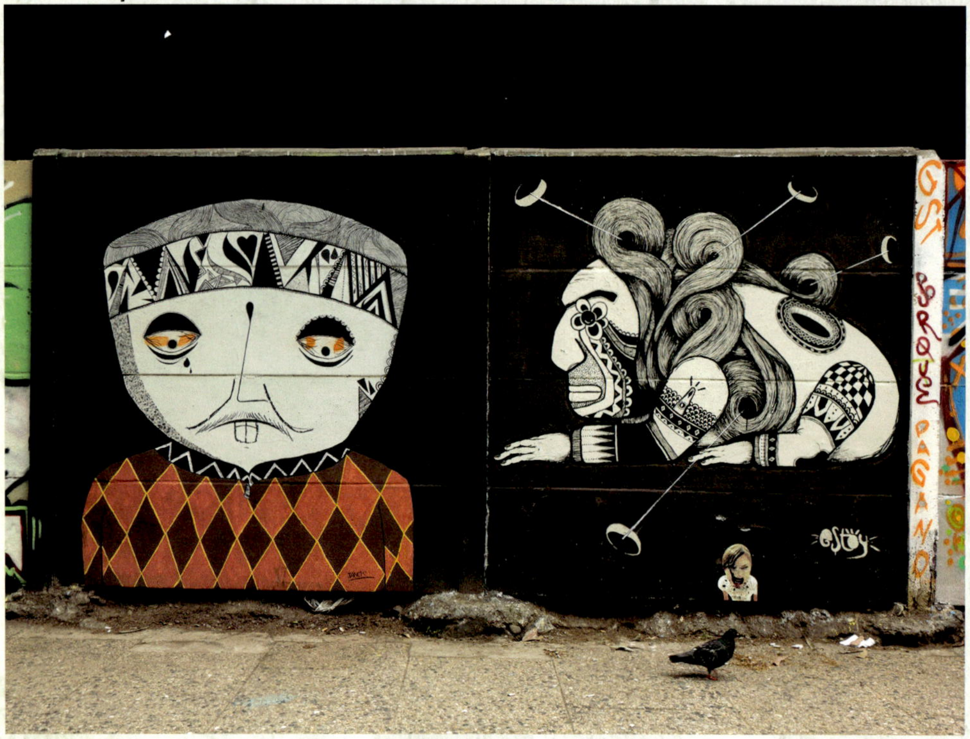

"You may arrive at a destination and see that an old lady has a big wall with awful bombs and tags and stuff, and you're like, 'Can I paint these? Look this is my drawing,' and she'll say, 'Oh, please do' and so she ends up like inviting you for tea and you meet all the people that live around there and they tell you the story of the place and give you the opportunity to stamp your own imprint onto the environment. I would rather work with the local residents as opposed to tag their walls, as the city is already so accelerated, so violent. When you do art in the street it can be in another rhythm, where you put a little more thought and effort into your work, collaborate with the community, and create another space in that same accelerated and violent city, and make some place better so that not only the residents but the commuters can look up and have a few moments of tranquility. That's really gratifying!" **LA GUATA FRIA**

Som – Fisura

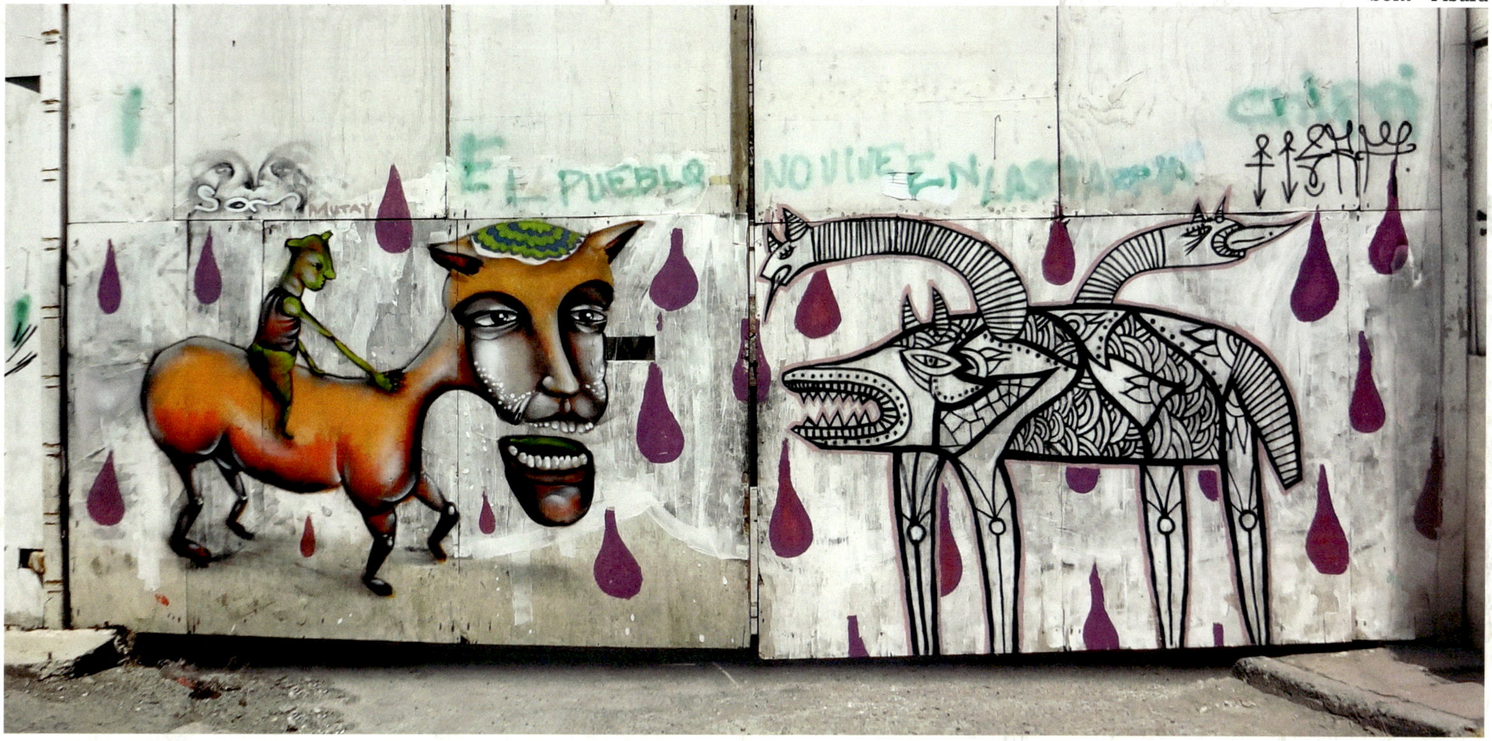

Senk – Jenny

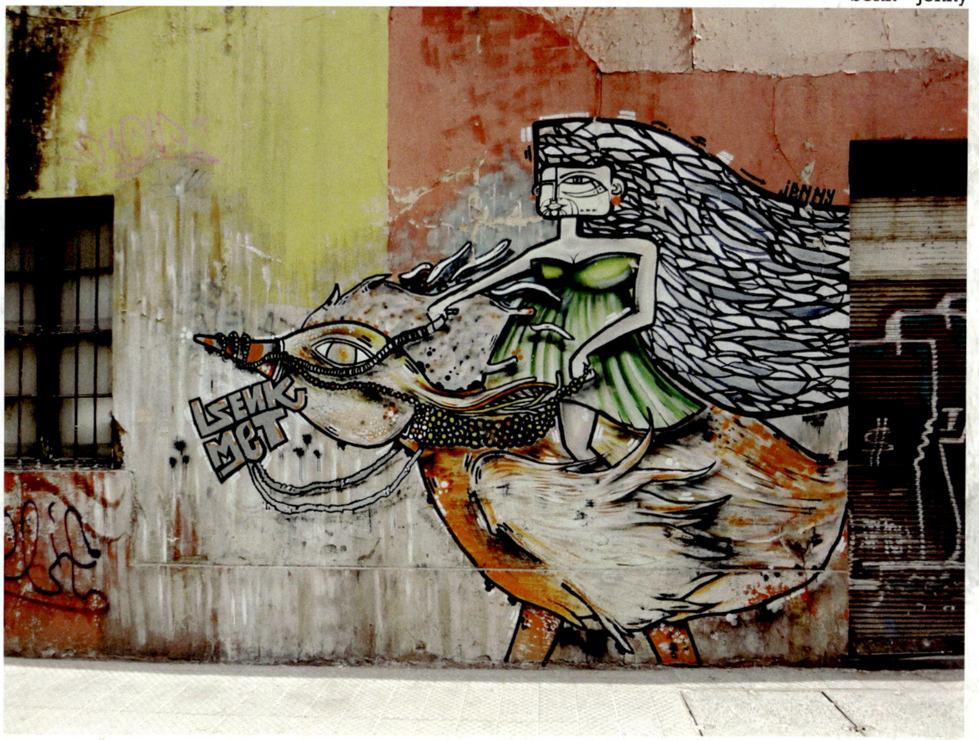

"The characterizing element of my painting is 'You like it or you don't like it.' I paint using white and black. In my graffiti, there is no ambiguity, there is no 'I like it somewhat.' When I encounter odd situations and get crazy ideas, I take them to the wall through my characters. I believe that the street is pure expression without the need to follow certain parameters. You paint whatever you want. It isn't important to follow a certain aesthetic or defined concept. On the streets, the idea is to go out and share your ideas, without caring what the neighbor or the person who studied fine arts thinks. Nothing matters. I find that street art is linked to the 'crazy dude' who likes to walk around with his hands stained, painting and being an artist. Perhaps I am classified in that category, because I paint with a brush, but I consider myself totally hip hop, and within my style, bombs are fundamental and cannot be left aside." FISURA

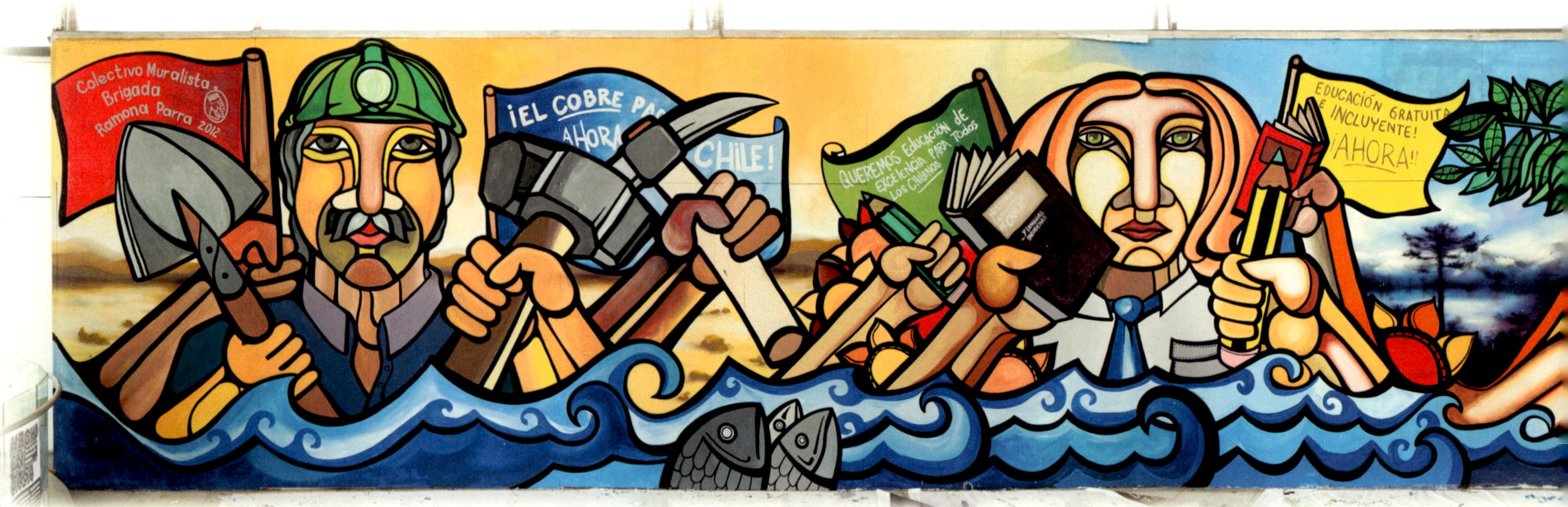

"We became communists as it was the only way to organize ourselves to fight against the military dictatorship. I was really young when I became a communist, and all the people in my school were communists. In those days, in the late '80s, the students were the first ones on the streets. We tried to capture the streets for ourselves. We were all frightened and it was really difficult, but we did it! Four years later Pinochet's reign was terminated.

"Our current president is a businessman; he is from one of the richest families in Chile. All his friends, who are businessmen, are now in the government and the general public don't know this. The state is run like a corporation and that is very wrong! But we will fight them. They can't dismiss us! The people are discontent! I would say that over 80 percent of the public are discontent!" **CAROLA DEL RIO**

"We are not artists, we are humble people. I have never thought of myself as an artist. I am a worker, and I take my struggles onto the streets with the Ramona Parra Brigade. The brigade formed in 1986. I was the last person in charge of the brigade in the year 1973 when the military blow came. I was one of the founders. The brigades formed from Arica to Punta Arenas. I was the communal leader, the regional leader, and lastly, the national leader. I had 150 brigades under my command. We are the old school brigade members, those that were exiled and later repatriated. I am also the last of the surviving artists who painted with Roberto Matta in La Granja on the mural *The First Goal of the Chilean People*, in commemoration of the Allende government's first anniversary. I entered the J.J.C.C. in the year 1968. From that time I began my struggle and education on the ideas of the moment, the ideas of Emilio Recabarren, Che Guevara, and Salvador Allende. I am a worker, and I have a basic schooling up to sixth grade. Muralism appeared as a phenomenon succeeding the great struggle on the streets that we had in Chile. In the beginning, we didn't consider that we did muralism—we thought it was a job with a function. Now, there are people that look back to that time and call it muralism and say that they are muralists. We don't want to cry or make ourselves victims, but the fact that we are laborers gets us discriminated against by those who have studied. The bourgeoisie underappreciates us and thinks us incapable of doing art. That's why I say that we don't feel like artists, because that is a category that belongs to the bourgeoisie. That doesn't mean that we see street art as inferior work. The name 'artist' places you on another plane, a superior one, and that doesn't interest us.

"Regarding the relationship between the communist party and the brigade, I can say that the communist party thinks they are the owners of the name 'Ramona Parra,' but the collective was born to promote unity and goes beyond the intentions of a political party. The group extended the message of the Popular Unity coalition. The Ramona Parra brigades began in the sixth congress of the J.J.C.C. and were brigades of agitation with the purpose of making propaganda, not for making murals. I want to clear something up: The Ramona Parra brigades no longer exist because the brigades were a body of propaganda for the communist party, which no longer exists. The collective muralist Ramona Parra Brigade is something that came about later on and it consists of us, the old brigade members of the 1960s and 1970s. We formed this open collective, because for us, culture doesn't have a religious creed or a political affiliation; it doesn't need to restrict. On the

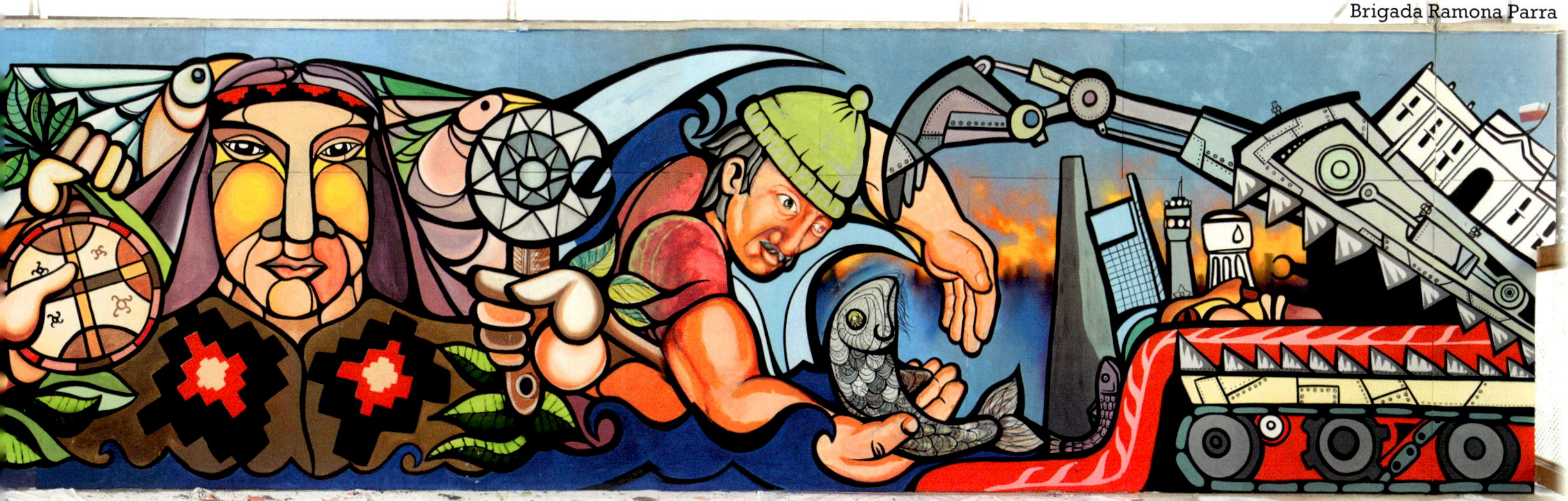

contrary, it has to include. We don't complain about our roots, but today we are free of the communist party due to differing opinions and viewpoints. It's nothing personal against the leaders of the party. I don't make personal comments on third parties. We are active on the street and we support students and workers in the struggle, but we don't get involved in politics. The struggle of the middle class has nothing to do with a political party. We are activists of the people, not of a party. Ramona Parra is not synonymous with the communist party. The brigade is something bigger that encompasses more people. When the brigade formed, it was made up of laborers, high school students, and college kids. Nobody had studied art. Our function was to develop political propaganda and our objective was to get Allende to the presidency. That motivated the creation of images and iconography such as the pigeon or the raised fist. The idea of the Popular Unity coalition was to unite causes around Allende. We would place a pencil in the raised fist and that became the icon of the struggle of the students. If we interchanged a shovel for the pencil, then that would come to represent the struggle of the copper miners. The fist is the emblem of the Ramon Parra Brigade, a composition that intends to reflect the majority of the Popular Unity: the laborers, the country folk, and the students. Our idea is always to unite and to disperse our message of unity, to make the world a better place to co-exist in. Our role models are people like Che Guevara and Salvador Allende, but our inspiration came from something that we felt in the heart. When you fall in love with a woman, you want to give her only the best. We fell in love with an ideal society and we are still in love, we continue fighting. We have been on the street for more than forty-five years, and are now trying to unite popular young street artists in Latin America." CHIN CHIN

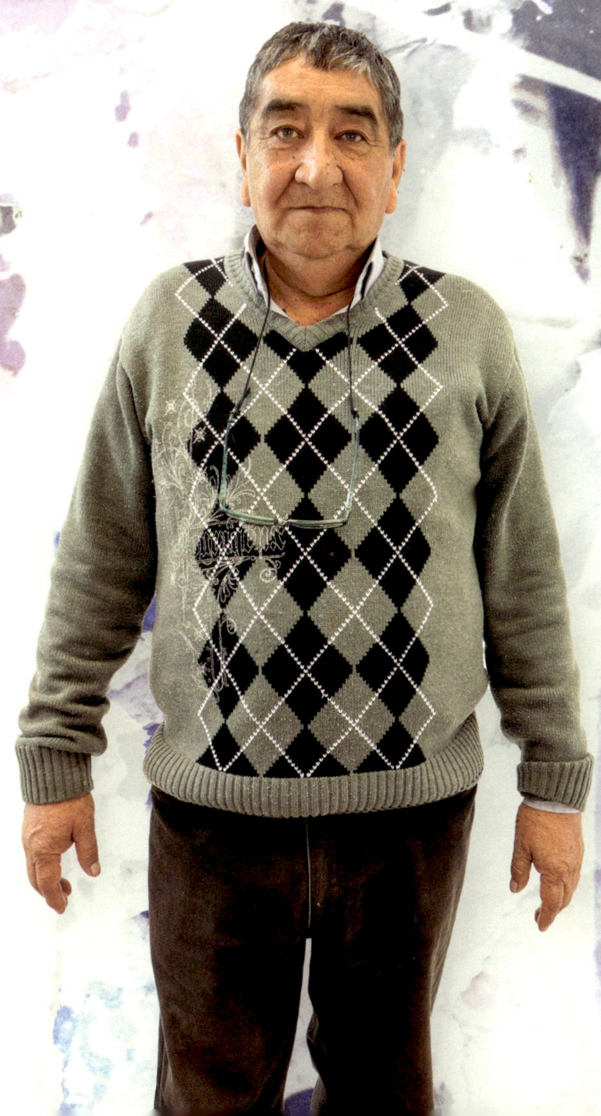

Imagine it,

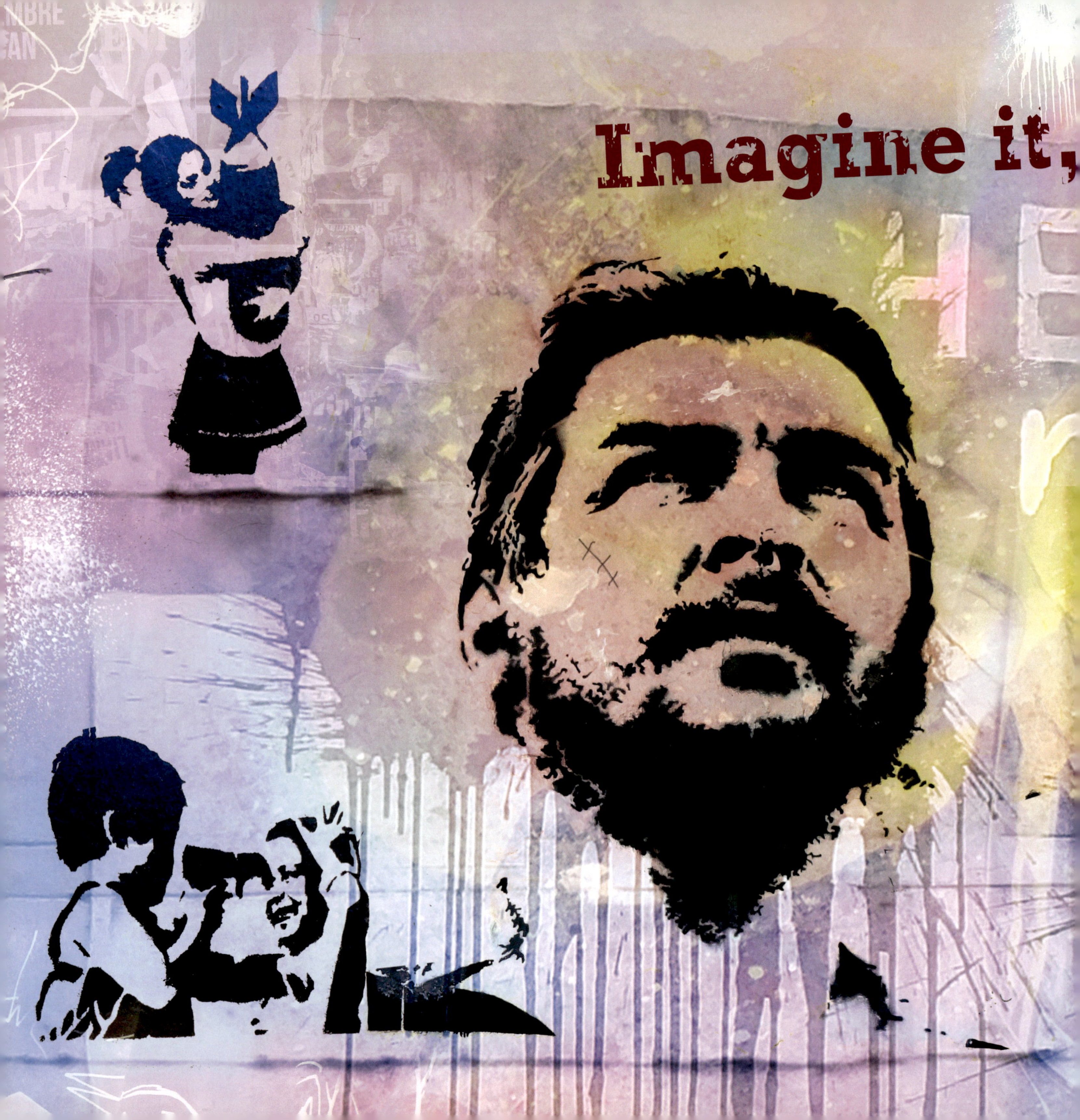

cut it, spray it, leg it...

"Aesthetic quality takes a back seat as I prefer to focus on the meaning behind the letters and images."
ALEJANDRO GANDARILLAS

"I have noticed a scarcity of stencils in Santiago."
ARTESANO

"What motivates me to paint are the things that I feel the city needs to see in a given space. My personal ideas do not move me."
ALEJANDRO GANDARILLAS

"The style of stencil art that we paint here in Santiago is devoid of a defined characteristics. It is very individual. Every person has their own style."
ARTESANO

"I often cut my stencils with cardboard. The downside is that it doesn't last as long and wrinkles up quickly, but I like the fact that it is easy to work with and permits less usage, so I am obliged to make more constantly and not repeat the same image for eternity." ARTESANO

"Here in Chile, the people that go around painting graffiti on the walls are called gangsters. In my opinion this is far from the truth, as someone who paints spends the little money they have left over to buy some cans of spray paint so they can paint graffiti with their friends. There is something honorable in that. Graffiti deserves a lot of respect for the time, dedication, work, and study that must be invested.

"I do not agree with limiting the definition of stencil art to one technique or form. The process used to achieve the stencil doesn't matter to me. I can stand in front of a strong light and have that light provide a shadow, and my own silhouette can be the stencil. I have many resources; I have paper, I have a projector, I have my hand, I have a collage of cut-up photos. In my opinion, what makes my work a stencil is the end result, the message. It's a quick technique that anyone can elaborate on without a set form. Stencil art is like screaming what one has buried deep inside and has always wanted to say. It's like vomiting, like a vomit-scream, quick and expressive." ALEJANDRO GANDARILLAS

ESTACIÓN CENTRAL

Area: 24 km^2
Population: 121,282
Average annual income: $21,601
Population below poverty line: 7.3%
Graffiti prevalence: 4/10

"I live on the border of the communes of the mountainous areas, which include Maipu and Estación Central. Estación Central has always grabbed my attention. All my life I have seen paintings and painted buildings here. The neighborhood has evolved. There are many good pieces, but there's also an abundance of bombing. It is a sector with a combative quality. I have painted a few pieces in this part of town that have been respected with the passing of time. I remember the old crews such as IMP or VBL. They showed me my first tags and flops here. In this neighborhood, there are some that paint wildstyle and there is an abundance of political murals painted by anarchists. Furias, Gap Crew, BRP, Splif Crew, Nogratos Crew, Howm and Alterna often paint here.

"Riding the bus through these streets to see the graffiti will always be a pleasure and the graffiti is always transforming, despite the intense surroundings. " GUZTOK

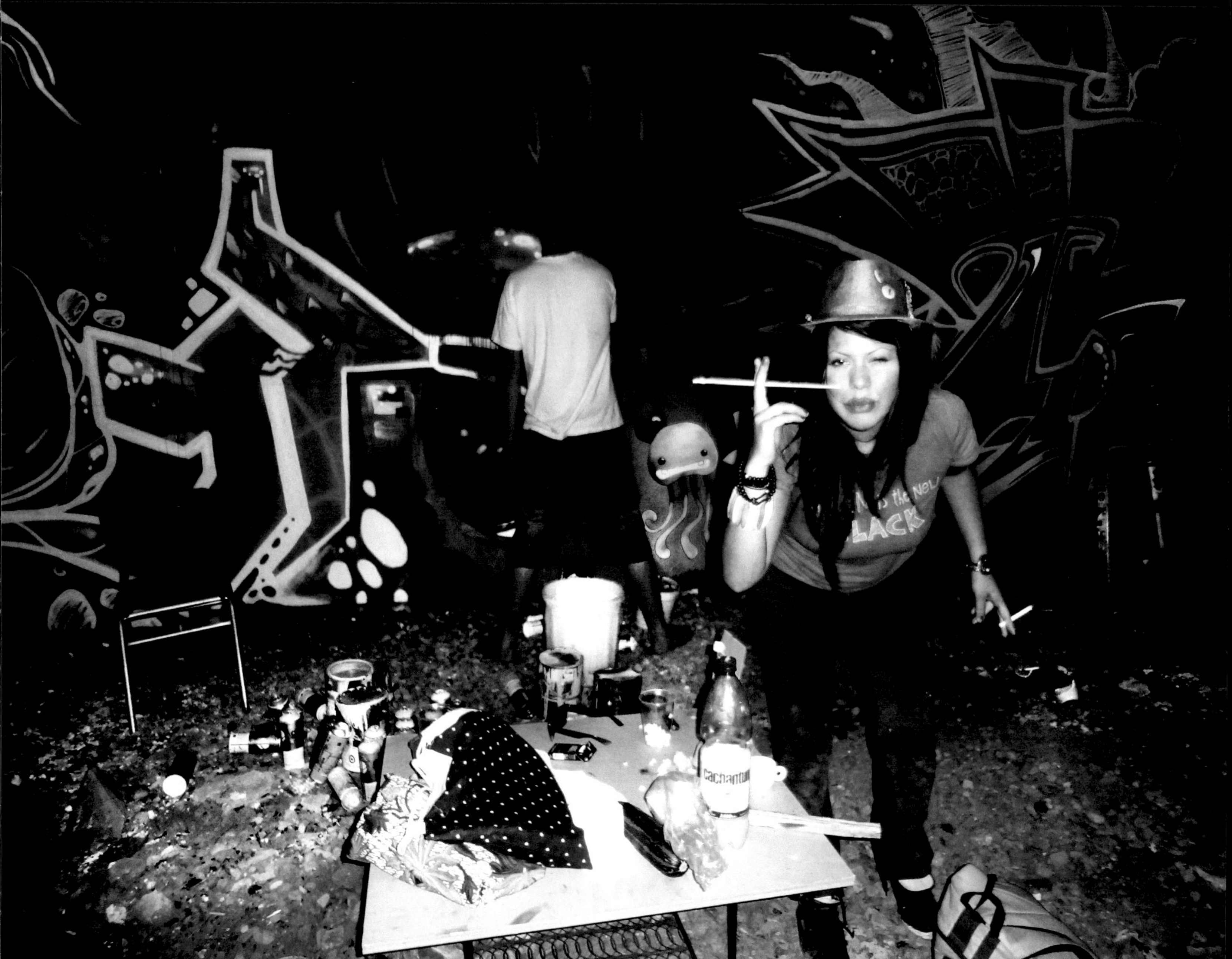

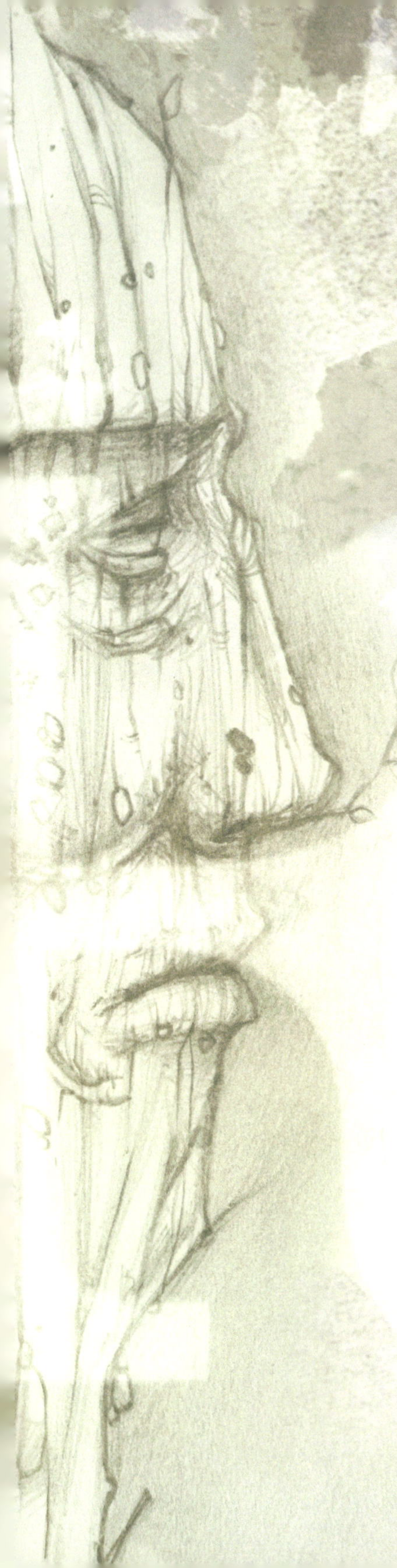

"Chile has a high level of graffiti in comparison to other cities of the world, not just South America. There are many graffiti works and many artists. Little by little, graffiti is being valued more, even if its real value, that it is given in other countries, goes unnoticed, here.

"There is a contrast between the old and new school here in Chile. The difference is in the uncertain materials that were previously used. In fact, I used to paint with only three sprays, all of a national brand, and they weren't good quality. Currently, there is more variety. More color tones can be purchased, and the prices aren't that different from the old ones. I don't think my style has changed at all with use of the new aerosols, but they have served the purpose of giving my pieces more detail. It's the same work, but with more detail, more evolution, and also, with brighter colors, as the national paints are less potent than the new lines of aerosols. Also, the new school has made itself well known through the use of the internet. The old school made themselves a name through magazines and the very street that they occupied, through people recognizing their graffiti. Today, there is more access to the internet, and therefore graffiti spreads through there. What has changed is that now there are many styles developing at the same time. Before, the Chilean artist would copy foreign styles. Now, now Chileans copy each other, and they are influenced by their peers. Currently, the influence comes from within the country, not from outside.

"I have some anecdotes. On certain occasions, I have been paid to paint, without my piece being an official job. I have also had paint cans stolen from me while I was painting. On other occasions, guards have passed by and tried to arrest me, so I have proposed this to them: 'Of my artwork turns out to be uglier than the wall in its original state, then I'll let you take me.' They come back later and they like it. I have used other materials besides spray and latex. I once made an intervention with clothing and paper. I have used magazine pages, newspaper. I have even painted with dog shit. And of course, I have also met different people and shared materials, thanks to graffiti.

"Regarding tags, I think it's a phase that is currently evolving. People that paint tags also paint graffiti. In the old days, people that tagged only did that, but now graffiti artists start by tagging, and then they get into graffiti and evolve. A tag can be just a signature, but it can also have a function or carry some type of content. It can communicate something to the public. It's part of street art, and it will always exist. People are always going to write on walls when there is social discontent. Regarding tags that contain a signature, those are just advertising done by the artist. It's related to the ego. Bombing is writing the author's name in big letters so everyone can read it. It's an act of pure egocentricity. It's similar to how politicians will advertise themselves, but in a different format. It's advertising and visual contamination. In the past, I would get angry when someone would paint a tag over my work. I think anyone would be annoyed about having their piece covered by someone else, with something of lesser quality. When I see that one of my paintings has been covered with something better, it doesn't affect me as much, because that's more acceptable than a tag or a bomb. Generally, when my graffiti is scribbled over with tags or bombs, I paint something new on the wall. If I see that they have destroyed a part of the piece, then I will repair it or paint whatever comes to my mind.

"Regarding other urban interventions, I think that stencil should be considered a form of graffiti, because it is done with spray. Stencil has a liaison with graffiti because they stem from the same root. In reality, graffiti is just graphology, part of letters and writing. With stickers and posters, it depends on how they are used, because many times people who advertise with posters cover up graffiti and that's when respect is lost and graffiti art is destroyed. When posters are used in a better manner, more creatively, that's when it's valid. Stickers are a part of urban intervention. I like to paste my stickers on the train.

"What will happen with the graffiti in Santiago, and it is already happening, is that it will strengthen and become more valuable. Also, companies are paying attention, as they use graffiti to advertise themselves to younger audiences. Maybe I don't engage in that, but it's great, because this provides jobs for graffiti artists. The positive side of this is that graffiti is being respected more and valued as an art form, just like all the other art techniques. I think people's attitudes have changed in regards to what graffiti is. Once, I was painting in another city and I was asked, 'What are you painting?' I said, 'A mural,' so they wouldn't be scared because, formerly, you would say the word, "graffiti" and they would look at you like you were a thief or a delinquent. So, I said, "Mural, graffiti," and the person said, "Oh, graffiti, how nice!" People changed their attitude completely towards graffiti. Currently, people that are outside the hip-hop or graffiti movement are gaining more knowledge and this is what I believe has caused graffiti to be regarded with more value. Having less ignorance helps in attaining more space for your work.

"My themes vary. I work with social and personal themes frequently. I translate or express my social critique within the wall. I also try to communicate with people through graffiti. This, for me, is incredibly important. My works are sometimes based on songs that I compose. My painting themes vary. I don't like to do the same thing all the time. If I choose a theme, I like to take it on from different angles.

"My source of inspiration comes from my opinions of reality and society. Part of my opinion and viewpoints are reflected through graffiti. Deep down the communication that can be achieved through graffiti is what inspires me. This is incredibly important, because through graffiti I am feeling, I do it by feeling and thinking about something. It's my personal story, my own thoughts, opinions, and feelings. Graffiti comes out from within me. It is a pure expression. I don't like to paint things that don't give me feeling. Even if the graffiti was requested by someone, I still give it part of me." **DENST**

Denst

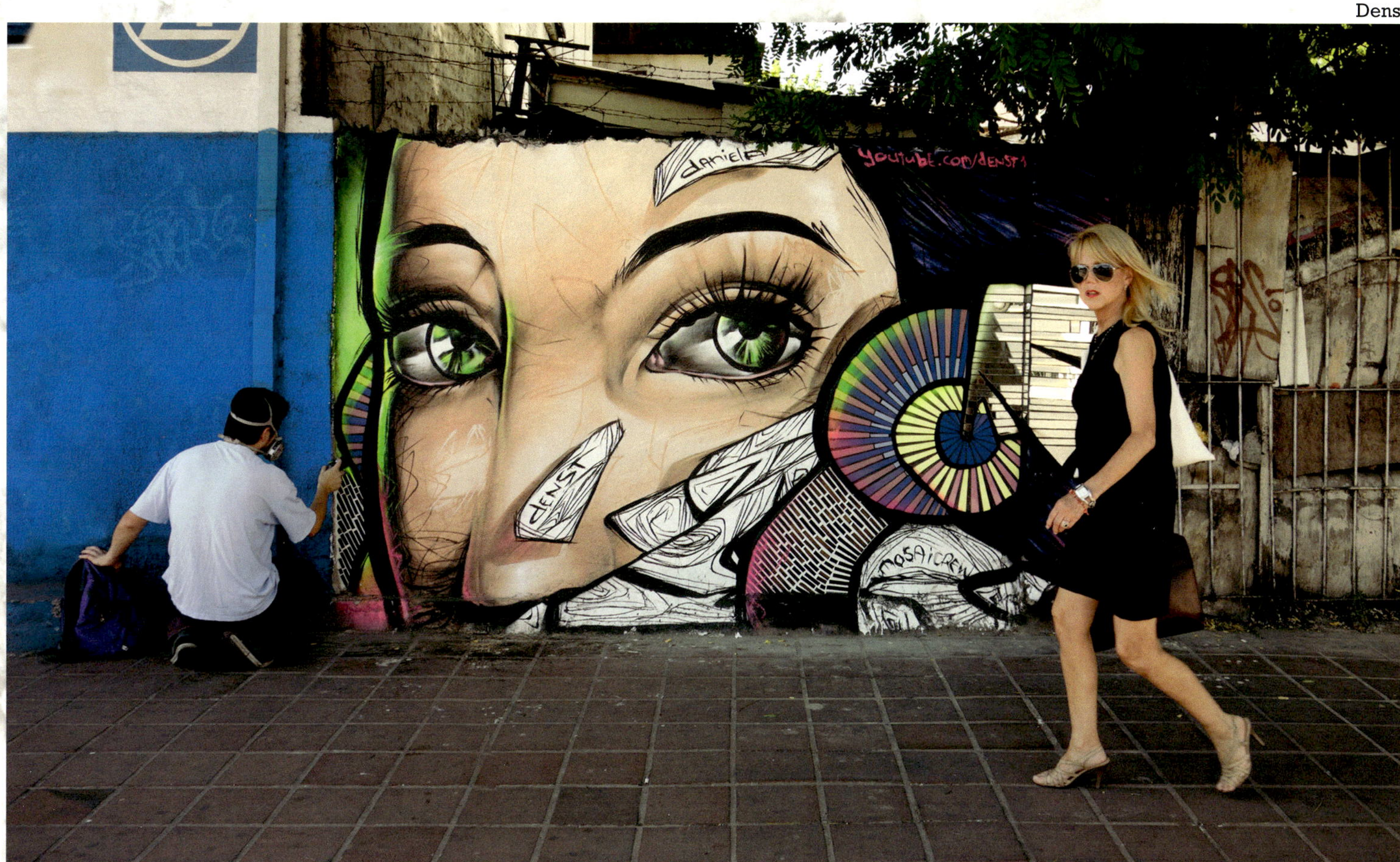

"I like to draw funny characters that look like animated drawings and that tell a story or present a message. I always make up stories and create the characters and situations that come up in my head. Why do I paint graffiti? Because it is a new form of expression that makes the most sense for the art that I make, illustrations. I love expressing myself on the street and going out to show my work in an open fashion, so that the greatest amount of people possible can view it. The messages that I deliver in my artwork aren't so explicit but have more of a double meaning. I love that my work intervenes the space that I am painting and that it serves the purpose of narrating something that can be interpreted as a story." **ACCK**

"The street is the street. You do whatever you want. If you are given permission, great, if not you do it anyway, and if the next day someone writes over it, it doesn't matter, because the streets don't belong to anyone. In a gallery, you are destined to do the work that the gallery wants. At a gallery, the spectator has to pay an entrance fee. On the street you don't have to pay anything, and you can enjoy art anywhere. Gallery artists aren't seen on the street, and almost nobody knows them." **ANGEL**

"Painting on the street was something that intrigued me since I was a child. I had an uncle who was a muralist and he influenced me. I then gravitated towards graffiti through some friends that I would hang out with. I always liked to draw, and at sixteen, I decided to try it on a larger scale. I loved it. It's painting what you want but extra large. The difference with graffiti is that, unlike canvas paintings, it doesn't have an owner. It becomes part of the place where you paint it." **DENST**

Hemse – Denst

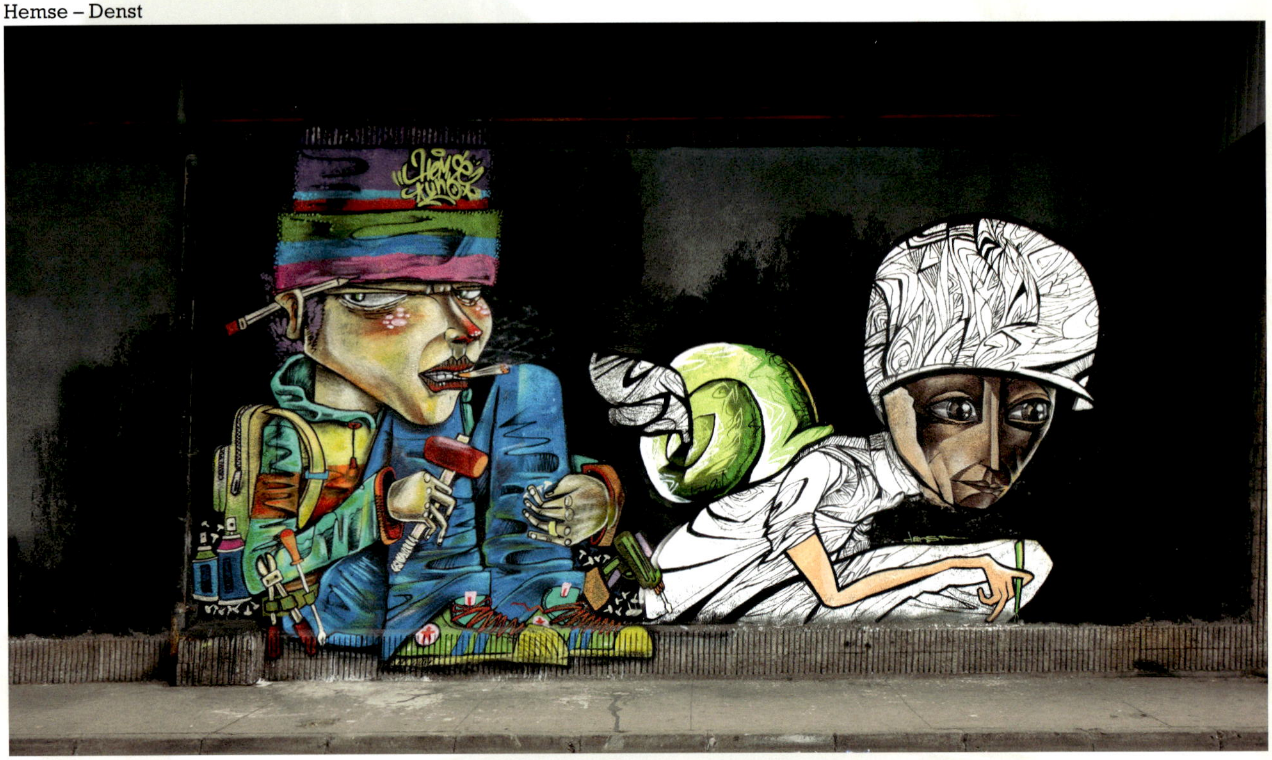

Zero – Teas –Yalus

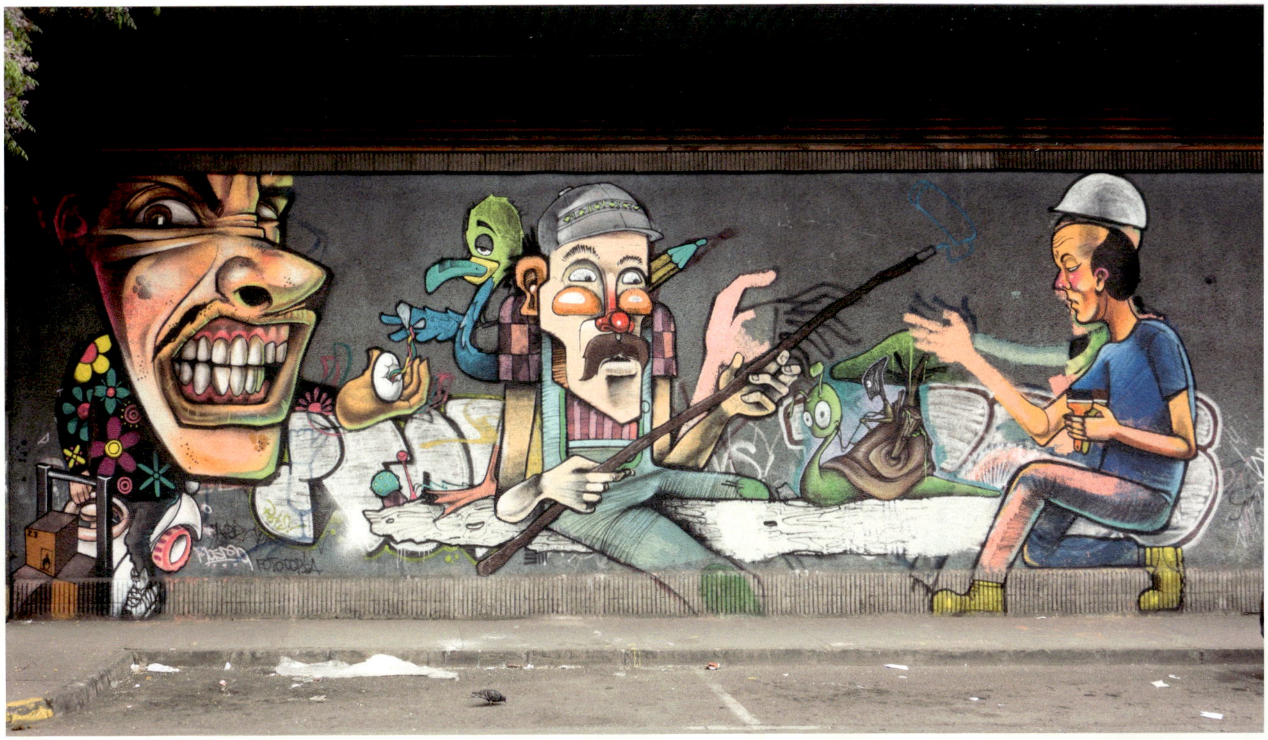

El Bigot – Senek

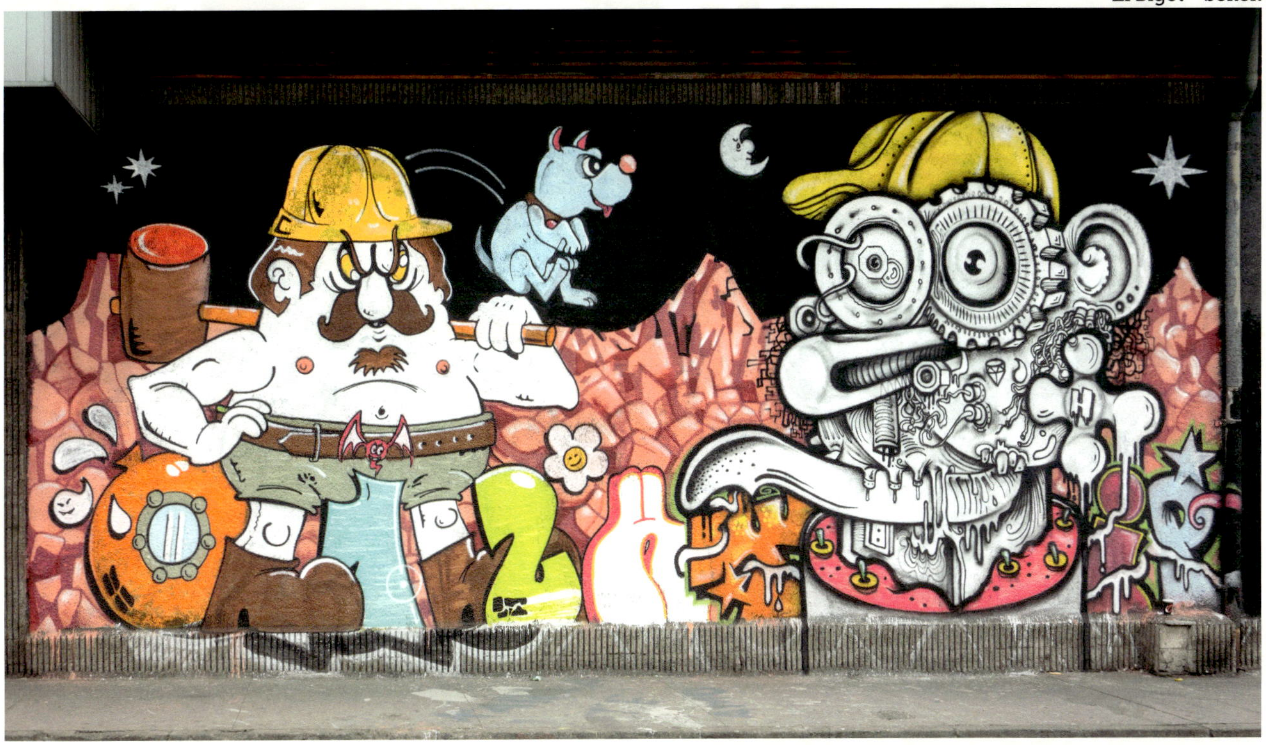

Area: 7 km^2
Population: 112,800
Average annual income: US $13,881
Population below poverty line: 20.1%
Graffiti prevalence: 5/10

“I grew up in José María Caro, and I painted there for many years, which allowed me to form a strong bond with the barrio. Around the year 2002, I met Snap, Año, and 16. Later on, and after joining forces with other friends, we formed 12 Brillos. We grew up together, painting graffiti. At first, we would tag our names, but as we progressed, we began to paint murals with content and images that reflected Chilean culture.

“José María Caro is an old barrio with a long history. It has a liaison to Pedro Aguirre Cerda as all that territory used to be joined into one. In the time of the coup d’état, José María Caro was one of the barrios that battled, giving it a great part of its identity. During the entire dictatorship of Pinochet, it was a neighborhood that was characterized by its resistance and oppression. When Chile went back to a democracy, it developed a stigma. Today, the barrio is associated with drugs and delinquency, but in reality, drugs were introduced by the police and detectives as a control method. In the more political years of the dictatorship, some residents committed savage and vengeful actions, especially due to hunger, scarcity, and repression by the police. This is why, when Chile returned to a democracy, the barrio kept that stigma. This produced a vicious cycle and some neighbors would shut themselves in more and more. They didn’t leave the neighborhood, and they began to isolate themselves from the rest, at the same time that the police labeled anyone fromJosé María Caro a thief.

“In José María Caro, there were many political murals. The majority were by the Ramona Parra Brigade, but today, there are barely any left. Later on, there came the era of graffiti and a group appeared called the ‘Legion,’ who were really good. Before, everyone would tag and bomb, but now neighbors don’t allow just anything to be painted. They make sure that paintings are beautiful and tasteful. People know us, so they don’t give us a hard time. They say, ‘Here come the boys to paint.’ There is one wall that we are always renovating every two to three years. On that wall, we try to portray different aspects of the social struggle that is lived in Chile, especially in Santiago, such as the march of the penguins, the stigmas of the lumpenproletariat, the police confrontations, and currently, it deals with the Mapuche resistance against the machine and the system.

“The barrio has many good walls. All of the houses were built a long time ago, before Allende, and they are big. After the earthquake, many neighbors renovated their houses and built new walls, hence each street generally ends in a big wall. Every time I walk through my neighborhood I feel that there is so much left for me to paint, and at the same time, I’m looking at many walls that are special to me. I feel a great attachment to this place and its people. It is here that I feel at home and not a stranger.” SEBAD

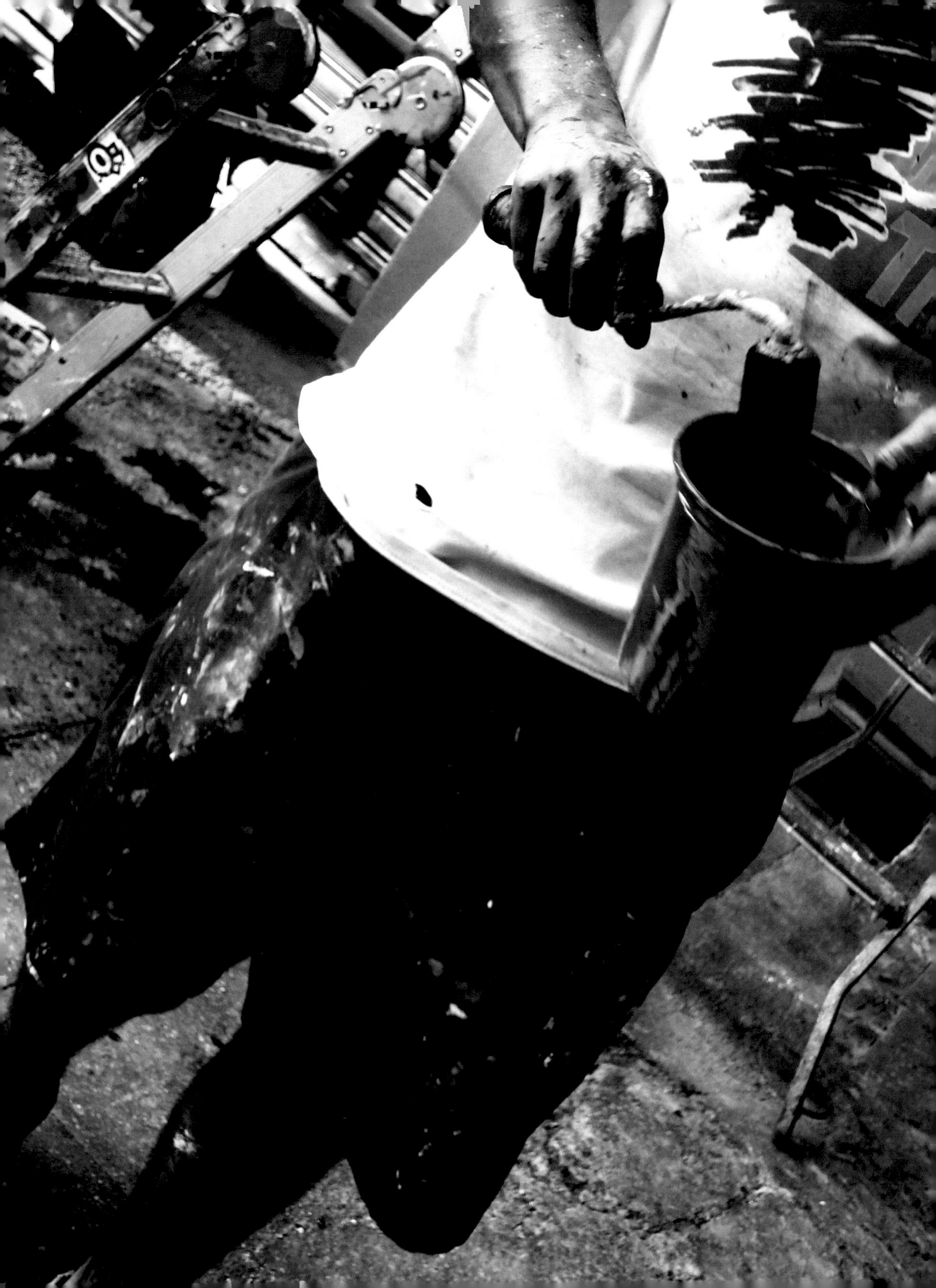

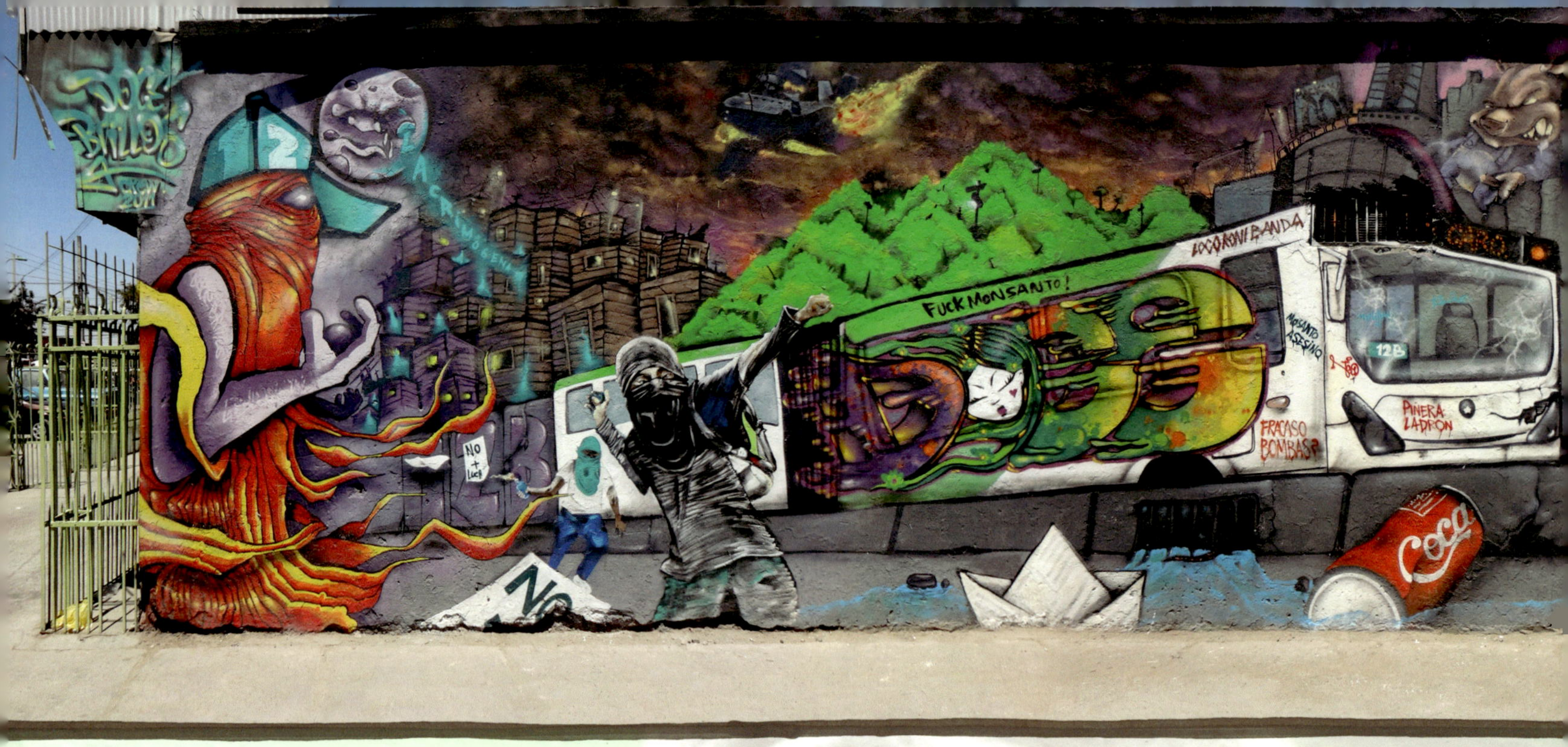

"The government's manipulation of the media has served as a great source of motivation to turn to the streets and expose what they attempt to hide."

"Some of us at times have had conflicts with our parents in that they want us to stop hanging on the street corners. Yet we receive more of an education from these experiences on the streets than within our own homes. In many different ways, the 'hood is an extremely important place to us because it's a way of life, it's where we gain our experiences. It takes balls to be able to leave the house to paint on the streets. We're not afraid of the streets because we're from the streets. We've all been born in these hostile environments, yet we respect and love this atmosphere because it is a part of us and we're a part of it.

"Therefore, we have a responsibility to our society and to our people to denounce and shed light on the issues that are not touched upon in the traditional media outlets such as television, radio, and newspapers. We want to be an alternative to the cultures within the neighborhoods, in the populations, and in the poorest areas. Our crew supports these aspects in that we aim to be a sort of relief for not only ourselves, but for all the people in 12 Brillos who work long and difficult hours for companies, which causes a great deal of stress throughout the week. Therefore, graffiti work on the streets is a form of therapy, a family, an army, not with a military-like discipline, but rather with a discipline of love and trust between all of us.

"We don't believe in celebrities, in stars, or the jet set. We have all lived through difficult situations in life because we are from the 'hood and come from poor families. We live in neighborhoods that border the edge of Santiago so we know the reality of life on the streets. Many of us have dealt with class discrimination due to our socio-economic situation, and therefore we want this to reflect in our work and in what we do.

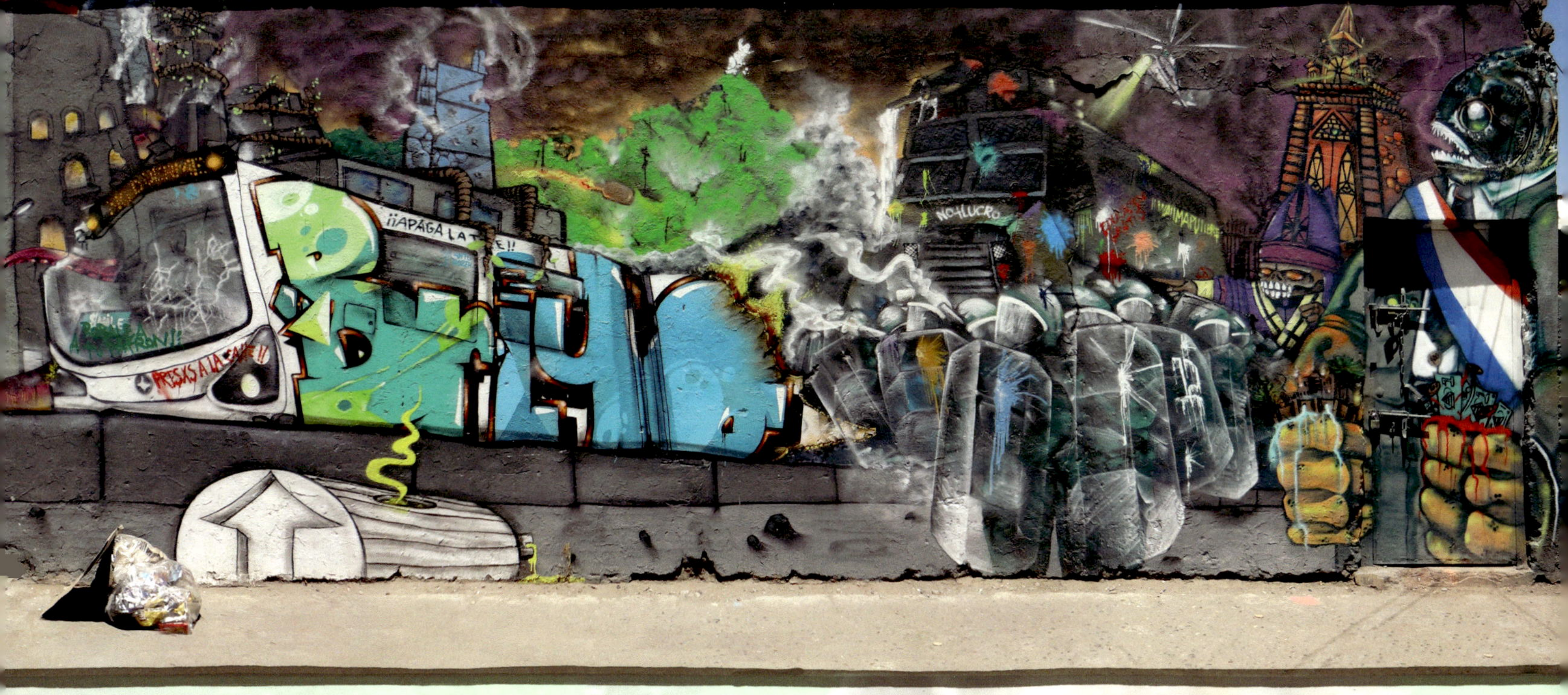

"Over time, our crew has begun to focus more on political activism through the implementation of murals. Lately, they have focused more and more on social issues —the real issues—yet never neglecting traditional graffiti aspects. In Chile, there is a very influential school of thought that has recently defined muralism in not only artistic aspects, but in political aspects as well. For example, the brigades, especially Ramona Parra Brigade, have served as a great source of inspiration for the Chilean graffiti scene.

> **"We want to provide a source of counter-information in the 'hood through graffiti."**

"Many of us have lived throughout this political mural movement that in one way or another has influenced our ideas in the visual and aesthetic concepts that we are now using. Lately, there has been a greater opportunity to collaborate with the people from the brigades, such as with Mono Gonzáles, who is one of its founders, as well as with others who form these newer brigades. The brigades are important in many ways, in that of recovering what is ours, in that of our Chilean identity, and in our identity as artists and as people of the street. Muralism, and not just for political emphasis, but for artistic emphasis as well, has had a large influence on us and for most of the artists in the present mural and graffiti scene.

"The majority of our experiences have been in our 'hood and in our town. We have always tried to convey a political message through our graffiti work. We especially focus on our work in the vicinities where I suppose we feel the most at ease and know that there is a greater need to culturally inform the people, for them to receive more information in addition to the news conveyed through the mainstream forms of media." **12 BRILLOS**

"I formed a crew with Wendy called Abusa. We joined forces five years ago after we realized that we complemented each other's work very well. We paint for the good of all people. Our idea is to renovate a space and make people feel like there is something new in their environment. We created a cultural organization to obtain funds from the government and to be able to finance our material expenses. Spray paints in Chile are very expensive, so if you like to paint often or paint big walls, then you must get a job, but then, all your time will be consumed with work and raising funds for materials. We knew we had to find a solution to this, so we created a cultural organization, and we finance our paint through it and also take on sporadic paid painting jobs. I teach graffiti workshops to boys and girls and always include a social topic such as violence against women, abuse in relationships, drug abuse prevention, and other matters related to abuse. I always deal with the subjects without going into very dark areas; I touch upon the subject by reinforcing that the person can be stronger and be free. The idea is to help people liberate themselves and help them feel less frustrated and stuck, and I don't want to approach the topic in a sad and dark manner. We also like to condemn social problems and situations that we believe are wrong. We try to make others aware of issues like child abuse, domestic violence, and social inequality. We like to go beyond the hip-hop and ego hype, because we don't like that stuff, and we don't believe that the ego exists.

"The wall is a huge platform to paint on and no format can compare in size. This is what motivated me to start painting on the streets, and everyone can see your work, unlike a canvas in a gallery.

"In São Paulo, Rio de Janeiro, and Belo Horizonte in Brazil, the scene is strong, but not as abundant as it is here. In Chile, people are gaining culture, but many are still not impressed by graffiti unless it is a colorful and polished piece of work. People don't like letters that much because they limit themselves to what they can understand. If they can't read a word that is written on a wall, they don't like it. That limits graffiti artists' possibility to live off of their work.

"Politics has become a little enemy of graffiti as many politicians are trying to prohibit the sale of spray paint to minors and they are seeking to control graffiti. They are placing greater consequences for engaging in it, and since Latin America is a bit more laid back in its legal system than Europe and the United States, these changes are bringing it up to par with their restrictions. Let's hope they don't succeed, haha." ANIS

"I know this is cliché, but graffiti is a lifestyle. When you get into graffiti you will ride the bus thinking about painting, the color, the texture. Anything makes you think about graffiti. This is great because painting isn't something that you just do on a wall—it becomes an activity that liberates you, and one that you can share with others. This allows you to express emotions and feelings. Painting is good for you. If more people discovered what it feels like to paint, I think that there would be more people painting. When you pass children a spray can, they want to paint on everything, because they feel the adrenaline of spraying their name, making their own drawings, and realizing how good it feels. I like to paint with kids because I feel like they are the ones who have taught me the most about graffiti. They aren't afraid to experiment. They do whatever they want and use their imaginations. They enable me to transcend the structures that have been created, where we tell ourselves we have to paint letters in a certain format, etc. I have learned that if I want to do it differently, then I can.

"To me, graffiti isn't just about colors; it's also an expression of emotions that bring life to a wall. You can take a wall that nobody knew existed, paint it, and suddenly, people begin to realize that the wall exists. You can give this wall an intention where you transmit messages through it. I think that graffiti has the same impact as a huge Coca-Cola sign, and it can garner the same response from people.

"We usually paint without permission. This began with the birth of our crew Abusa, because we would go out to paint spontaneously, and we would look to see that no one was coming. We then began to take more risks and paint bigger works without anyone bothering us. We began to abuse the fact that no one would say anything and that there were no consequences for our actions. Being a woman has its advantages when it comes to the police. In the past, when we have been stopped by the police, we have told them that we had no idea because it was our first time painting. We've also had some bad experiences, where we have been detained at gun point by the cops, but it's part of the story. We have never had to pay a fine or stay in jail. We only had one moment where we were held up for investigation, but it's funny because we have never had major problems as we always use our feminine charm to get away clean.

"The graffiti in Chile is mutating. We don't want to paint graffiti from the Bronx anymore. We want to paint what reflects our Latin roots."

"Abusa will abuse spaces, materials and moments. That's what characterizes us; we like to enjoy and take advantage of circumstances to the max. Day to day, people abuse your time, they abuse your money, they abuse you with publicity. We think we can abuse them with graffiti. I think that people in Chile are increasingly accepting of graffiti as art and it has a great graffiti scene. Chile has a strange society, as it is a bit pessimistic, but recently, I have noticed some changes with the education system and the public's discontent with politics, and this has opened the door to adopting a more liberal way of thinking. When we start to desire a different education, we also begin to yearn for a different kind of life.

"We have more and more crews painting graffiti, which is something that reduces the egoism associated with graffiti. Many artists are all about "I"; I did this, I painted this. When you work with a crew, you have the mentality of, 'We're working together to create something better.' It isn't my name, but ours as we become one and lose the ego. Chile has a lot of constructive collaborations, and participating in a crew has helped me grow artistically and it has given me the opportunity to step out of the same character that I would always paint and try new things instead." WEND

12 Brillos /Abusa Crew

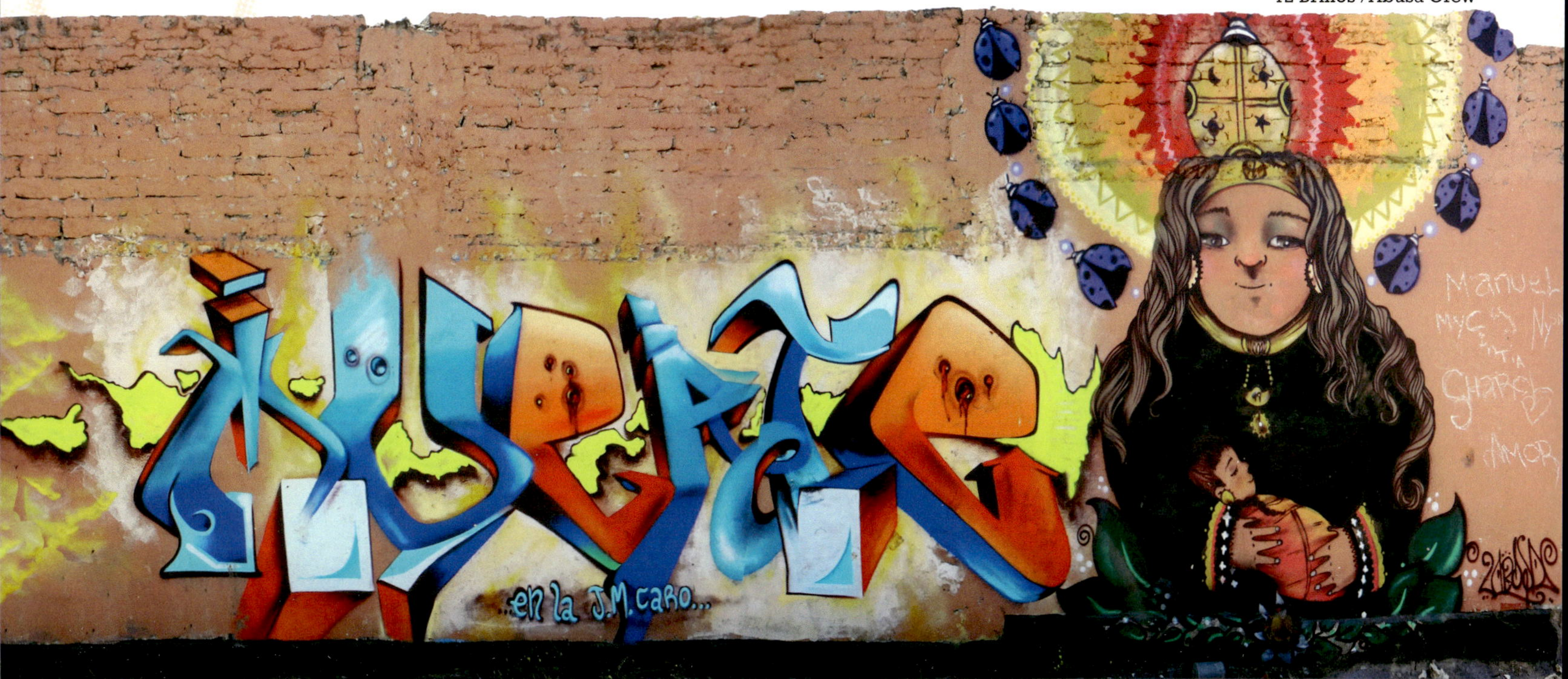

MAIPÚ

Area: 135.5 km^2
Population: 525,070
Average annual income: US $25,664
Population below poverty line: 9.1%
Graffiti prevalence: 5/10

"In Maipú, you can paint peacefully. Years ago, painting had to be done in a hurry and at night. Nowadays, people offer us space on their walls, and they even look for us. The police appreciate when something good is being painted and when it's not good, they don't cause any dramas. The residents in this barrio tend to respect us. They have evolved with the graffiti over the years. Two years ago, my graffiti would last between two to four years, but they do not last that long anymore. New artists have arrived with new ways of thinking and ideologies, and all they care about is trying to erase you off the map and showcase their work instead. The new pieces that are created by people who know what they are doing are amazing! However, the new works that are painted by novices that have their head in the sky and think they are the center of the universe don't contribute to the scene. They are filling everything up with lifeless paintings and disrespecting the system that is based on respect and evolution that has existed for more than twenty- five years. That sucks.

The guys that paint here often, amongst others, are HW and MRK who are comic muralists, as well as Zero, Baresk, Kecha, KIF, SFC, Bres, Trebol, and Angel. All of us are part of the graffiti lifestyle in Maipú, and all of us live within the commune." ANGEL

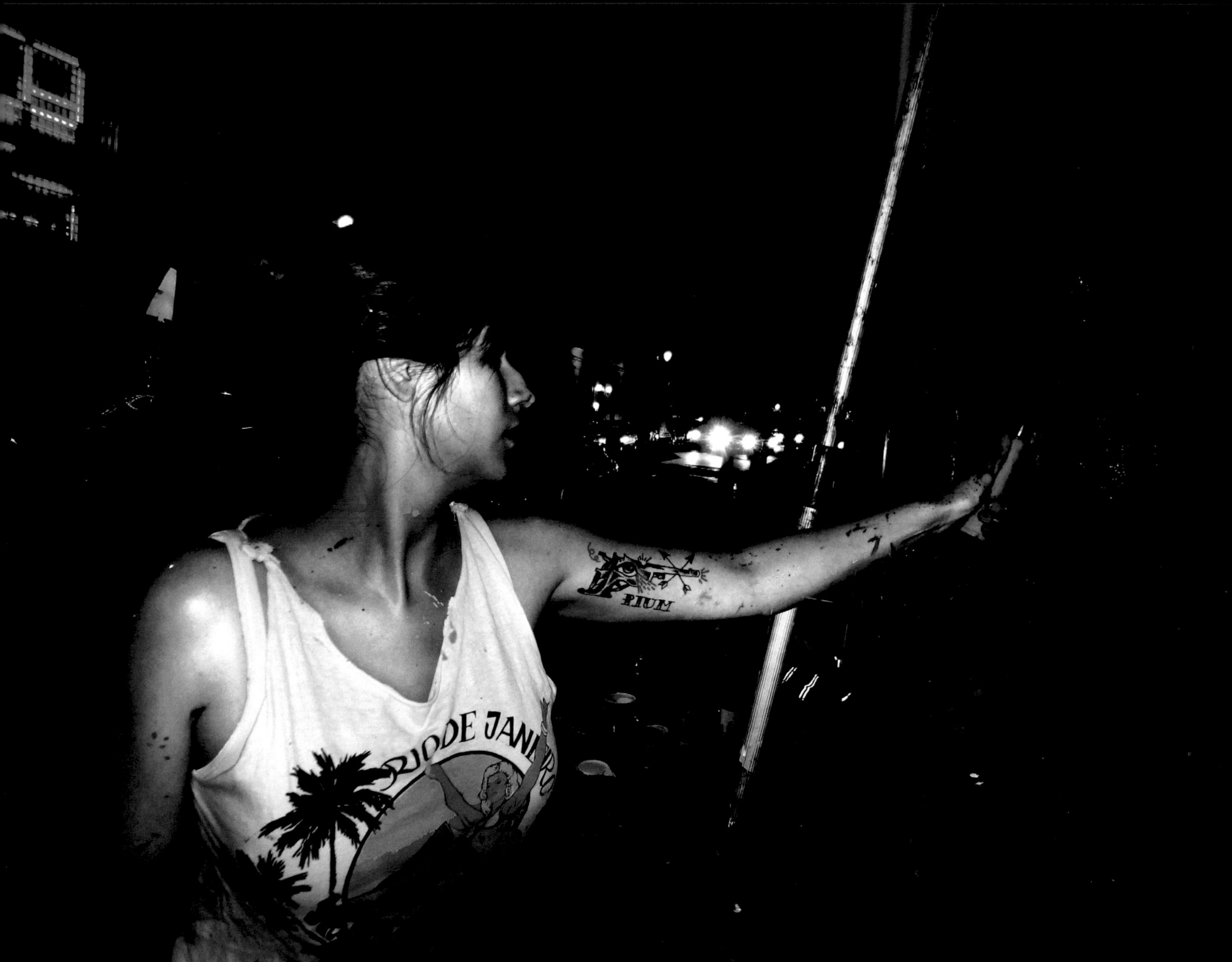

"Not just anyone is born with the desire to risk everything to paint, the desire to leave everything on the wall, but in Santiago there are many people who paint with passion and with love for art. Even if materials are scarce, people paint. They are incredibly motivated." KARIM

"Once, as a kid, I starved of hunger at school in order to save up and buy three spray cans. I then stole paint off my grandmother and painted my first graffiti. It came out horrible, but to me it meant the world. The following day it was painted over." SGWOR

"Graffiti is my greatest passion in life. It's about enjoying those moments facing the wall. The end result is not as important." SEIS DEDOS

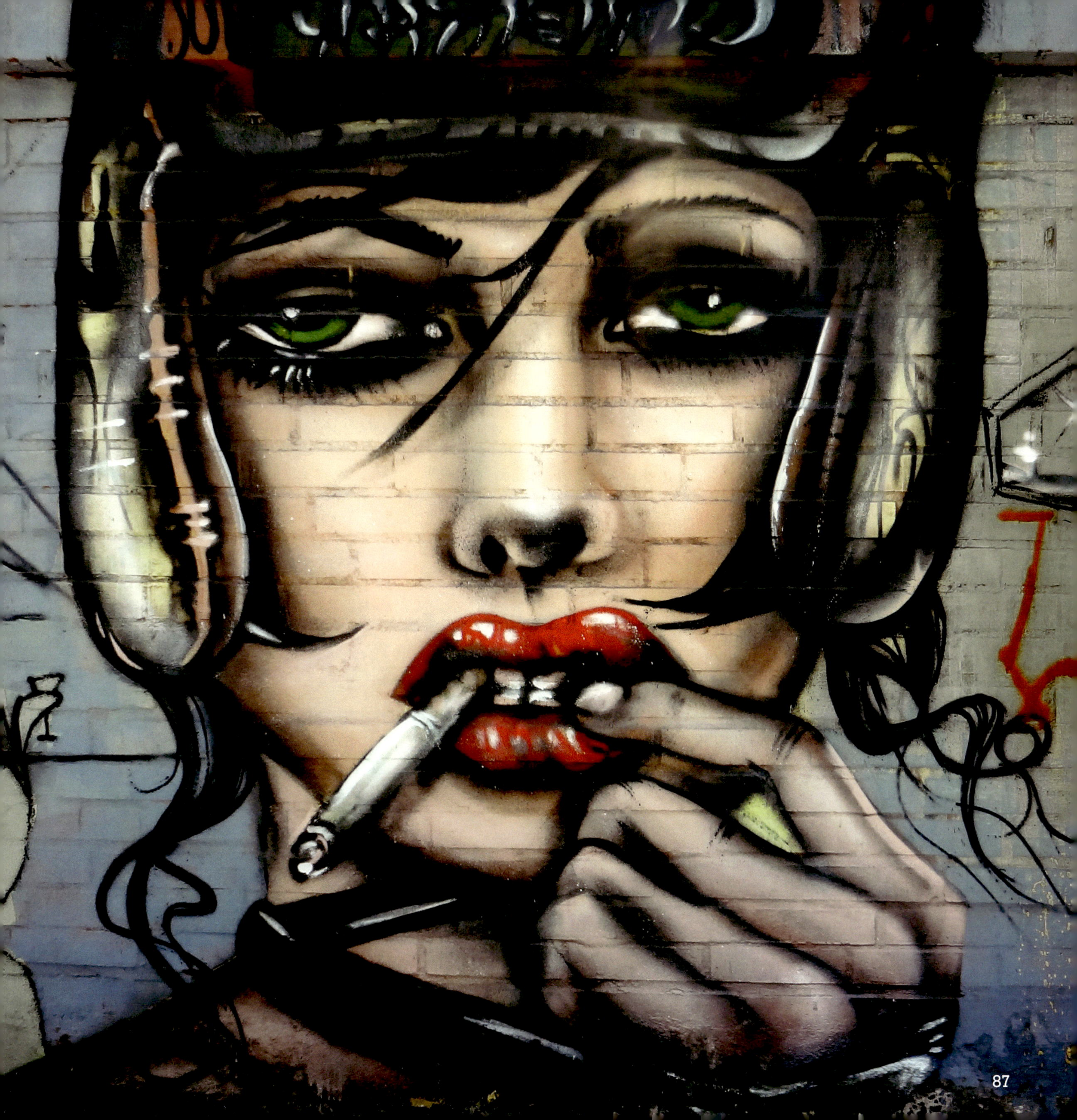

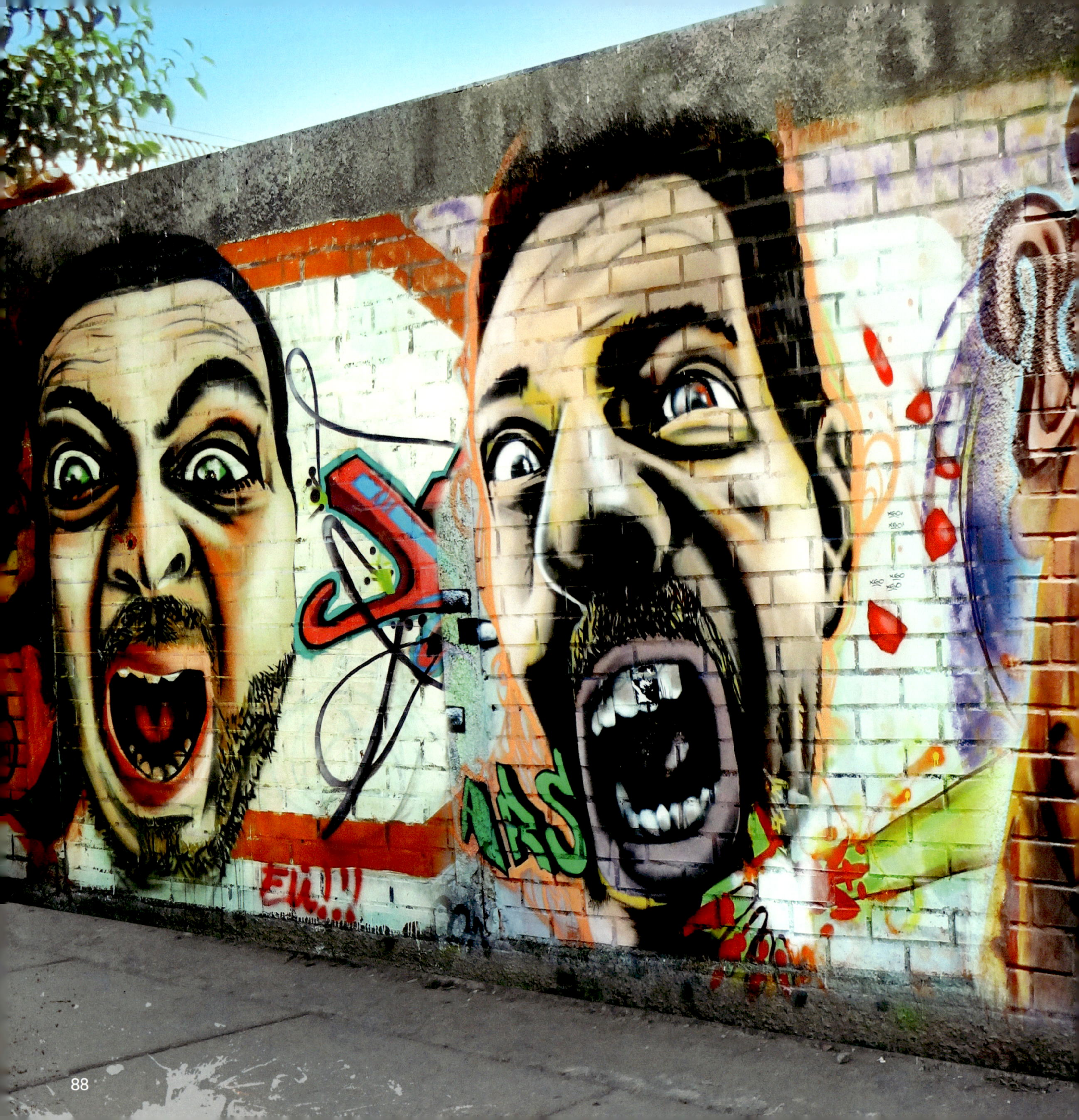

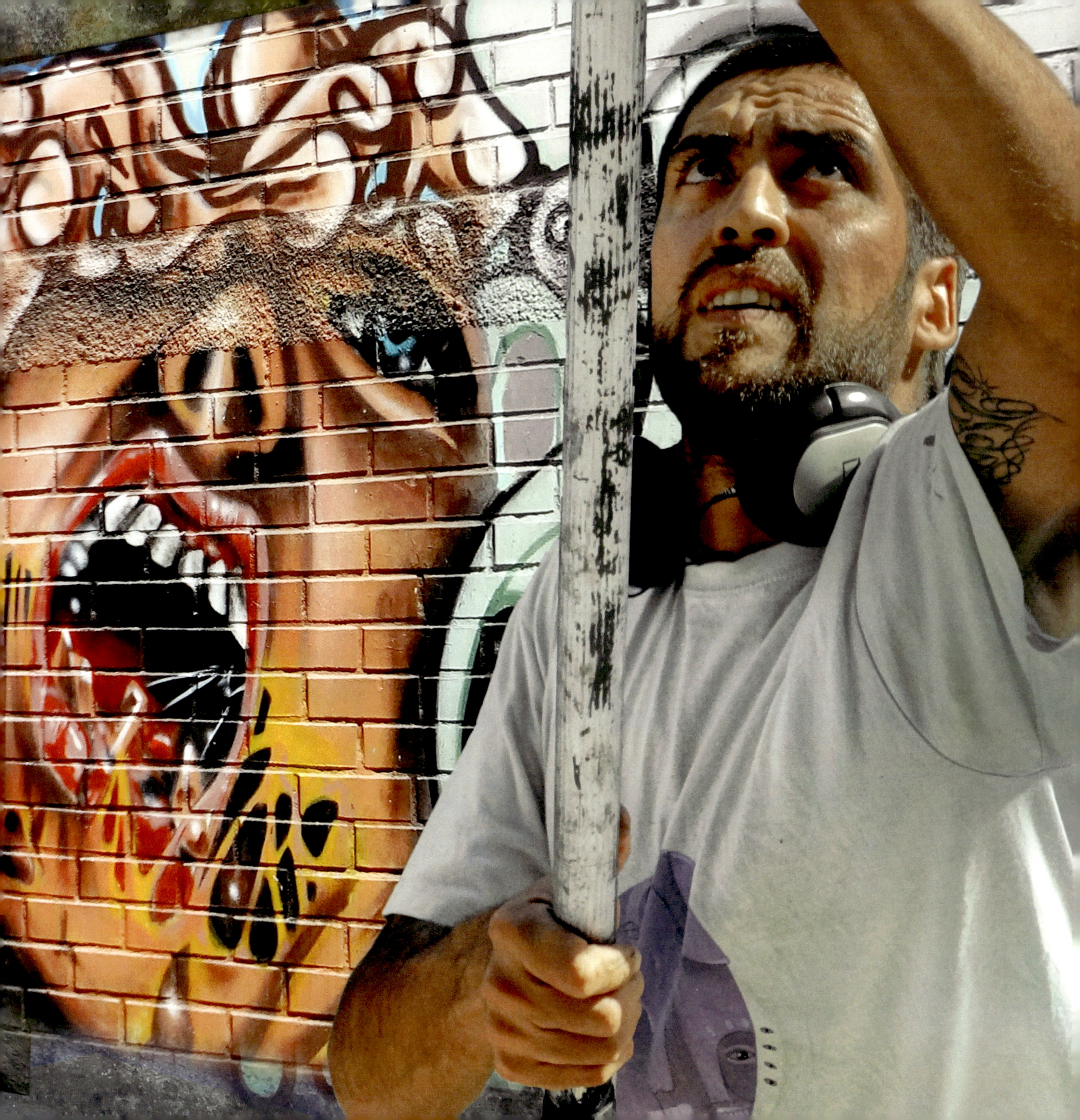

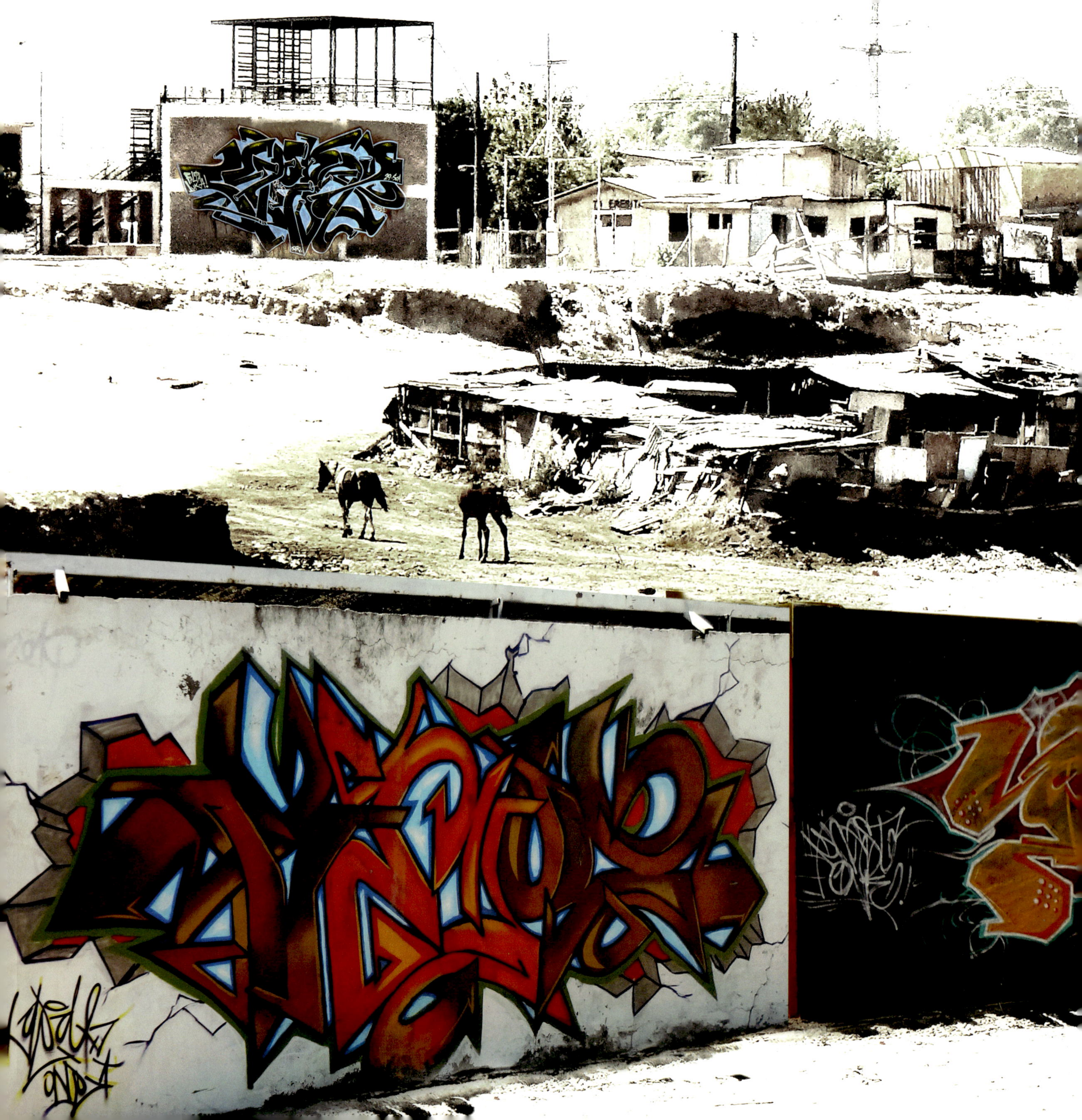

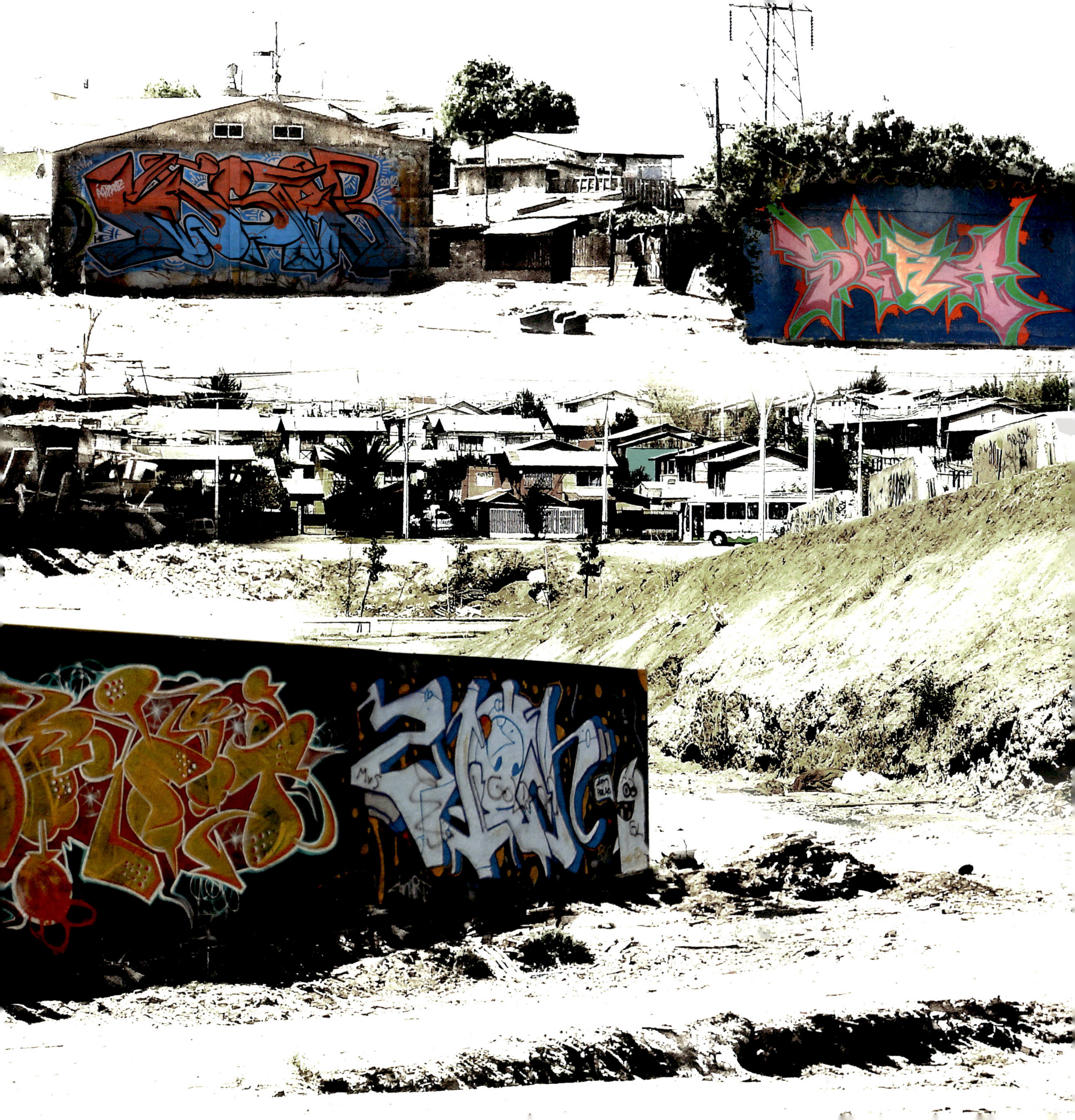

MAPOCHO RIVERA

Length of river 110 km^2
Graffiti prevalence: 6/10

"Artists usually paint illegally in the Mapocho. There are a few who have painted with permission granted by the municipality; however, the majority paint without authorisation. So many artists have painted here. The ones that I recall are Aislap, Conpaz, Cekis, Grin, Derick, Sick, Piguan, Agotok and Ramon Parra Brigade. These guys have painted the biggest and most visible pieces along the river bank

"There is far greater police vigilance in the part of the Mapocho that flows through the center of town. The police tend to get annoyed if they have to go all the way down the river bank to arrest us, so that is an advantage. During the rule of Mayor Zalaquet, all paintings were removed. The municipalities' attitude towards graffiti varies depending on who is in charge." DENST

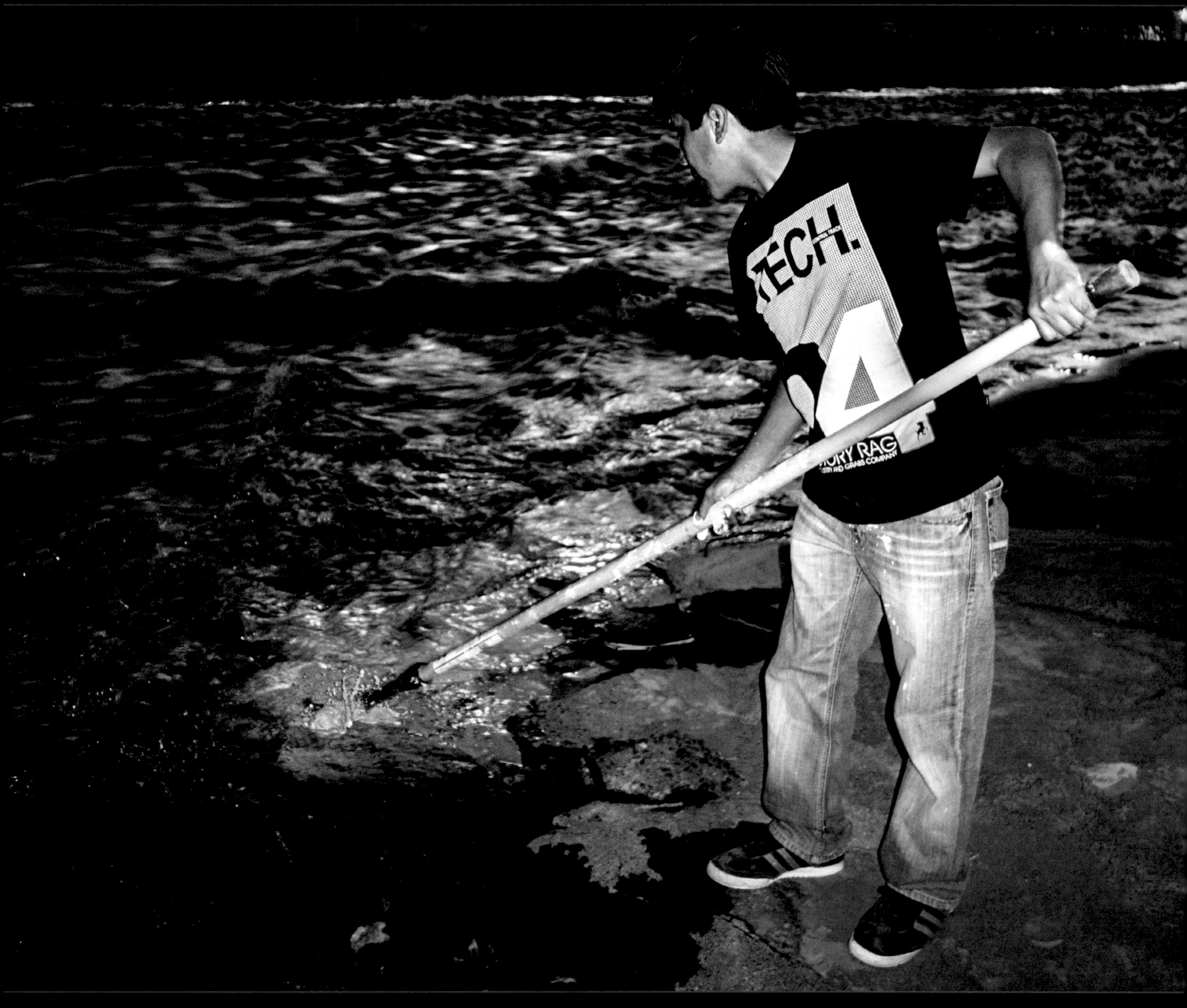

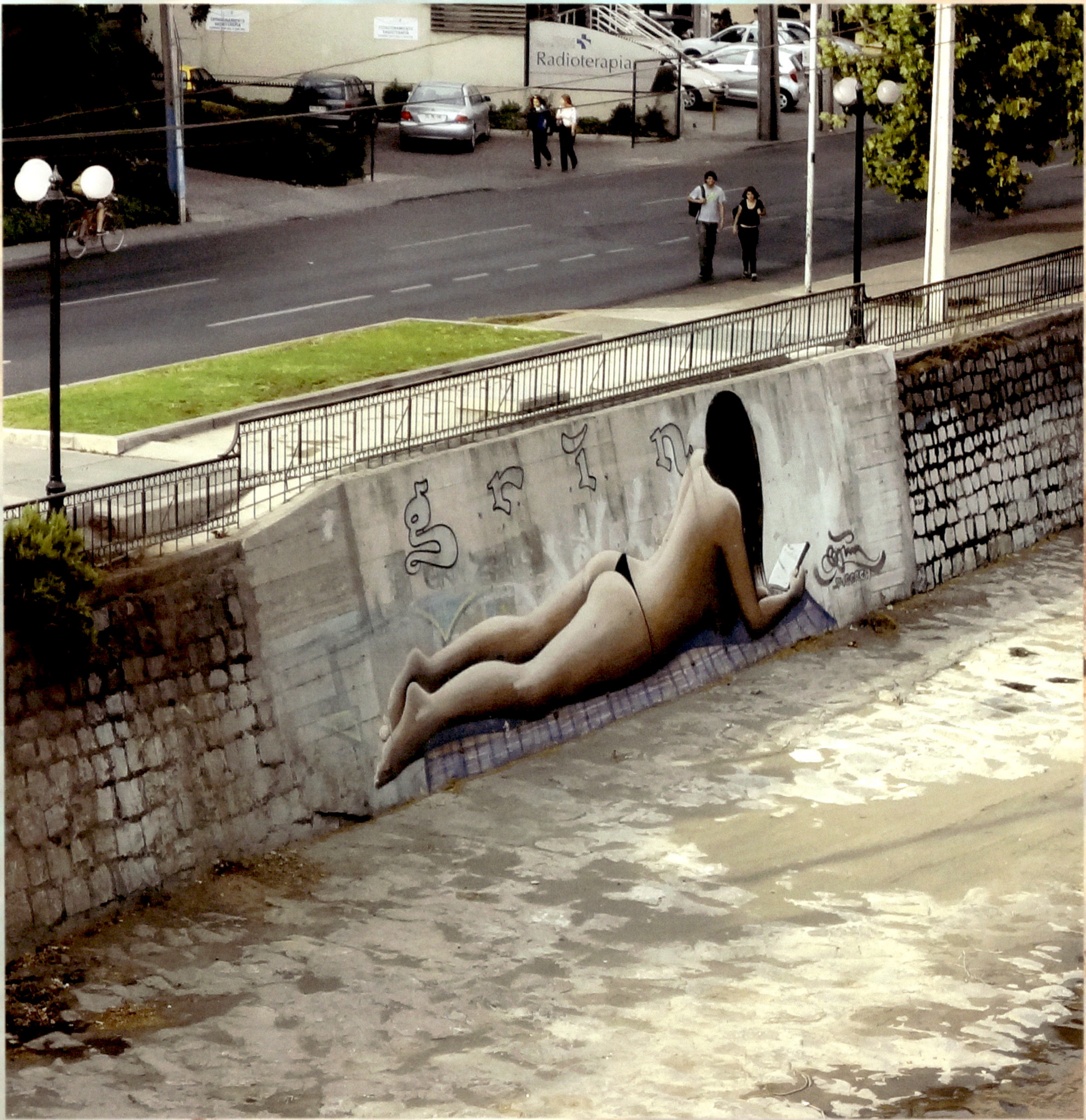
Radioterapia
grin

"We Chileans are good at inventing things. Idiots from Europe come over and don't understand how we paint with latex, roller brush, bag techniques, and other inventions. Beginning to paint with bad cans helps, scarcity also helps—it's either that or not painting at all. If you have talent, you will do it despite the odds. It won't be the same quality of painting, but it will have the same impact.

"Graffiti is a man's world. It is entertaining; difficult and hard when it comes to criticism. It is very competitive even if no one wins anything. It is pure respect, status, and level. I like it and it is pleasant, that's why I got into this, but at the beginning I was absolutely scared. There are few women in graffiti, not because the men won't allow them to paint, but because women won't take the risk. Women generally don't like to get dirty, but it's all the same to me, it's always been the same to me, so it didn't cost me anything. When I began, I thought the men would exclude me, but the opposite happened. They included me without judgment.

"When a wall is painted in the city, things change. I was on the bus and would see certain walls, and I would say, 'Cool, now we're nearing that area where there is a wall that I like and I look at it, again, and I find something new on it, every time.' I think that this is a service to the people. I like the idea that graffiti is a gallery that is free to all. I like knowing that people fall in love with a wall that you painted.

Painting on canvas and on a wall is different, yet the difference isn't in the piece, but in the sensation and the conditions. There are people passing by all the while, there is noise, you are outside, there are police. These conditions aren't present at home. The pressure under which you work is beautiful. The love that I feel isn't for the drawing, but for the experience of having painted a wall and for the people that were with me." LUNA LEE

"I began to get to know the national scene little by little. I arrived on the scene anonymously, but after the success that I had with *Los Muros Nos Hablan* (*The Walls Speak To Us*), everyone wanted to meet this man who takes photos of murals and graffiti. The idea was that only those who painted were well known. My objective is to cherish something that will later evanesce, giving it an ephemeral quality.

"I will never sell pictures of graffiti. They are available for publication because the photos belong to the painters. What I do keep under lock and key is a type of inheritance that I received—some thousand photos of the graffiti that was painted back in the day, a product of the old school, From Santa Isabel to the works at Plaza Italia. To those that investigate the Santiago scene, I will say this: never forget to pass by Santa Rosa. There is a phrase that has been repeated to me various times: Santa Rosa, Saint School. It is the crib of Aislap and Agotok. It is an immense avenue of pure graffiti. Many walls have died, but fortunately new ones are always born, and that's what we're doing, registering that work." LEON CALQUIN (PHOTOGRAPHER)

"I never paid much attention to graffiti and tags, because I don't paint hip hop, I paint for Latin America. The Negotropica Brigade is different, and this is noticeable in Lo Prado. There we have what we call El Cordon Lo Prado (Lo Prado Rope), a series of murals, many of them within barrios where only the people who live there see them. There, they take care of us and understand us. I like graffiti, I find them beautiful, but we paint within the muralist brigades, which are very communist, and we move in a different circle. In that circle there is the Ramona Parra Brigade, Elmo Catalan, La Garra Pata— all with the same style: human shapes struggling, made with a gilded edge and detailed. This is a more narrative type of painting. I have been painting for twelve years with my brothers and with them I decided the type of characters, trace, theme, and signature that define us. I believe that graffiti and muralism are mixed together, nowadays. Everyone knows each other. I have painted with Abusa graffiti artists, and we made a mystical and amazing mural which I really like." TELLY GACITUA

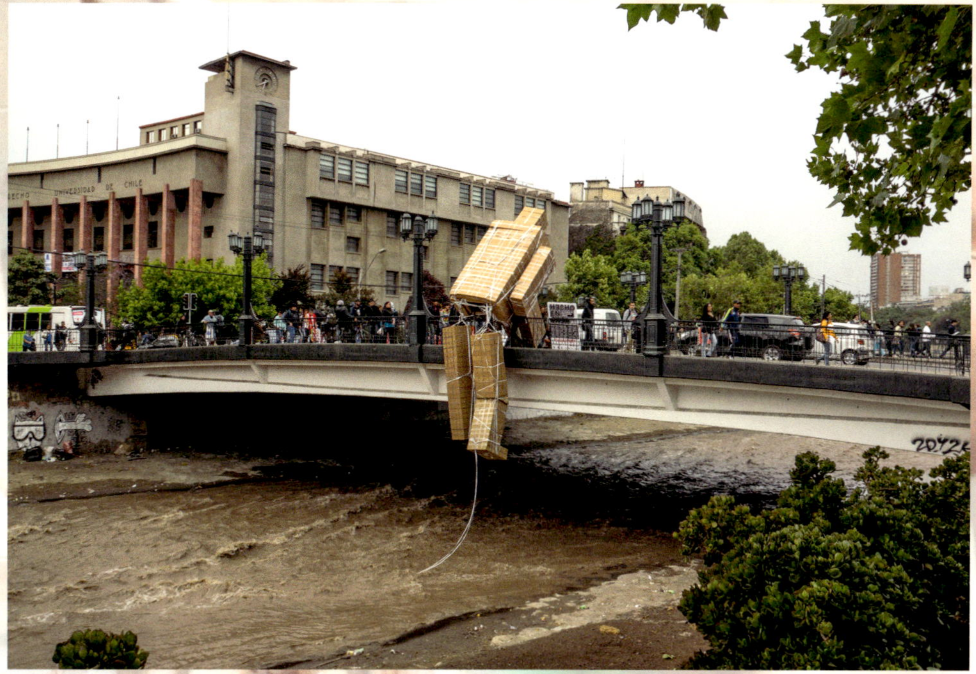

Piguan

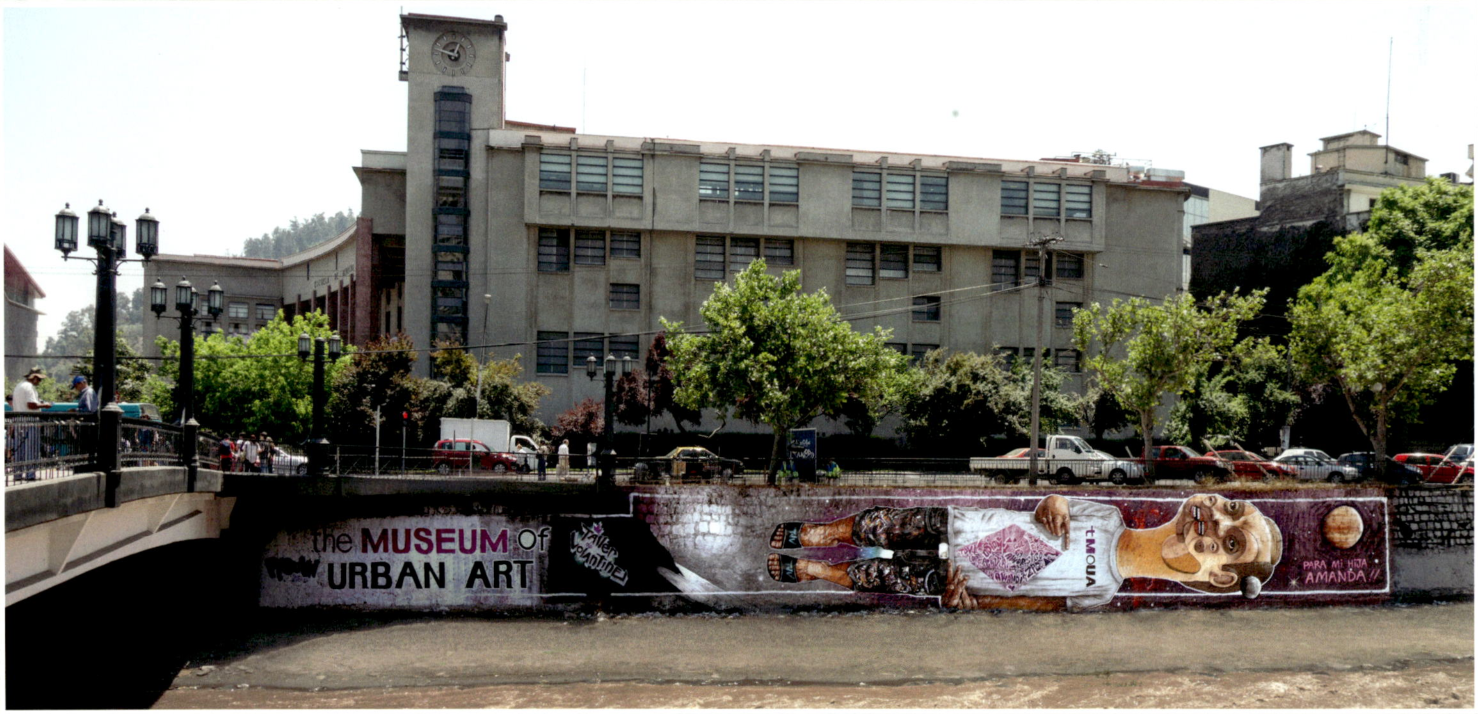

Agotok

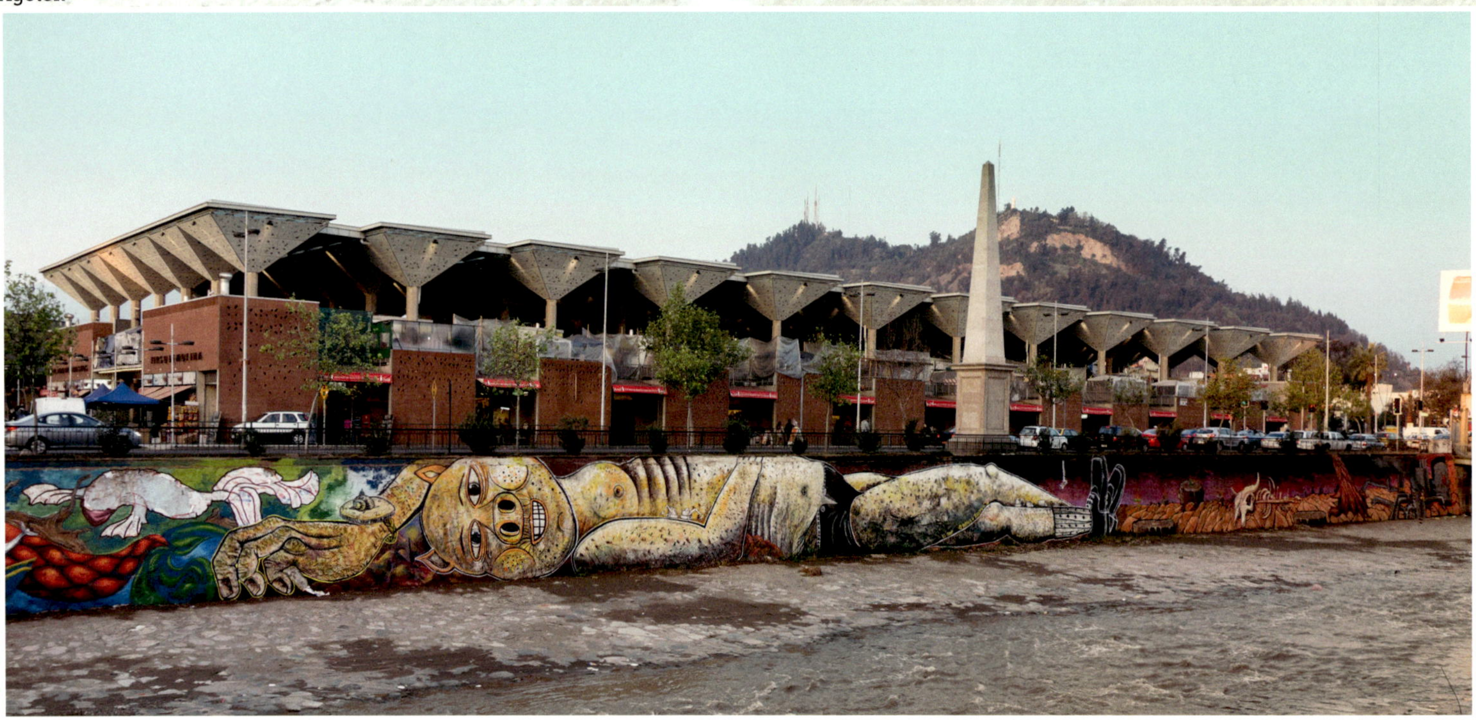

La Robot de Madera – Elliot Tupac – Charquipunk

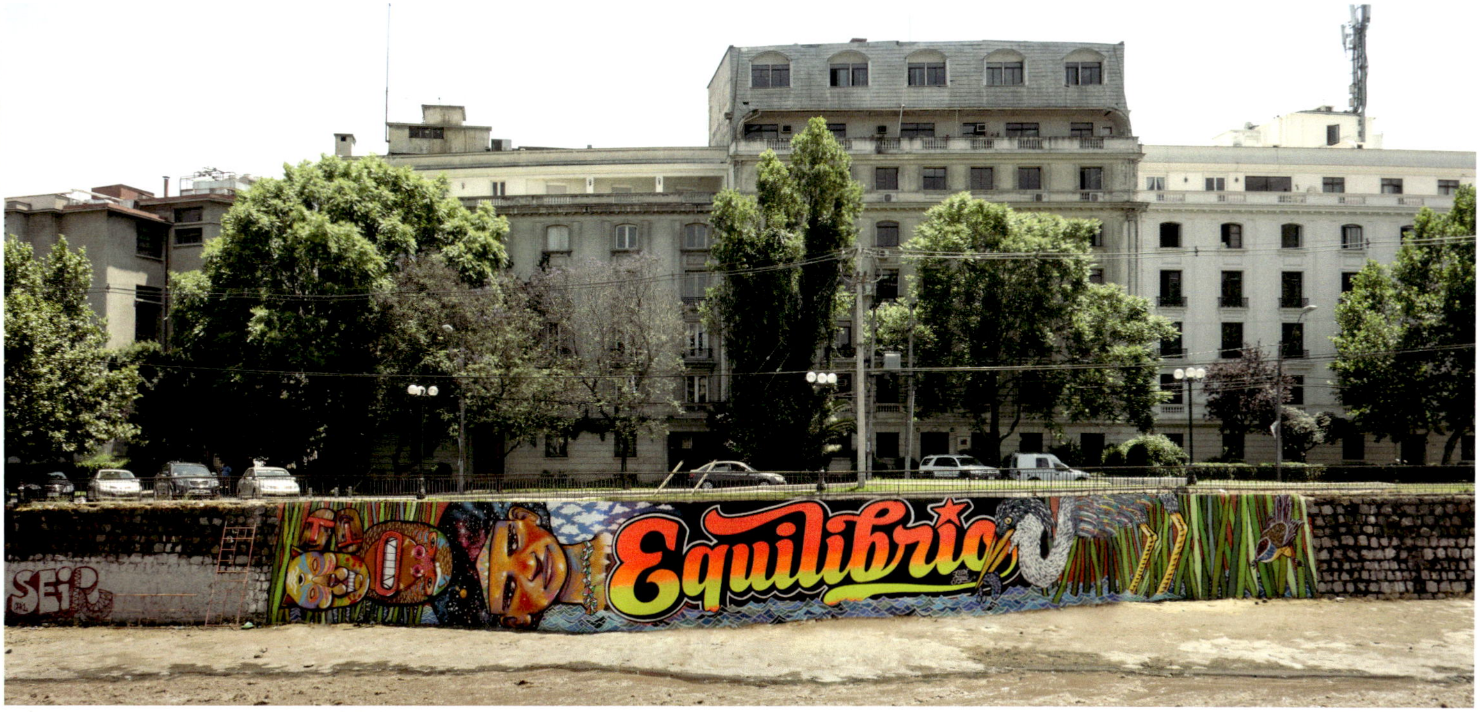

Unknown

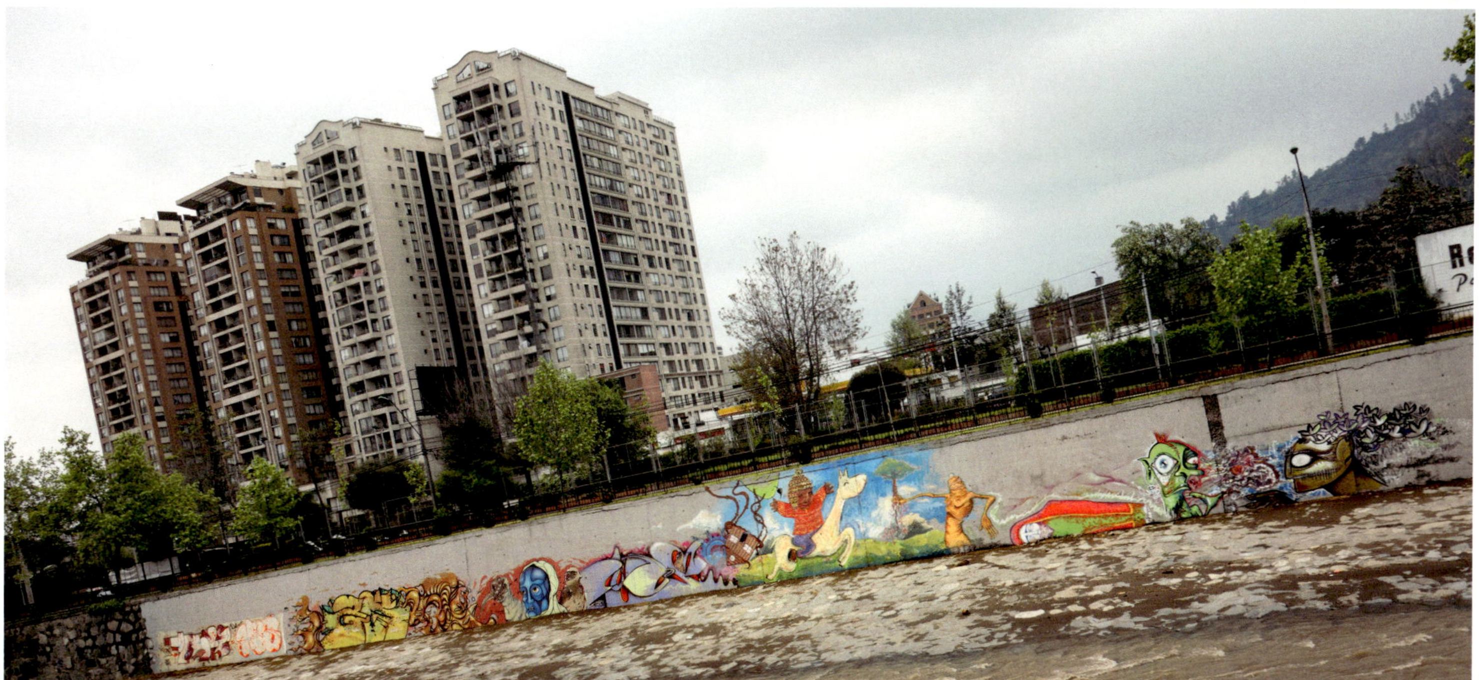

Patronato

Area: 2.6 km^2
Population: n/a
Average annual income: n/a
Population below poverty line: n/a
Graffiti prevalence: 9/10

"I live in this neighborhood and paint often here. I feel really comfortable walking around and painting here. There are a lot of immigrants living in Patronato. There is a mix of Peruvians, Ecuadorians, Koreans, Chinese, and Palestinians. We all live together harmoniously. A lot of money circulates in the neighborhood, although it doesn't show on the outside. Patronato is a residential area with plenty of commerce. During the week I walk around networking in order to acquire painting jobs over the weekend. During the weekends, my relationship with this neighborhood is about painting, sometimes commercially, other times illegally. The police are not really bothered when they see someone painting in the streets. They're used to it. Sometimes, they will ask you for your ID.

"There are lots of different types of walls and also many shop shutters to paint and many spaces and corners to intervene. Generally, the graffiti here tends to be left untouched, especially those that are recognized to be great works. However, the artists tend to repaint their own works very often. I feel that the residents are very fortunate to be able to enjoy the ever-changing artworks. My crew (BAM) predominantly paints in this barrio as we all live in the vicinity. Others who often paint here include my girlfriend Naska, Piguan, and Mutay. Patronato merges into Bellavista, which is a mecca for tourism, hence a lot of tourists spill over into the area and the works tend to have a high profile internationally as the tourists photograph the works and spread them all over the internet." SANTANA

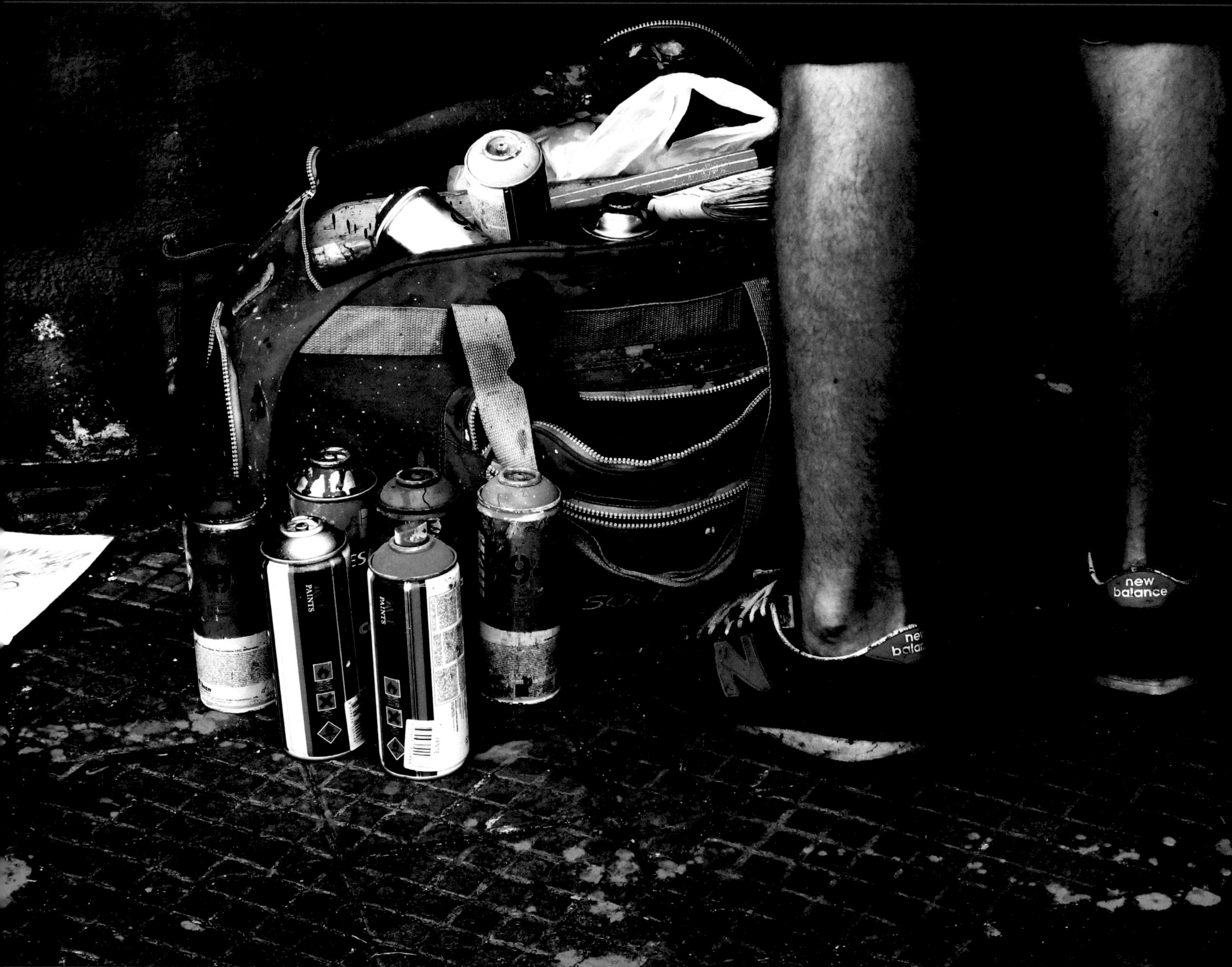
new balance

"If someone sprays over **my work** I would truly find it disrespectful as I put a lot of dedication, **effort, and love** into what I do. I certainly paint on the streets with good intentions in order to intervene in the place and **to beautify** it. If I did see somebody destroying **my graffiti**, I would certainly **break his jaw,** hahahaha." SANTANA

Santana – Naska

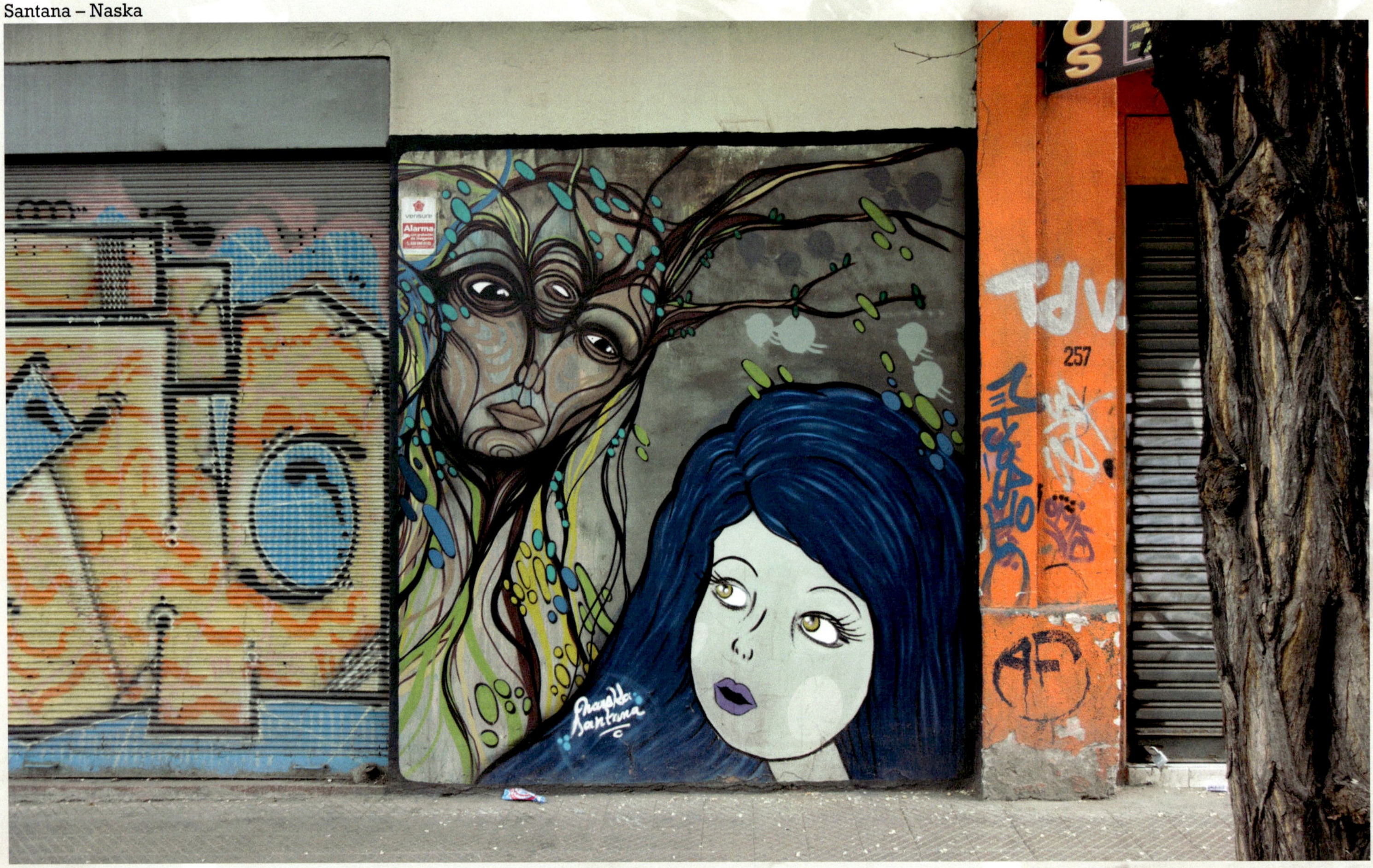

Piri –Santana – Faya

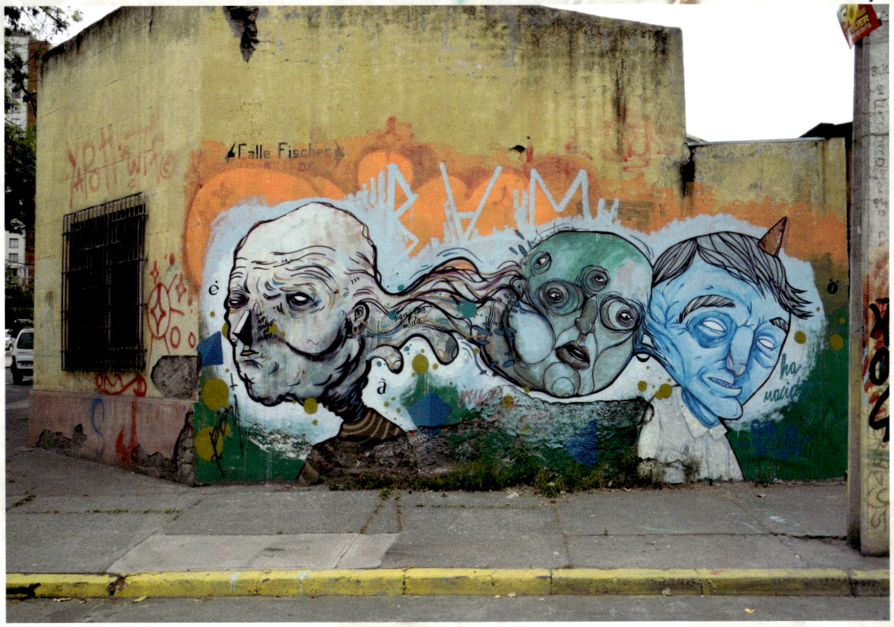

Faya

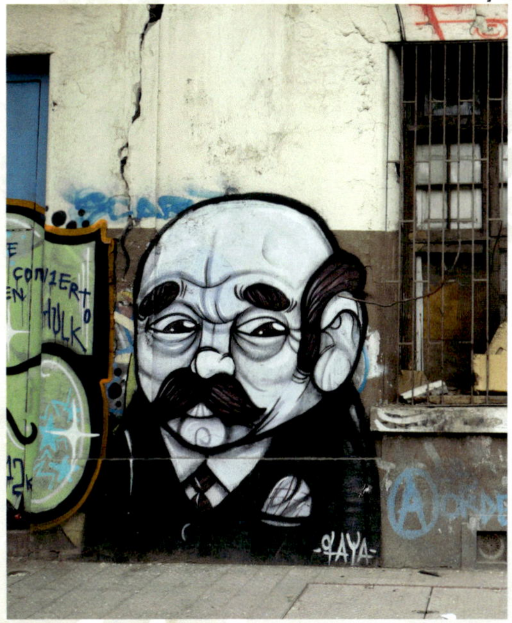

Santana – Faya

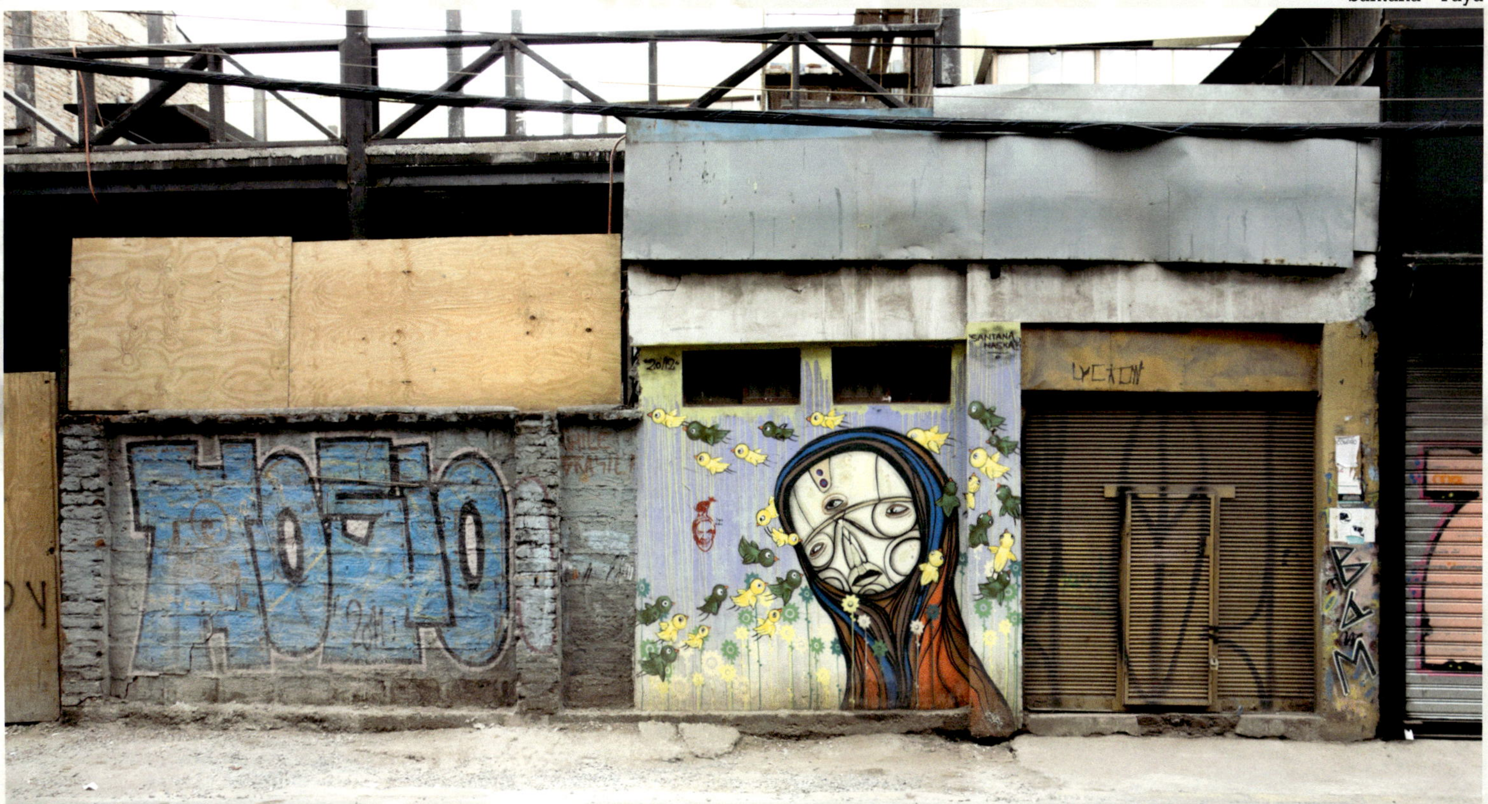

"I don't think the **educational** system is opening up to **graffiti**. Currently, there exists a contradiction, because the educational system hires graffiti **artists** to teach kids how to paint so that they lose **interest in drugs.** When these kids turn eighteen years old, they want to paint graffiti and the same **government** will erase them and punish them. **It's stupid.** I believe that both the educational and political systems **have no idea** what graffiti is, and they put on this show to pretend that they **cater to the youth.**" GUZTOK

Faya – Guztok – Santana

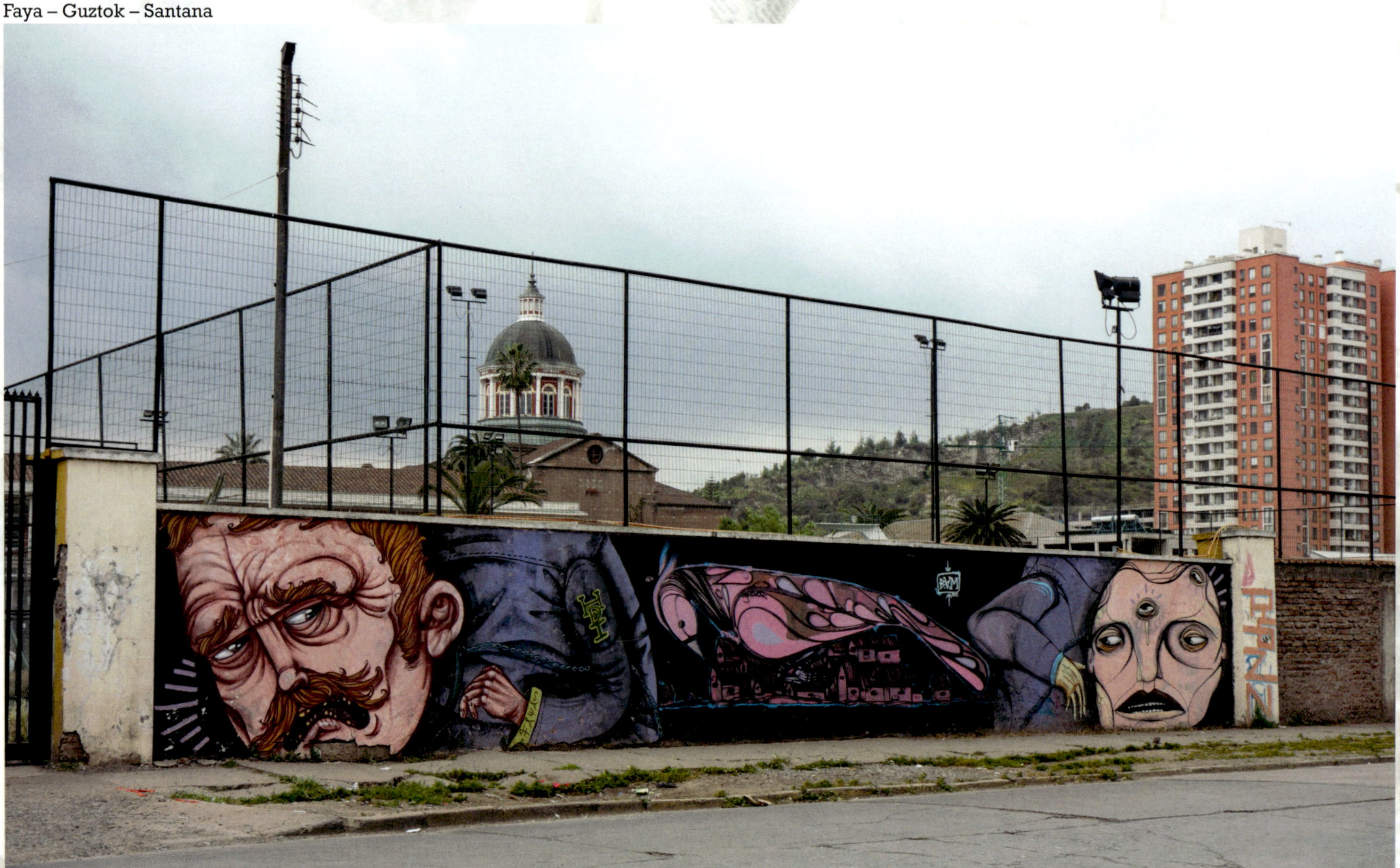

Santana – Faya

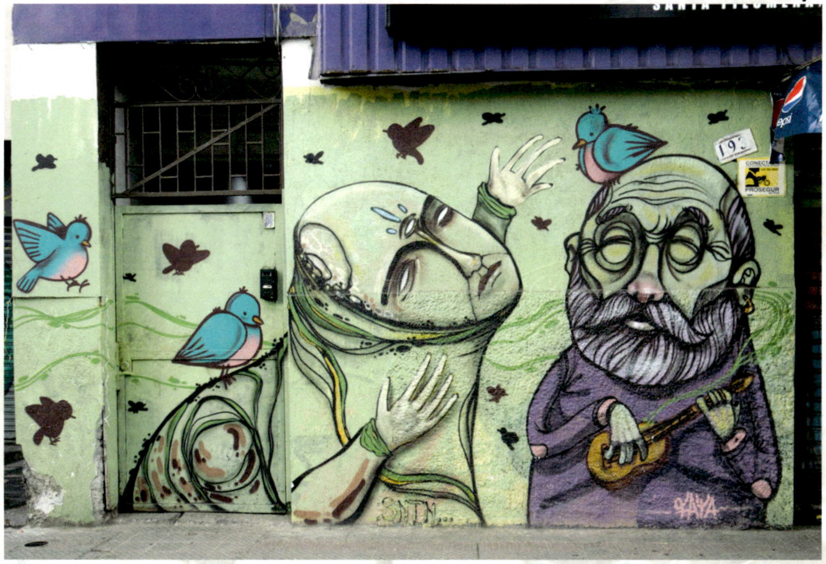

Piguan – Naska – Santana

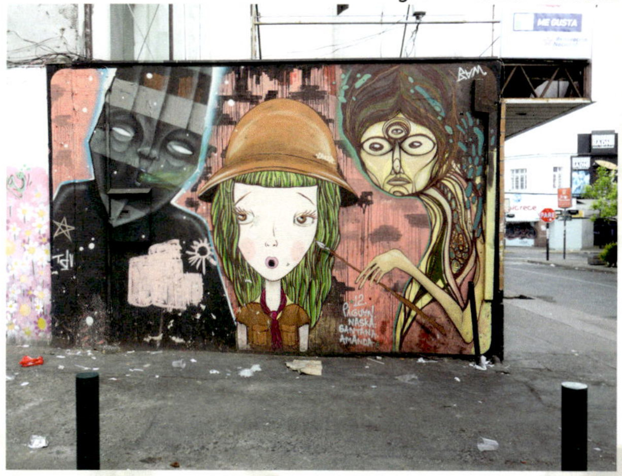

Santana – Piri – Faya

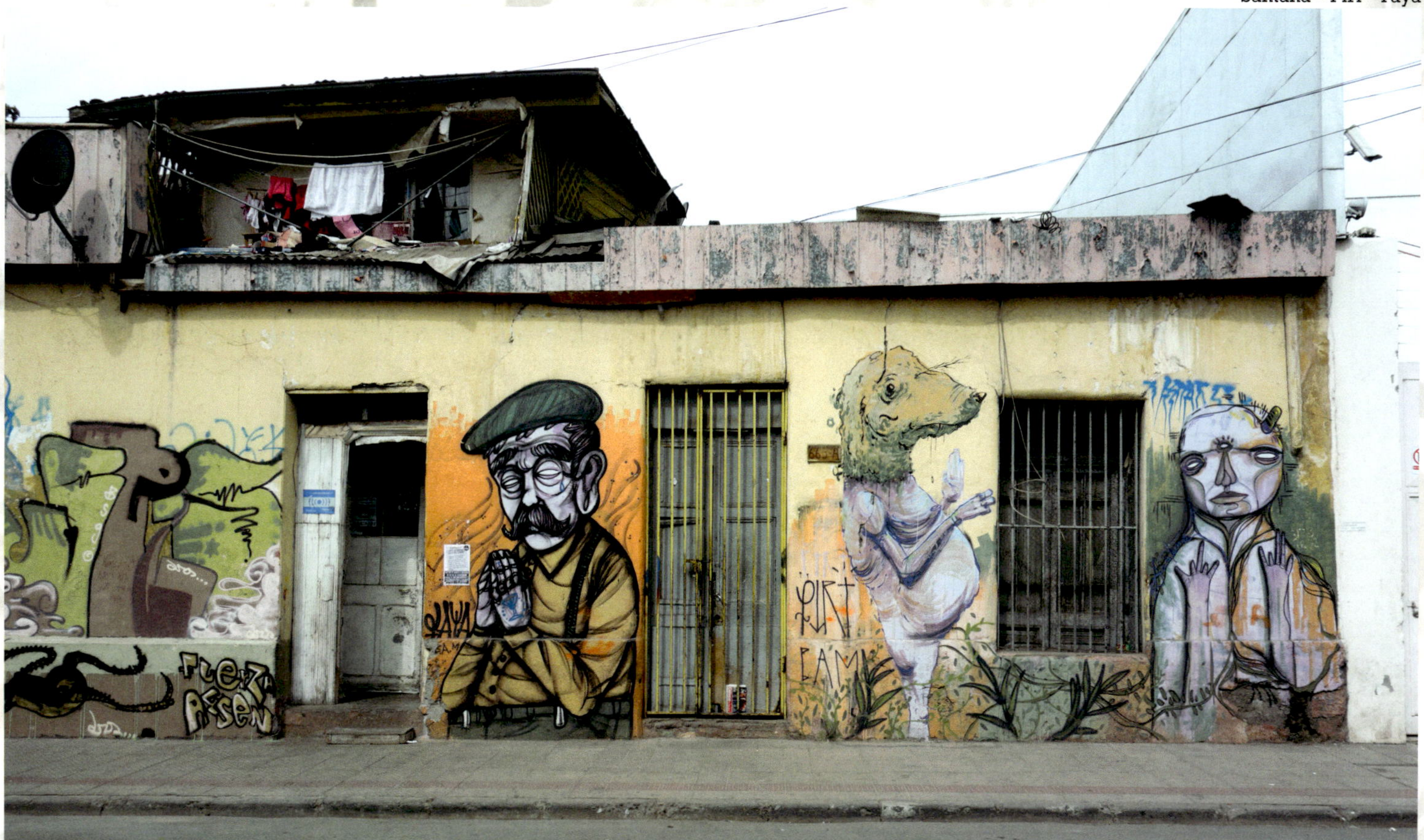

"Painting should always **have a reason** for being — not a fixed reason **that is forced** on everyone, but an individual reason through which the artist can develop his vision **to approach society** and himself. The creative process is **a binary one:** it starts at the microcosmic level, **which is you,** and extends towards **the macrocosmic** level, which is the universe. This establishes a **balance** at the moment **of creation."** PIRI

Santana – Piri – Faya

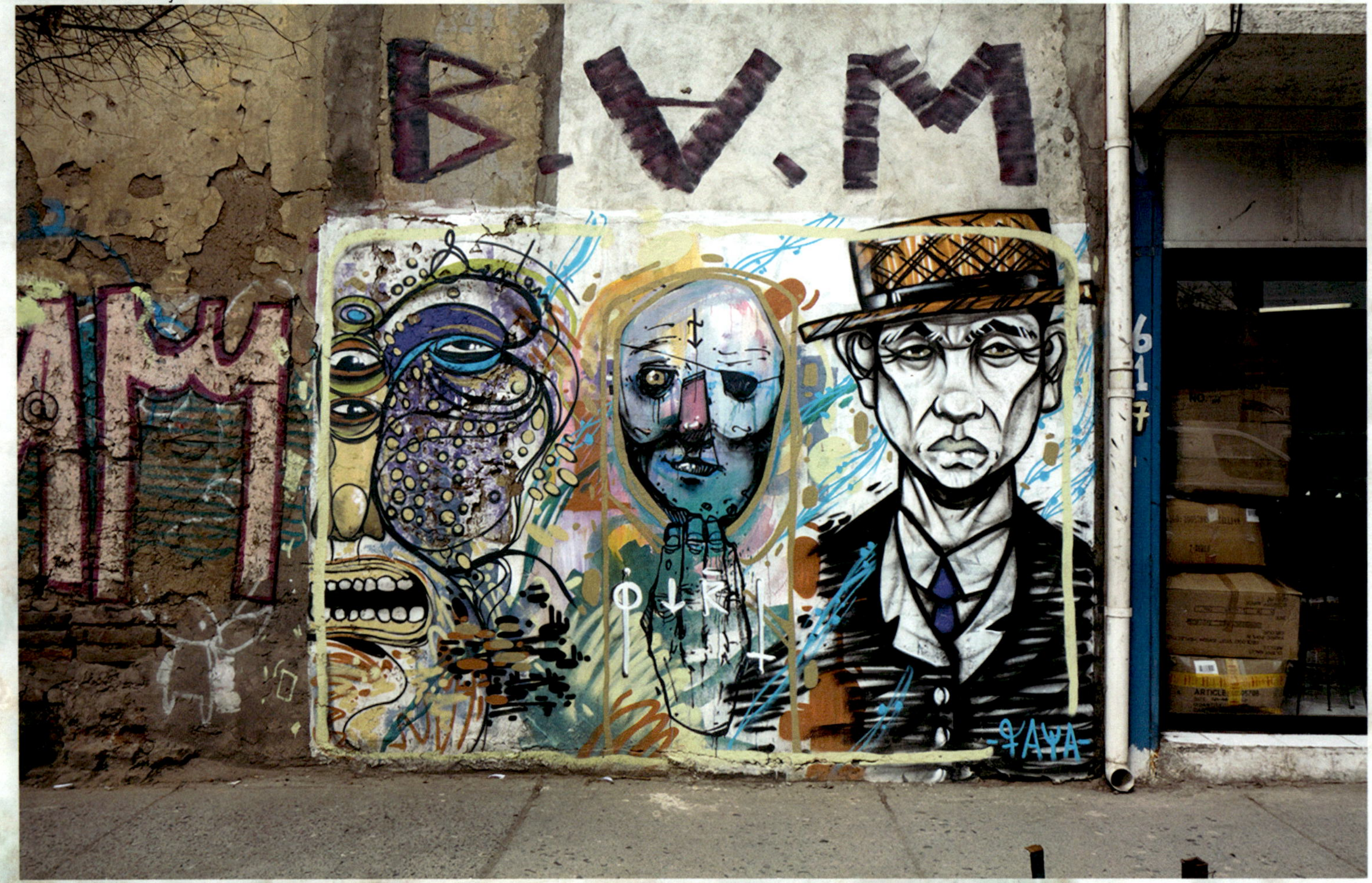

Piri – Santana – Faya – Guztok

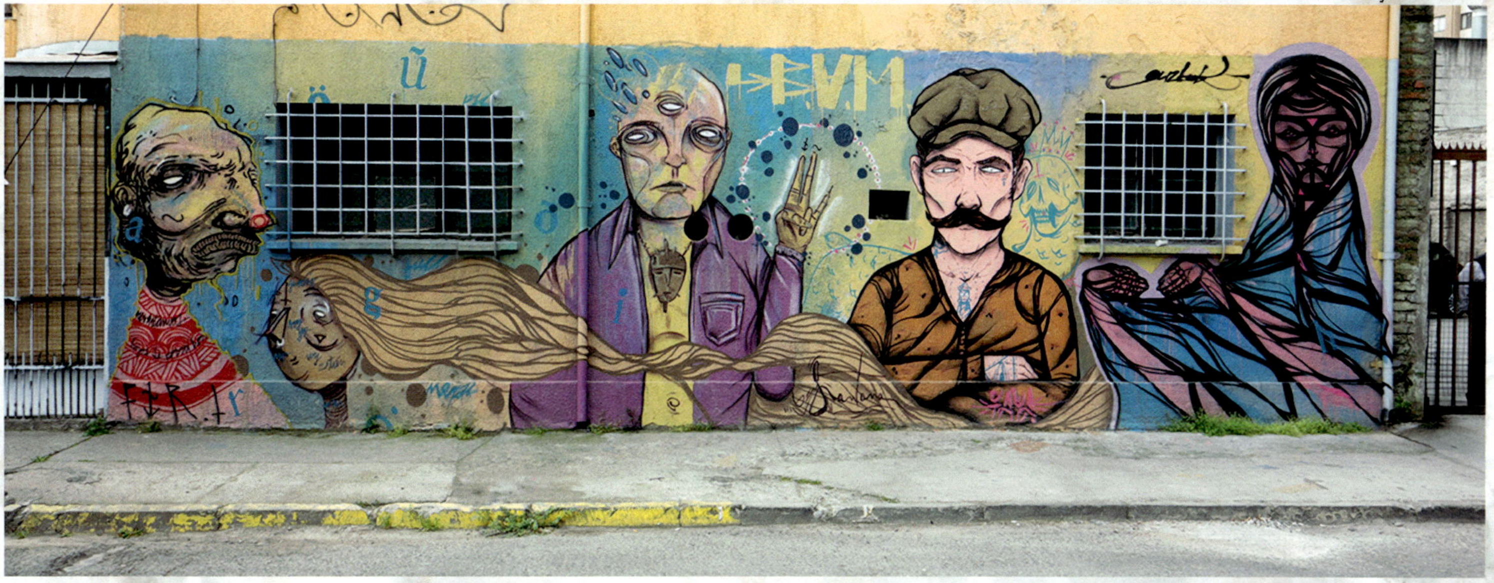

Santana – Faya

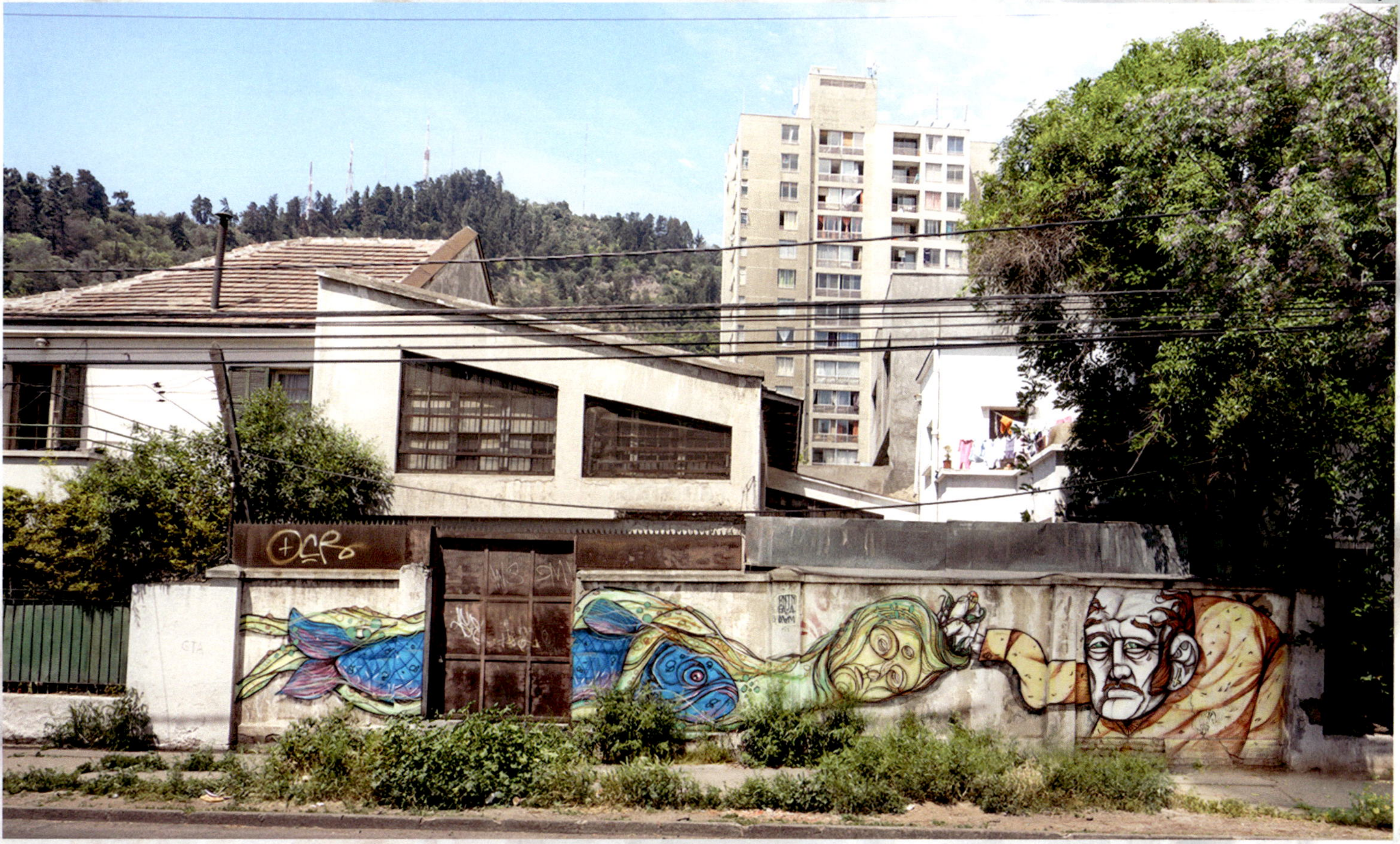

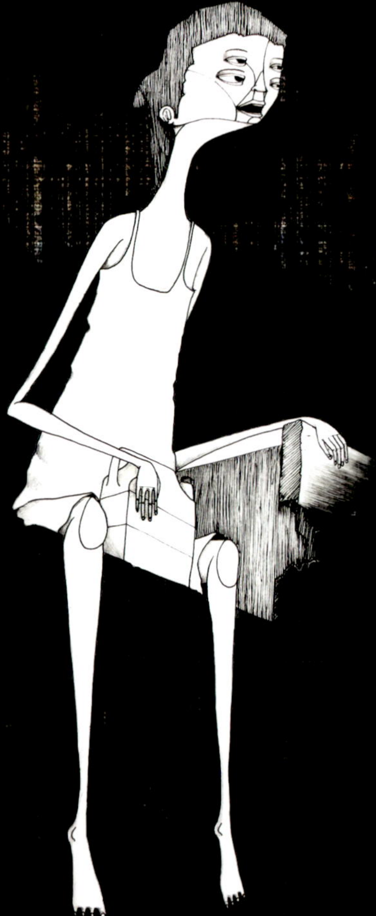

"The best time to paint is during the day, when it is legal in Santiago. At night, the police will pass by and arrest you." **VADE(TIPS)**

"The only thing that I try to achieve with murals is to beautify the spaces by which she walks. If she gets to see a painting when she is older and can reflect on it and understand it, then I will leave her a hidden message in the work so that she can decipher it. It's about valuing life more and making life more enjoyable for my daughter. There are many people who don't need to be exposed to negative things, but would rather have positive things that can make them see life in another light and make them happier to go about their day." **PIGUAN**

"The walls that are in a good location are the ones that we choose to paint. We generally paint illegally. We arrive, paint the wall white, throw on the background colors and then when we begin there is always someone who thinks you're going to paint something hideous. When they see that you are working with dedication and that you are serious, they support you. Our technique is to arrive with all the personality in the world. People will see you painting with confidence and conviction and they will think, 'This guy has permission, he's authorised.' We try to create something folkloric that offers some type of protest. At times, you can't explain the concept of a painting, but it will always be rooted in protest. This is why it's social. What moves us is injustice." **AGOTOK**

"With every passing day, graffiti becomes a bigger part of my life. It's a necessity, like a drug. No matter how much you plan before hitting the wall, what you want people to see and think about you will subconsciously be reflected in your work. No matter how much I want to come off as aggressive, I will subconsciously reflect something more passive, more natural, and juvenile, because that's what really identifies me." **NASKA**

Santana – Naska

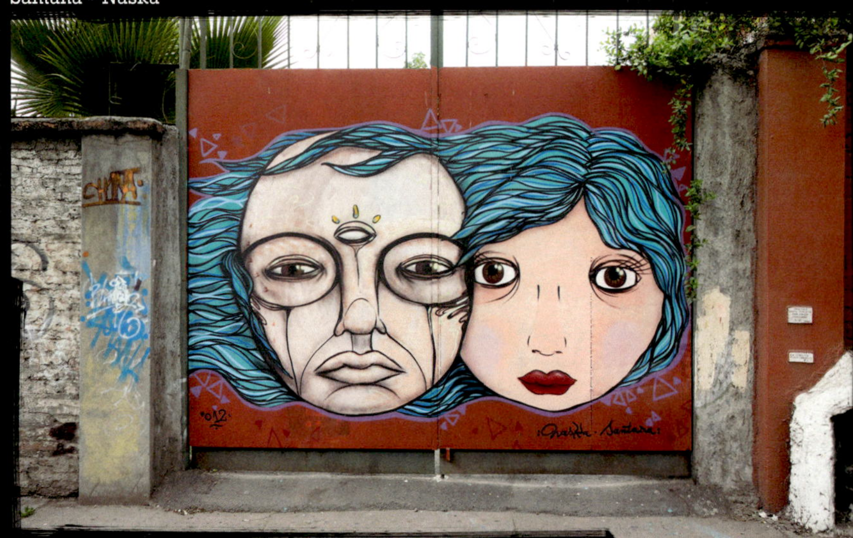

Piguan – Faya

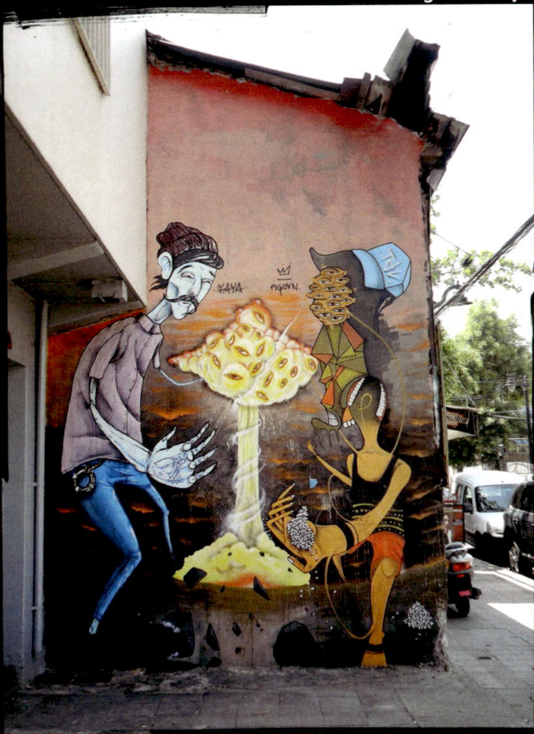

Piguan – Faya

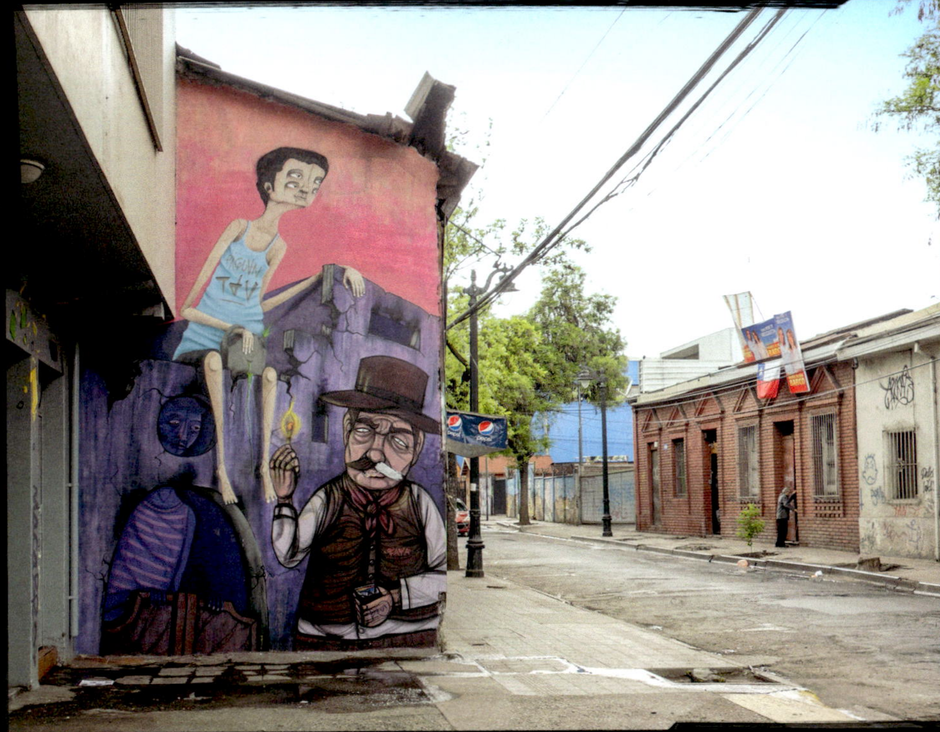

"My style is very juvenile, even if I don't want to come off like that. I believe that the majority of youth like it and are attracted to it. If I want to leave a message on the wall, I will do so, but my work isn't always related to politics or protest." NASKA

Santana – Naska

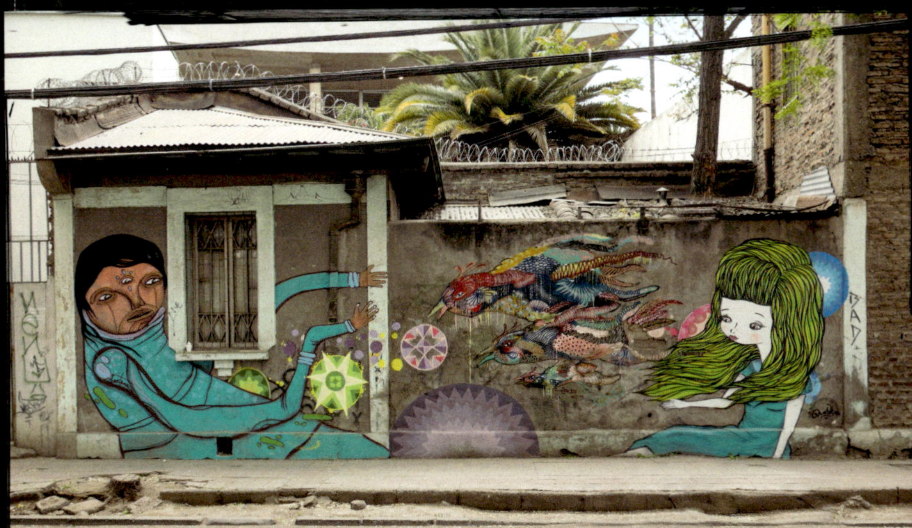

"Talking about female graffiti artists, I would like to see them break away from the traditional butterflies, flowers, birds, and mushrooms. A woman can paint amazing works, because we have many things to say. Women are more delicate, intuitive, and loyal. A woman who has a child and raises him well is courageous. I once set out to paint at eight and a half months pregnant. I was a week and a half away from giving birth. The press came up to me and interviewed me because they couldn't comprehend how I was there. I was only painting, and to them it was impressive. I will take my son out to paint when he is older, obviously." SOL RECICLANDO MUROS

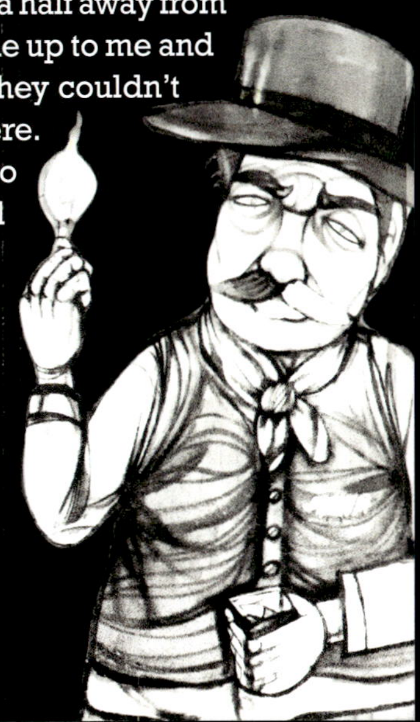

Las Condes and Providencia

Area: 113.8 km^2
Population: 376,000
Average Annual Income: $64,162
Population below poverty line: 2.6%
Graffiti prevalence: 2/10

"These adjoining barrios are amongst the most affluent in Santiago. It's a unique part of Santiago in which many buildings were erected in the '50s. The majority of its inhabitants are families and senior citizens, I also live and paint here as there has been a rediscovery of this zone that was once impossible to paint in. There are graffiti artists who feel that painting here doesn't do much for their street credibility, I really don't care about 'street cred.' My interest is in evolving as an artist and staying focused on my artwork.

"In Providencia and Las Condes doors are opening and there are an increasing number of commercial opportunities. When painting here, we try to maintain a relationship between our work and its surrounding architecture. This pleases the residents and also looks good in the photos we take of our work. With each passing day, this neighborhood is evolving. The residents are beginning to open up to street art and so is the municipality, which is commissioning increasingly more artists to paint here. There is still very little graffiti in the area, probably the least amount in Santiago. However, I feel that if you are lucky enough to paint here, the artwork really does stand out. The quality of works is high, and lately I have noticed that the best national and international artists are painting here. Virtually each time I paint, a resident will approach me and offer me another space to paint in and that experience is shared by my friends who paint here." ZEWOK1

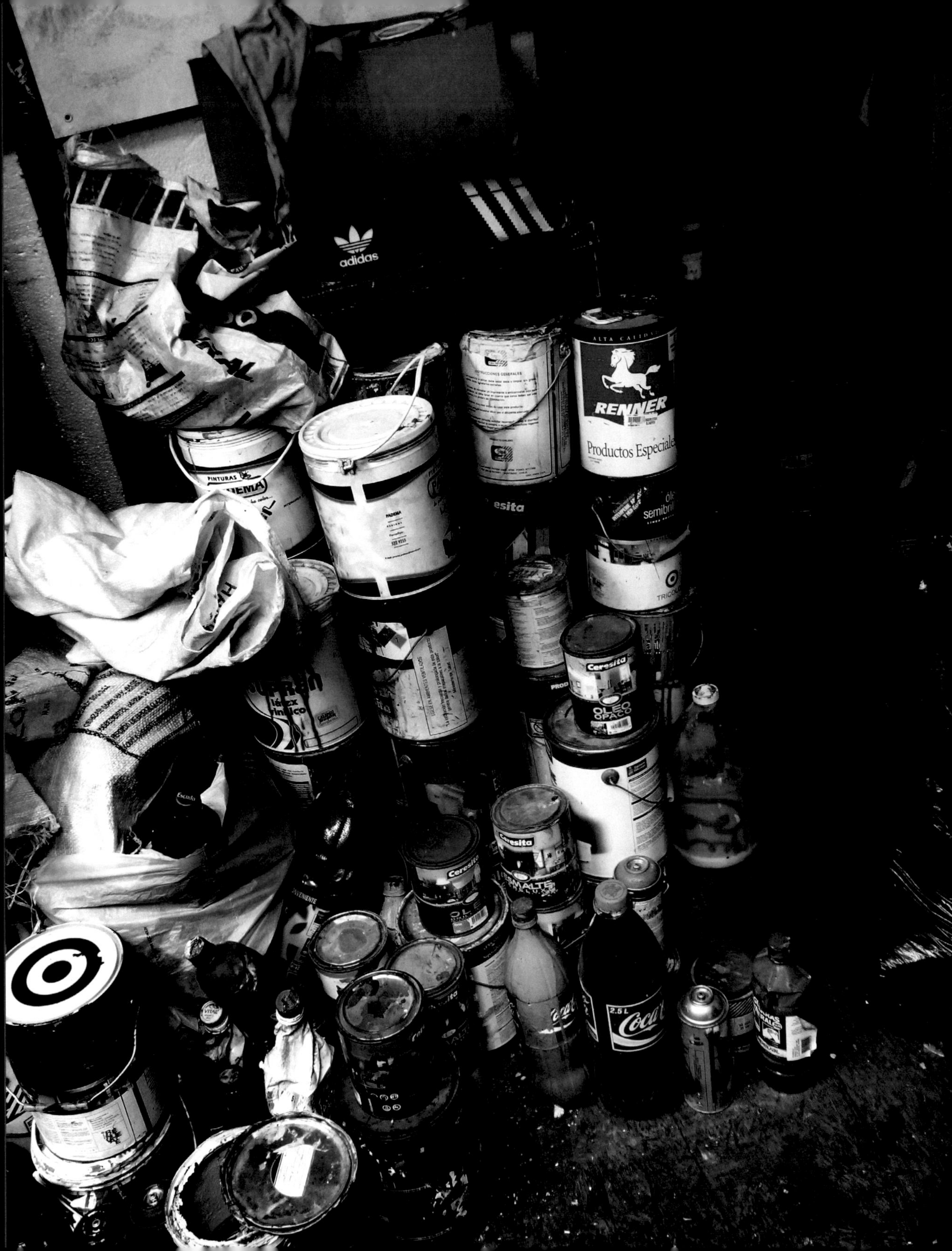
adidas
RENNER
Productos Especiales
Ceresita
OLEO
OPACO
Ceresita
Ceresita
2.5 L

"We had always wanted to do a piece together, and we realized that we had the same aesthetic and we worked in a friendly and visually appealing manner together. We then uploaded the pictures on the internet and little by little our friends began to ask us to paint their rooms and their walls. They would buy the materials for us, and we began to paint interiors exclusively for an entire year. We continued to paint together afterwards, since we had chemistry. This created an environment where we could learn and share generously. If Coni was working on something, I could butt in and intervene it, and it was fine. Sometimes, Coni would have an idea, and I would execute it or vice versa. It would be like a tennis match of ideas. Everything we have learned has been in the practice; we never sat down and said, 'Let's paint murals.' It just happened. Everything has been experimental. We see our work as something that is in constant evolution. Estanpintando is a creative initiative where anything can be done and where we don't limit ourselves by saying, 'I am a graffiti artist, I am a muralist, I paint street art.' We don't like to trap ourselves in any one description, because for us creativity is most important and it opens up opportunities. At first, it was murals inside restaurants and houses. Later we started painting on the street.

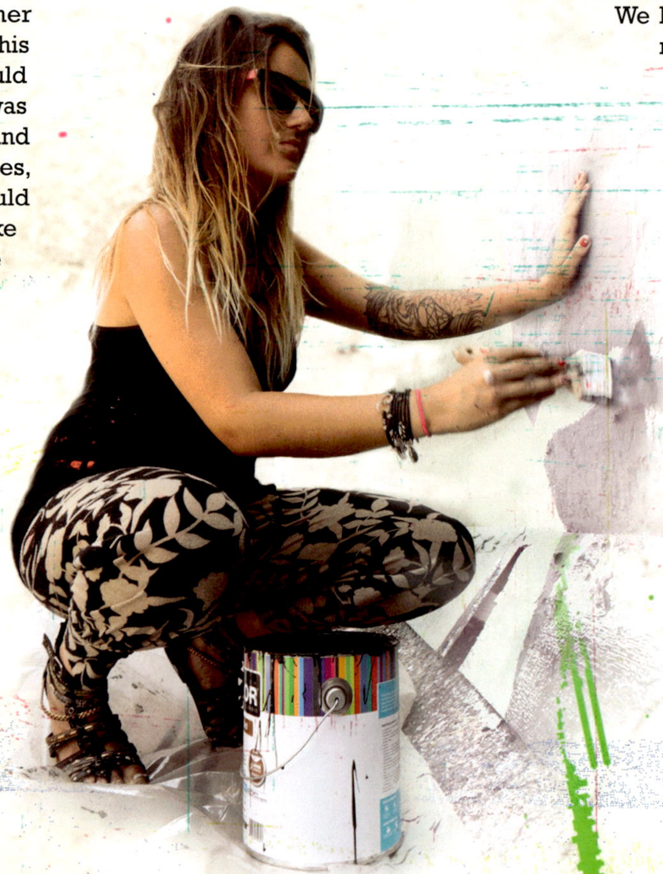

"When you put your heart in what you do, it is noticeable, and that attracts not only money, but also other possibilities. We have been painting full time on the street for two years. We are workaholics. We started painting houses and five months later we began to get clients. Benetton called us. We've also worked with other brands such as Foster (clothing), Home Center Sodimac, Lemon Stones (beer), and Mystery Land (a music festival). We have really liked working with them, making things that many people can see and enjoy, and at the same time, permitting us to make what inspires us —art—into a lifestyle. We learned to create an estimate and be professional, to charge for our work, and see it as a job, not as a hobby. We don't believe that because we are artists we should be paid less, because we value what we do. We have gotten many projects. We painted a jail with the prisoners, we painted a pool, clothing, on the street. Before Estanpintando, I was working as a waitress and Coni was making handmade trays to sell, trying to save money in every way possible. This is why, for us, it makes us proud to do what we most love and be paid for it. What more can we ask for? It's as if a surgeon didn't get paid for doing surgeries.

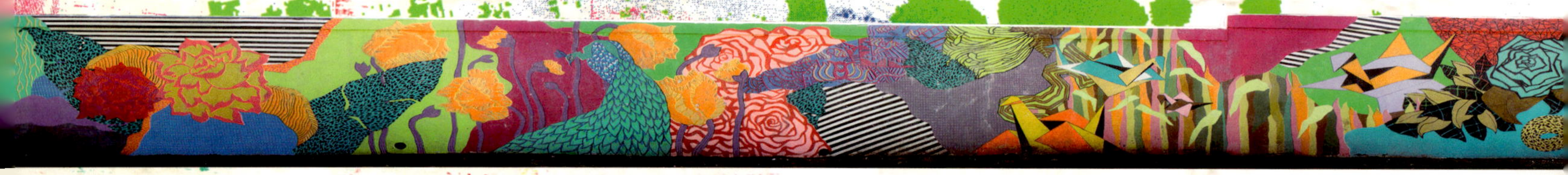

"We think that there is an evolution in the art of Santiago. People are putting more value on it. I feel that there are many more opportunities for young artists to market themselves, whether they engage in street art or something else. Nowadays, there are so many alternatives that allow you to spread your work free of charge; this needs to be taken advantage of. For example, social media allows your work to be seen not only by your friends on Facebook, but by people in other countries on the other side of the world, who can enjoy your work and critique it. It's diffusion, it's free, and it really helps the young artist. There are so many technological tools, like taking a picture of your mural with your cellphone and instantly uploading it to the internet. We are proof that this works. The public is more receptive to the new forms of media, new experiences, and new interventions in the city. Brands are also conscious of this and are looking for new ways to reach consumers without being aggressive or resorting to the traditional forms of marketing. Today, brands look for genuine examples, real representatives of the product or service that they produce. They use 'ambassadors' for a reason and their publicity campaigns don't idealize one consumer prototype. They are more real because the consumer needs to feel closeness with the brand to purchase it. This phenomenon is something that everyone can take advantage of and if, for example, you are a graffiti artist, there are brands that can fund you. We have never directly searched for a sponsor. Different brands have called us and, according to the project, we have accepted some, always thinking about what will benefit our work. At this stage of the game, there should no longer exist a prejudice in which we label the artist who works with brands as a 'sell out.'

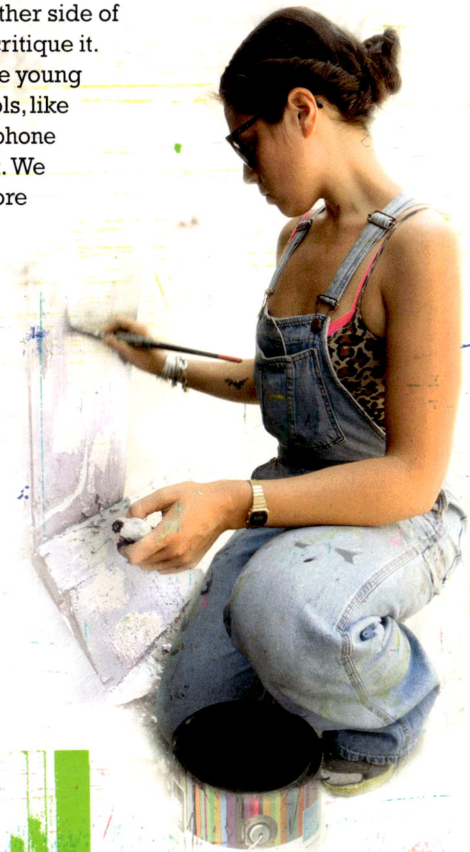

"Since we are two heads, we never sketch. Creating a preliminary image on a tiny piece of paper is difficult and we like to improvise at the last minute. We see the context surrounding the wall, and we get inspiration from that. For this reason, we always demand from our clients 100 percent liberty to choose the colors that we want and the figures that we draw. We take control of the entire process. It's impossible for us to say, 'The mural is going to be like this.' It is difficult to put two heads on one paper.

"Part of the sacrifice of Estanpintando is having left behind the life of the independent artist. Each one has her studio, but we are loaded with projects, and it costs money to develop a personal piece because each work of art requires time and solitude, locking yourself in your studio for hours and days. It demands dedication. It's true that valuable alone time is sacrificed, but this moment has provided us with the opportunity to work together, and we are taking advantage of it. We once appeared in Benetton's style blog; they liked our work and called us for an interview. They wanted to do a feature on us and asked us if we

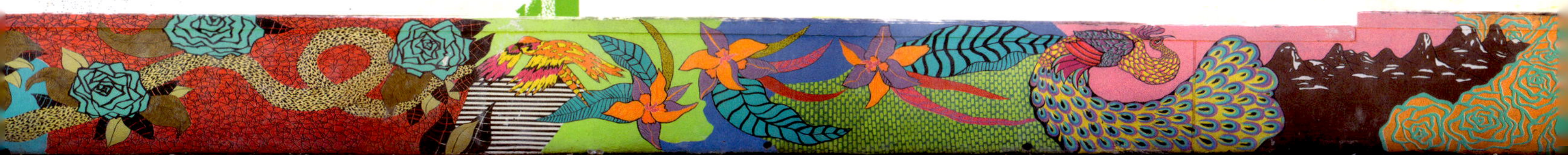

had a location in Santiago that we liked to paint, and we proposed the military school. They liked our proposal and began the process of obtaining permits from the municipality and financing the project. For us, it was a very important door to our work, because it was an incredible discussion. We had always cared about registering our work, making homemade stop-motion videos to encourage people to get involved, because people don't realize all the work that lies behind this. That's why we created a Facebook fan page, Instagram, Twitter, Tumblr, and all the pages available to spread our work. Benetton's feature was an amazing diffusion of our art work. The newspapers ran an article about a major urban intervention funded by a brand. Benetton gave us total liberty with the design and never told us what to do. They trusted us. Thanks to this, many people got to know us and at the end of the day, your artist portfolio is that: painting on the street and showing your work. Little by little, people began to respect us.

"In general, there is a stereotype about artists: he is a little crazy or somewhat bohemian, he works as a waiter and paints his canvasses. However, we can also be organized, serious, and professional. People noticed this with us as we have been working with different brands who have financed our projects. It's crazy, but it happens every day. It's impressive, you don't realize it, because you are always painting, but suddenly, you say, 'What I'm doing is amazing. It's the best.; There are people who send us messages wanting to paint with us. On the street, they will stop us and thank us for giving the city some color. People want more paintings, and this is why they are investing more in art, architecture, and decorating offices. The market is opening and so are the opportunities to paint. Before, everyone was focused on studying for a career that would generate a good income, because they followed a form of thinking that is now obsolete: that to make money, one has to have a traditional profession. I am an artist. I live off of my work, and I am an example that it can happen. It's a good thing that people realize this, so that tomorrow they won't fear living off of art, as many people will tell them that it can't be done. The younger artists should know that there's money and that they will be able to live off of graffiti and street art. If you like to use pastels, use pastels. If you like to paint, paint. The important thing is to do what you like and don't do something else for money or fame. Those things will come if you do what you love.

"In regards to graffiti, we are happy using cans, but we love brushes. We like painting on the street, as it calls upon pictorial concepts, just like the work of Santiago Salvador or Yaikel. We find this friendlier and more intimate. We like to see the paint and feel it. The aesthetic of pure graffiti, with the use of shine, seems like a print, like a plastic effect. This has to do with the technique. We respect graffiti, but we see it as something different from what we do. For example, whoever wants to tag can do it, but in a place where no one else has painted. At the military school, we discovered a pillar that was scribbled entirely with pure shit. For what purpose? If there was an entire team working for a month, making something beautiful so that people can enjoy a place that previously looked like a dump, why are you tagging on it? I think it has to do with respect. I am all for everyone doing what they want, but without stepping on anyone's toes. I still think it's strange that graffiti artists have a signature that they want to draw all over Santiago and that they think the more tags that you generate the more respect you will achieve. For me, respect is about being great, being an amazing illustrator, to create a spectacular drawing that will leave your audience speechless. If you want to work with typography, make big letters with pretty colors, so that it gets people's attention. But to scribble just for the fun of it? I don't see any meaning to tags.

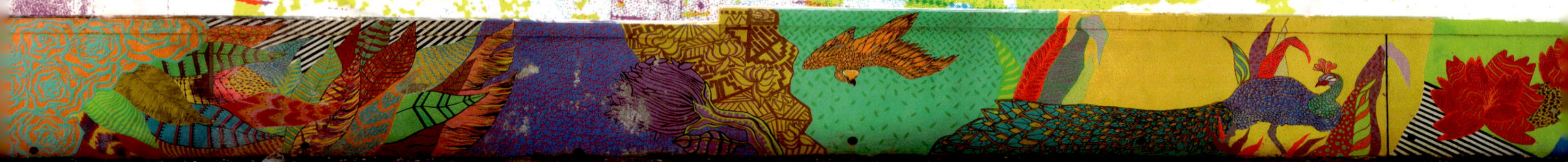

"Despite the evolution of graffiti in Santiago throughout many years, we feel that our work is different than the majority that already exists, as ours doesn't address a specific political theme or social protest. We seek a transversal discussion that will be enjoyed by different people of varying origins. Many brands have come to us in search of an alliance that will allow them to reach people through art. Obtaining governmental support here is very difficult, therefore a great way to get money for big projects is through sponsorship. We have learned to rid ourselves of the local stigma on forming an alliance with a brand. There is a difference between the thinking of graffiti artists and us; the graffiti artist will never join forces with a brand. I think that mindset is medieval. Furthermore, the brand gives you the liberty to do whatever you want. Someone told me, "That's money laundering," and it may be, but people will keep laundering money and evading taxes, and if it's done through art to favour the city, I don't care, because I am being financed for an incredible project. We don't just do projects with brands. Often, we have been catalogued as the Benetton girls or the Home Center girls, but we also work on social projects even if we have sometimes left those to the side. It's our job and we need to pay rent and for food. We are both doing this. We are 100 percent independent, and we are proud to be living off art. Don't come here pointing at us telling us what we have to do. Everyone makes their own decisions. It is idealistic to think that one will live as an artist and that people will always buy your work directly. It doesn't always work like that, because it is difficult to sell work. If a brand comes by and wants to work with you and give you money for it, why not?

"If we had to give new painters a message, we would tell them to do what they love, whatever that is, but always respecting the older artists and the people who work with different concepts. One is never the owner of truth. You must know that you are starting from the bottom. You must look around and admire others for their work and effort. We are not in agreement with the outlook of, 'Here I am, this is my truth.' There is a little bit of everything, and everyone thinks differently. As long as you do something that makes you happy, you will not fail. This is a moment when creativity is gaining courage, so the key is to be sure about your ideas and be confident in what you are doing, persevere on the road that you are following to obtain your objective. You must be constant, because this line of work can give you really good months and months in which you won't have anything. The liberty that comes with it, however, doesn't have a price. To paint outside, you have to respect this profession, be professional, studious, converse with other artists, learn from them and be humble. It would grab our attention to be included in a book on the Santiago street art scene. It is a good sign that different things are being done and that not everyone follows the conventional path. It is very valuable to show that." **ESTANPINTANDO**

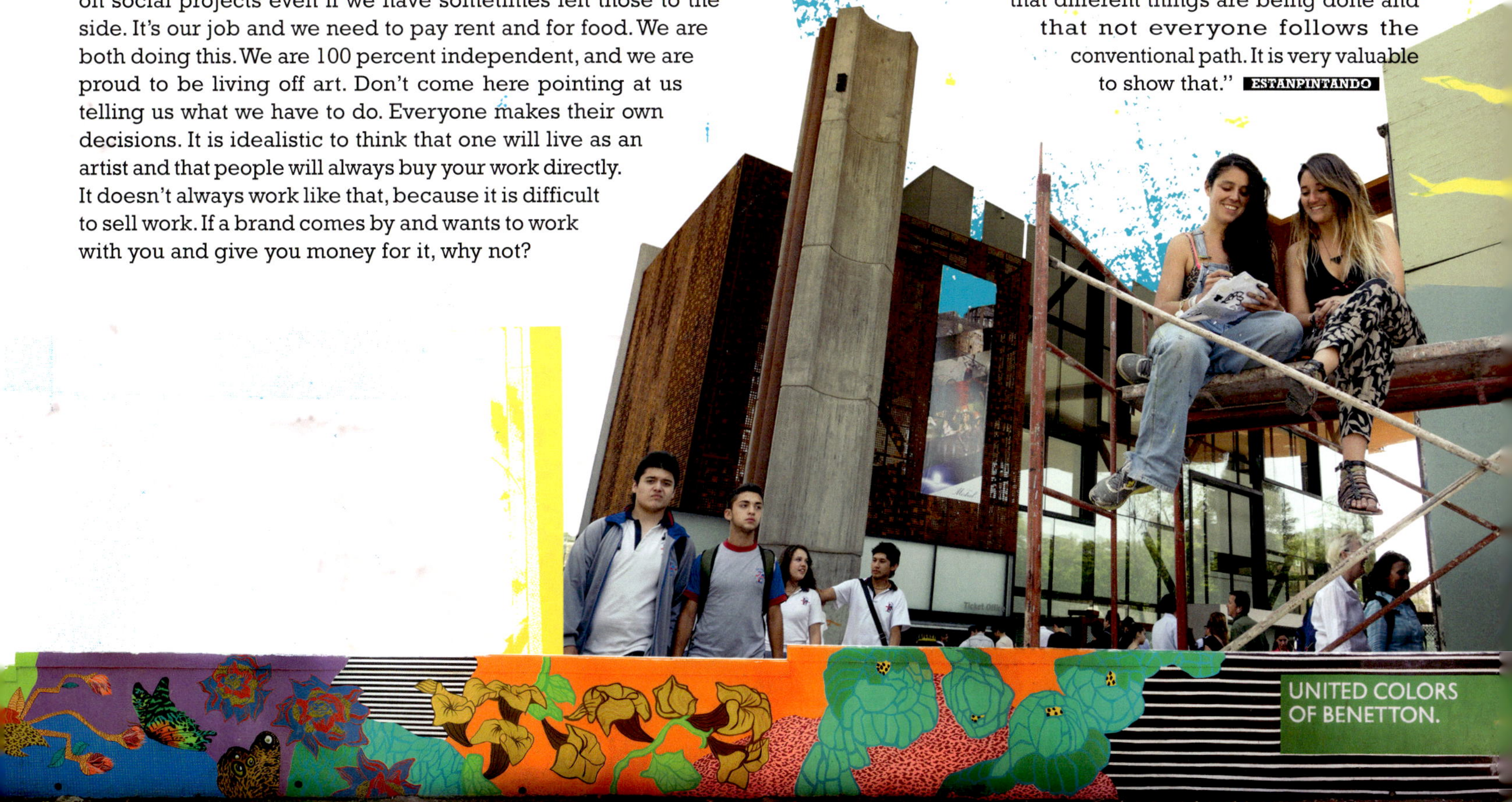

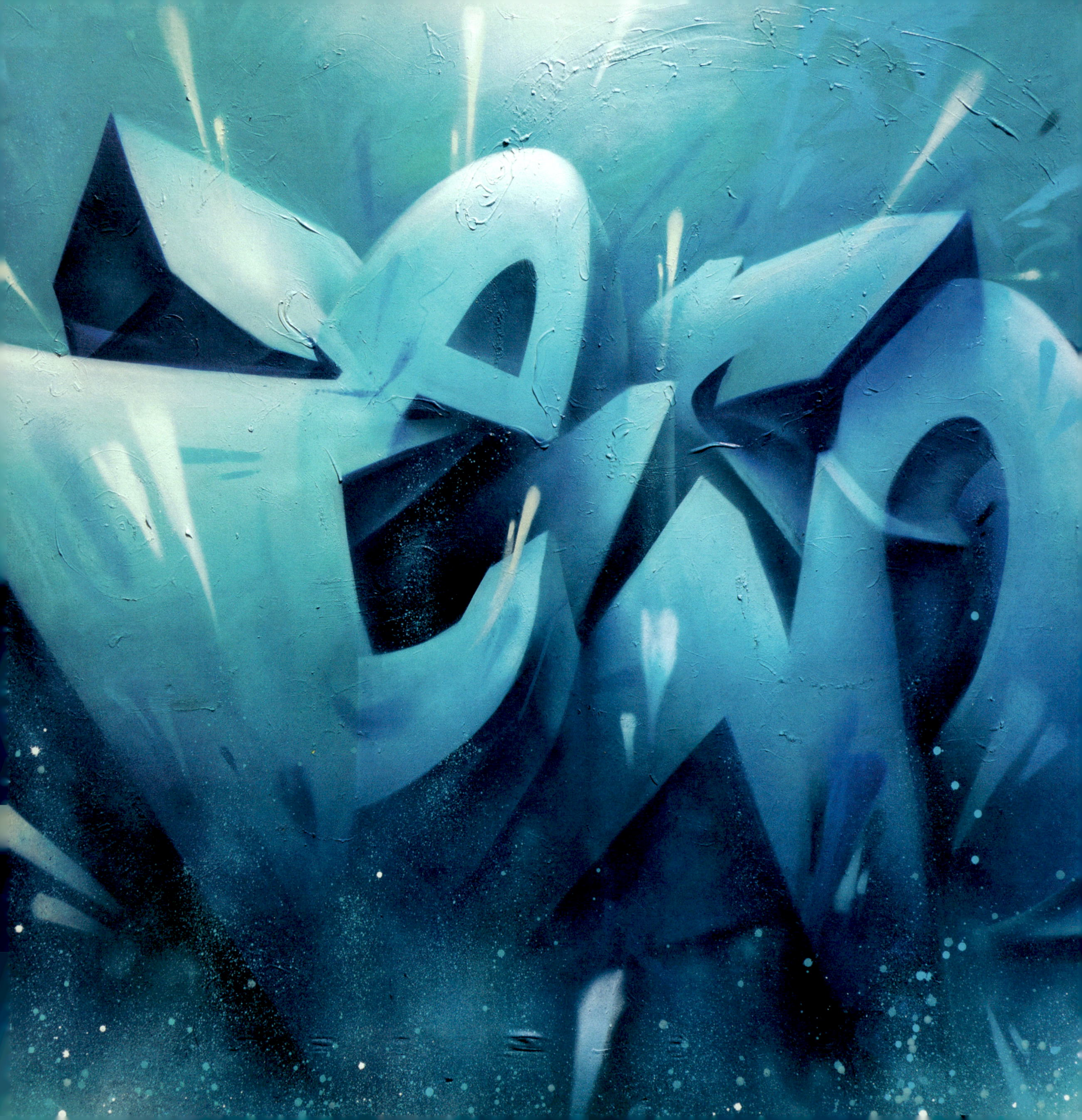

"**Believe** it or not I tend to stumble across unwanted **canvases** on the street. I'll take them **home,** spend a few hours spraying on them, and **sell** them off at $20,000 US **a piece.** The advantage of being a graffiti **artist** is that you're free most of the time to do what **you want.** No bosses! **No suits!** Just a lifestyle where you pursue your hobby of painting. The **hard part** is keeping disciplined. As with so much **freedom** and **no routine,** it's easy to lose focus. But the rewards **are high.** The pleasure of **appreciating** my finished pieces gives me enough **juice to stay** on track." ZEWOK1

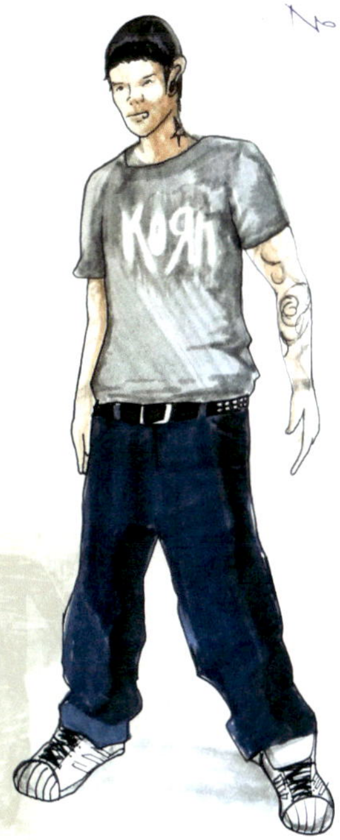

Zewok1

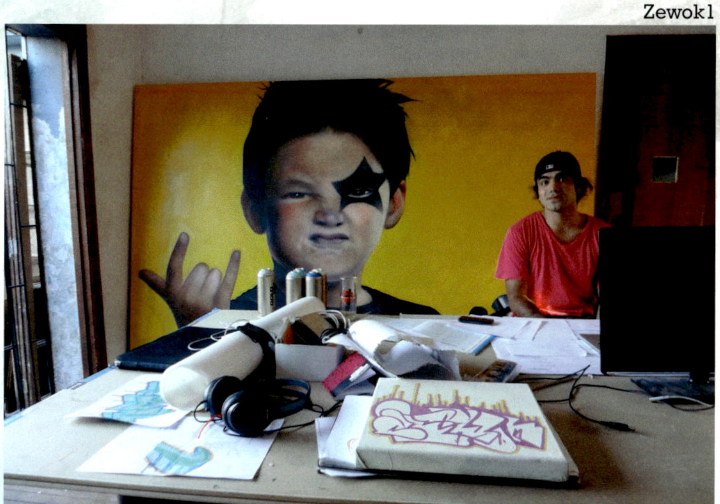

Zewok1

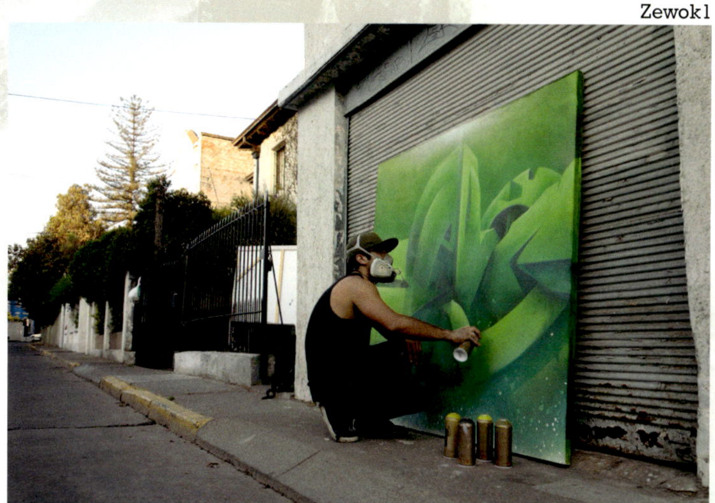

"Liberty, simple liberty. You do what you want when you want. Sometimes, I will go out with my backpack that holds two spray cans, a bottle of latex, caps, and a paint roller, and sometimes a ladder, and I stroll through the streets until I find a place that grabs my attention. When I do, I bomb it. Sometimes, I will bring a design, but the form of the space allows me to improvise, lengthen my bomb, paint in great heights, intervene the space inside. There is a clandestine atmosphere to doing something that no one else does. Some will yell at you, and others congratulate you on the streets. This mix of sensations decompresses me and lets out stress from work and the pressure of daily living. It's like a sigh, except the sigh stays there until someone paints over it, or until it gets erased." ASPE

"For us, it is necessary that the visual proposition, whether it be a mural or graffiti, binds itself to the processes or necessities of transformation for each location. When art is on the street, it doesn't have ownership. The street signifies twenty-four hours of daily propaganda and direct communication with the barrio and with the commuters. We want art to be of the masses, just as publicity sells you something or tries to communicate something to you. Visual advertising is ninety-nine percent of what we see, and it saturates us to death without respect for humanity. It's a form of contamination. Our objective is to conquer the wall, leave a message, and democratize the wall. I believe this has to do with the system in which we live in, a communist system, where the main idea is selling. Street art has the role of continually bringing ideas to people's consciousness. This is why we do street art, so we can conquer more walls and leave a message." OLFER

"Nature is one of the things that inspires me. The seasons of the year, the deterioration of things, I believe there are many pictorial lessons in the objects that surround us, from shades, tones, and forms to artifacts. I believe that's what motivates me the most, having that experimental projection where things flow and destroy themselves. The most interesting and beautiful aspect of graffiti is getting to meet painters and share with them, relating with other artists and sharing the gratifying moment of painting on different walls. What most fills me and what most attracts me to art is the feedback of people who are also painting, who are trying to grow and destroy their fear and ego, that ego that only makes you compete with yourself. I believe that the scene in Chile is in all its glory as there are many artists who are creating amazing works, generating ideas that complement with more ideas to create a bigger nucleus. We work in teams and have things clear, we have fewer fights, we get to the places we want to go faster, and we make society more intelligent." FOSER

"I began by creating flops, scribbling with brushes just like everyone else does. Then you get the hang of it and place goals for yourself. It all comes down to that: evolution. It's like life: you begin by scribbling, which is like walking, then you begin to paint flops and this is like running. I love typography, although I can't explain why. The great thing about graffiti is that you are always trying to evolve your process, to advance. It's all about finding somethin to break from the boring routine. That's the idea, that each wall is different, that each wall makes you feel and live different things." EYNOR

"The scene in Chile is really good, in my opinion. Everyone is painting and there is a good level of talent within the graffiti community. I believe there should be more spaces to do this. What most interests me is painting and discovering new techniques, learning from paint cans, learning about color, trying new locations, trying to achieve something with minimum resources. What I intend to do with graffiti is provide some tranquility to everything that happens in the city, whether it be with fish, with an image of Buddha, or with a gesture of good faith to the people." PAPES

"I believe that we are laborers just like everyone else. All we do is paint in public places, all day long. We are workers just like the people who work in construction or in banks, except that we paint on the street. If this is art, someone else will say it is, because I consider it a job equal to any other. Things will always happen in the street. Sometimes they're bad experiences, sometimes they're good; they're all experiences, regardless. That's life. Sometimes, you will experience things that mark you or things that you didn't expect, like people's gratitude or someone offering you a drink or food. One time, when we finished painting, a woman invited us to a barbecue and we ended up inside her house, sharing with her family, the same people that come up to you on the street to start a conversation with you. These are the processes that we seek and need, because when you're on the street you need to establish dialogue with the people that pass by your wall. We must seek and enjoy these experiences. People come up to you, but if you don't open up to them it is difficult for someone to comment on your work and tell you what they feel when they see it or ask you to explain what you are trying to do. The more we experience these type of interactions, the more we are going to enjoy this type of work. We seek to be seen. That is our reason for painting on the street." DEGRA

"Street art has few or no limits. It is about going out into the urban space and choosing whatever you want to intervene." ZAINES

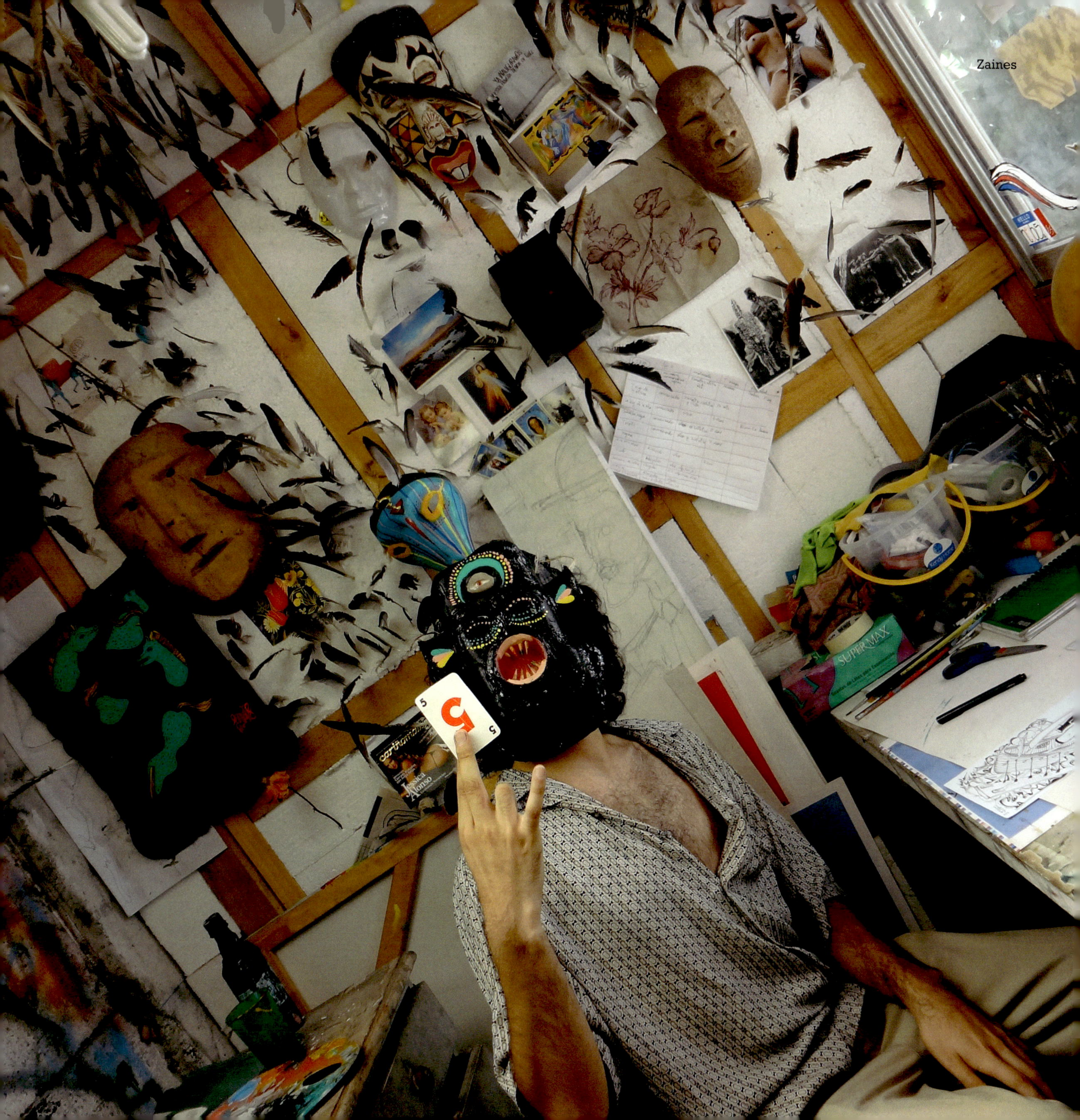
SUPERMAX

QUINTA NORMAL

Area: 13 km^2
Population: 104.012
Average annual income: US $17,919
Population below poverty line: 10.8%
Graffiti prevalence: 7/10

"This is my barrio, the one in which I was born and raised. Here I know many people, both good and bad. This is where I paint graffiti and where I learned my trade. My barrio has many paintings. Police can't do a thing—only observe and shake their heads. There are paintings of all types, sizes, and textures. Quinta Normal is a place for bombing. When you get a good spot, it's yours for life. Some of the other walls alternate between different graffiti artists. In my barrio, there are artists that produce very elaborate works and others who go around bombing everything. In Quinta Normal there are old school graffiti artists who have evolved through time. The new artists have far greater access to information than we did back in the day. This allows them to generate good works at a higher level more rapidly. The main artists who spray around here are Nehs, Setiob, Saes, Linos, Dolor, Boster, Dhaig, and Hemse. My barrio is very good for graffiti artists. There are many walls available, so all the artists that live here are content. There are no obstacles to painting; you just arrive and paint, and when you've finished your graffiti you celebrate." CUB2

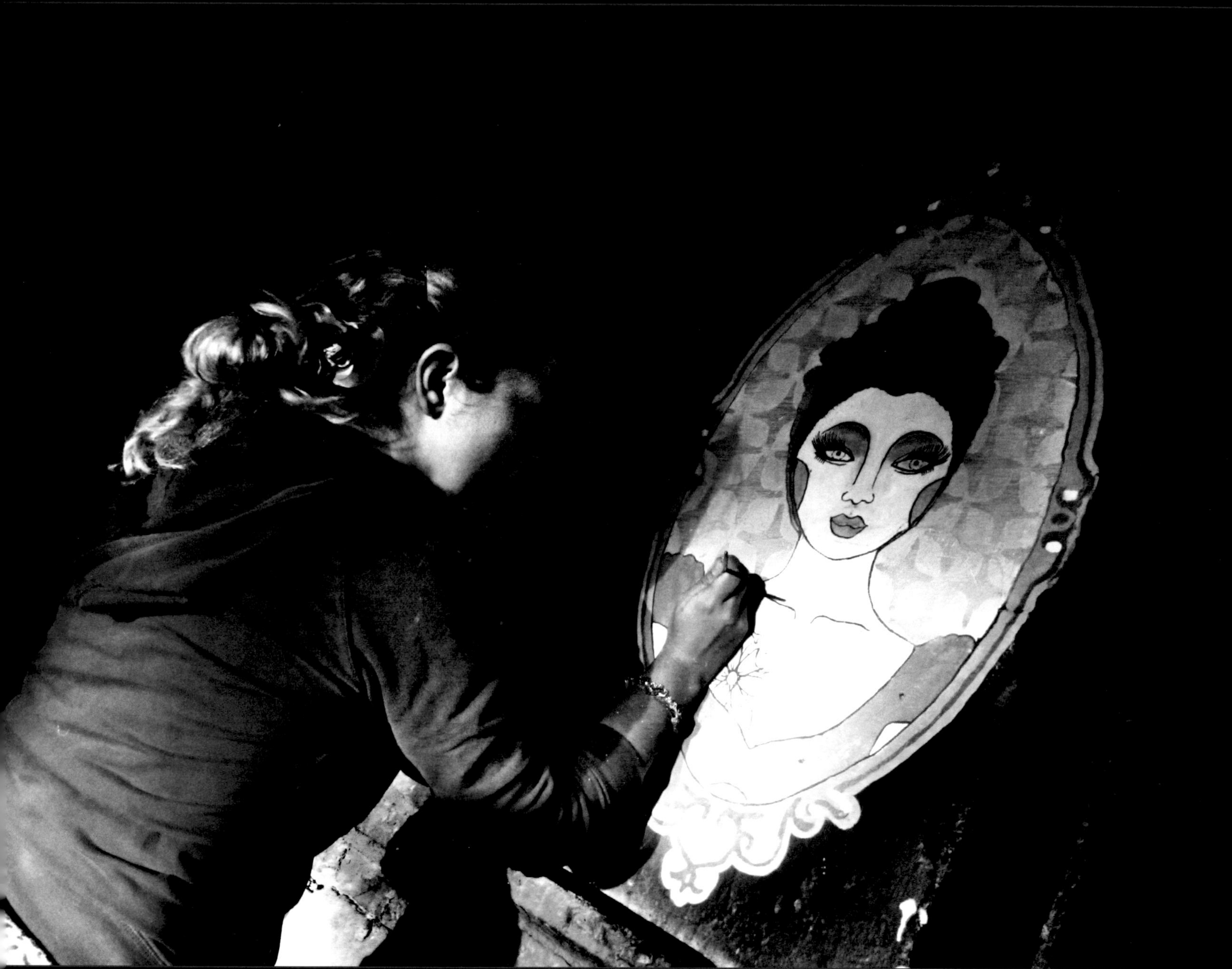

"The press do not show the truth of what's happening. Our idea is to display social and political facts and communicate something that is different than what is in the press.

"It's a way of saying 'We're here and here it is, this is what's going on.' But many people look at us and say. 'Ah, they are causing trouble.' But they don't have the context no the vision of what's really going on and what is motivating us to do things.

"Sensationalism on television and in newspapers is massive in Chile, and people believe a lot in the media. The media is like a mafia! So we show the public something totally different than what is shown in a newspaper. The news is very invasive. Here media is like a capitalistic society: they sell you all the dreams. It's like they sell you everything. You can have this, you can have the LCD, you could have your house, you could have your bed, you could have everything. Go in debt! Go in debt and you're gonna be fine, just like a rich man, but of course, then you're not gonna be able to pay for the shit, you're gonna lose everything you have. So they sell you dreams and people in the end are not worried about their own dreams, they are worried about how to pay for their material things, which doesn't matter in the end. It's like, 'I have more than my neighbor.' That shit is completely influenced by the media. It's superficiality and they sell you dreams.

"We show the true reality, dude! The cops abuse their power, dude. That's what we show. We want people to realize that the good guys are not good. They are not a 'friend on the road'! No! We are not kidding. They are the enemy on the road!

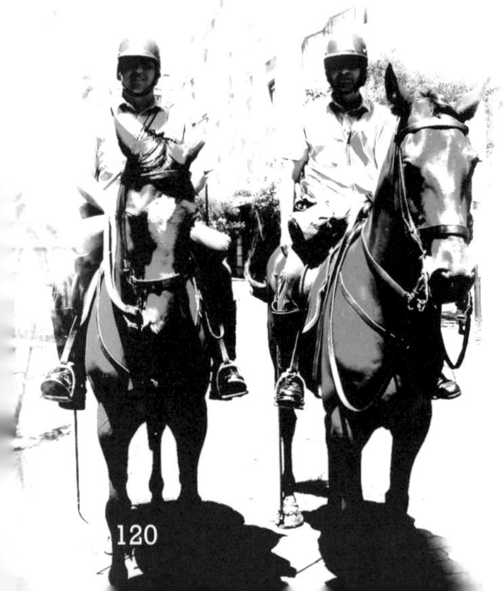

"We are a group of twelve and each one of us goes out and pastes in his neighborhood. We're all from different parts of town but when we get together we often go downtown and look to paste in areas with the most passersby. We try to cover as much space as we can. We are planning to paste in Valparaiso, San Antonio, and other regions as we have got the images, we got them! What we lack is money, the fucking money!

"We're common people. The difference is that we're delivering a message to the people, but we're very normal. Besides photography, we all have lives. Nothing is easy over here. No one is going to fix things for us. Some of us have children. Some of us sadly have to work to bring money to the table and our spare time is dedicated to taking pictures and study. We like to be focusing a hundred percent on art and not having to depend on money for stuff, but sadly we have to work to sustain all our things. But we're lazy just like any other person. The only thing we do different than the others is paste pictures on the street and take pictures. But we're just dudes like everybody else. We get home tired and we eat.

"Our fellow students have a different perspective on photography. They focus more on advertising. The dudes want to earn money from photography. What we do doesn't attract them. They think that we are lowering ourselves, and they don't want to get involved. But we don't care about money. Even if we had more money we still wouldn't care. Money does not equal happiness but does help, of course, it helps a lot.

"People sometimes think we're wasting time and perhaps we're not respected by other photographers for what we're doing. We know we have a long road ahead of us. It's going to be difficult, but we have a sense of unity and we're all friends and we're all paddling in the same direction. That's how it is right now, dude.

"One more thing — Fuck the police! We're against capitalism and cops." **ENGRUDOORS**

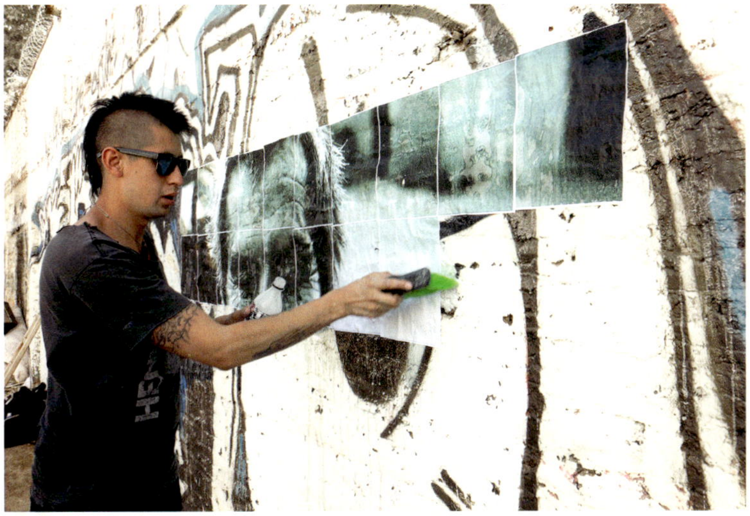

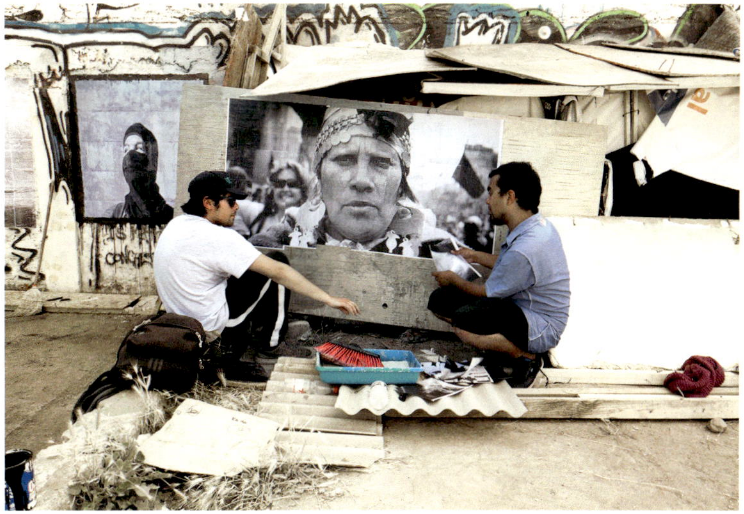

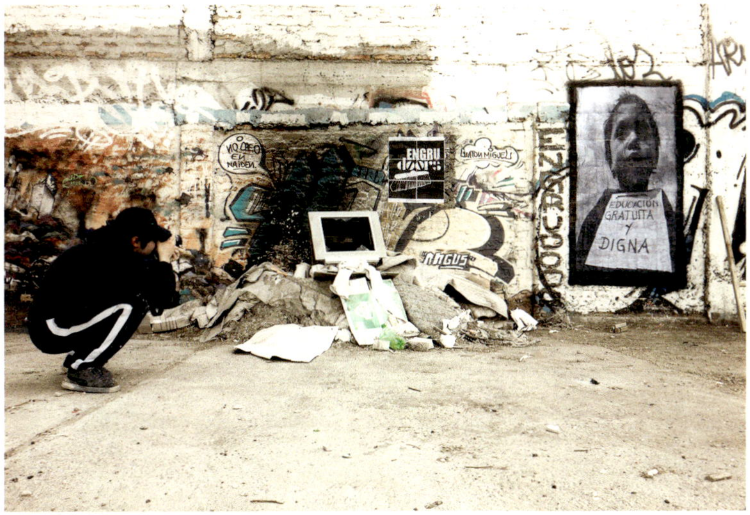
EDUCACION
GRATUITA
Y
DIGNA

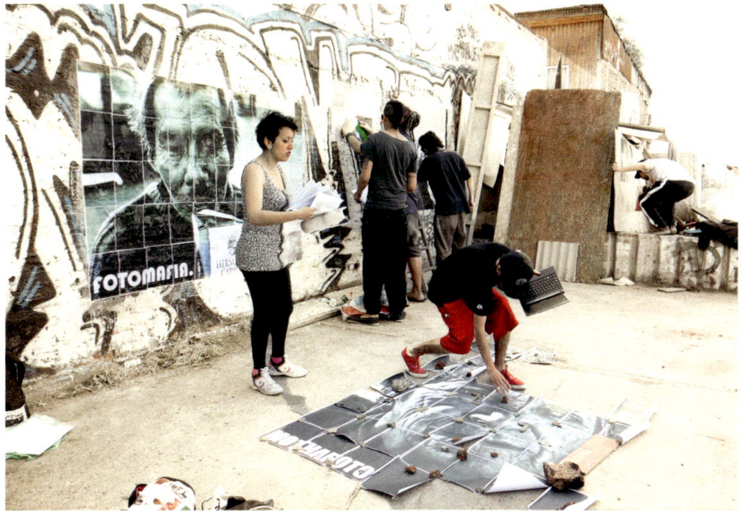
FOTOMAFIA.

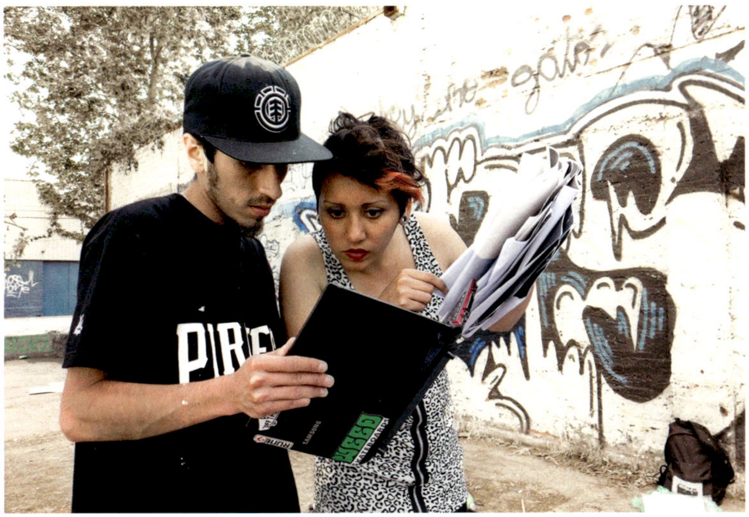

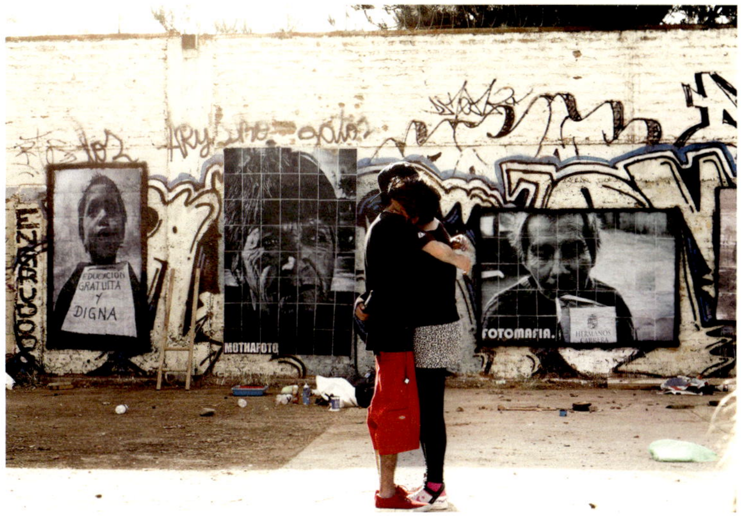
EDUCACION
GRATUITA
Y
DIGNA
FOTOMAFIA.

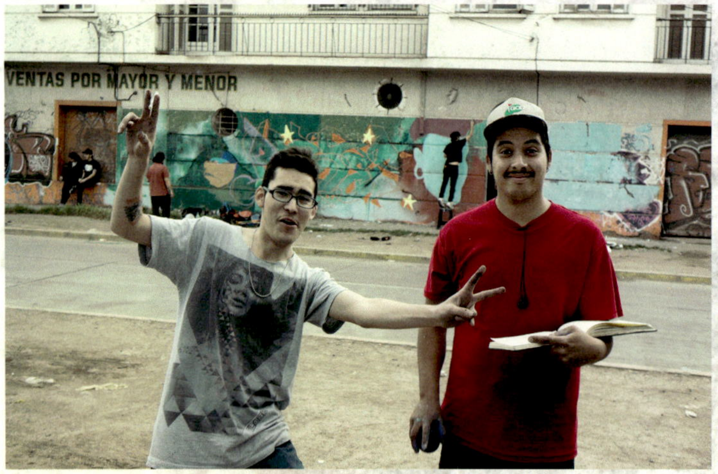
VENTAS POR MAYOR Y MENOR

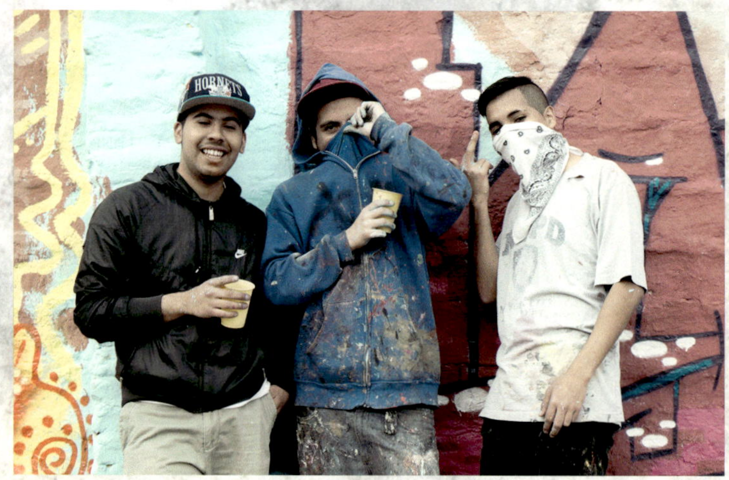
HORNETS

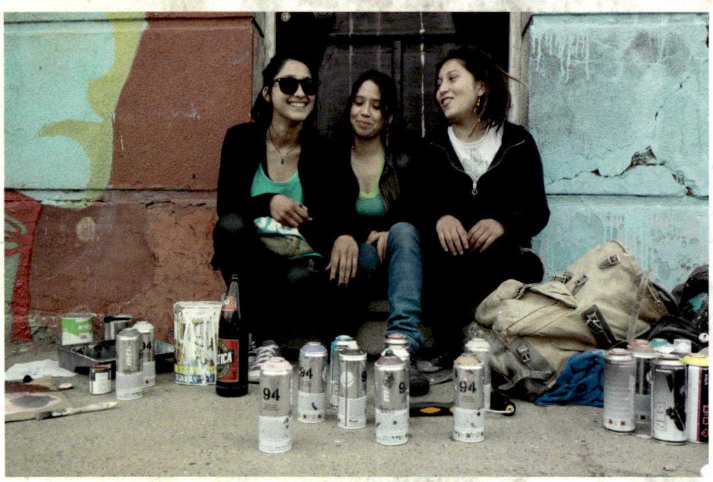

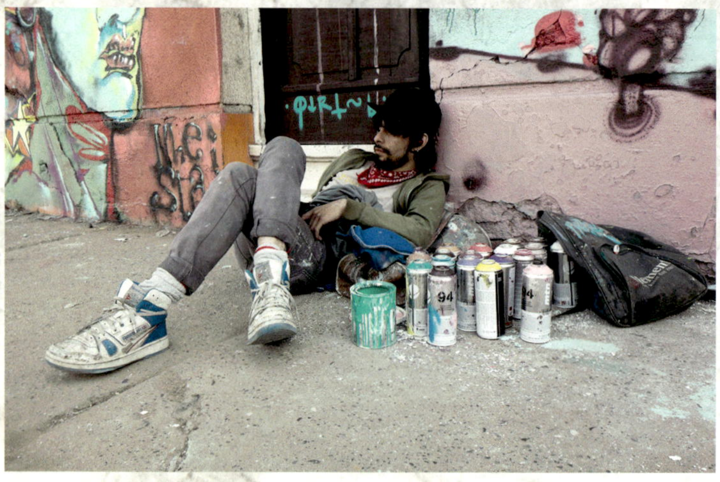

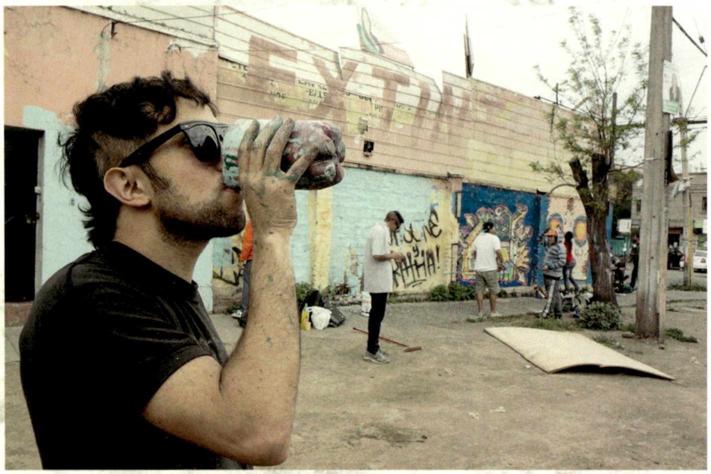

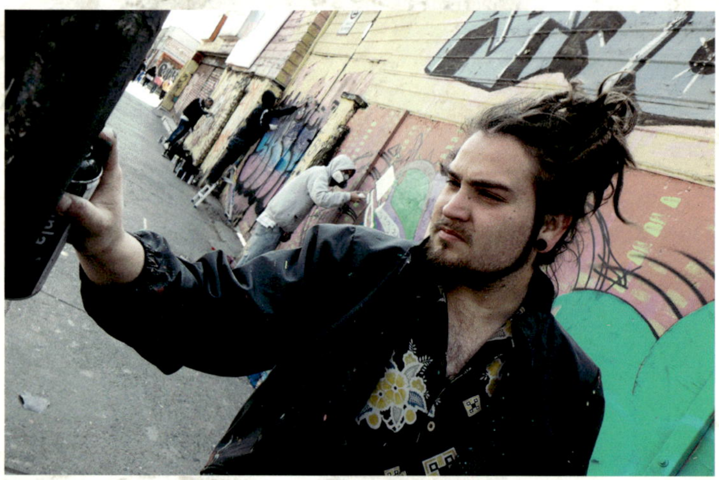

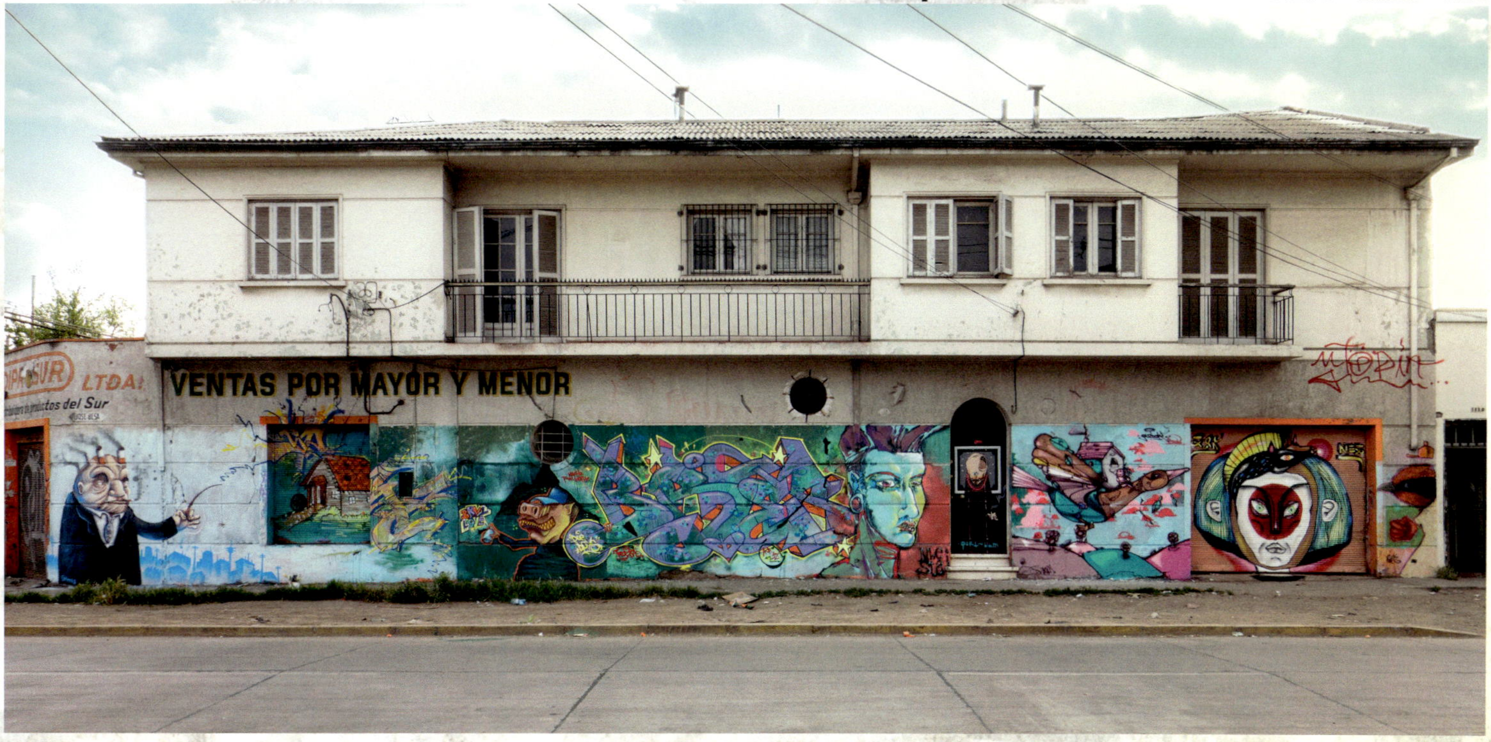

"Persevere in your technique and style, apply color, strength, and identity to your work. Deliver messages. Put up on the wall the things that you have seen and liked. Make the world vibrate." VISION

"My friends took me to paint for the first time. For some time, I had been painting in the neighborhood, but on this day they told me that we would go to Bellavista, and this is when my perspective on the topic changed, because I saw that really great work could be accomplished. In this moment, that neighborhood was like an open-air museum. I also met people and witnessed different styles, causing me to develop more feeling for the technique. To paint is also to meet people. You start off painting with intense emotion and then you realize, 'I do have a role within my surroundings,' and this is when you try to begin communicating with the people who are living there. You are generating a space, perhaps you are invading it, maybe you are improving it. But I'm never aggressive. If I paint something, I want to generate conversation with the people, and it's possible that they may not understand what I mean to say, but just the fact that they stop, stay a while and look, creates an empathy with the wall." SOFRENIA

"Graffiti is on the street, and it's not just the wall. Things happen to you, you meet people and see new places. At the end of the day, the tag becomes your brand. Suddenly, people don't know you by your name, but by your tag. Then they'll ask you, what's your name? There comes a time when other people, who do not belong to the graffiti world, will begin to call you by that name and that's when it sticks. It's more than just a tag or an alias, it's you—period. I like to share abundantly, and I find conversing with others very fulfilling. There are people who will criticize you constructively. A critique, be it good or bad, is always necessary. You can't expect people not to say anything. By expressing something on the streets, you will trigger positive or negative feelings in others.

"I feel there is still a lack of education when it come to graffiti here in Chile. When graffiti is shown on television, it is mainly associated with crime. Commuters cross the street when they see you because they are scared of you." HAP

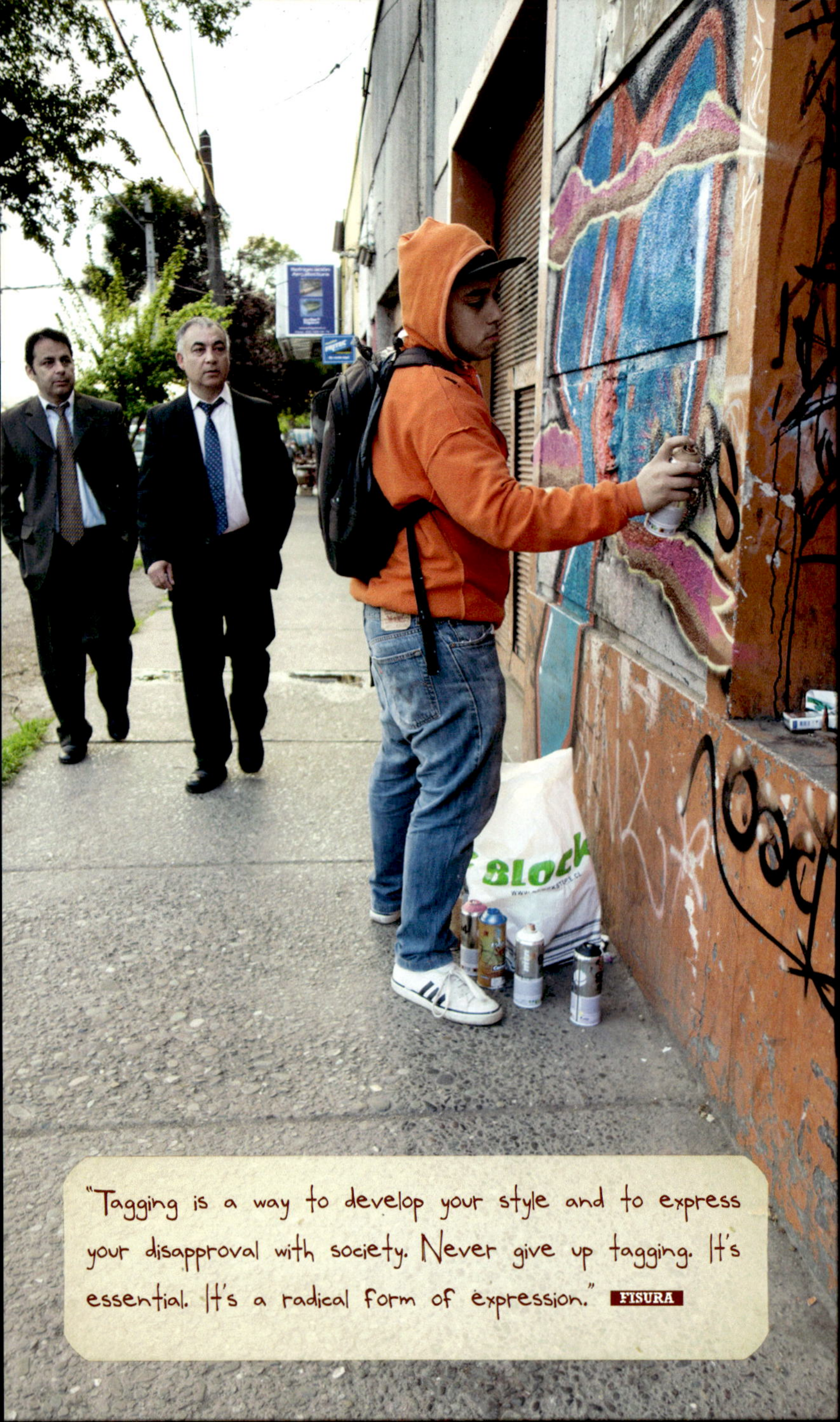

"Tagging is a way to develop your style and to express your disapproval with society. Never give up tagging. It's essential. It's a radical form of expression." **FISURA**

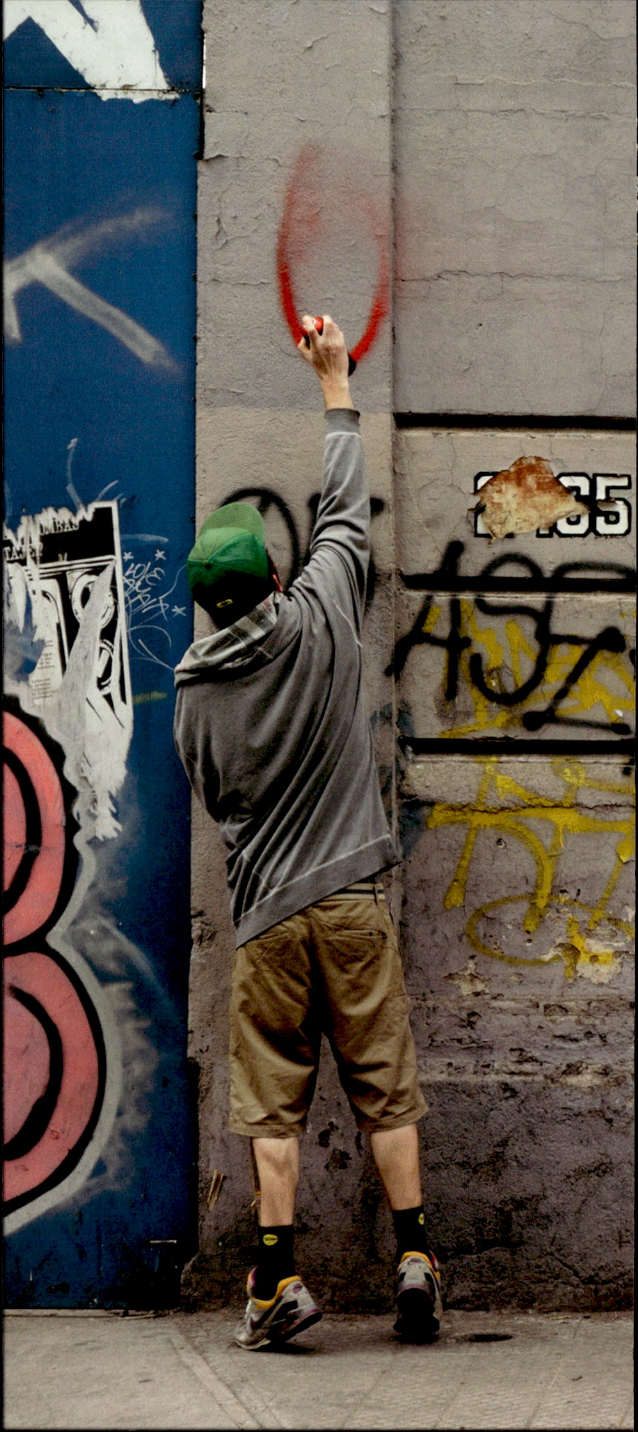

"I don't like tagging as it is dominated by the ego. Writing my name everywhere so that everybody knows who I am doesn't encourage evolution." **FAYA**

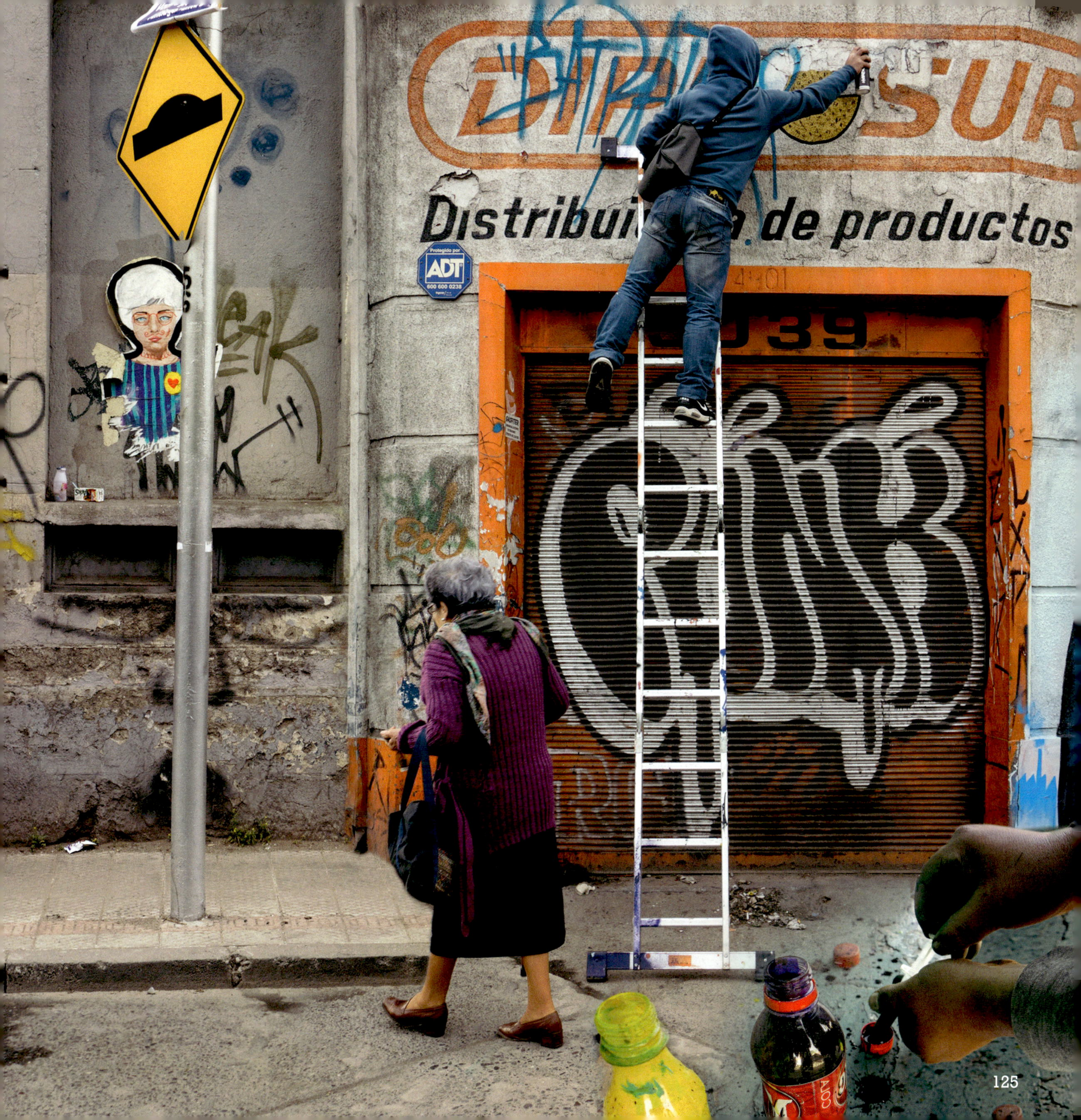
Distribui
de productos
ADT

"In some communes, the municipalities are more helpful than in others since they allow you to paint and don't repress as much. They don't see it as something bad. They see it as positive for young people. There are also communes that are against any artistic expression that is public, and those are generally the communes with more money. There are also other institutions that work with artists that come from graffiti or street art backgrounds. Then there's the example of the subway: they hired street artist Mono González to decorate a very important subway station and in my case, they let me paint a wall that was supposed to be temporary. Two years later it is still erect and belongs to a collection of murals in the subway stations. This mural in Quinta Normal Station took me two weeks to paint with the help of two assistants, I mainly used acrylic paint and a few spray cans." **CEKIS**

"I believe that graffiti is like a self-sufficient beast that doesn't need the galleries to be exposed. I see it as such a huge monster that it can pass as a gallery itself and not be domesticated under the seal of art. When you realize that your thing is painting on the street, that is what you must do. Now, if someone comes along and says, 'This is art,' perfect. I'll sell it to a gallery. I have to pay my bills. Yet, you're doing your thing, not with the intention of attracting the attention of the galleries. I don't believe in this discussion of whether it's art or graffiti, if it's more important, or not more important. It doesn't have meaning. The meaningful thing is to do what you love. Later on, if someone wants to put a label on what you do, that is external and separate from you. And if you benefit, then good for you. If a brand trusts me and gives me the liberty to do what I want to do, and if I like the brand, good. I live in a capitalist system, and at the end of the day I will have to pay my bills with money. If I'm approached by Nike because they're making a pair of sneakers with my drawings and I will be paid as much money as was offered to Os Gêmeos, then, hell, yes, I would probably do it. That's the way it is. Time goes by and people have to begin to worry about other things, not just the cost of paint cans. You put on the idealistic fight that you won't sell yourself, but you're buying the cans from those idiots. So, to make the fight really idealistic you would have to buy pigments at a hardware store and paint with handmade paintbrushes." **YISA**

"Graffiti is a lifestyle. You can make a living out of it and do it anywhere in the world. If I have the opportunity to travel and pursue painting, that would be amazing. I am usually looking to paint big pieces, but it is difficult to find sponsors that will give you the support to do that. Recently, some idiot called me and asked me how much I charged for a graffiti and if it was cheap. If that's what he is looking for, I don't wish to work with his sort. If I'm going to live off of my art, I honestly hope that it's because someone values my work and says that he wants to work with me because I'm good, not because I'm the cheapest." **ZEWOK1**

"I am pleased by the possibility of commercializing graffiti. After all, you invested many years of learning on the streets and buying paint cans. Furthermore, there is a process behind your work. We want to live off our artwork. I like to paint accessories, such as bags, and it would be marvellous to have a line. That's what I would like to be doing in ten years. I know many who say that graffiti belongs to the streets, but it's necessary to generate an income, make projects, and apply for funds." **ENEY**

"For me, graffiti is a lifestyle. For example, I always notice walls when I'm outside, and my mom and my friends tell me that I'm the only 'ridiculous person that notices walls.' A person who doesn't engage in street art, doesn't notice it. I wake up on a weekend with the strong intention of painting. If I travel to another city, I will take a can or markers with me, because that's what I go to do. By the way, many graffiti artists are heads of a family and have other responsibilities, yet they make the effort to keep painting. That is invaluable, because here in Chile, nobody lives off graffiti, as artists do in other places, such as in Europe, where street artists have children and live off their work, allowing them to have economic stability and pay for rent, schooling, food, and other things. Here in Chile, there are people who stand out and have made a name for themselves, who have proved that they are serious. In comparison to other countries, we don't have many opportunities. We all work in what we can or in the area that we majored in, but very few dedicate themselves completely to graffiti. Independently, nobody began to paint thinking that they would earn money for it. Everyone who ever thought of painting was motivated by something else. Money is a medium by which I can have certain things, but it is not my main motivator. Maybe I'm a hippie, but money comes and goes. It's all about knowing how to live." **ANTISA**

"You will have more opportunities as an artist if you know how to use all the different types of paint such as spray, brush, roller etc. I always try to use all sorts of materials, then go over it with spray at the end, as spray is easier and quicker and I can therefore finish all my paintings in a day. A person who uses only one tool, because of convenience, is limiting themselves. I have even painted walls by mixing latex and oil paints, which generally are not mixed." **PIGUAN**

Cekis

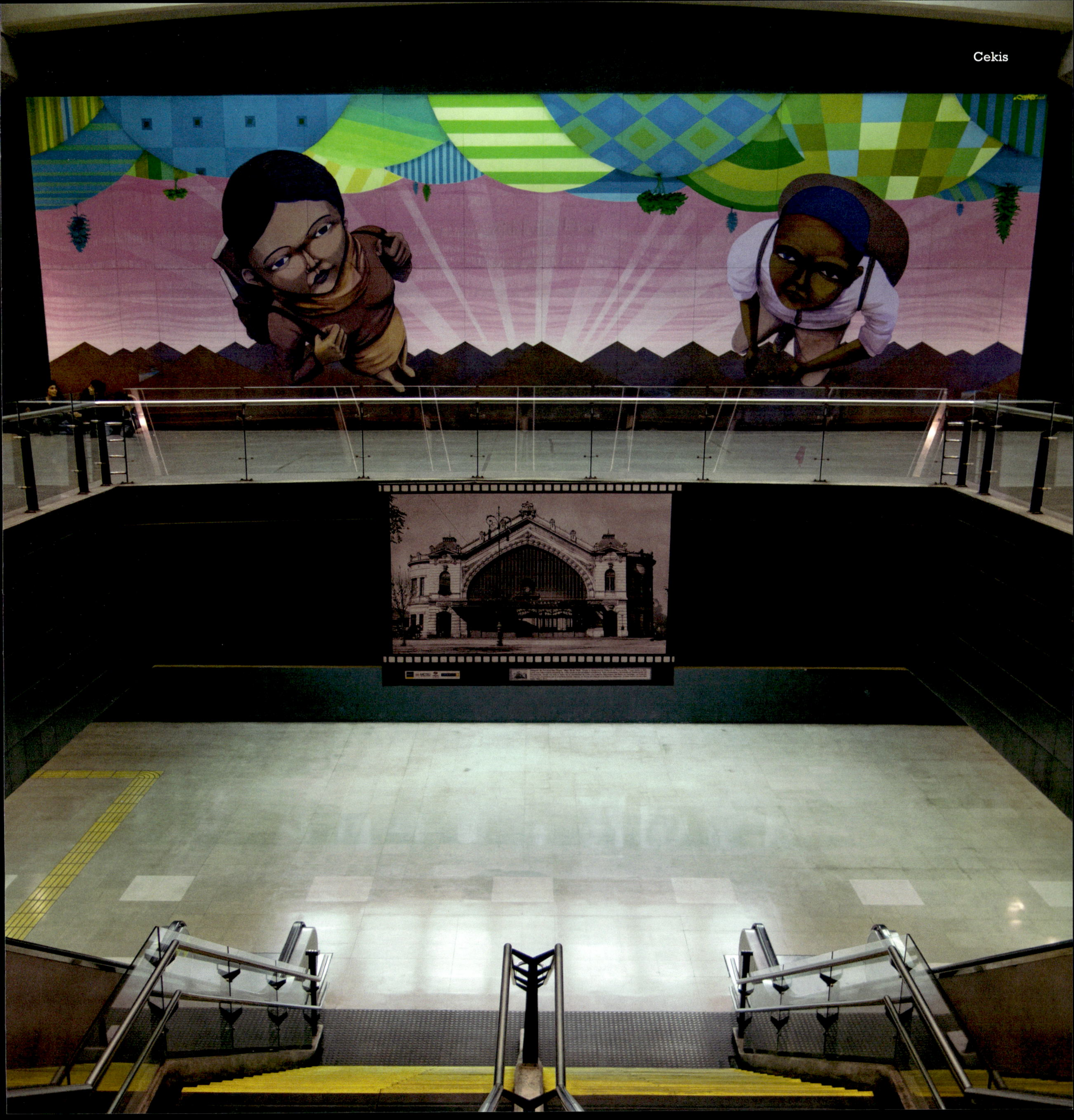

RENCA

Area: 24 km^2
Population: 133,518
Average annual income: US $17,278
Population below poverty line: 19.2%
Graffiti prevalence: 5/10

"In my opinion, Renca is a lower middle-class neighborhood. There are areas where poverty has lingered for many years. I grew up in Renca, and I have a permanent and close relationship with this 'hood. Here you will come across important graffiti artists. There all sorts of walls, such as houses, abandoned buildings, and on highways and there are many walls available to paint on. I have seen murals and graffiti works that have been up for more than ten years. By the same coin, I have also seen graffiti works and murals that last one or two days. They generally last longer on the main streets. The artists that often paint here are Sol ReciclandoMuros, 3k15, Hafroh, SHP, Guido, VKH, Mufe, Nase, and Dezman.

"The prevalent technique in this commune are tags. You can also find artists that are constantly reflecting social struggle in their murals and unite every so often to construct new themes and display them on a wall, whether it be the recovery of our origin, race, political thinking, history of communism, or personal thoughts and expressions. Even though Renca has had a good start and good artists, I feel that it isn't growing with sufficient maturity and consciousness.

"The police's protocol is the same in Renca as it is in the majority of the country. They will fine you or give you a warning if you are breaking the law. Although, many times they will see you painting and they won't tell you anything, while on other occasions they will stop and ask for identification and ask you to put your hands on the wall.

"I feel taken in and supported, respected, and cared for by the locals. It is gratifying to go out into the streets of Renca and be greeted and congratulated for what I do. I hold on dearly to this affection that nourishes and nurtures me, so I can keep going on this path that has given me many good experiences."

HOE

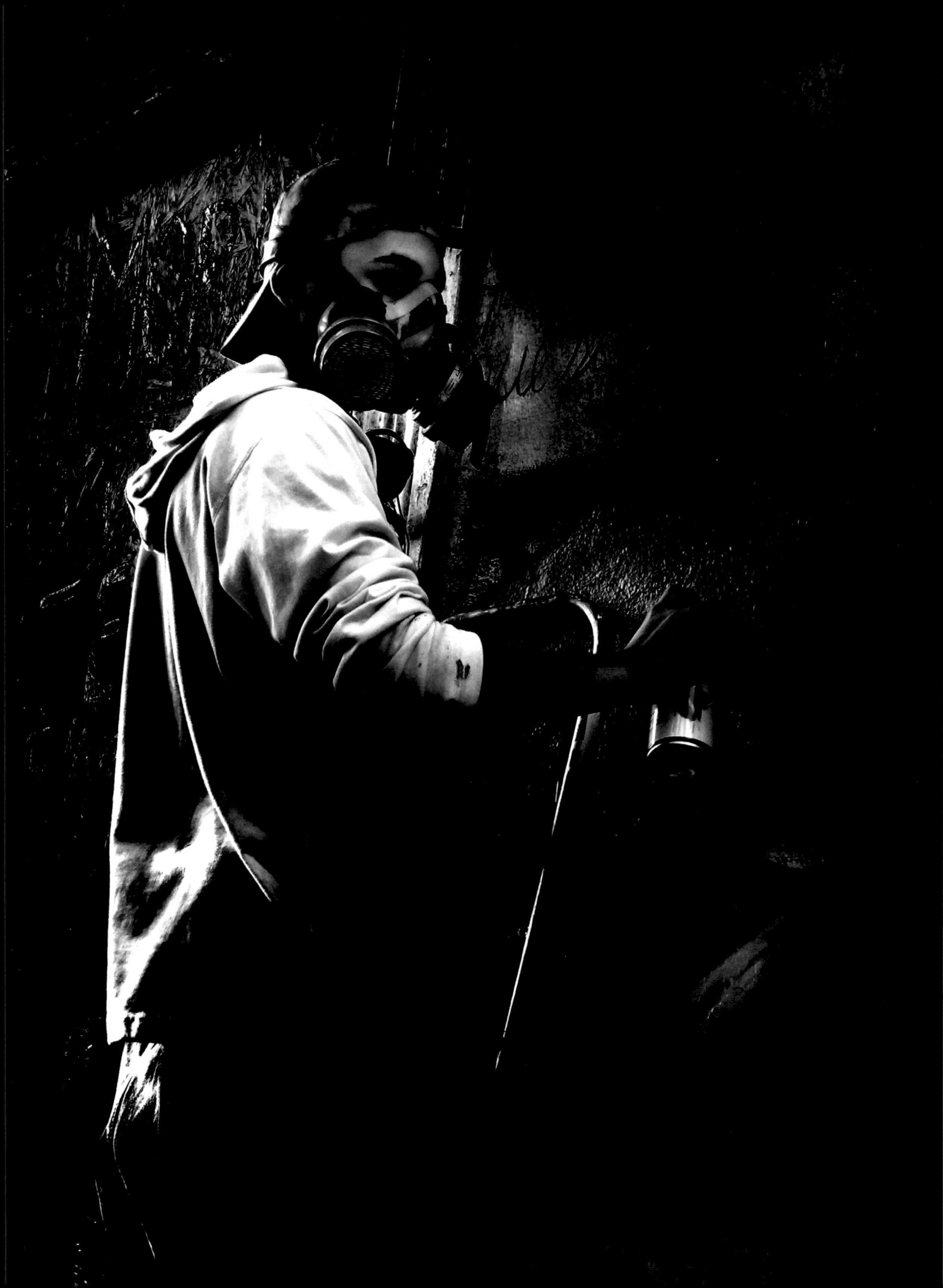

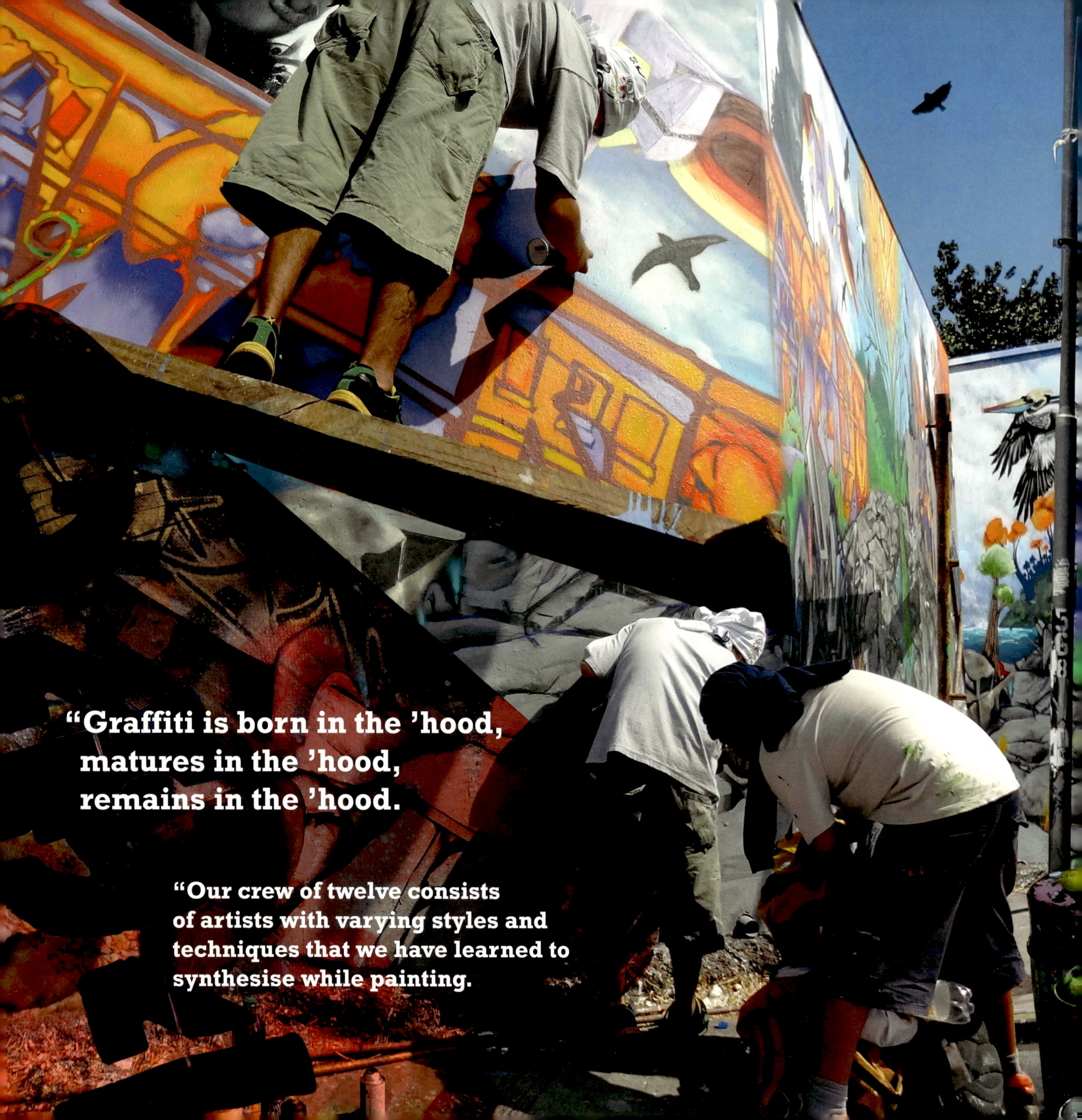

"Graffiti is born in the 'hood, matures in the 'hood, remains in the 'hood.

"Our crew of twelve consists of artists with varying styles and techniques that we have learned to synthesise while painting.

"We are all from the lower classes, and the 'hood is an important part of our lives and our perceptions. It has a massive influence on our graffiti." 12BRILLOS

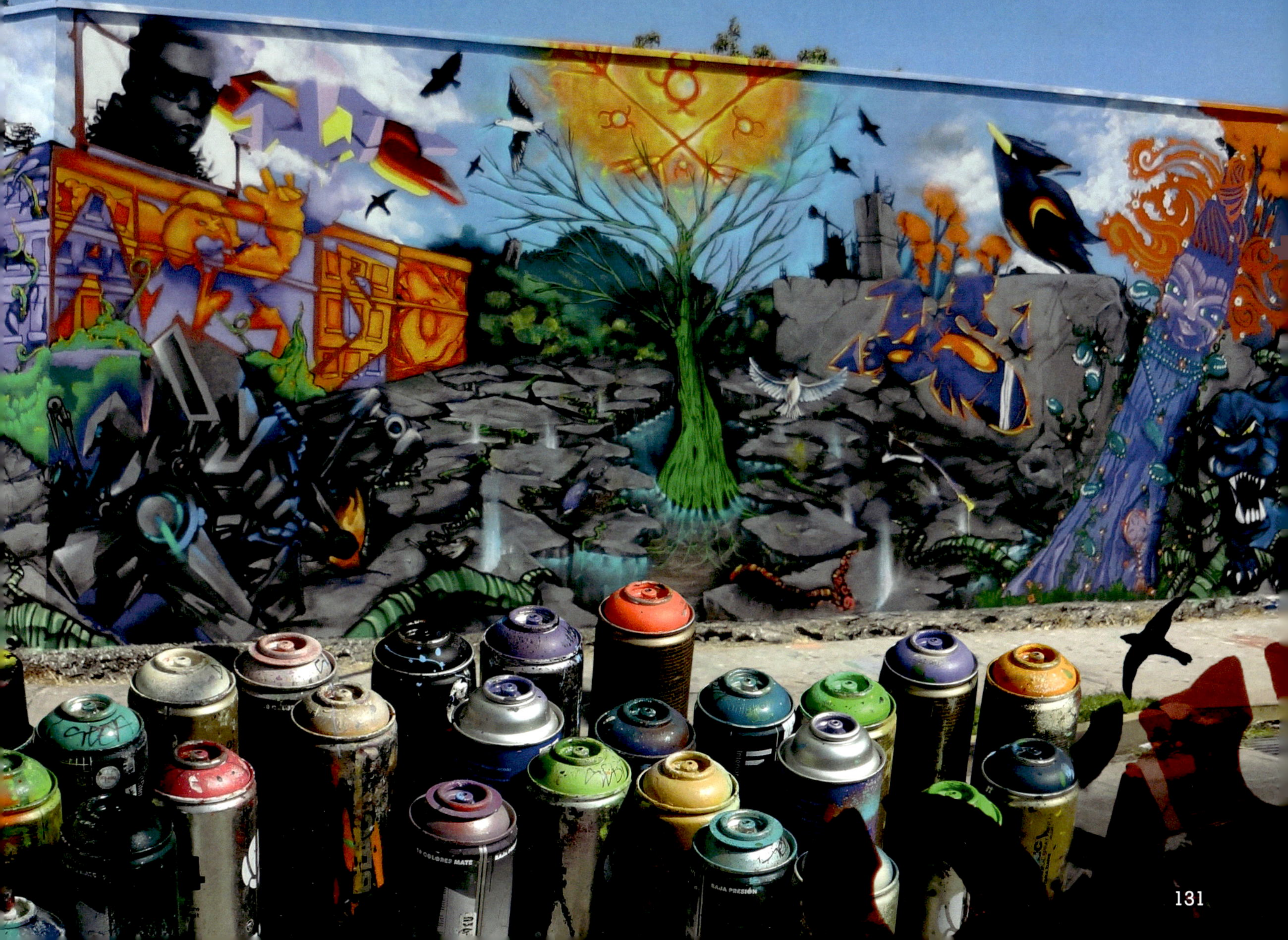

"I began to paint **faces** so that their **eyes** could transmit what **I felt** in the moments that I **painted** them." HOE

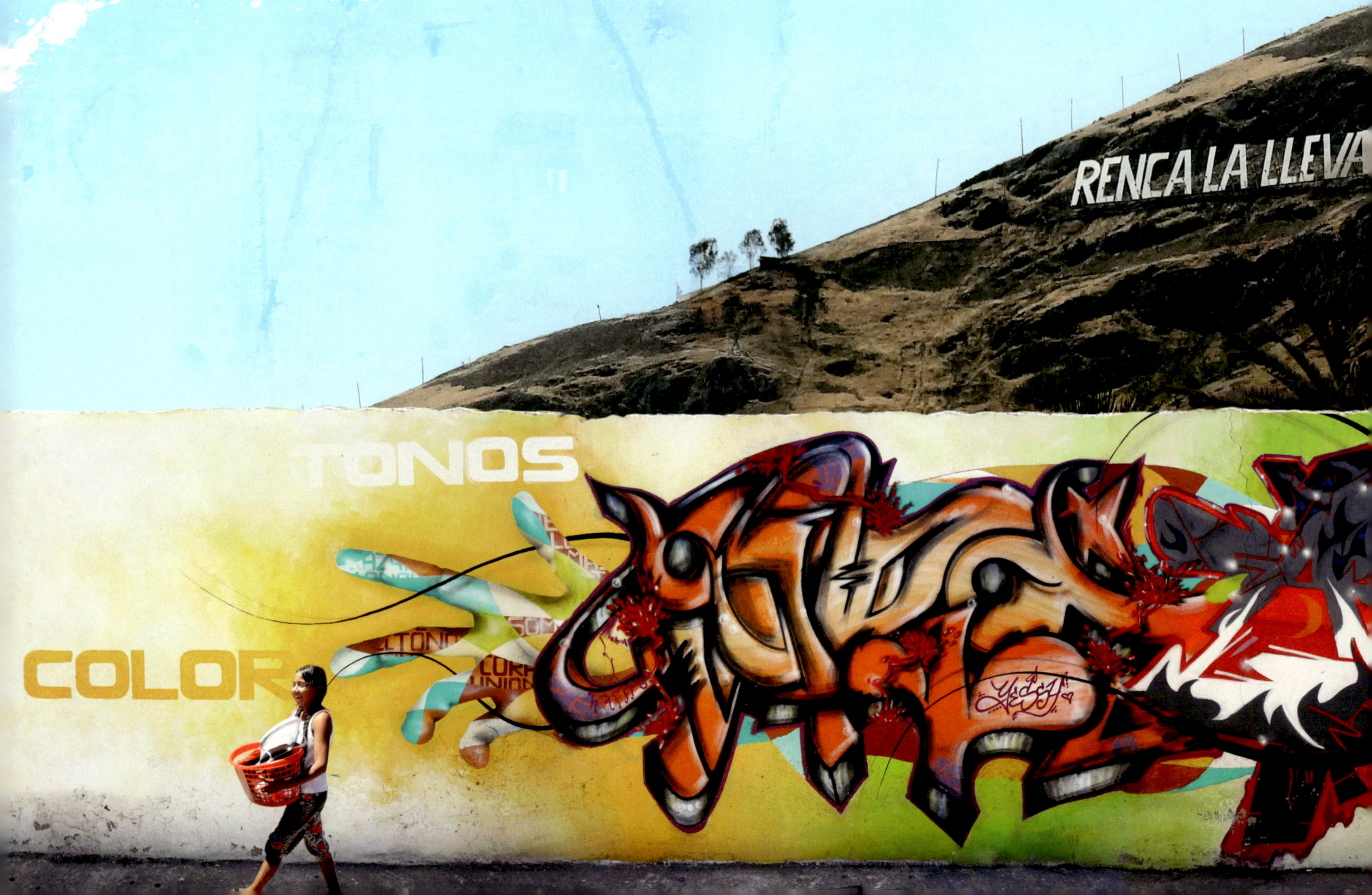

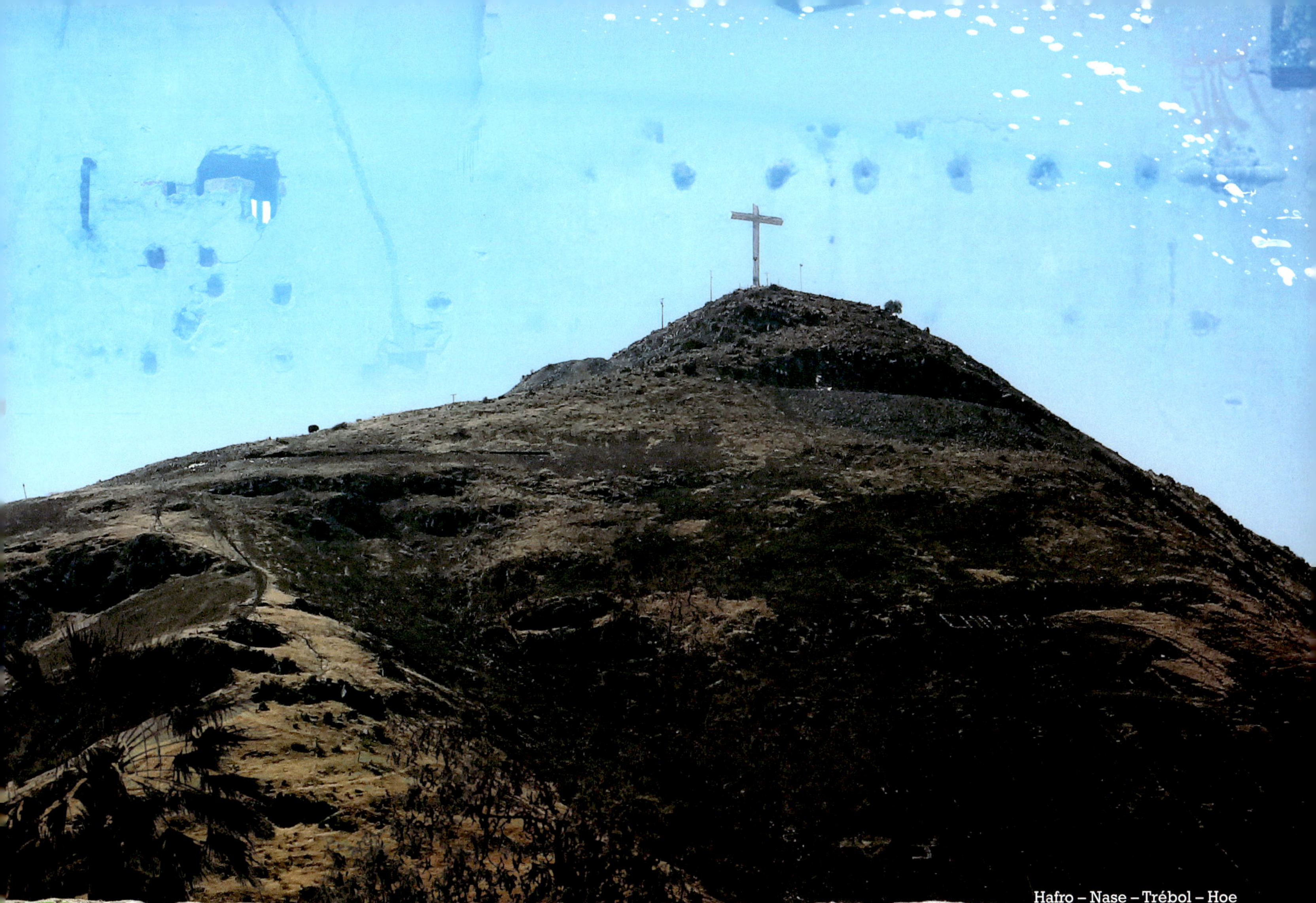

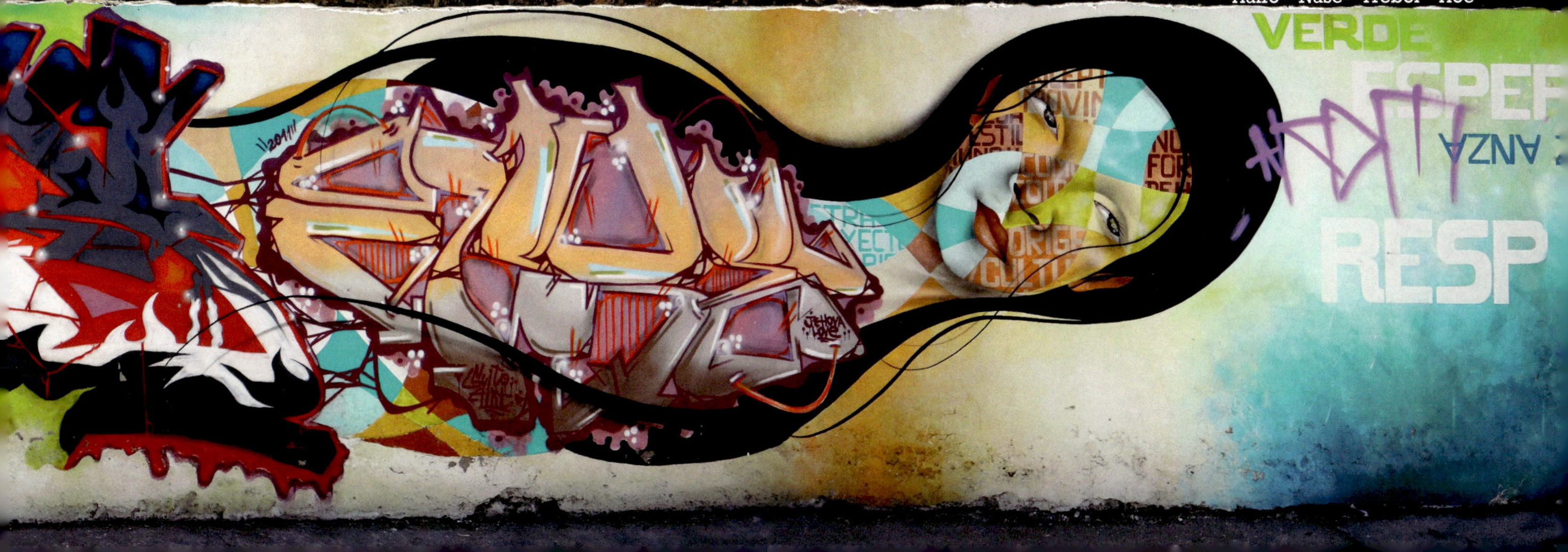

Hafro – Nase – Trébol – Hoe

SAN MIGUEL

Area: 10 km^2
Population: 78,872
Average annual income: US $39,670
Population below poverty line: 2.5%
Graffiti prevalence: 9/10

"The muralist project, the Open-Air Museum, in San Miguel, was founded in the month of March in 2009, after a series of conversations between Roberto Hernandez Bravo and David Villarroel Fuentes, both residents of the San Miguel barrio. They visualized the realization of murals that would serve as a reflection of Chile in its bicentenary, which would be painted on the blind walls of the blocks of the apartments, situated on the northern, narrow, rural path of the Avenida Departamental. These neighbors had a dream in common, of changing the gray reality of their barrio and converting it into a tourist site and an example of renewing an entire community through art.

"The residents' interest and the need to stop and eliminate the deterioration of the buildings of the San Miguel barrio, brought about by decades of contamination that generated overpowering scribbles and posters, were the engine of the community initiative taken on by the Mixart Cultural Centre. They worked patiently for three years to transform the neighborhood into a real gallery of public art, with free admission, without a schedule restriction, and for the enjoyment of the entire local community, commuters, and visitors.

"Today, the Open-Air Museum in San Miguel has become the greatest expression of collective street art in Chile, where techniques of muralism and graffiti share the stage and intertwine in original works developed by the best national and international artists, both new and established, who agreed, in advance, to have their creations validated by the residents of each wall. This unique cooperative participation creates a shared feeling of belonging between the murals and the local residents."

MUSEO A CIELO ABIERTO DE SAN MIGUEL, CENTRO CULTURAL MIXART

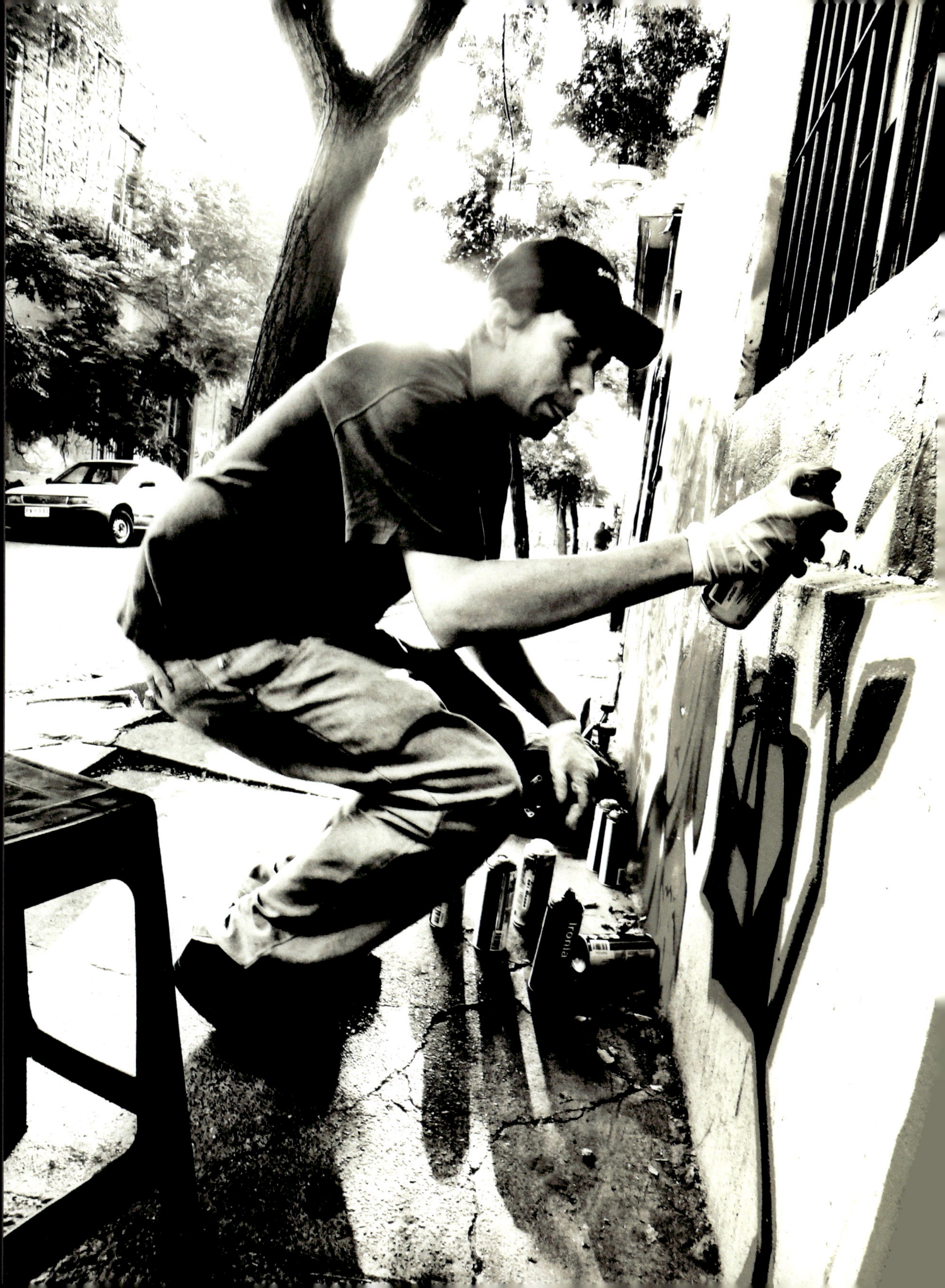
Ironia

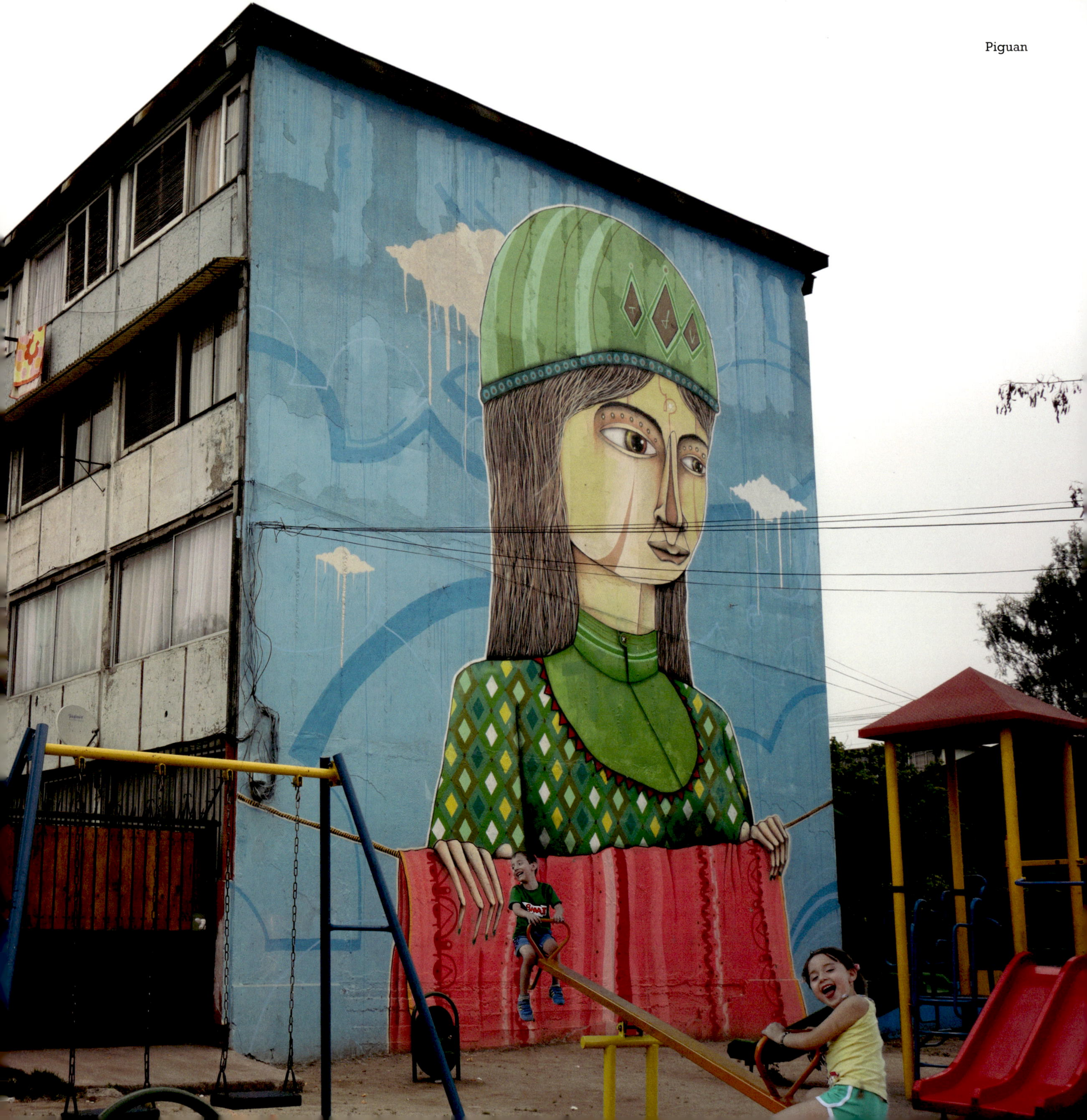

Piguan

Jamberta

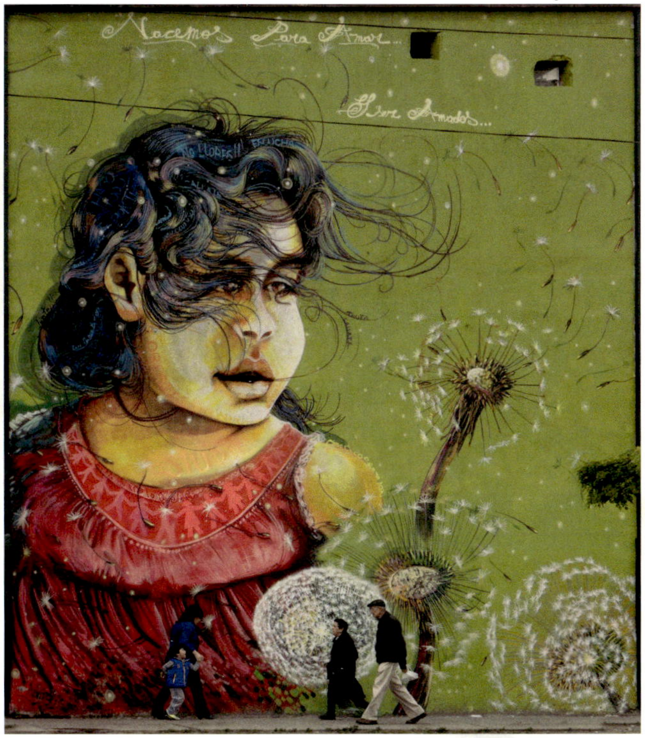

Jorge Kata Núñez

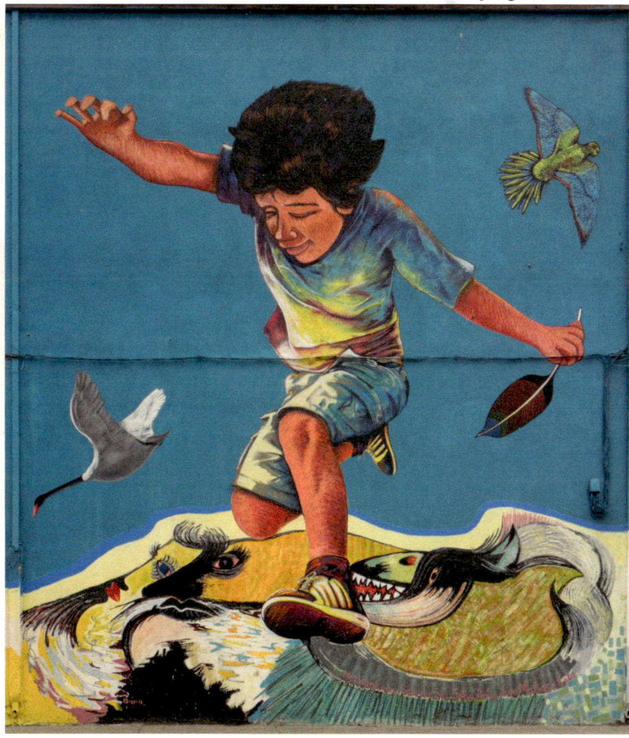

Crazis Crew

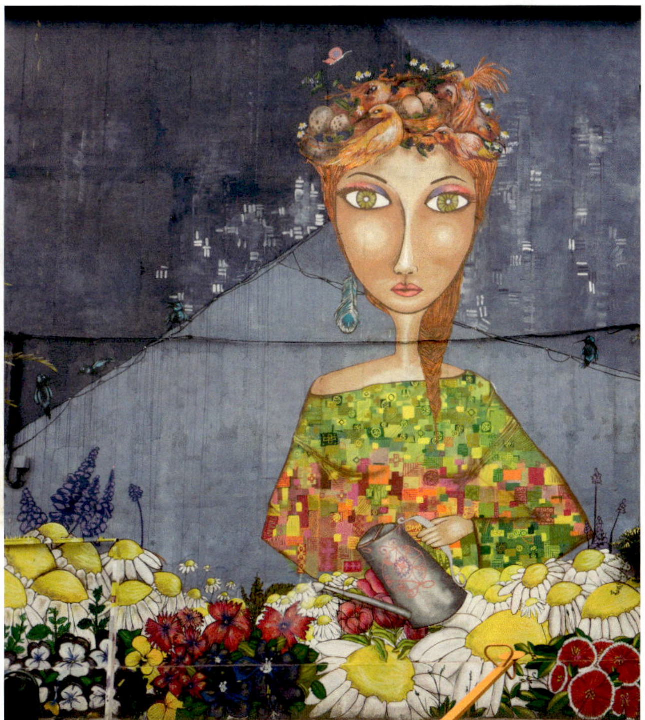

La Mano

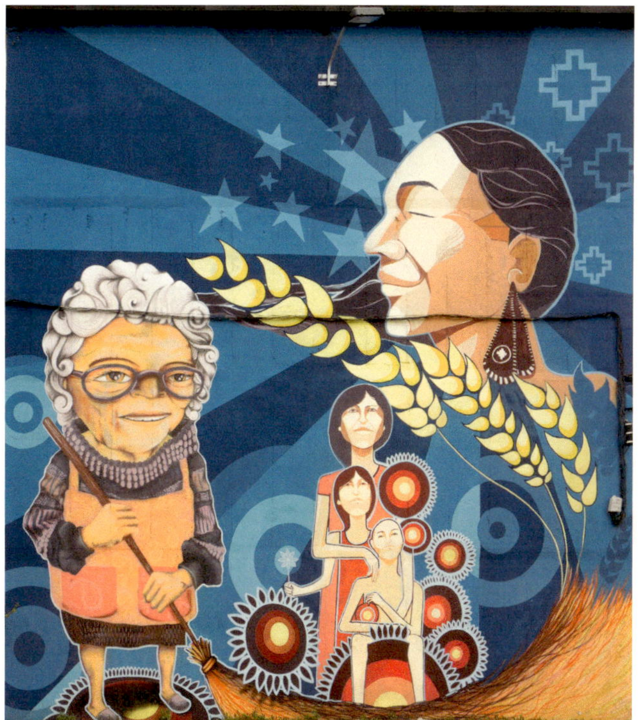

Alapinta

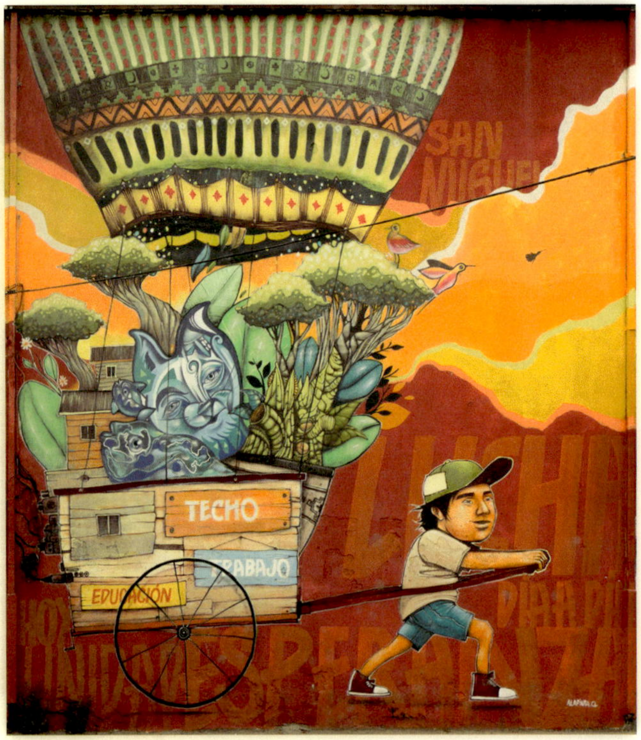

Salazart – Oet – Drk

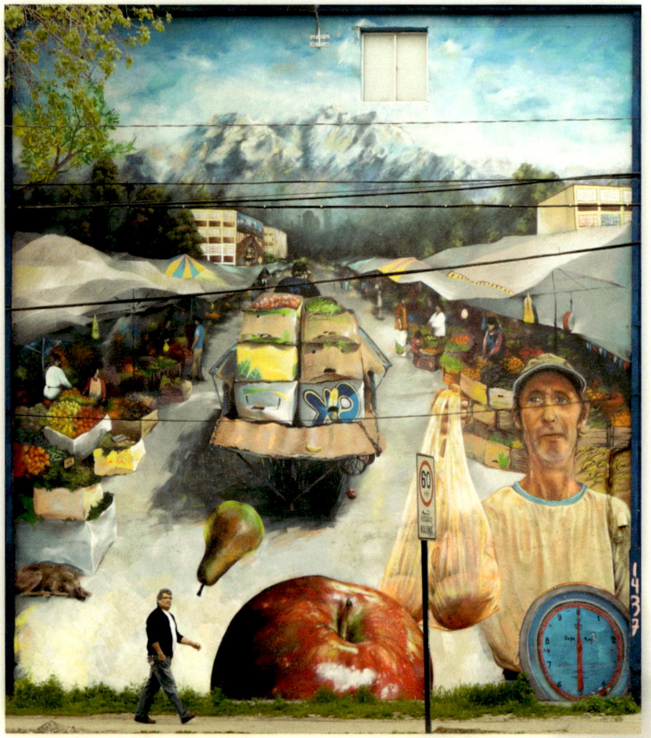

12Brillos

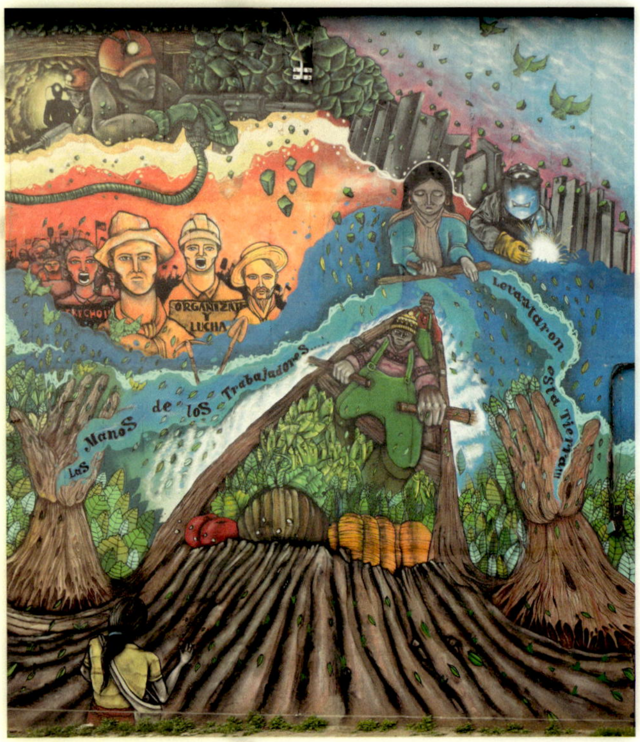

Depanité

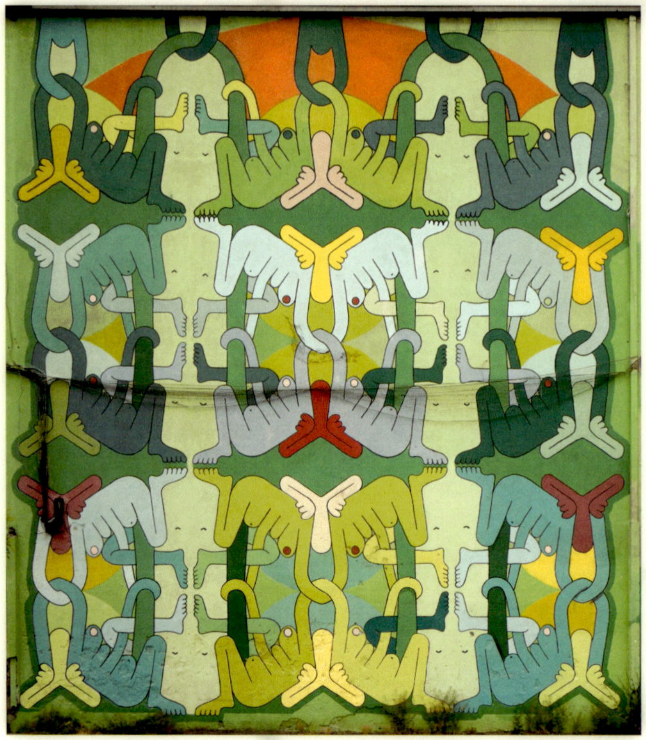

Morbo

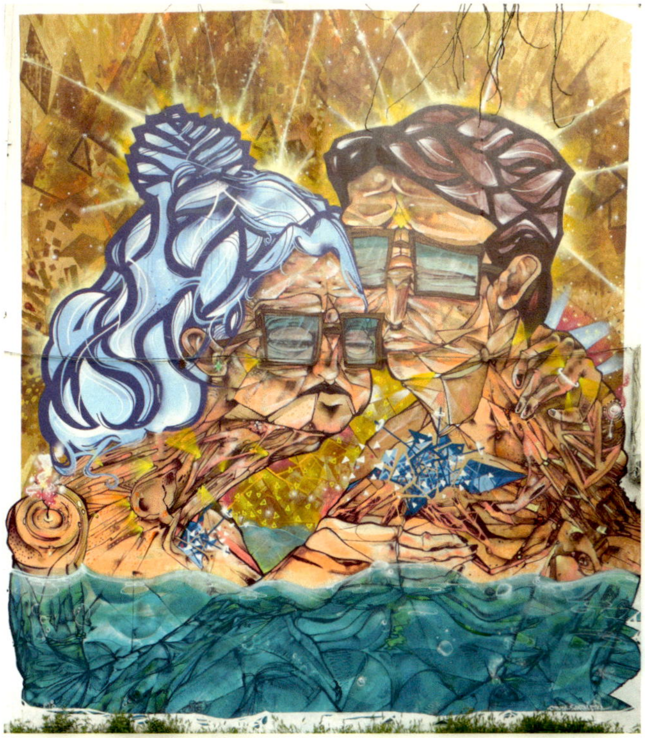

Vida Ingravita

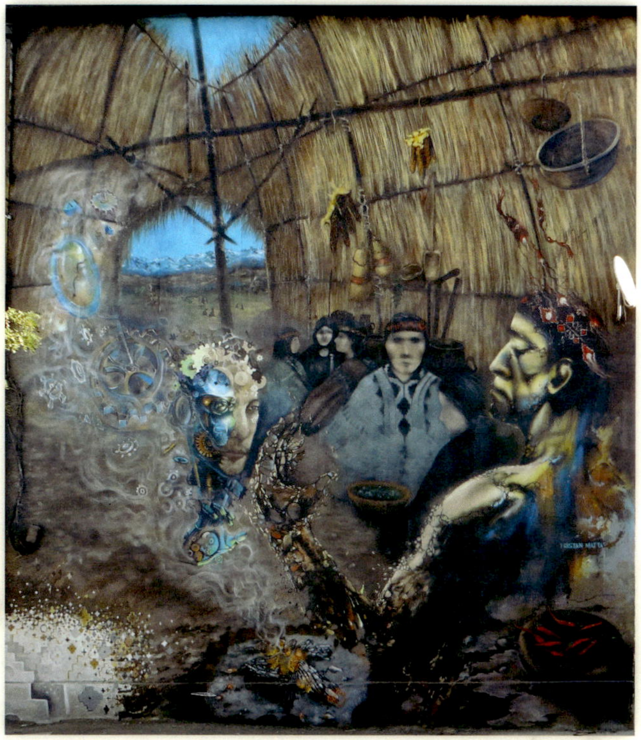

Aislap

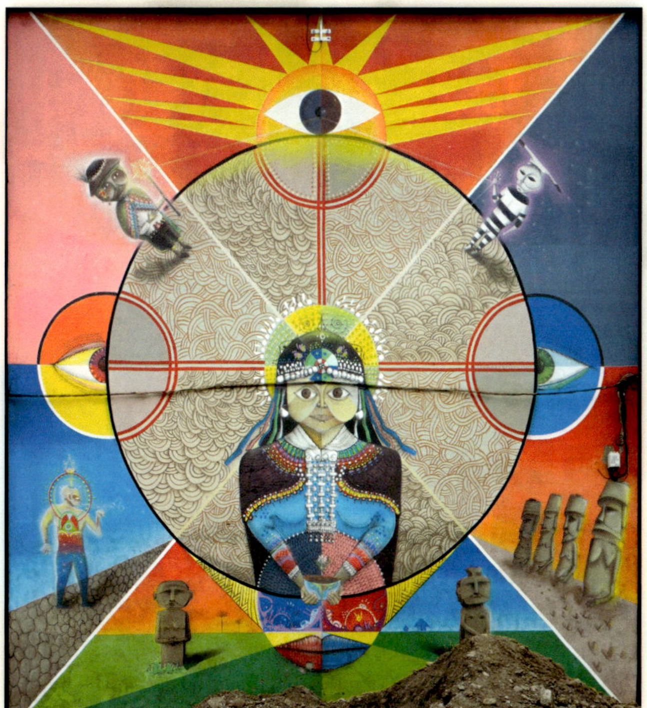

Ha crew

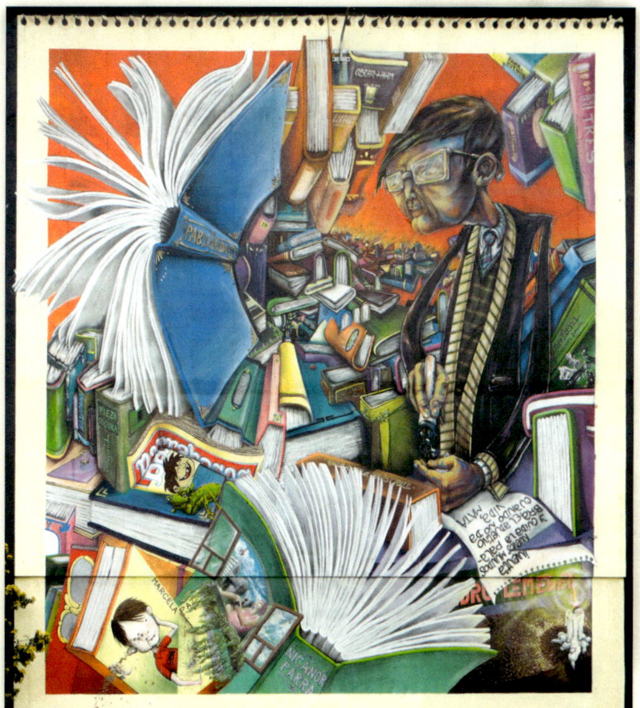

"My first encounter with a wall of massive proportions was in San Miguel, a commune with a project instigated by the local community center to paint more than twenty big walls. High-caliber local artists such as Mono Gonzáles, Alapinta, and Inti as well as those from further afield such as Seth and Roa have been invited to paint here." CHARQUIPUNK

OPEN AIR

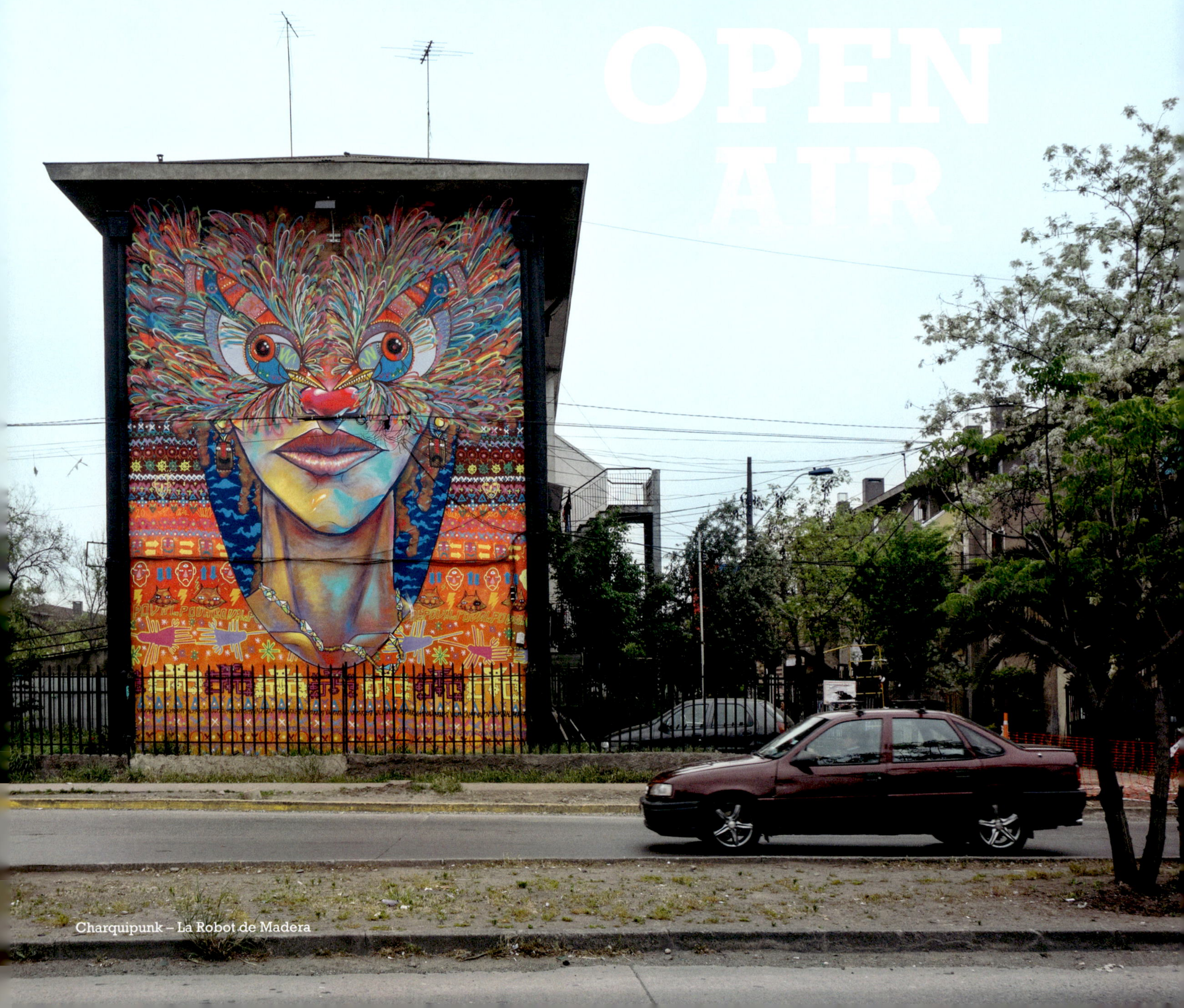

Charquipunk – La Robot de Madera

"When painting on such a large scale you need to make a design decision based on the viewing distance, as a big wall has two distinct viewpoints that must be accounted for. When viewed closely, the passerby pays attention to the finer details. When viewed from a distance, the artwork is often viewed in a fleeting moment, so must have a big impact. There are also technical issues to resolve, such as proportions and composition. To resolve the proportions issue, I use the scaffolding as a grid. I often have to walk away a fair distance from the wall to view the wall from another perspective each time I paint a new step." **CHARQUIPUNK**

MUSEUM

Aislap

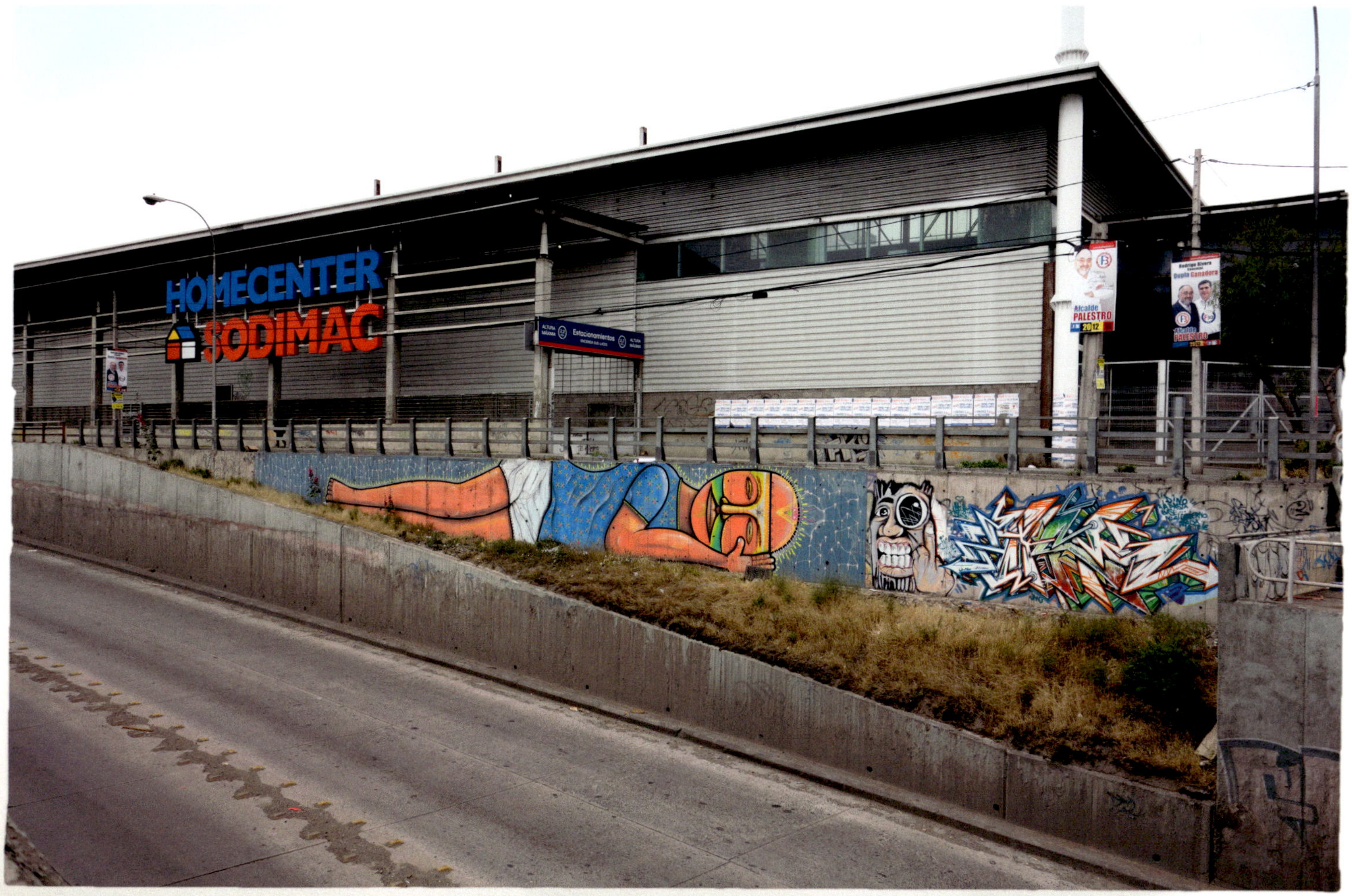

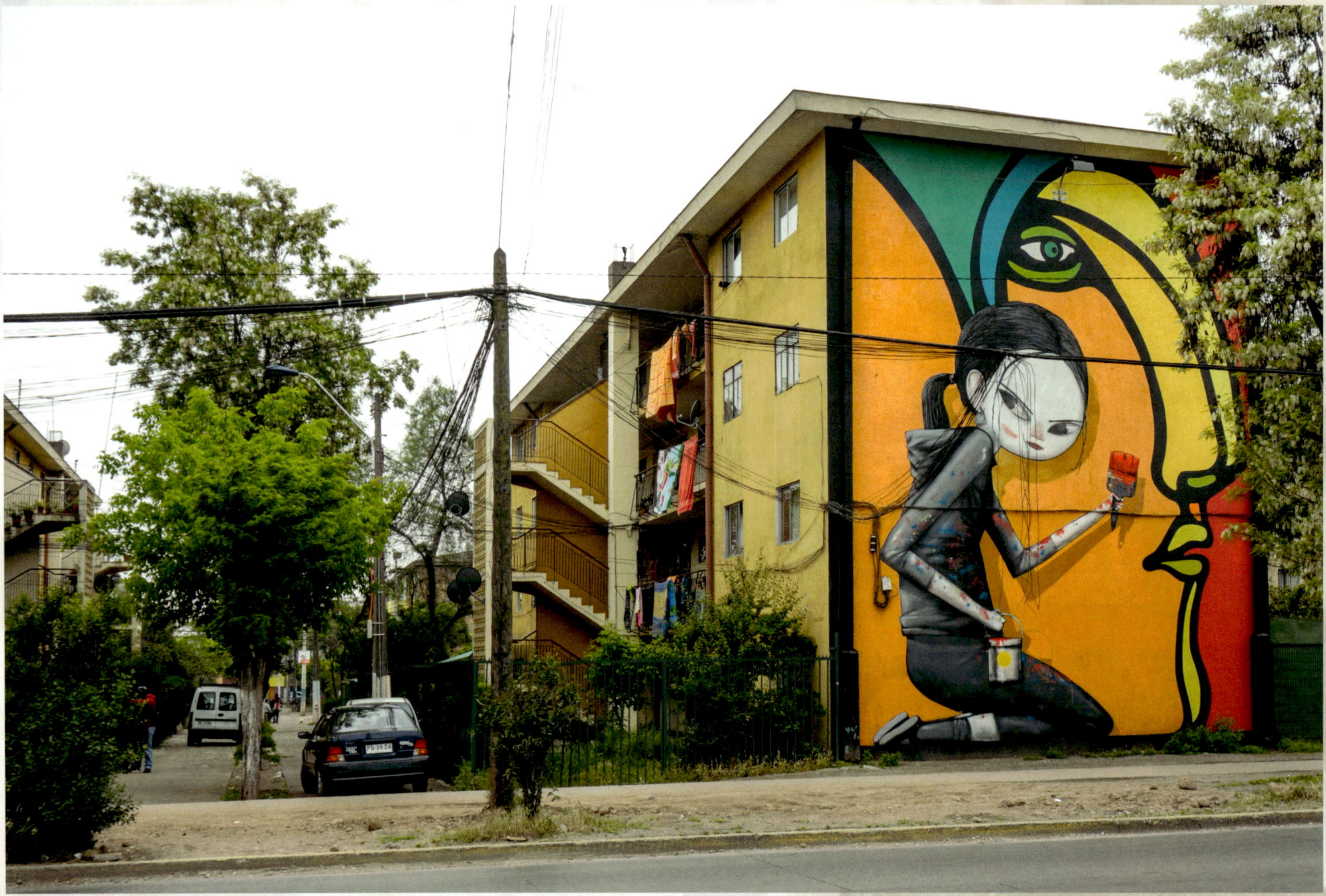

"Mono is not only a major artist of muralism, whose formal and aesthetic contribution is dominant in Latin American art, but also a man of conviction for whom painting is primarily a social act. Mono is part of a generation of mural painters for which the street is a way to fight for an ideal, against the system. I found out while working with him how much painting in public spaces is a social and political act. There is no need to write slogans to give sense to a wall. To show that there is an alternative to consumption and mass culture, by creating a poetic and colorful piece of work in a place where art does not usually penetrate, is a political act. This is the whole meaning of the Open-Air Museum of San Miguel: to offer an ambitious and generous art project in this popular district, restoring life to the old walls of this community.

"It was my first experience in painting such a big wall, and I learned a lot from Mono's expertise and techniques. Working in San Miguel with the painters of the projects, the people in the community, and Mono was an experience that changed my way of painting and my understanding of painting in public spaces.

"My characters usually speak to the social and cultural situations where they are painted. In this collaboration with Mono, I wanted to represent my vision of the Ramona Parra Brigade. A young girl, proud, stained with paint, eyes full of defiance, in a grey and monochrome suit that contrasts with the pure and bright colors of Mono's character. My modest tribute to Chilean muralism." SETH

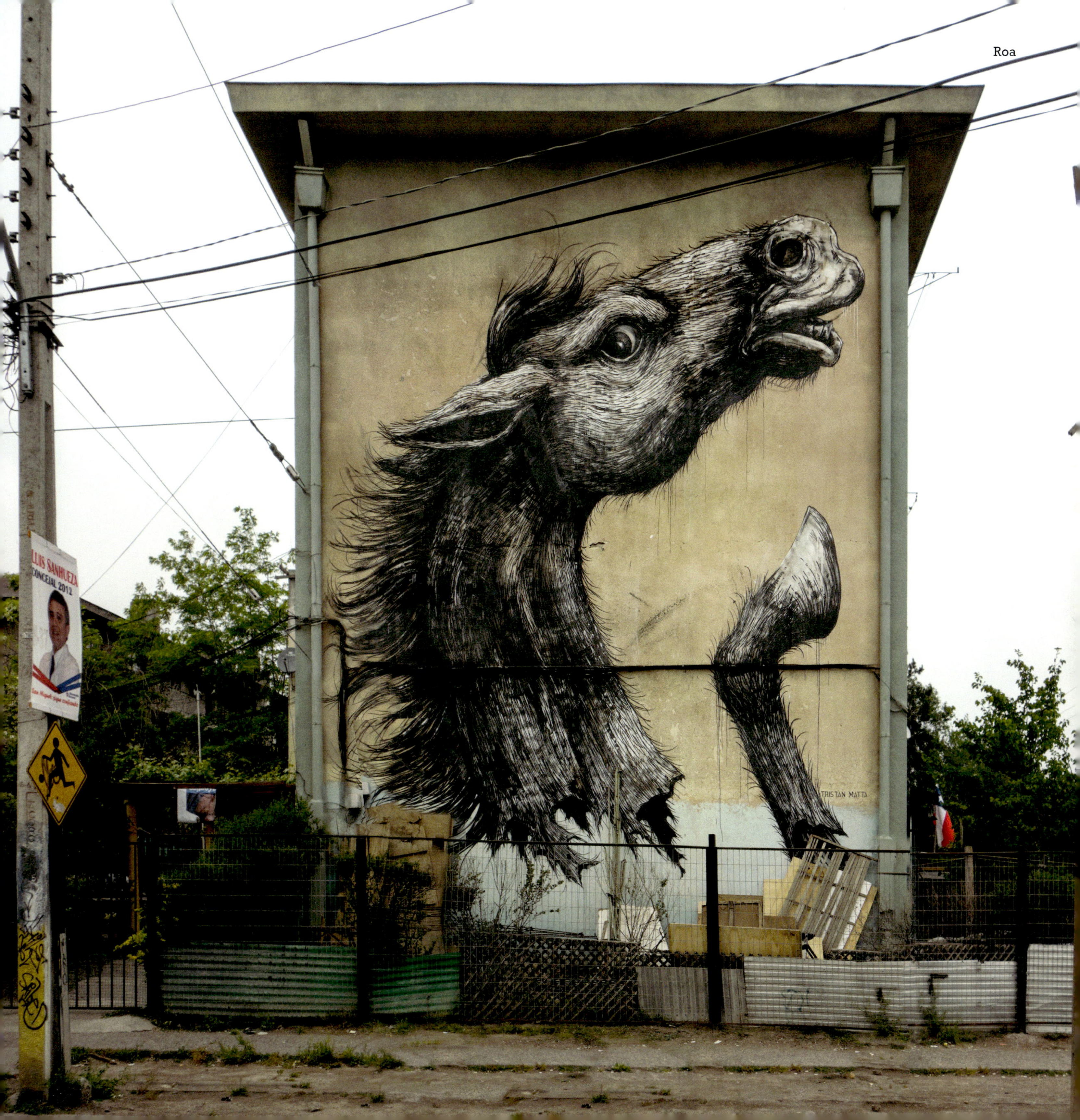

Roa

SALAZAR ART

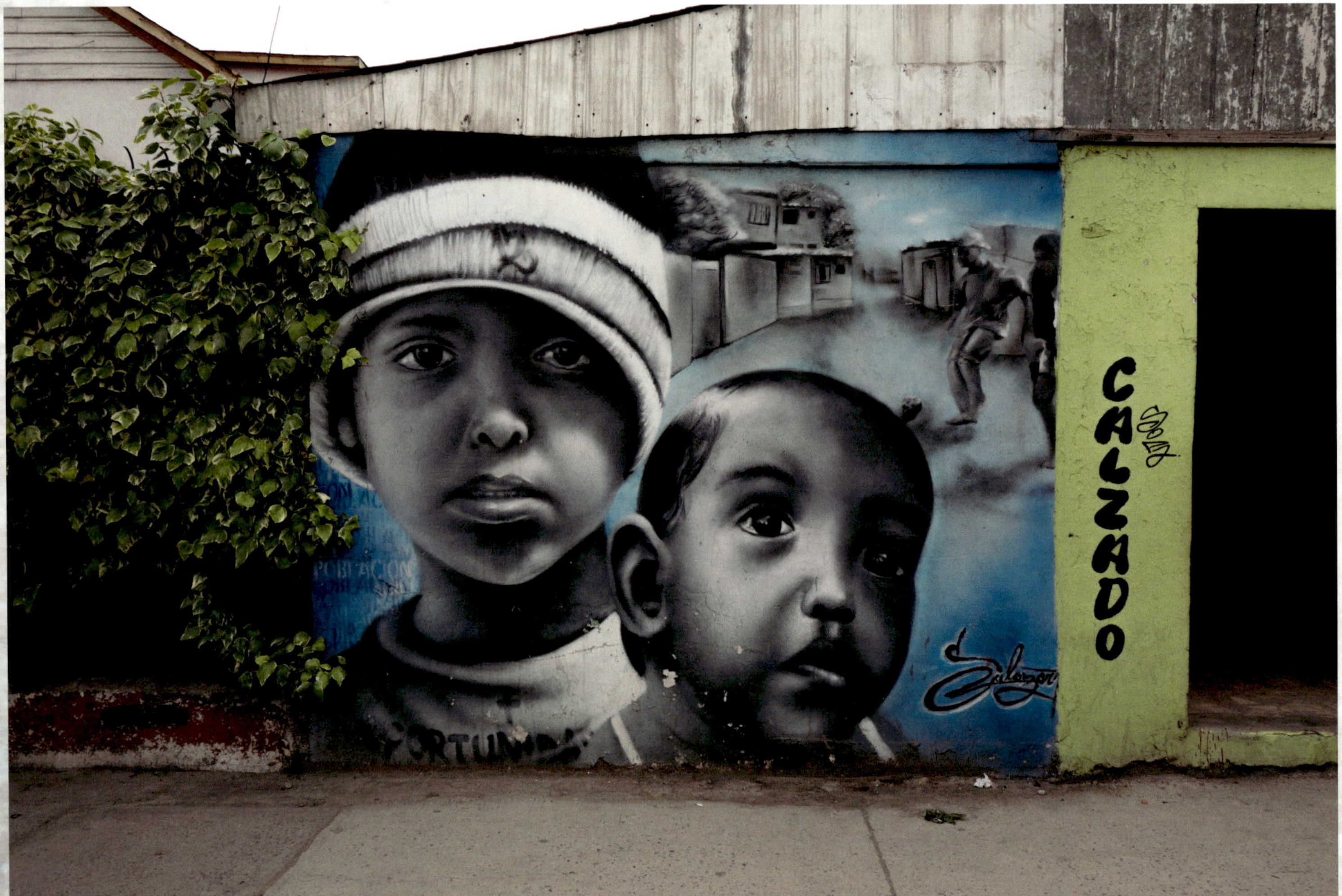

"When I was little, I became fascinated with the idea of a graffiti next to a face. I would see this type of graffiti and be captivated. From this moment, I began to experiment with those types of pieces and, little by little, I began to realize that I wanted my work to be more expressive. This led me to leave typographic graffiti aside to move on to a more figurative side of street art. I also liked to challenge myself to paint something more realistic, with more detail. Each time, I would increase my demands, trying to outdo myself in the search of a coveted perfection.

"Truth be told, I do not have an established theme. It all depends on what is going on in my head. All I know is that my graffiti must speak for itself, and it must move the viewer independent of the theme that I choose.

"When I lived in Santiago, I really liked Departamental and its surrounding neighborhoods. This was due to the fact that it was my barrio and one must begin at home.

"Honestly, I prefer small works. It is a constant challenge to achieve an excellent piece with just caps and spray. You run more risks of committing errors, and this makes it entertaining. Lately, I have been working on bigger pieces and working in greater detail. I believe that the viewer finds this more attractive." SALAZAART

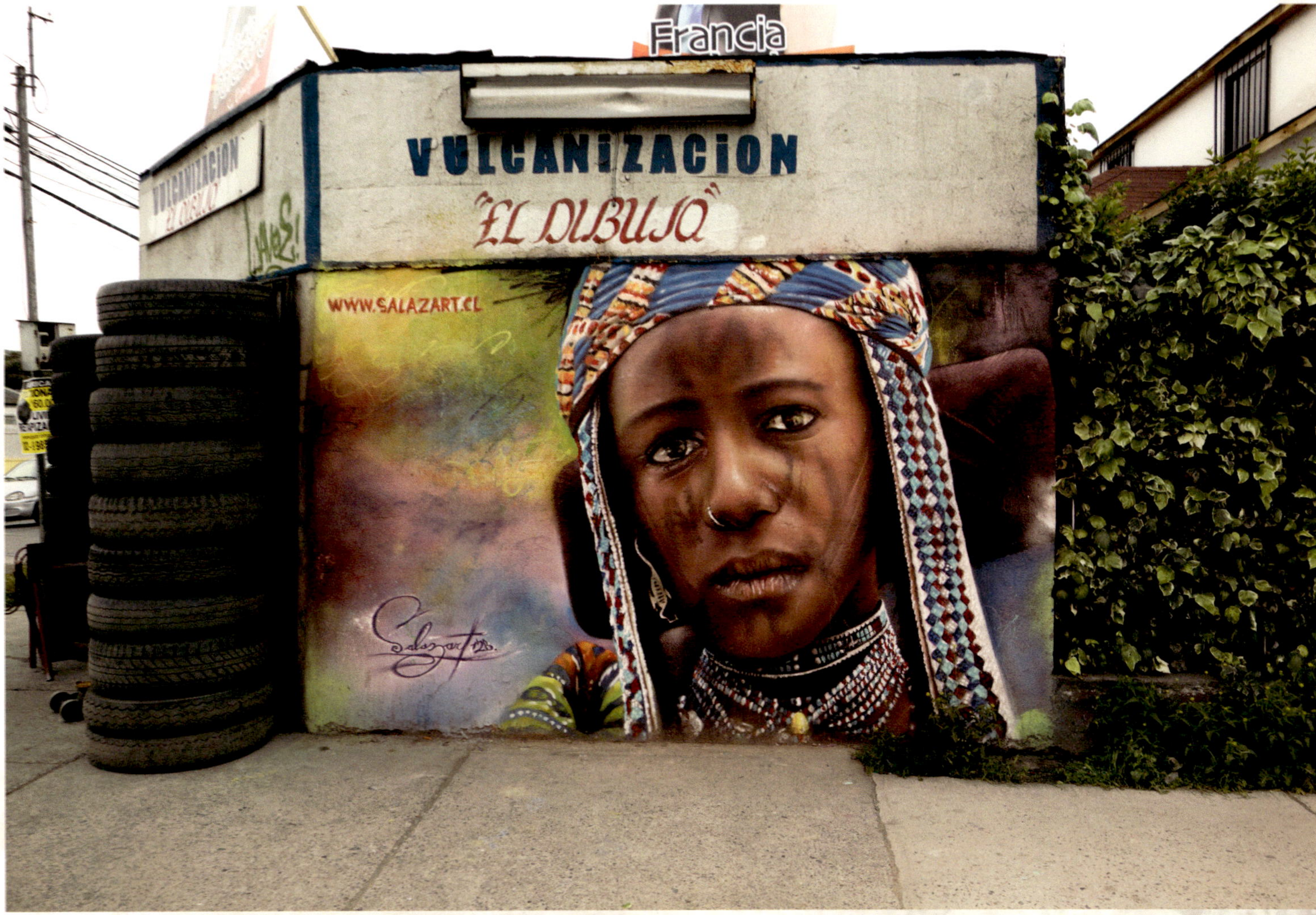

SANTA ROSA

(Photos taken on and in the vicinity of the main Road)
Length: 21.4 km
Graffiti prevalence: 9/10

"I have a close relationship with Santa Rosa as I have lived here for twenty-three years and I know many of the locals. I often paint façades and storefronts for the residents. Santa Rosa is generally a middle-class zone. It contains old neighborhoods with many professionals and retired elderly residents.

"There are many concrete walls and gates to spray on. There are about three to four available walls per street. There are also bigger walls, as there are many factories and industries. The length of time the pieces last in this zone is dependant on the graffiti and the artist. If the piece is elaborate, it will last. If the artist has a good reputation and has been around for a long time, plus he respects the other works in the zone, then his graffiti will definitely last a while. In Santa Rosa, you will generally find typography, big flops, and an elaborate wildstyle piece every now and then. Previously you would find more elaborate graffiti, and today you will see more bombs and throw ups. I believe that the locals interact positively with the existing pieces. From 2001 to 2010, there were a large amount of elaborate pieces and there was a notable dedication in each flop, graffiti, or character that was painted. There were many well-painted, big flops with many colors, from artists such as Aislap, Saile, Agotok, and others. Today, the ones of Agotok stand out most. There has been a further evolution in the style of graffiti from 2010 to this day." MUFFE

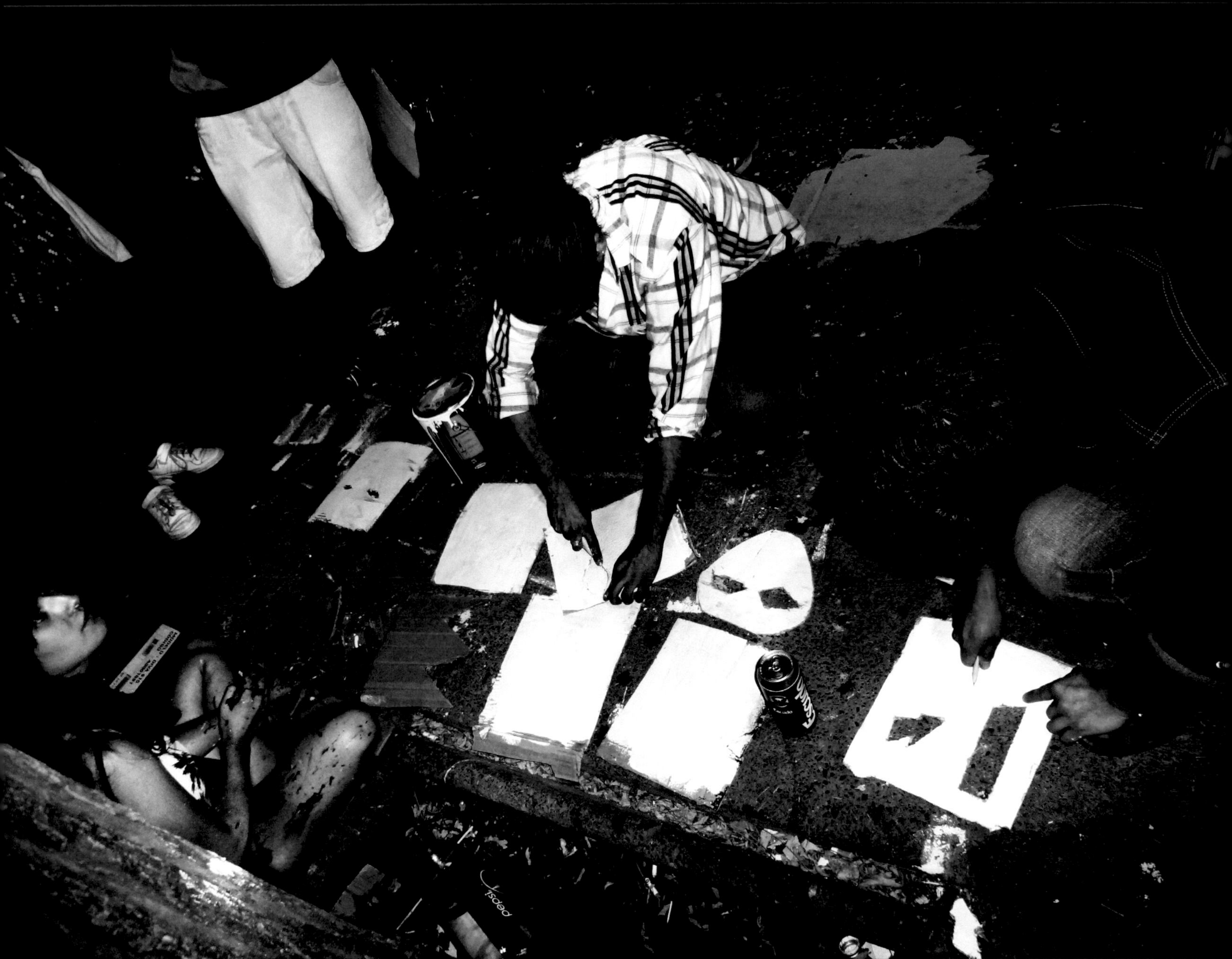

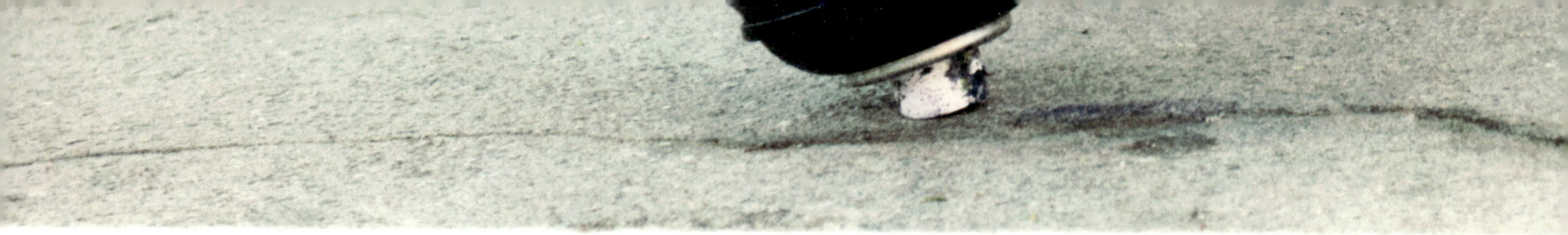

7 PFP 3100

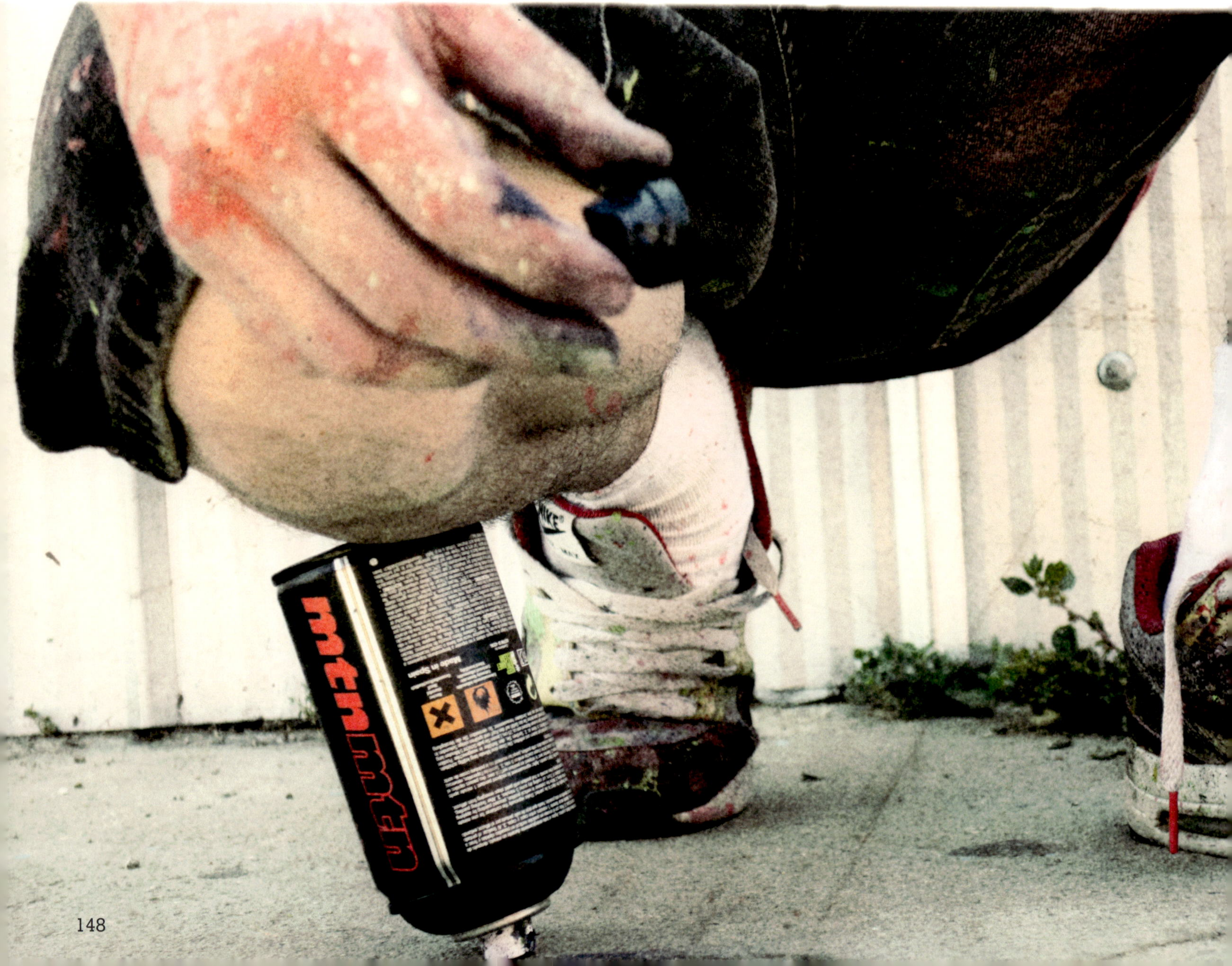

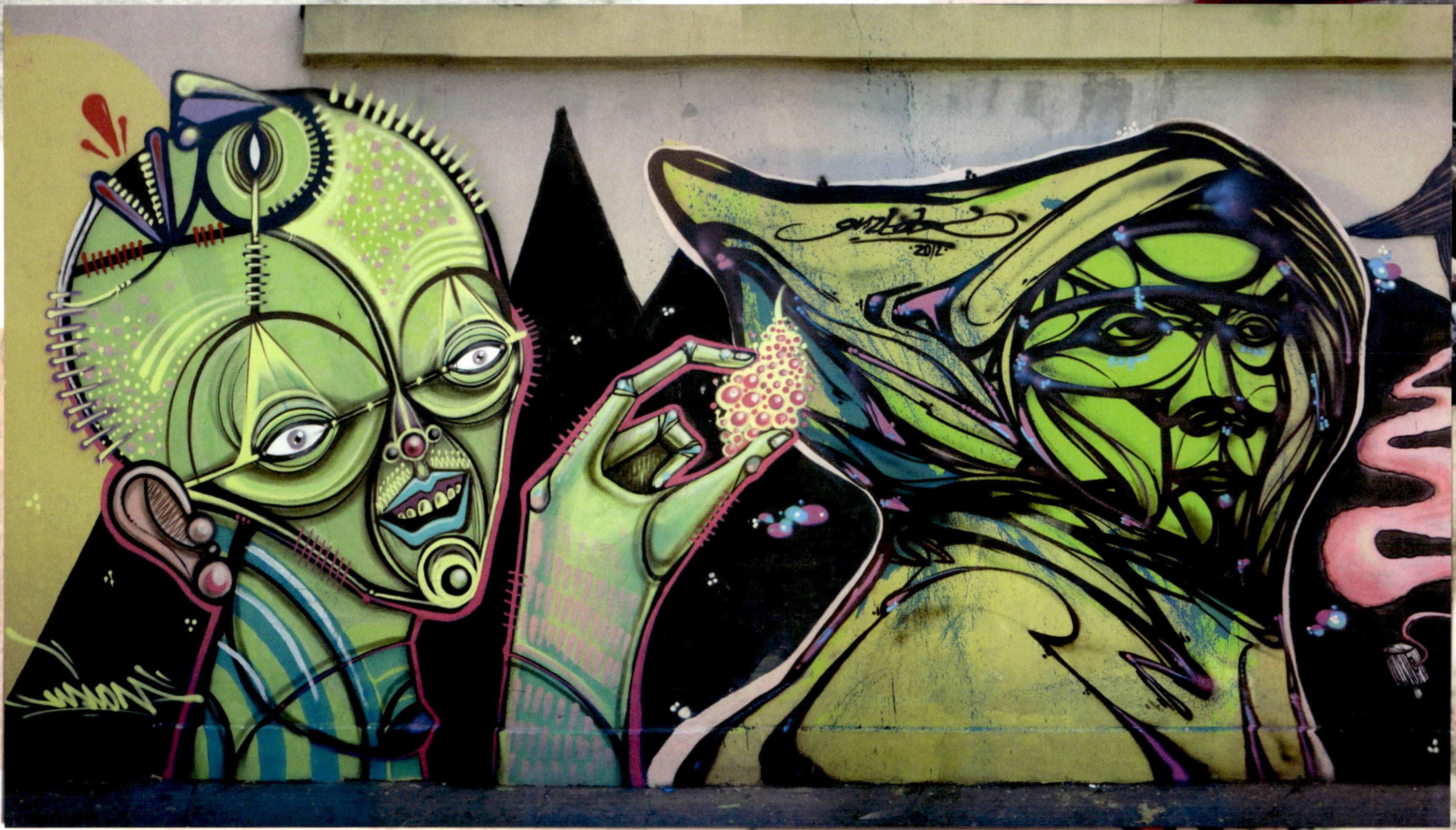

"There are places where we will never be able to paint, but nonetheless graffiti will remain in its birthplace, the ghetto." GUZTOK

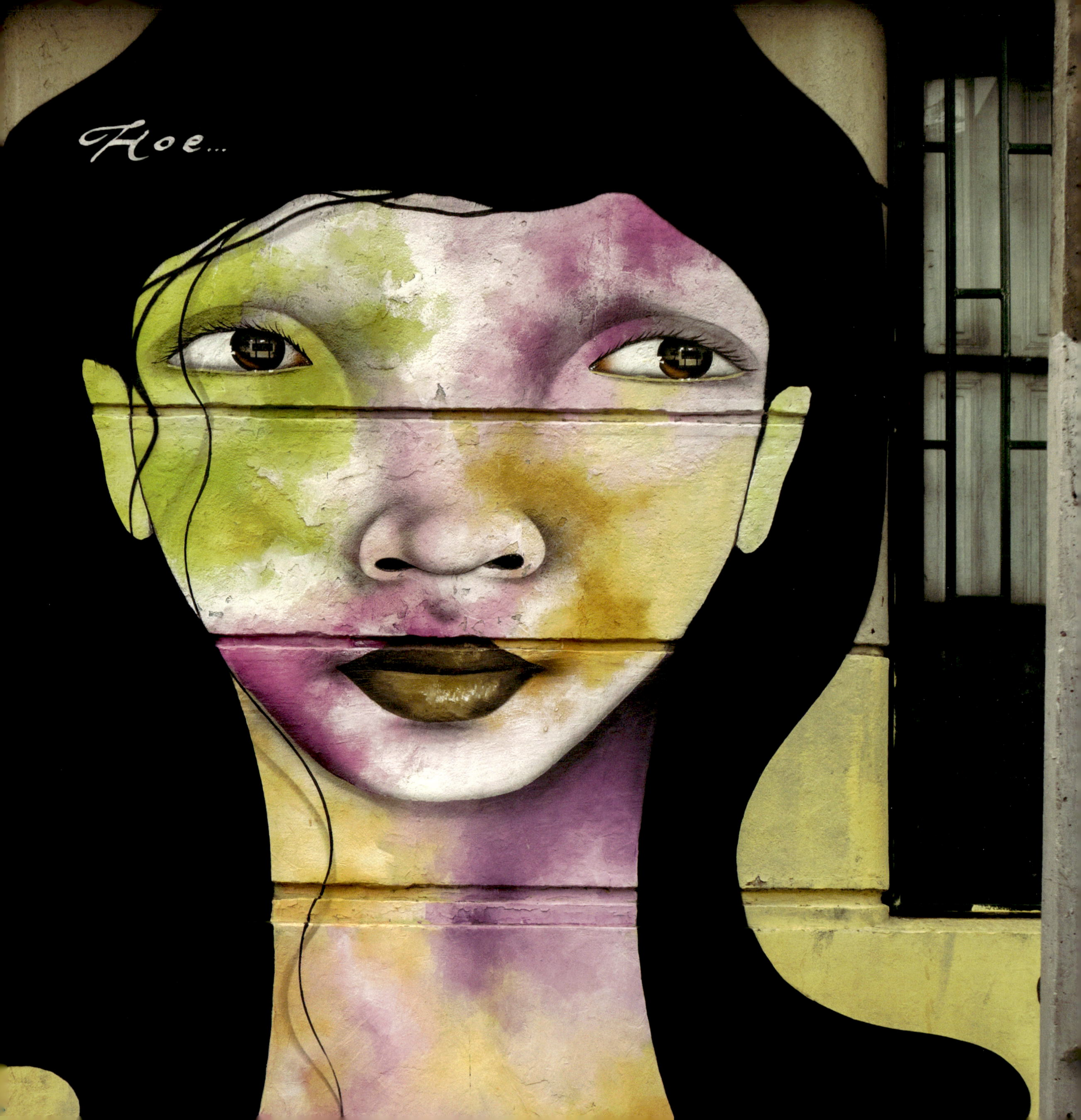
Floe...

"The first graffiti artists—Cekis, Saile, Grin, Horate—were my inspiration. I then began to discover new things. Later, I met Sol from Reciclando Muros, and she motivated me to get into muralism, because until then I had only painted with spray. We became friends, painted frequently, and mixed our styles. She was very important for me because she changed my concepts. From there, I began to pay more attention to the origins, the BRP [Romona Parra Brigade], and the methodology they have of inviting people to paint who have never created a mural or a graffiti.

"I have always thought that the eyes are the windows of the soul. I began to paint faces so that their eyes could transmit what I felt in the moments when I painted them. If I want to convey the poverty of a barrio, I can do so through the eyes.

"The experiences that I cherish the most are the ones that occur when I set out to paint by myself, under a bridge or in an abandoned place. In reality, I am never alone, because there is always someone who lives in the places that I paint. I have encountered kids inhaling neopren [glue] and they are out of their minds, but they become curious when they see you painting. I also have conversations with grandparents who tell me why they are living on the street.

"I am always painting, I dedicate a hundred percent of my time to graffiti and muralism. As long as I strive and have perseverance, as long as I love what I do, things will happen for me. I know they will come and I wait for them with patience.

"I always tell the new graffiti artists to feel when they paint and to always convey a positive message. Whether we like it or not, our messages pass on and can impact children who nurture themselves with their surroundings. We have to take graffiti and murals as a responsibility, because they are being shown in public." **HOE**

"I began to paint with latex and shoe paint, which I believe is the best learning path. Now, I'm painting with cans, but I don't stop using the brush, because I believe that it is powerful and differentiates our work from Europe or the United States, where the can reigns supreme. We aren't afraid to mix materials and techniques together on one same wall, including dripping cans, brushes, latex, splashing water, etc. We are not so structured. We are very liberal with what we use.

"I consider myself a painter, not a graffiti artist or an artist. I paint on the street, and I like to work on murals. I get my inspiration from the country folk in Chile, workers, fishermen, and our Chilean roots. I am always trying new things out, making sketches, looking, and I always have a sketchbook handy, so that I can draw anything that catches my attention. I like animals and fish. Painting is pure observation, learning to observe and imitate reality at all costs. That's what I do, and what I expect to be great at in some point of my life, whether it's on the street, on carton, or on wood." **FAYA**

"I like to intervene in urban spaces and create a shock in everyday life through messages. Furthermore, expressing yourself on the street gives you much more meaningful experiences than when you paint on canvas. Most times, when you do it with love, you feel that you leave an important fingerprint to those who pass by. It's like a donation to the commuters. I intervene with extensive use of symbolism, yet in a subliminal manner. My goal is that the viewer who observes my work feels pleasure, tranquility, and equilibrium. I'm interested in creating pieces that initiate meticulous observations, instead of a brief glance." **JUANITA PEREZ**

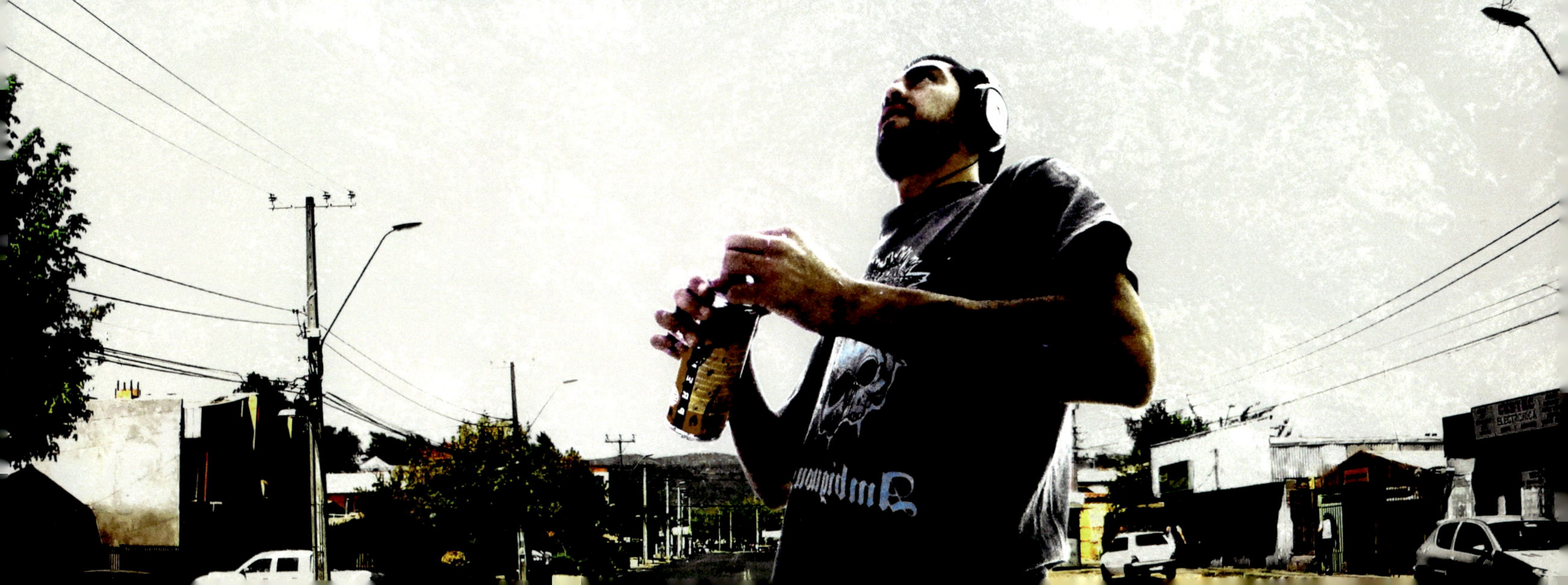

"When I began to gain interest in the street art in Santiago, I would pay too much attention to the images, and I would force myself to decipher the signatures, identify traces and styles, decode messages, and hunt for meaning. Soon, observation became insufficient as an investigative tool, so I became intent on getting to know the people behind the movement. I began to conduct interviews, basically a bunch of questions. In little time, the interest for the image transformed into a second dimension. I still like to look at graffiti and murals, they brighten my day and are like clouds of visual oxygen in the middle of publicity saturation and gray cement. But even more interesting is following street artists in their daily affairs and sharing with them. It didn't cost me much to discover this hidden facet of street art. Painting on the street is different from doing it in the studio. A studio is a home, a containment space. The street is the street, synonymous with exposition, full of chaos and randomness.

"I recall the case of a graffiti artist, Vamy, who likes to paint illegally, and if it's on the roof of a building or on the top of a subway wagon, even better. What mattered to him was the level of difficulty of the piece he worked on. On a cold night in June, while we were waiting for the bus, he said, 'Look,' and asked me what I thought of a work of graffiti on a balcony of an abandoned building. I told him that I thought it interesting and had good typography, albeit a bit simple. He responded, 'Yes, they are simple, but imagine how difficult it must be to maintain the pulse of your hand and your calm when you're at that height. You must be cold-blooded to make a graffiti like that one. I think it's an excellent piece, especially the intended mission.' 'Mission?' I asked him, 'Yes, graffiti is a mission, I'm talking about the vandalic type. There is a need to resolve a much bigger problem beyond that of paint. It has to do with the times, with meeting those who live and work in the surrounding area, taking into consideration access ways, escapes, and many more things. How do you think he got up there? Surely, someone helped him climb to the roof of that kiosk and then he climbed up to the balcony. That's how I think and see all the time even if I'm not painting. I'm always identifying good spots, places to climb and ways to break in. That's living in graffiti.'

"Another case is Kilo. That guy, who I met casually at a farewell dinner for a friend, had a very particular pastime: painting on walls in abandoned places that are far from the public's view. This person told me that he began to paint on these walls because his canvasses were too small and he felt the need to experiment on a bigger format.

"Yet, he felt shy, incapable of painting like graffiti artists who paint in plain sight. That's how he began to search for abandoned locations, far from the hustle and bustle of traffic. At first, he was disappointed, because all he found were cracked walls that were dirty and about to collapse. However, with time, he adapted to the forms and the patches of the locations he found. One day, while he was retouching a wall, he heard a noise and felt a hand brush his back. He almost died from fear, but calmed down when he realized it was an old man. He lived in the location and had his "nest" on the second floor of the abandoned house. He just wanted to tell the painter that the image he had painted on the wall was very beautiful, and, additionally, he wanted to know if he had a cigarette. The painter took his carton out of his pocket and gave the old man a cigarette, lighting another for himself. They later went to buy a box of wine, bread with tomato and ham, and they remained in conversation the rest of the afternoon. So, the old man told the painter his story, about his childhood in the countryside, his life in the city, and the reason he had ended up on the streets. 'These experiences are the ones that fill me,' the painter told me. 'Those in which you meet people who live on the street, because they have another point of view on things, they're behind the curtain, in a different frequency.'

"I can't stop commenting on the experience of my muralist friend and tattoo artist, with whom I lead a workshop. Puxo is a guy with many travels under his belt, 'a worldly guy,' as we like to say. This characteristic always called my attention, awakening in me a healthy type of jealousy, because I believe that there is nothing better than traveling. When you travel everything is new, everything becomes unique and, therefore, valuable. I don't want to say that this sensation of permanent astonishment can't happen in our daily lives—as a matter of fact, I think that's where the key to a happy and exciting life lies, in surprising ourselves constantly with those things that surround us in daily living. However, when you travel to another city or another country and see other scenery, smell other smells, see other clothing, and get to know new traditions, astonishment blooms naturally, without effort. The thing is, Puxo is always traveling, and he does it thanks to his murals. I remember that he told me one day, 'Those of us who paint on the street always fall on our feet, like cats, wherever we go.' At first I didn't understand this comment, but with time, as I noticed how other graffiti artist friends that go to expositions or that simply venture to other latitudes to paint made connections, I could understand how this movement worked like an international network." **BRIAN GRAY**

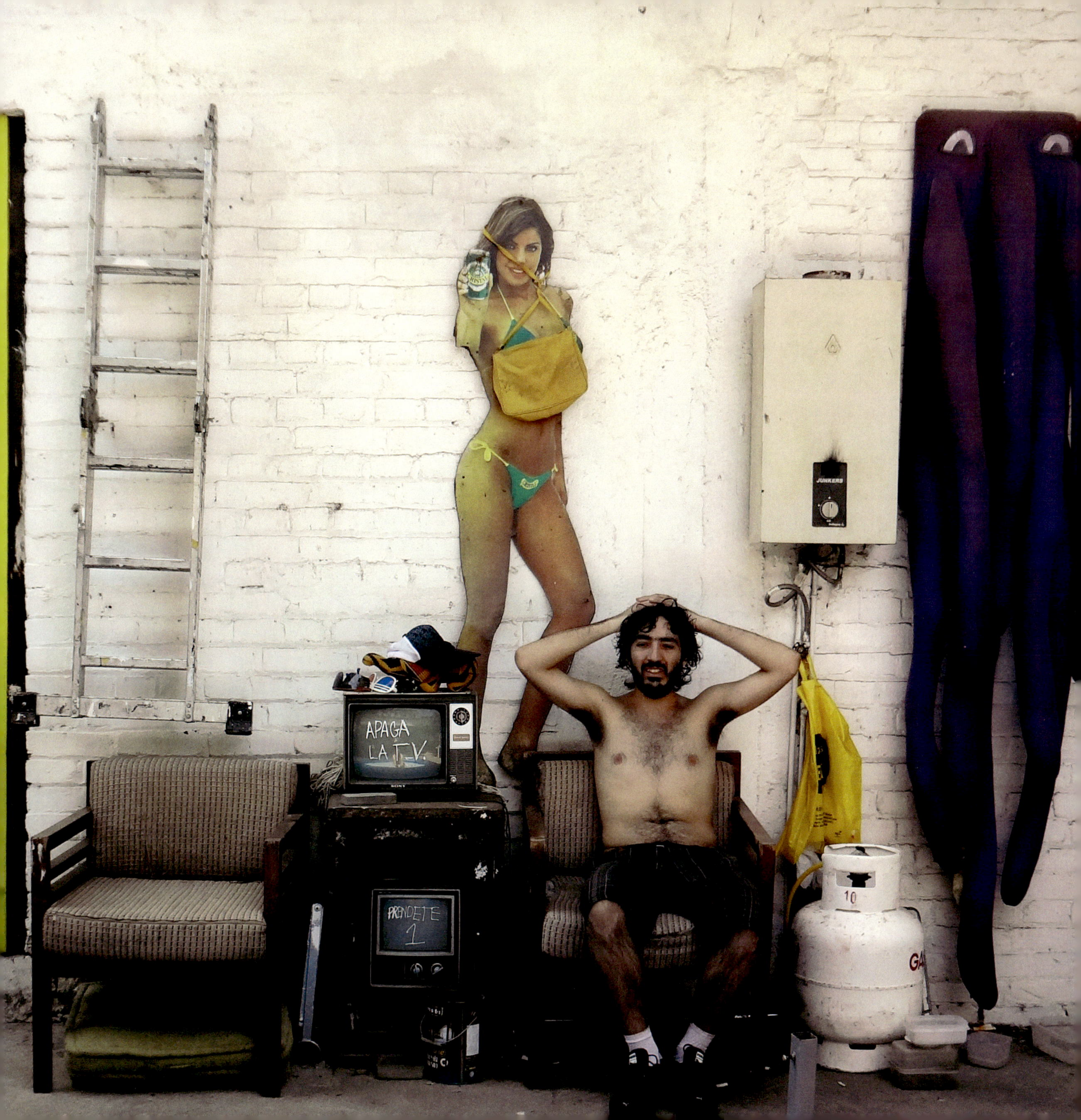
APAGA LA T.V.
PRENDETE 1
JUNKERS
10

BARRIO YUNGAY

Area: 0.72 km^2
Population: n/a
Average annual income: n/a
Population below poverty line: n/a
Graffiti prevalence: 8/10

"The Yungay neighborhood is located in the western part of Santiago. It is a traditional neighborhood with unique characteristics due to modernization. Its name comes from a plaza where the famous Monumento al Roto Chileno, an homage to the Chilean people, is located.

"I live and paint often in this neighborhood. Graffiti in this zone is well established and various graffiti artists live in the vicinity. Here, you will find works from 12Brillos, KGB, Piguan, Brigada Negotropica, Azucar, Pium, Tenam, Coas, Sofrenia, and other emerging muralists and artists who are dedicated to street art. The neighborhood's evolution continues to grow, as it is an ideal place to paint with its many small streets and abandoned corners. The style and techniques found in the neighborhood are varied, from wildstyle to characters, from abstract to bombing, and productions. Spray, paint, rollers, and paint brushes are the tools of choice. In this neighborhood, you find a new and original wall to paint each time you walk around, as its infrastructure is spread out between the old neighborhood and new constructions. The residents appear to be really open to street art and are very used to it and in many cases proud to be living in this region because it can be seen as an open-air gallery due to the abundance of graffiti. Forget the paid galleries, the quality here is often higher, and the work bigger and more impressive." HIPSO

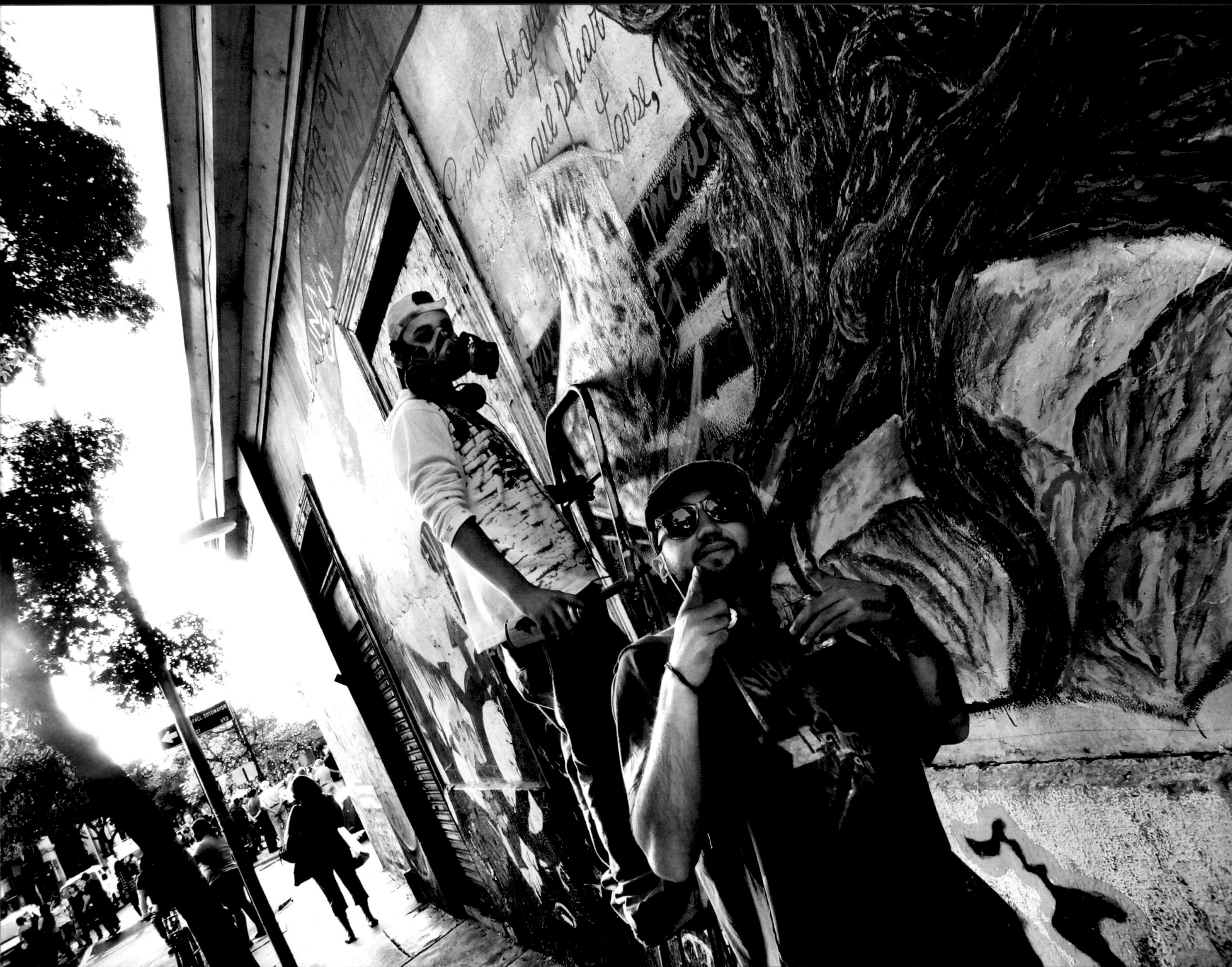

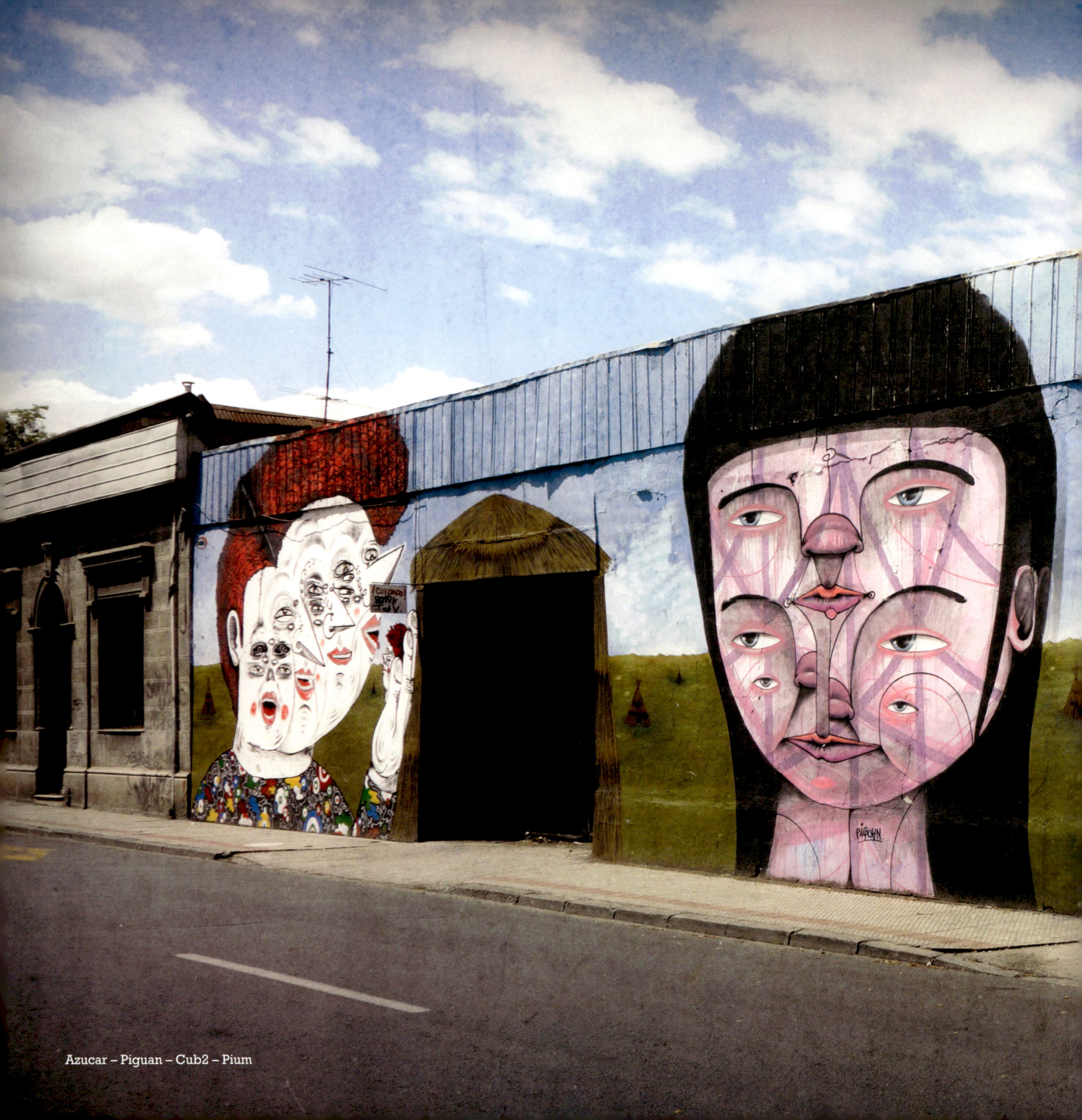

Azucar – Piguan – Cub2 – Pium

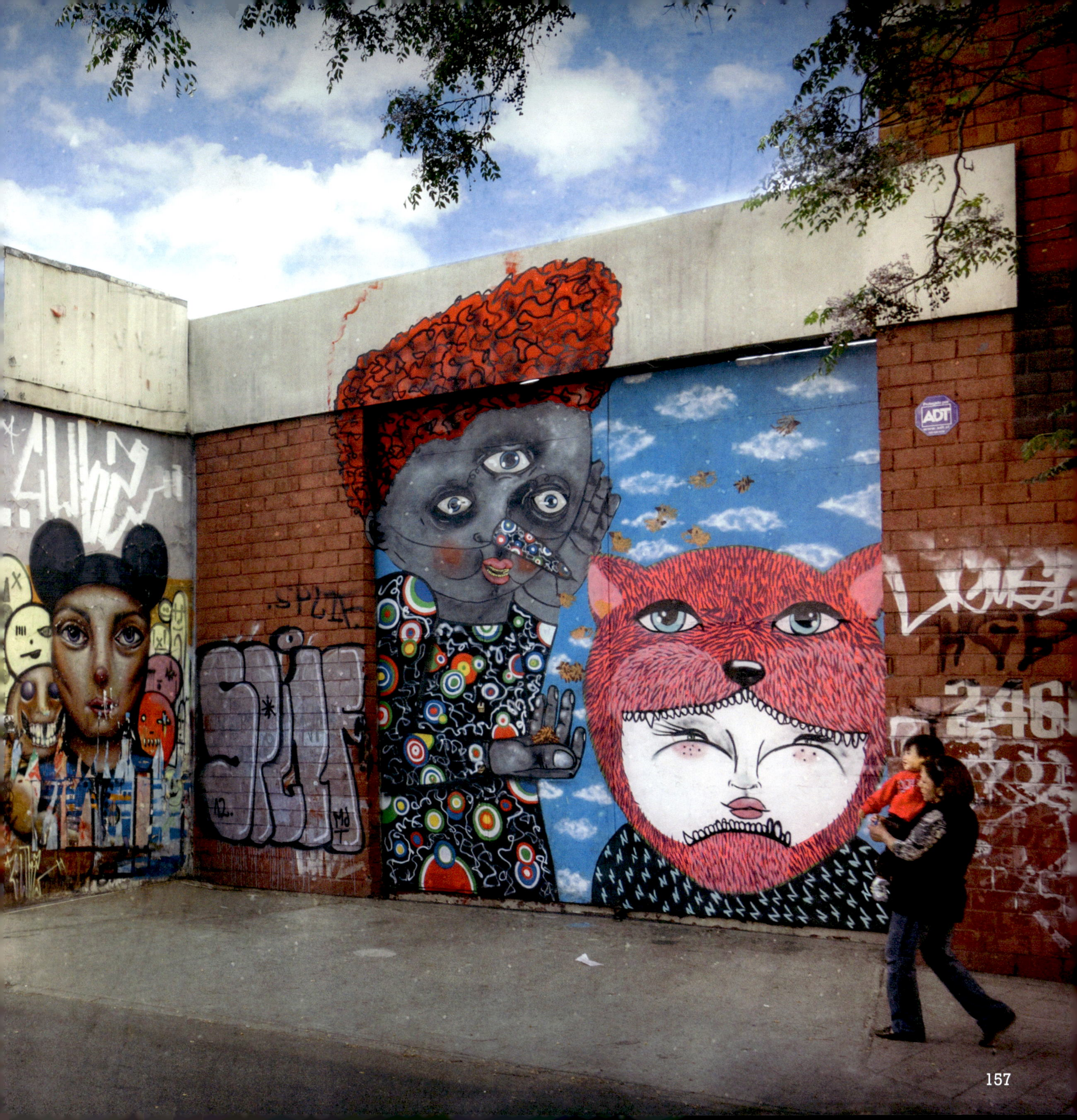
ADT

"Movement united with depth and perspective, that's what I want to achieve. Thus, the spectator can view the the process of my completed works." GESAK

"Many times I approach a wall, and if I see that I won't have a problem, I will paint it. Other times, I ask permission. I also paint at night, illegally. I wouldn't be able just to paint legally, because illegal painting provokes other types of sensations. For me, the equilibrium between painting calmly while sharing with people and painting at night with more intimacy, where you risk more and there's room for spontaneity, is fundamental. It's that adrenaline, mystery, and intensity." BISY

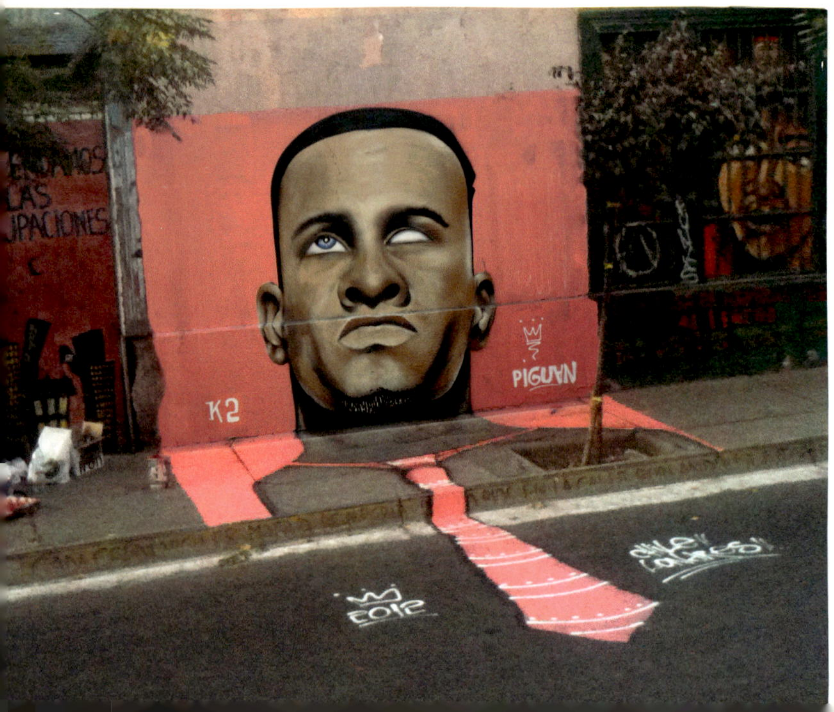

**"It's a gift for the people.
I don't do it for the money.
I do it because I am free and
I wish to express myself."** HEMSE

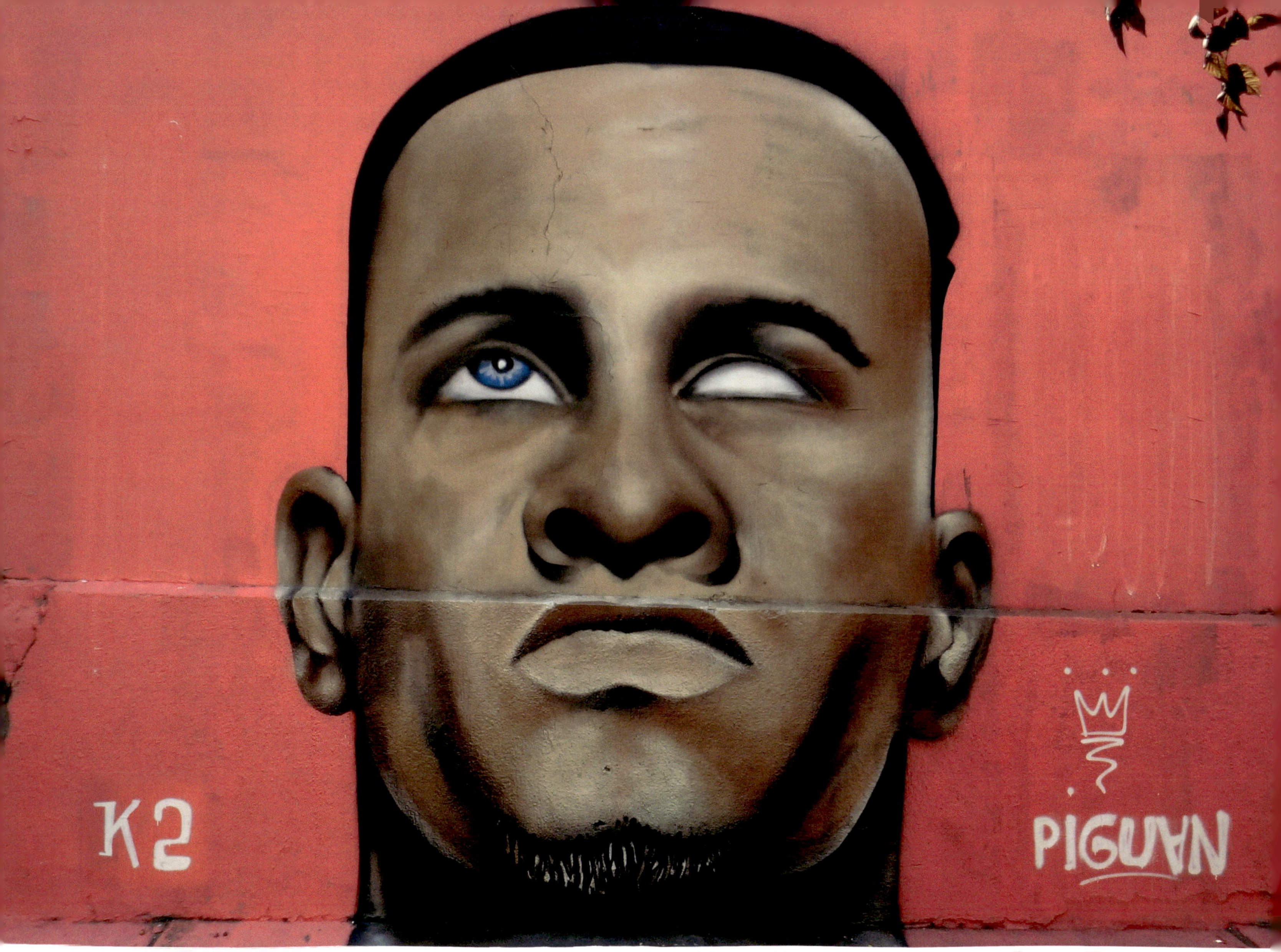

"Having spent the majority of my time taking photos of other artists, I was desperate to get my hands dirty and paint. My experience was never going to be complete until I picked up a spray can in Santiago and got to work. There were two things that struck me. First, the overwhelming gratitude of passersby. Second, the sense of satisfaction at sharing a piece of art in the public domain." LORD K2

"I would search the streets, go to factories on my bicycle to see if I could find buckets and dry rollers that could be revived with some hot water. I have painted walls with a mix of latex and oil. If you have a messed up roller, you use it and come out with a new texture. People will say, 'Water with water and oil with oil.' I tell everyone, learn to use all types of materials." PIGUAN

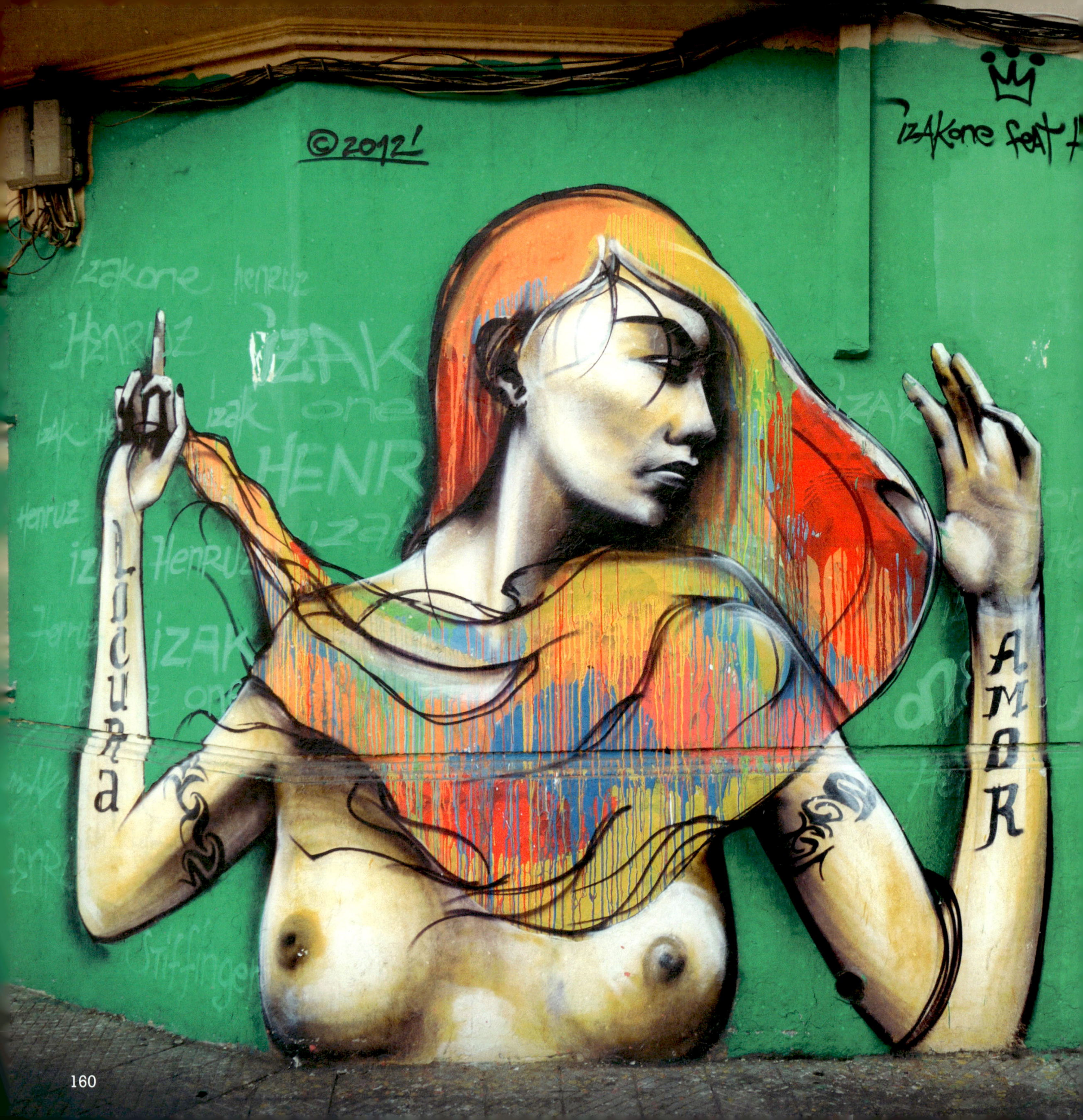
©2012!
izAkone feat
Locura
AMOR

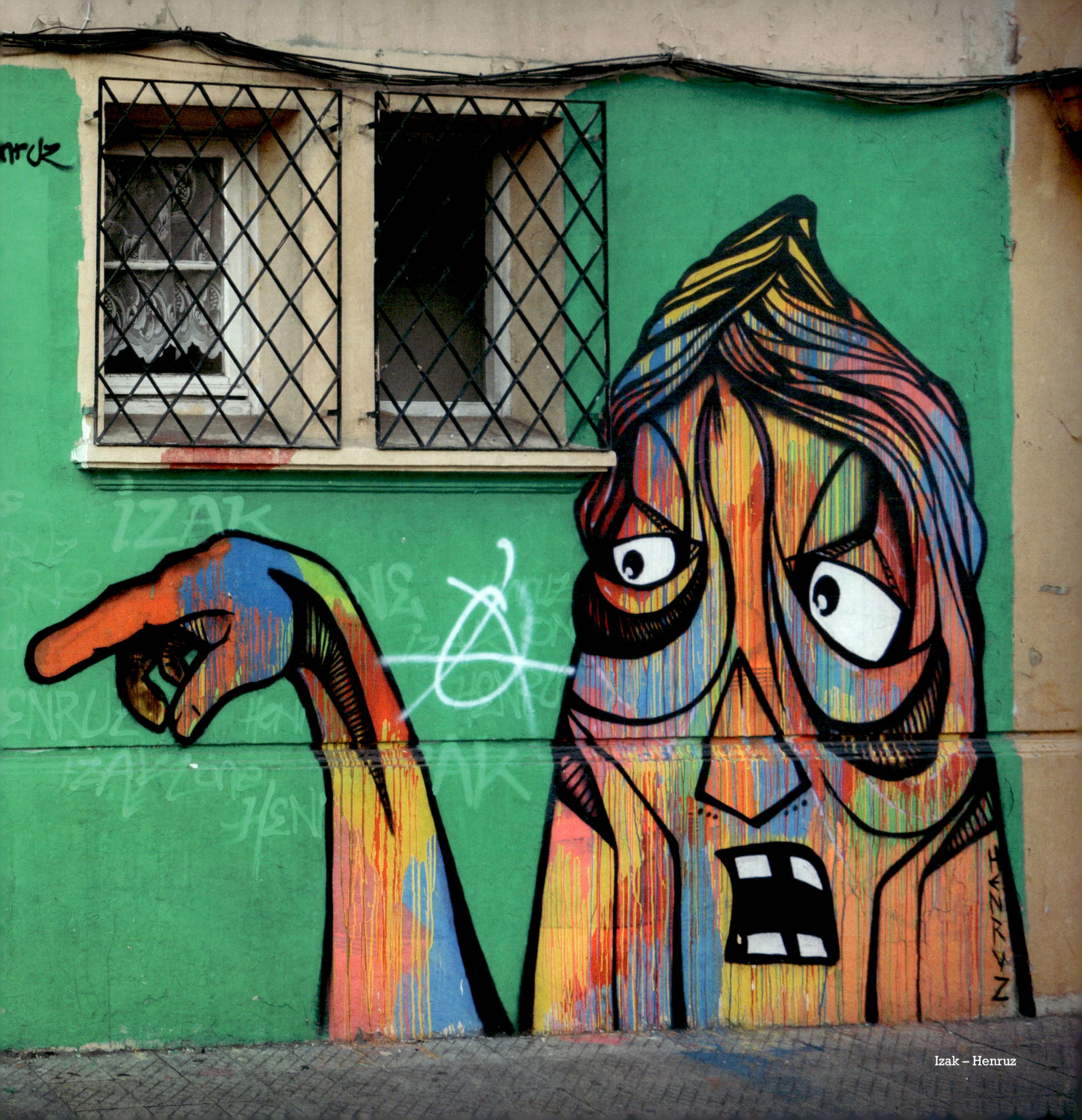

Izak – Henruz

"After accumulating so many paintings, I did some introspection. I realized that what I do is capture what's lacking in my surroundings, because what I depict is mostly nature. I try to introduce fantasy and imagination to survive within this gray world. Some say that painting is an escape, but for me it is a form of living well with life just as it is, gray, but from a fantasy world. To be able to pursue this, I created this visual style. At first, I painted with plain colors, then I rose to the three-dimensional level, and in this manner, my paintings became more realistic, more tangible, a portal to another world." **SOFRENIA**

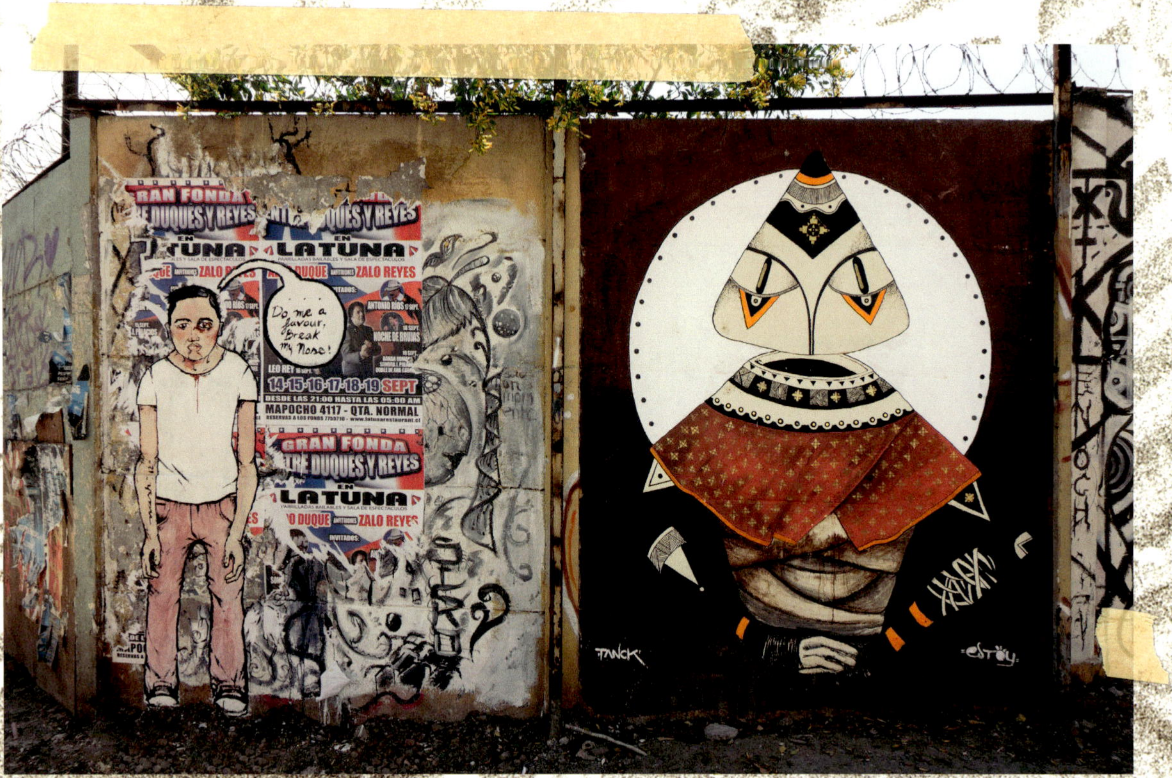

Tanck – Estoy

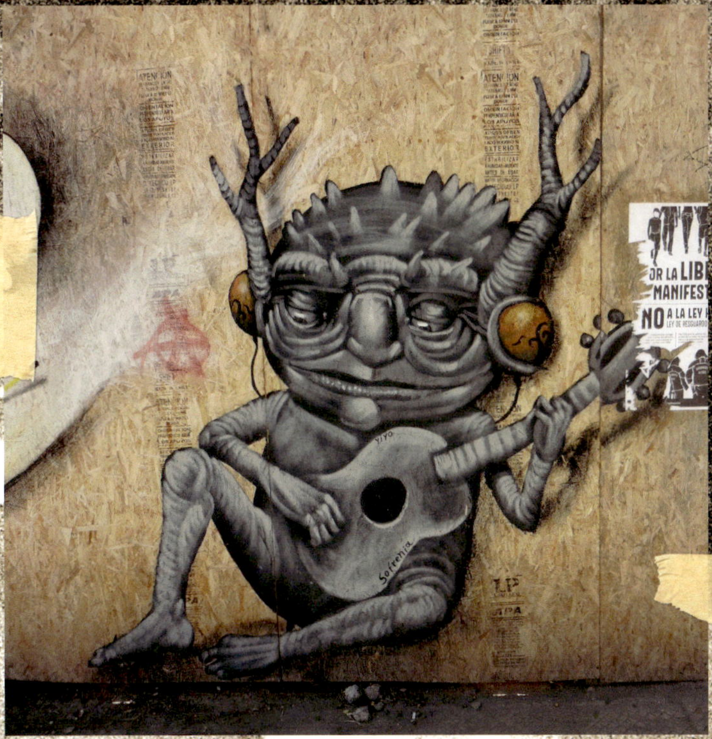

Sofrenia

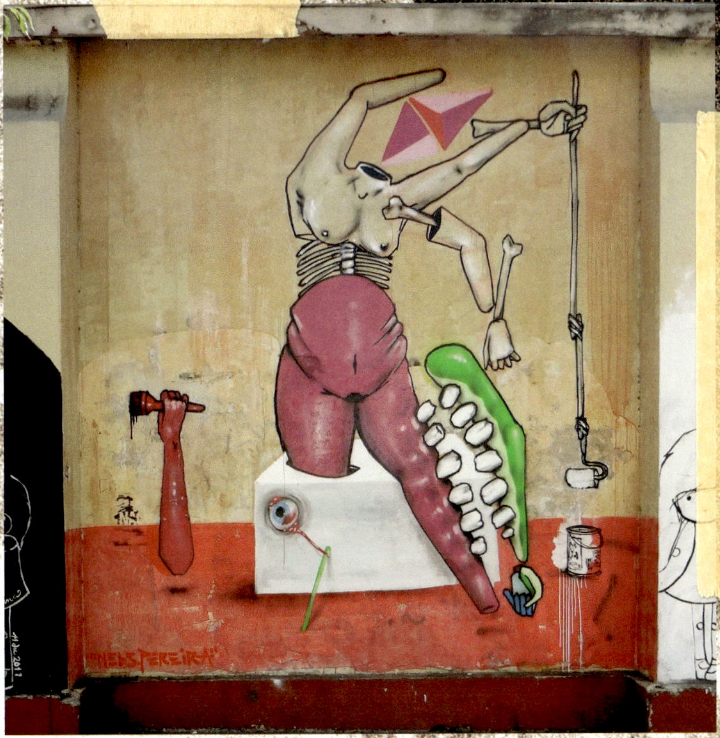

Nebs

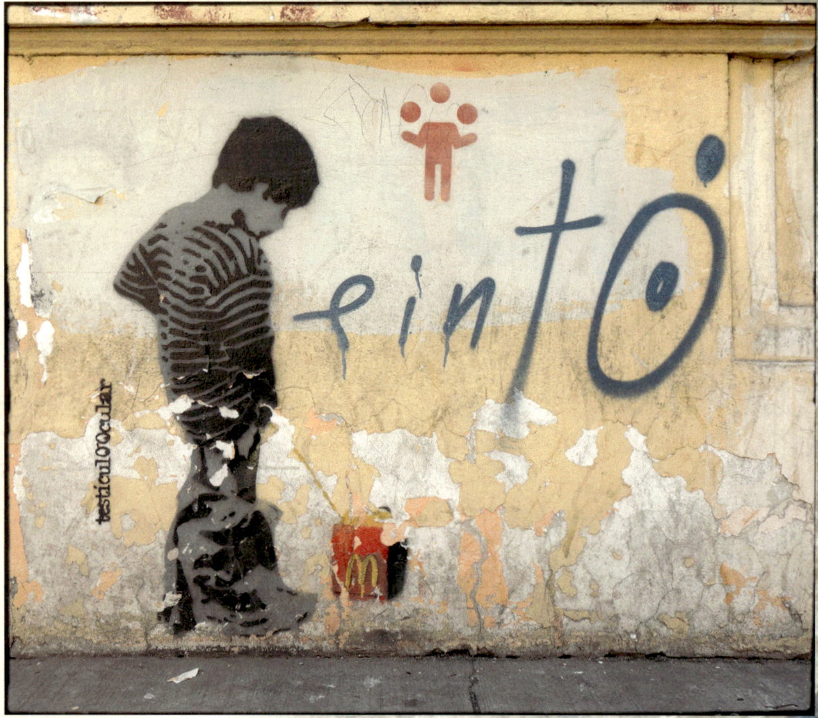

"Graffiti is the weapon I use on the street." PINTO

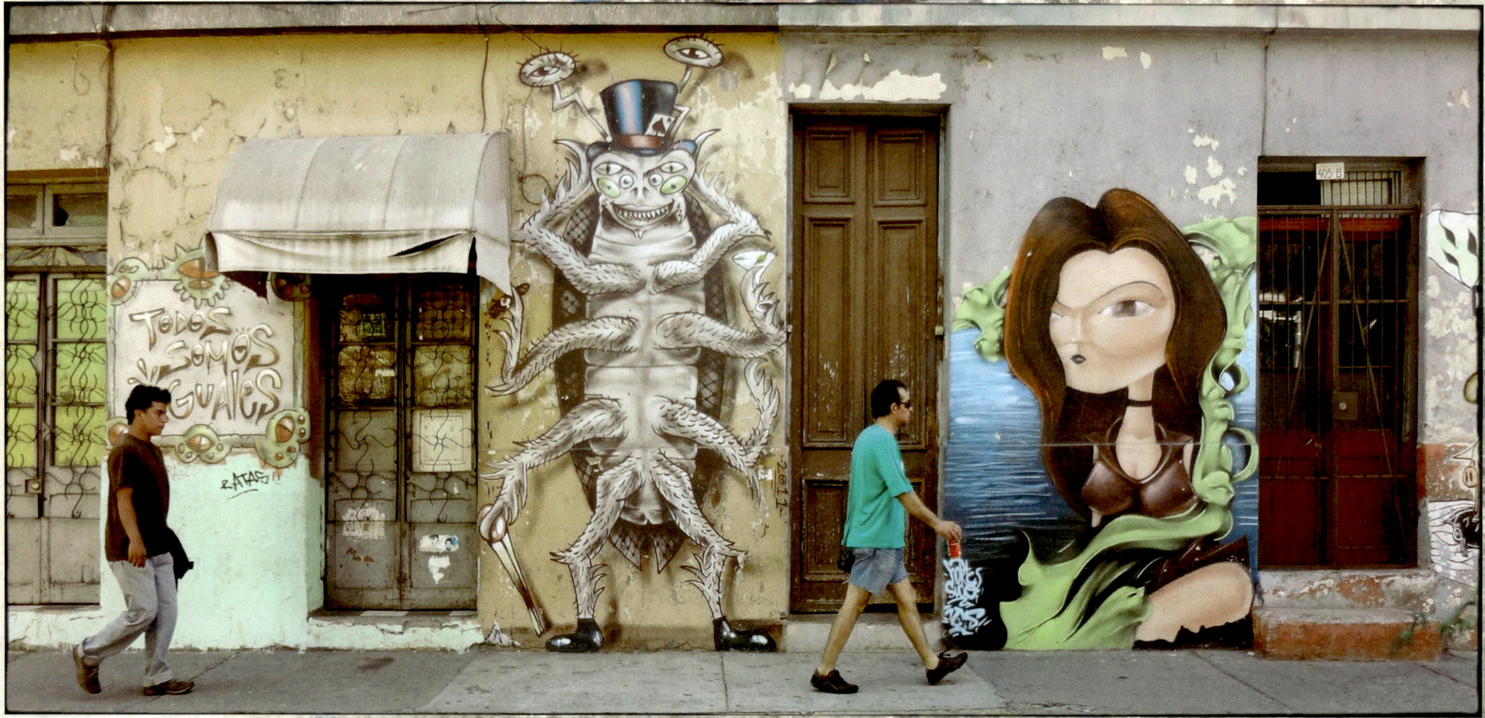

Piojonewen

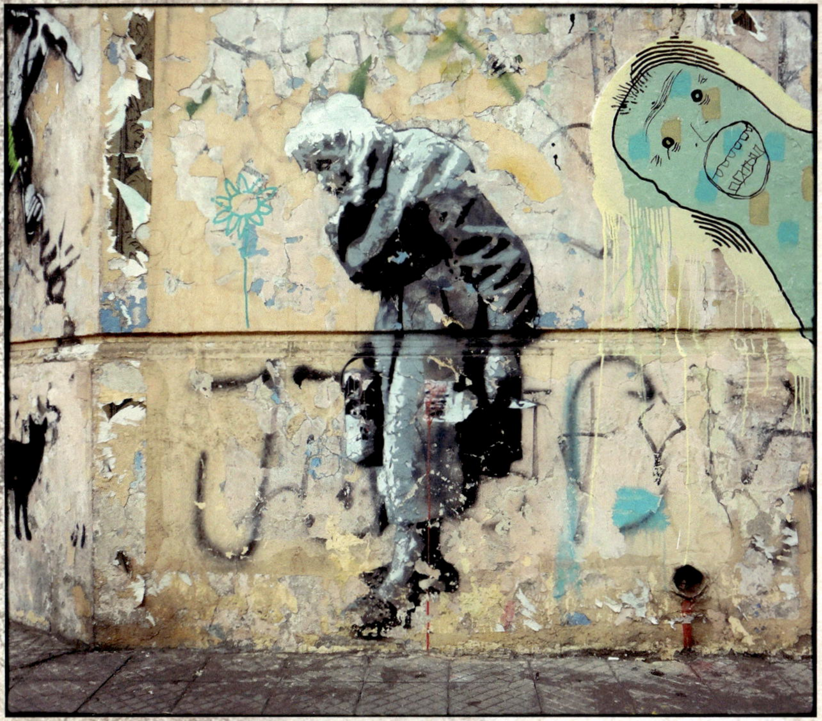

"I don't paint for the fame! The canvas wasn't big enough for me to liberate the load that I carried on my back. I have many things in my head that aren't easy to release through conversation, writing, watching TV, or partying. So, I paint on the wall. I want people to gain consciousness through my work. Some attain this by music, but I do it by painting. I am unhappy about people being force-fed shit from the mass media into their heads, treated like puppets. I have noticed it, and this is my weapon for expressing it on the street, I feel it is my responsibility. I like bold colors and terror—heavy stuff. There is a stencil by Nosferatu that reads, "blood sucker." Vampires without respect! There is a social message behind it, wanting to show that those dingbats want to suck our blood. You are a professional, I am a laborer. Painting also helps you unload that. I'm not resentful, but I can tell that there are more restrictions for laborers than for an idiot who had doors open for him. Chile is overcome by painting, and this is why I like to put on a strong image, an image that makes people think, that clashes, and that people will despise." **PINTO**

"I met a friend, Capitan Cochayuyo, in college and as we conversed about our desires and the ideas that we could share, the theme of stencils came up. It was something that we both had a passion for. From there we began to come up with images, without reason and with no theme. Our main goal was to appeal aesthetically, but the work that followed was intended as a rebellious or critical act. As I said, they were born from an aesthetic desire, to appeal to the people so that they would stop on the street to observe these big works with admiration and take a break the monotonous daily commute. Generally, stencils come in a small format, but in our group we try to make quick stencils that are invasive and large-scale, that disturb and grab people's attention even if they are passing by for a split second. First, we would think of the idea, we would choose an image, and then we would work on it with a program if we needed to mix images. From there we would apply a filter and choose the colors that we wanted, three or four, depending on the project. Then we would project the image on the wall and we would set out cartons to later mark them with felt tip pens and cut them out. Now the end result is rebellious, and a process is being generated where the art is being moved from the gallery to the street, from the street to the gallery, and techniques are being combined. There is a synchronicity going on and although it is not yet concrete, it is a very interesting process that has to do with brushes, graffiti, and stencil. I think it's valid. As long as it carries a message, as long as the image makes people feel certain things, then we are talking about art." **PIOJONEWEN**

"I like everything connected to urban intervention, everything that comes out of the gray or the ordinary of this society. The first thing that I like about it is that it's accessible to everyone. You just ask permission to paint a wall, or use an abandoned one or bomb one in the middle of the night. In a way, it's like you're stuffing people up to their ears in art. Not just the ones that want to view art. The second thing is that graffiti has become my perspective, my point of view. It's a way of laying out my ideas, my needs, my projects, my formation as a person. It's one of the things that I most love about this life, being able to take a can, my cans of paint, rollers, and sketches and go out into the street to paint. I don't see myself doing anything else. The two material things that I love the most are my spray paints and my bicycle, two tools that help me commute around this city and see it from different angles than most people see it. When I was about seven years old, I began to pay attention to what occurred on the streets, to notice graffiti. I feel fortunate because graffiti found me." HIPSO

Hipso

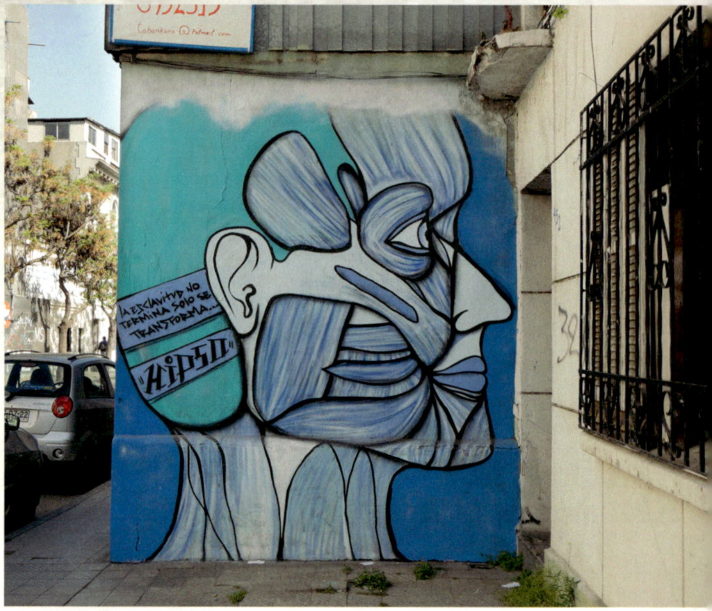

"I like to add color to the neighbourhood, a constructive noise that contributes something to the city, so that children can see beautiful artworks that makes them happy." ALTERNA

Coas - Hipso

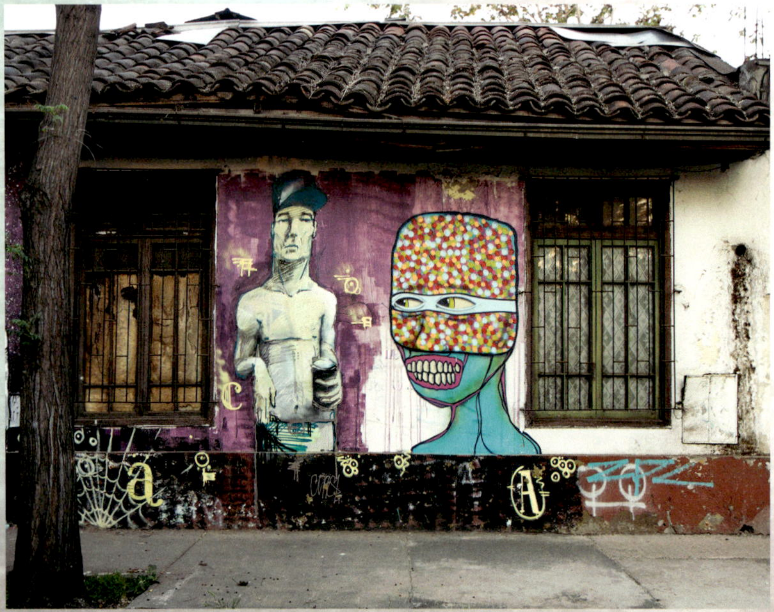

"I like to paint legally so that I can work calmly and dedicate time and energy to my works, but I don't have anything against illegal graffiti. I like both. I find that there are some artists that have style and attitude when they work quickly. In my case, it's a matter of expressing myself and showing my work so that people can see it and appreciate it. I like the movement of the street, the stories that happen around a wall; this is why I continue to paint. I am inspired by music, other painters, my friends, and people that I know. I can paint a work that reflects the friendships that I have. I really like people that do something and have a passion for that thing, because this inspires and nurtures me. I seek for people to view my artworks and feel better, feel full, be touched to a point of sighing. This is what I look for, to provoke an emotion, whether it be love, rejection, anger, or anything else." YALUS

Spam

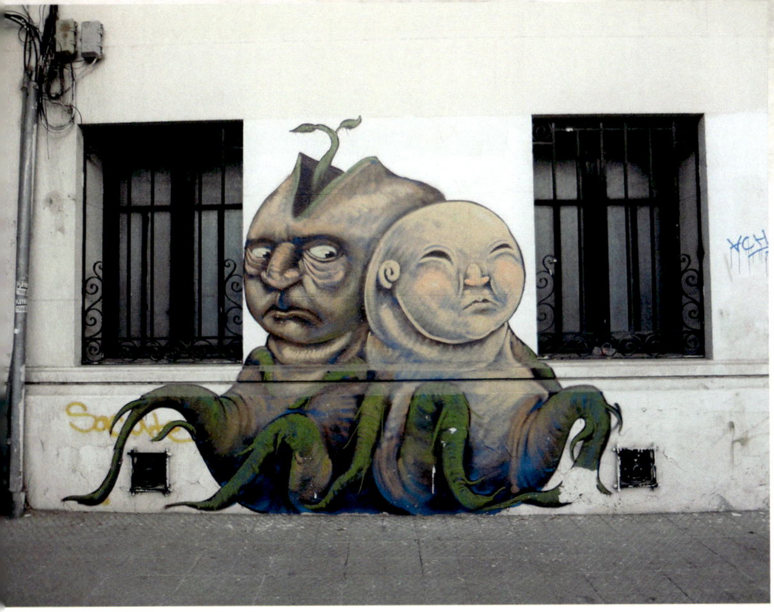

Spam

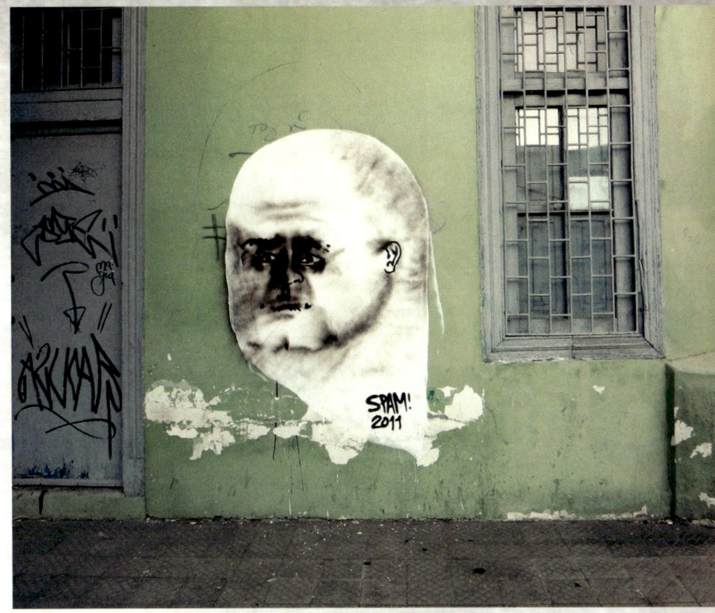

"People come up to you to talk and they may not understand the paintings, but they make an effort to understand them, and this is what I want, for people to sit and think." INJUSTICIA

"Graffiti is a form of expression and communication. It is the art of the twentieth century. We live in a technological age and spray is a technological object that requires a meticulous industrial process. People prefer to see graffiti on the street rather than to go see a painting in a gallery. Graffiti has been established in Santiago for a long time. The level is really good, and there exist many possibilities when it comes to materials. I also find that much of the graffiti in Santiago is influenced by what is painted in Europe or in the United States. I believe that people are realizing that originality goes beyond influence or technique. They're noticing that they must opt for a more innovative proposal that transmits new concepts, forms, and different techniques. Many times when one paints on the street it has to be done illegally and this causes clashes with other people. To produce a more elaborate piece, it is necessary to have permission, and it is easy to obtain it nowadays." LE DORIAN

Naira

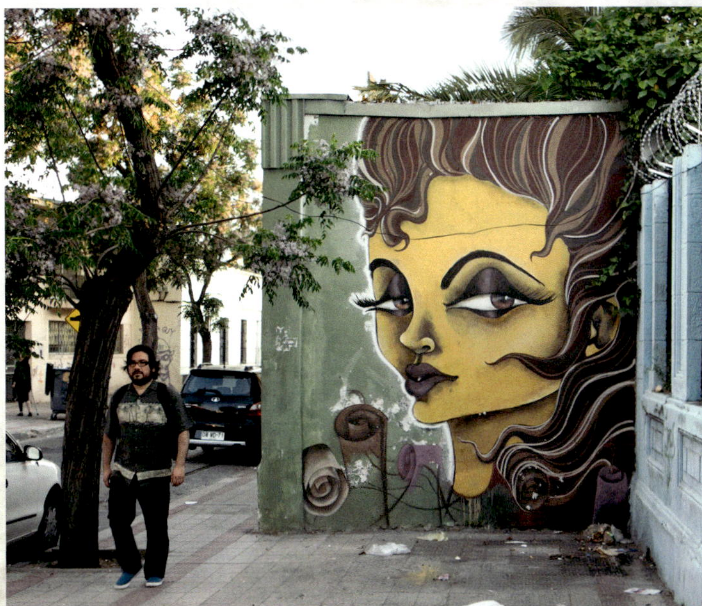

"12Brillos have seized the mansion at Cueto 993. Thanks to squatters rights, they are now the proud owners of their new home. Feel free to drop by and pay them a visit. They are a hospitable bunch."

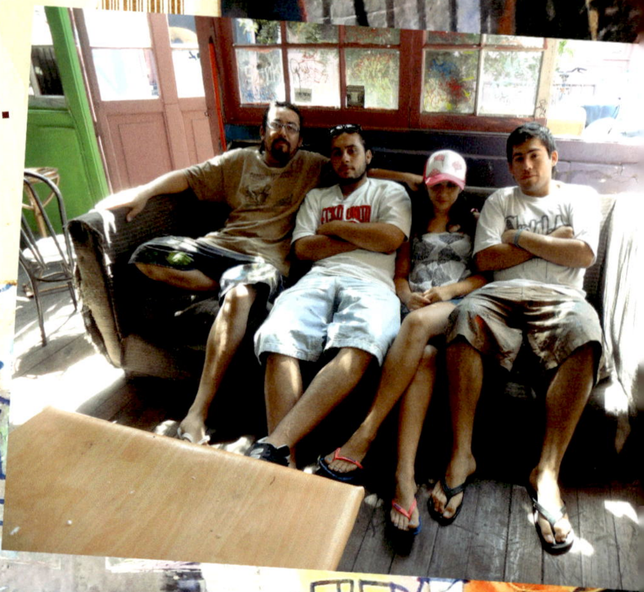

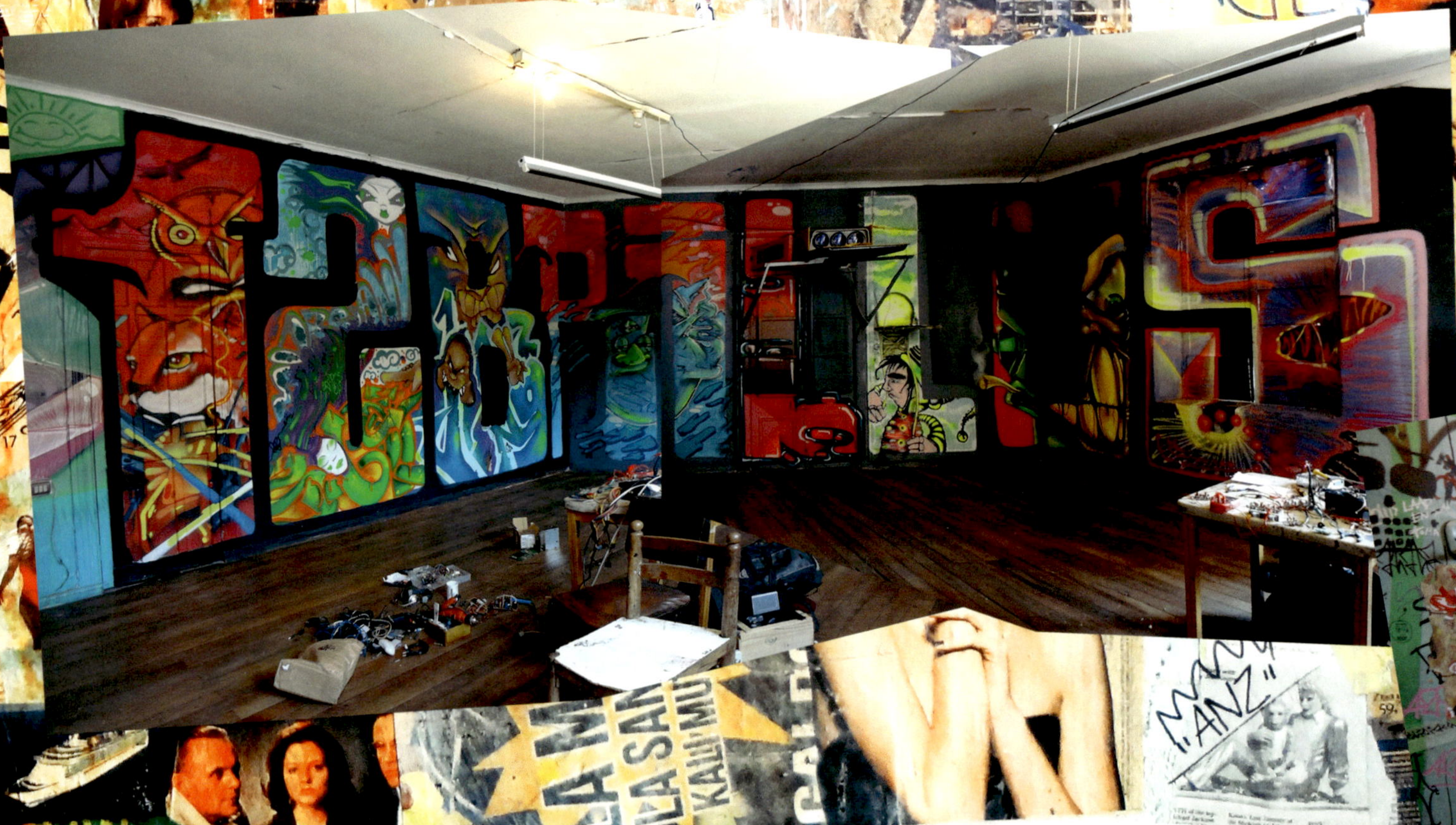

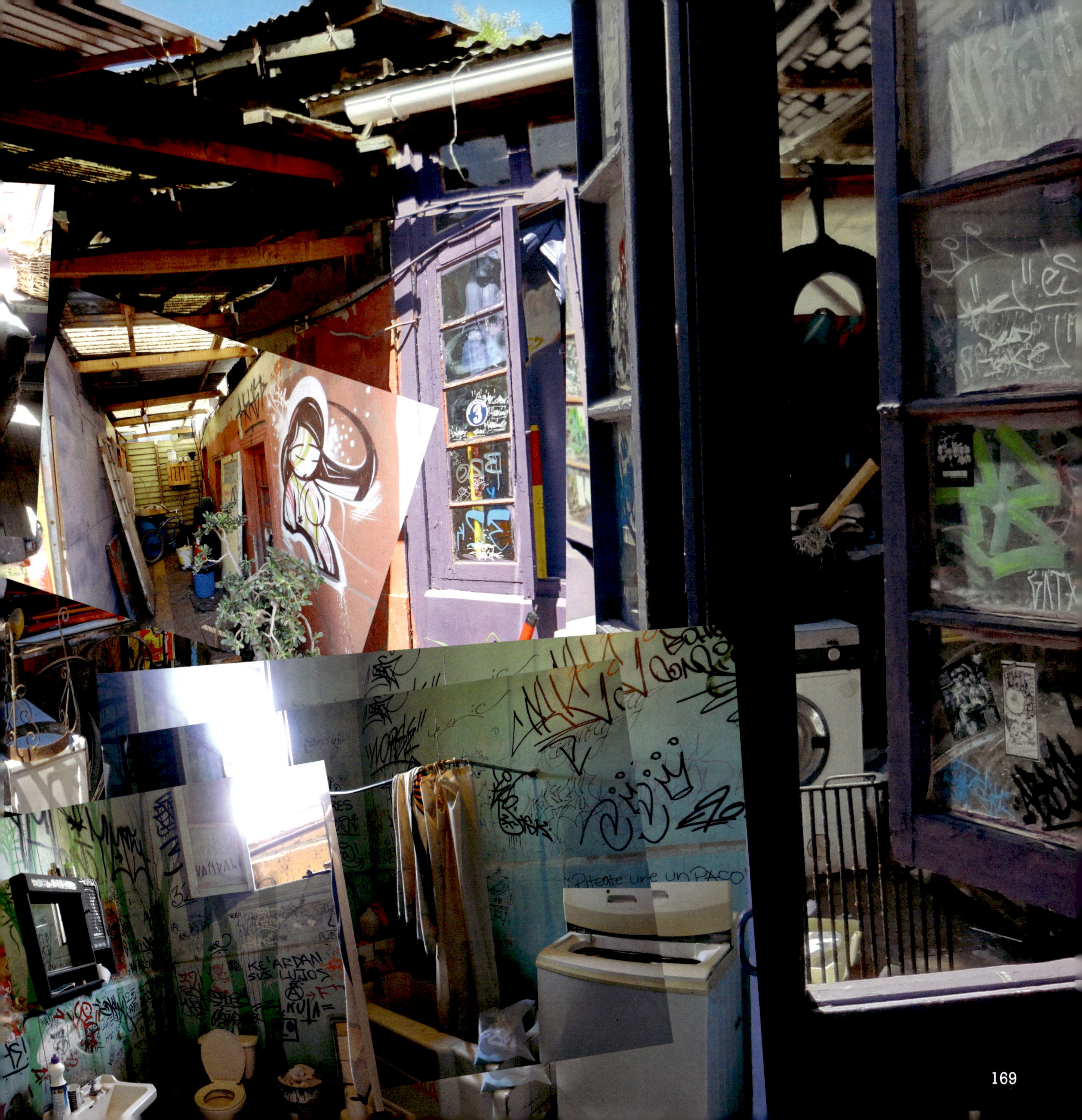

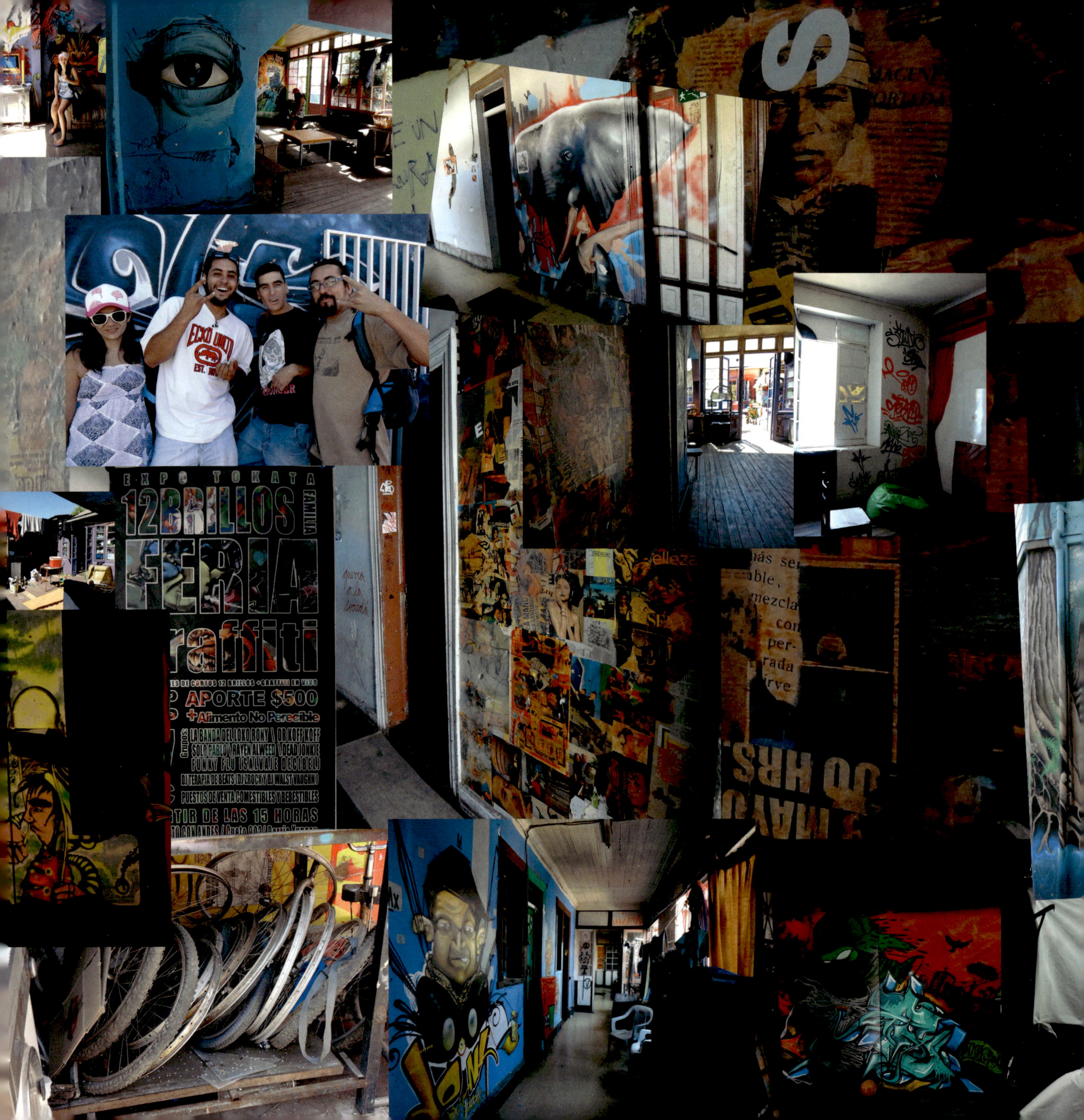
EXPO TOKATA
12BRILLOS
FAMILIA
FERIA
raffiti
ES DE CORTOS 12 BRILLOS +GRAFFITI EN VIVO
APORTE $500
+Alimento No Perecible
Grupos: LA BANDA DEL LOKO RONY \ DR KOFF KOFF
SOLO PABLO \ RAYEN ALWEED \ DEAD JONKIE
FUNKY FLU (SALVAJE DECIBEL)
DJ TERAPIA DE BEATS (DJ ZROCK Y DJ WALST VAUGHN)
PUESTOS DE VENTA COMESTIBLES Y BEBESTIBLES
RTIR DE LAS 15 HORAS
ECKŌ UNLTD
EST.
HRS

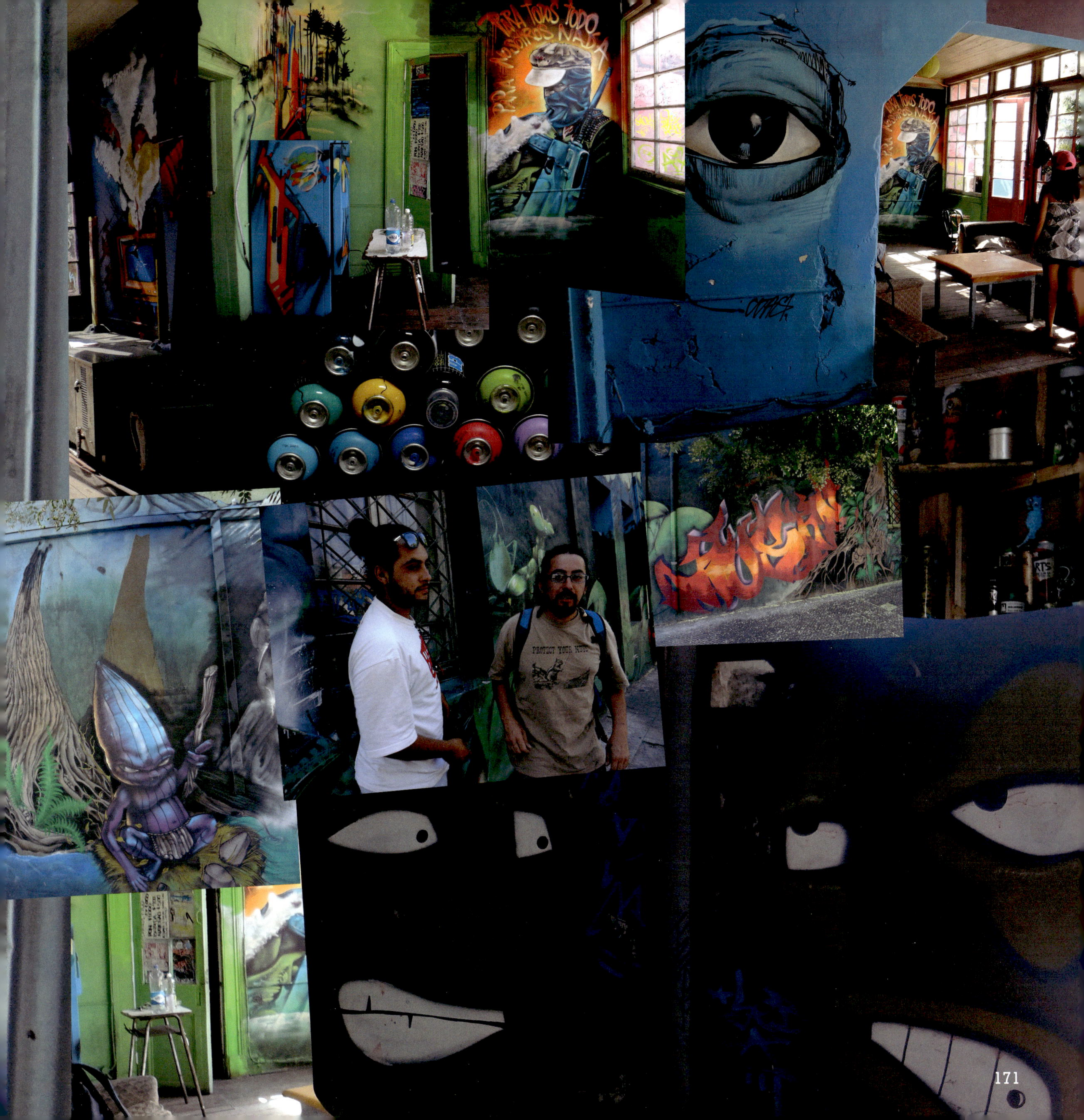
PARA TODOS TODO
PRA NOSOTROS NADA

INDOORS

"Most Chilean graffiti artists paint indoors. Some maintain the same style both indoors and outdoors but most differentiate between the two as outdoor painting tends to have a different purpose. A mural is designed to be appreciated in a fleeting moment, therefore it is often bold and striking. When one looks at an indoor piece, he usually has more time to appreciate what is drawn and pays more attention to the finer details, therefore indoor pieces tend to be far more elaborate.

"Graffiti artists use all sorts of mediums to paint on. A factor that tends to distinguish them from other artists is that they often find things on the street and paint on them, such as discarded plywood, advertising bollards, wooden planks, and other abandoned materials. Naturally, this keeps costs to a minimum and can enhance the piece due to its urban appeal.

"Another big reason for painting indoors is that it offers an avenue to make an income out of painting. Graffiti artists often hold exhibitions and sell their pieces for varying prices, often depending on their reputation on the streets.

"In Chile, there are a large number of talented artists who have a lot to sell, but unfortunately many of them struggle to sell their pieces as the demand isn't sufficient enough. A handful have moved oversees and doors have opened." DENST

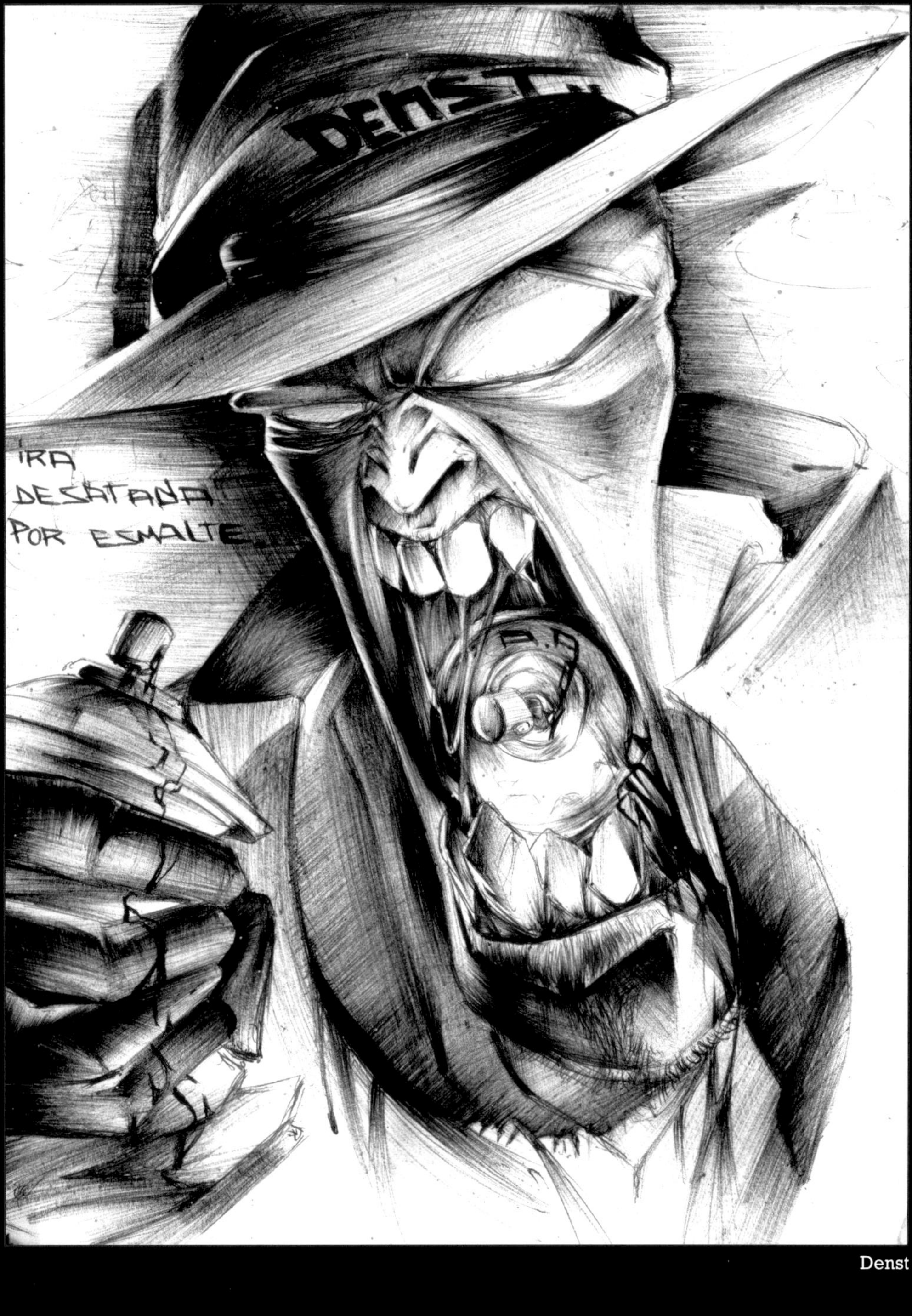

Denst

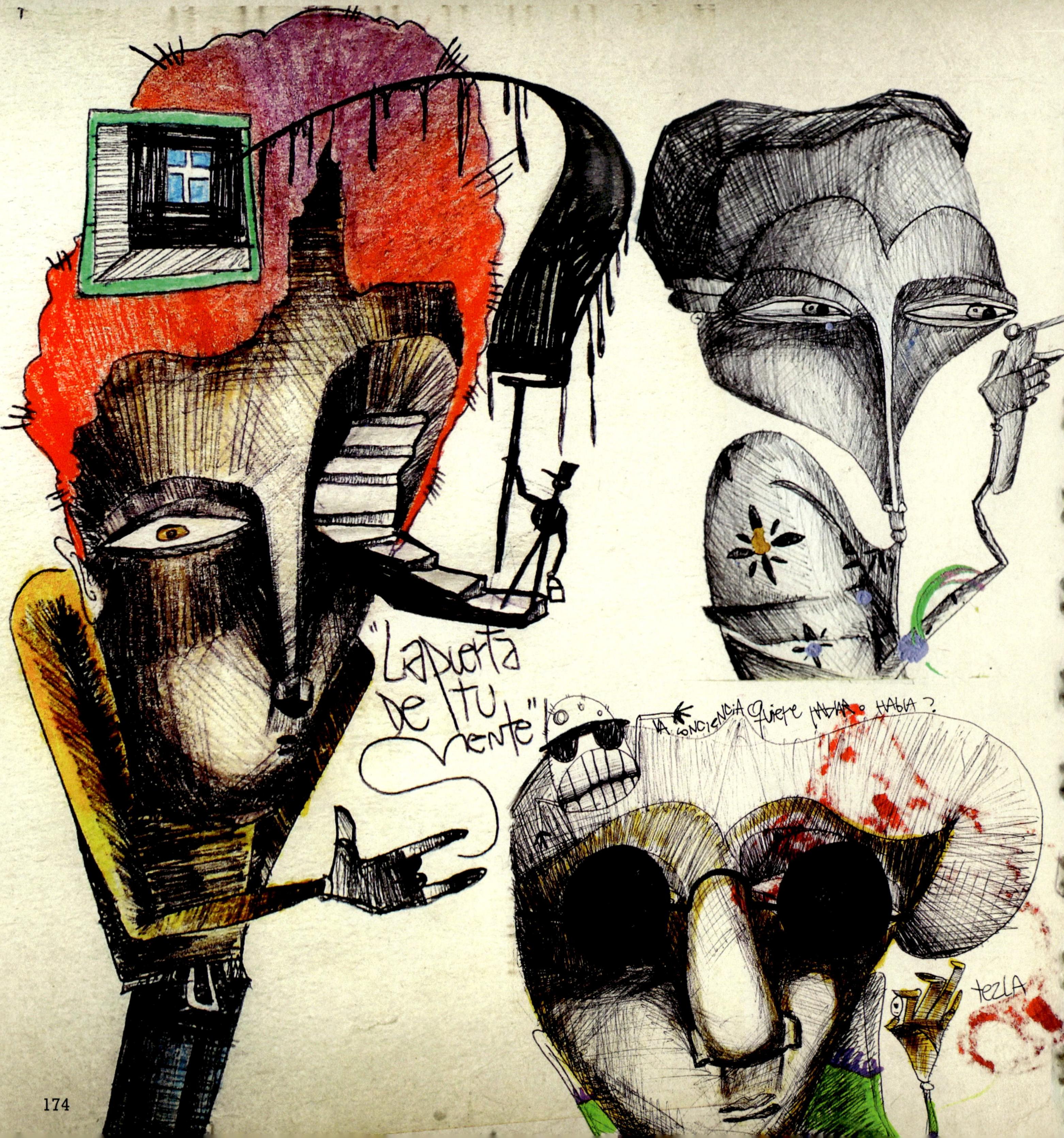
"La puerta
De tu
mente"
LA CONCIENCIA quiere HABLAR o HABLA?
TEZLA

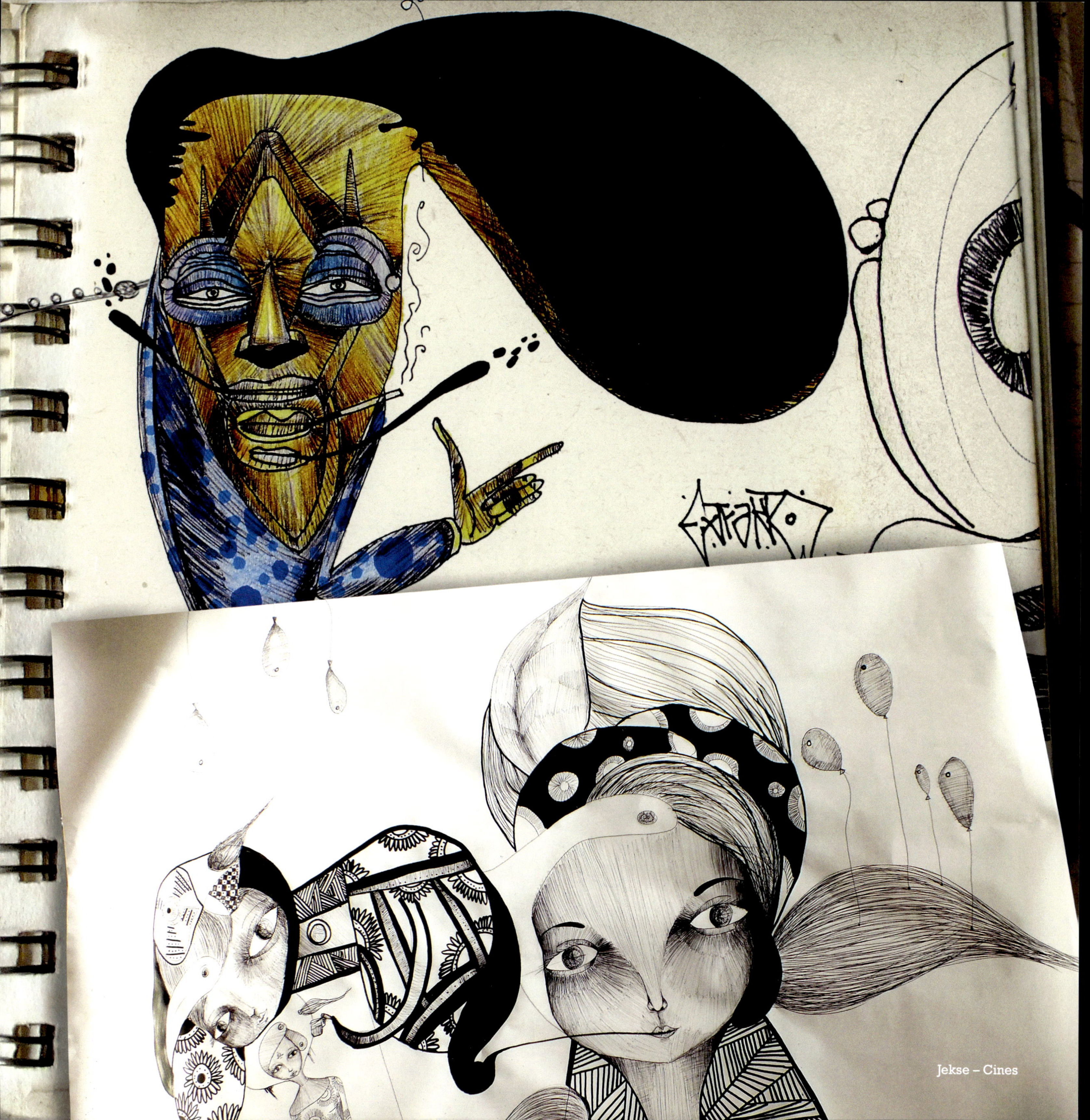

Jekse – Cines

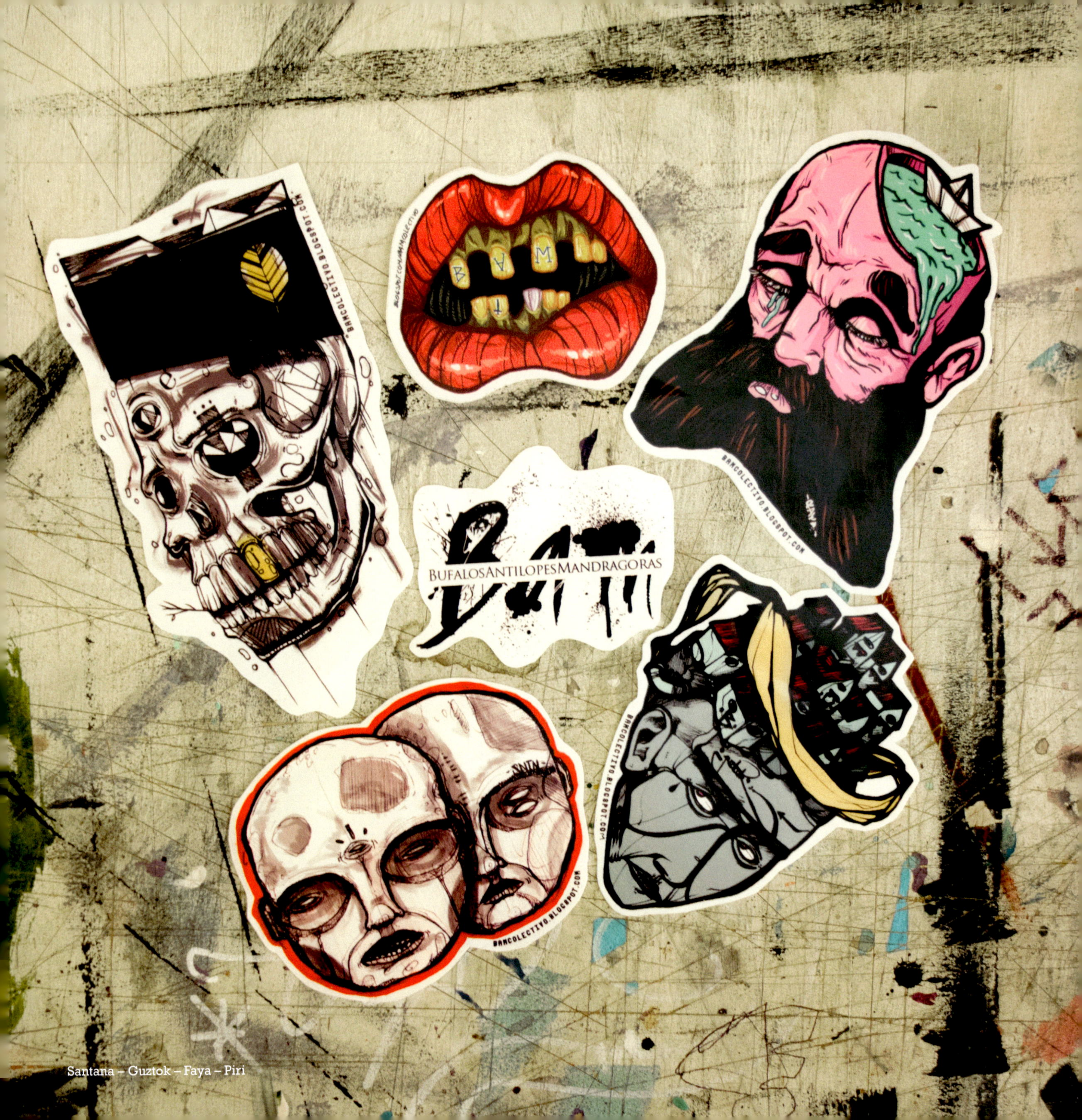

Santana – Guztok – Faya – Piri

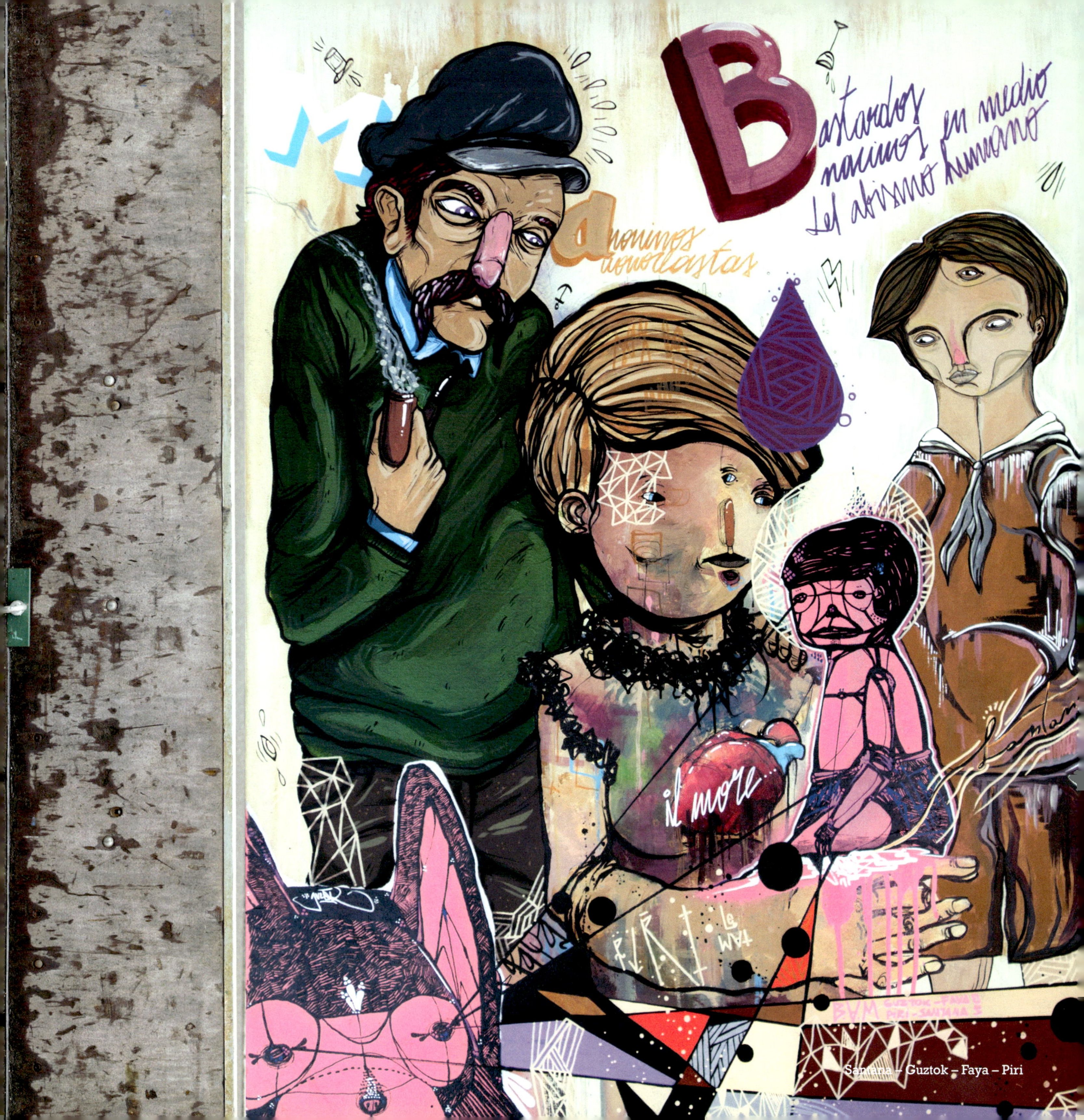

Santana – Guztok – Faya – Piri

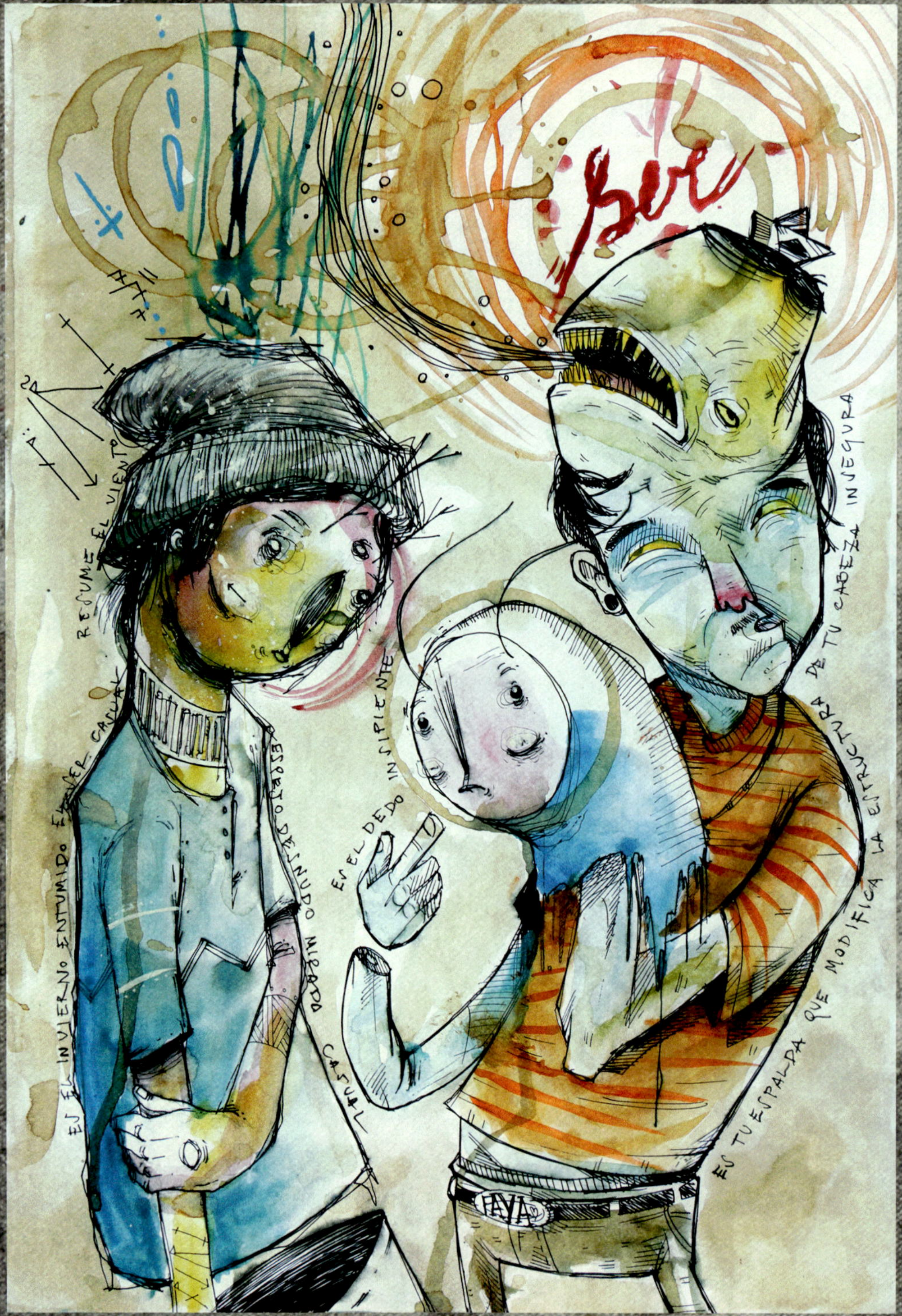
ser
ES EL DEDO INSIPIENTE
ES TU ESPALDA QUE MODIFICA LA ESTRUCTURA DE TU CABEZA INSEGURA
FAYA

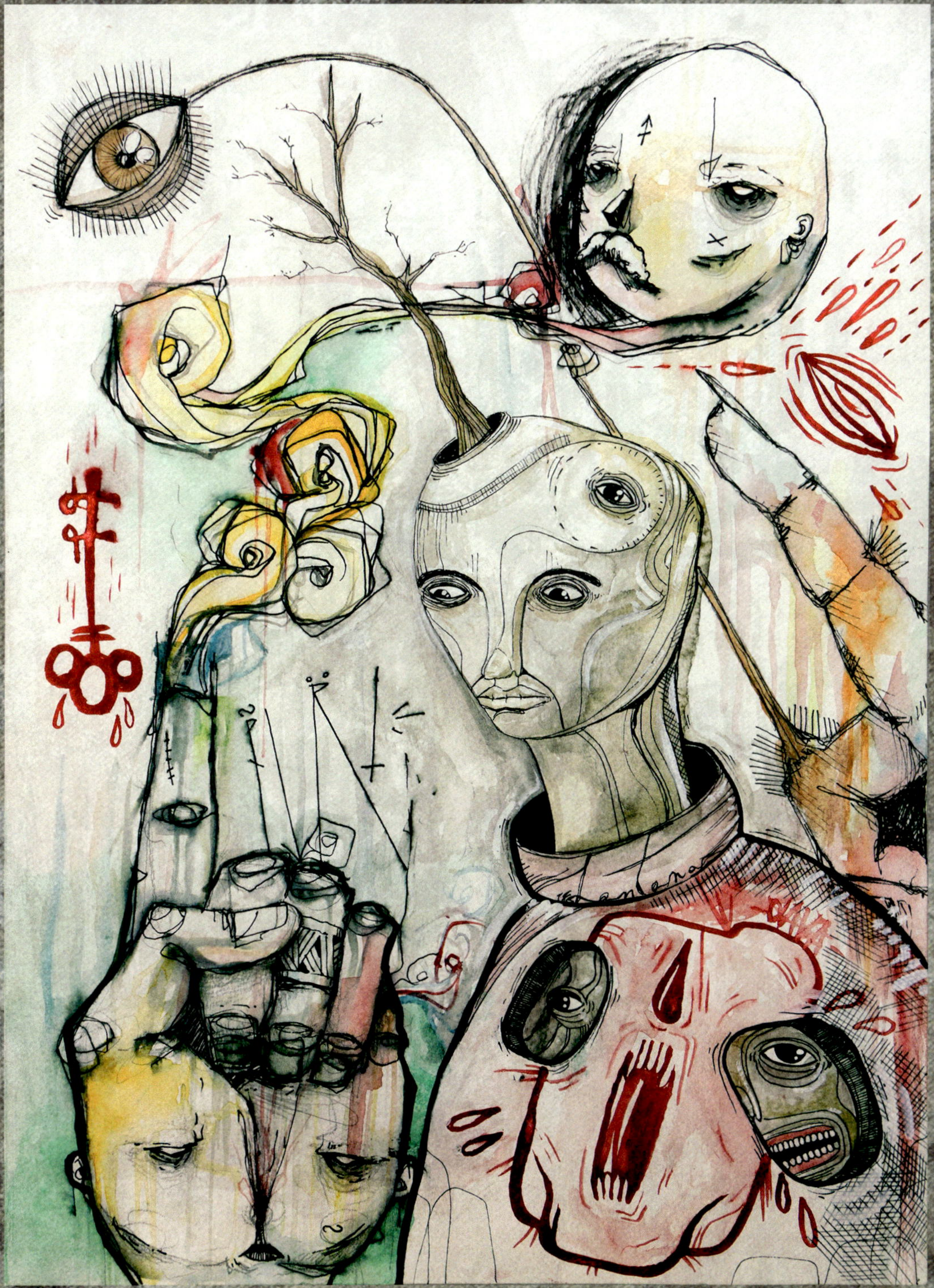

Santana – Piri

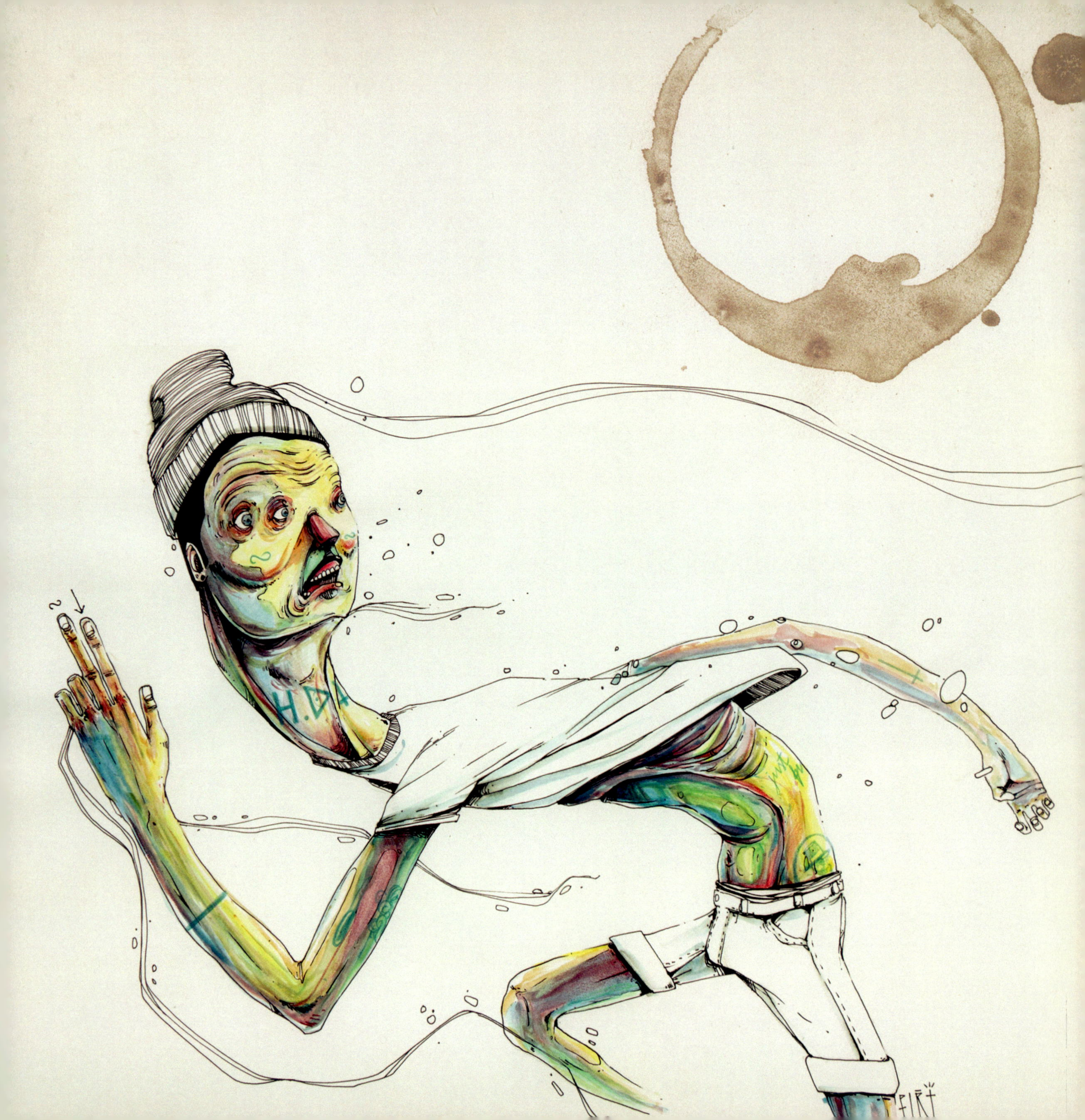

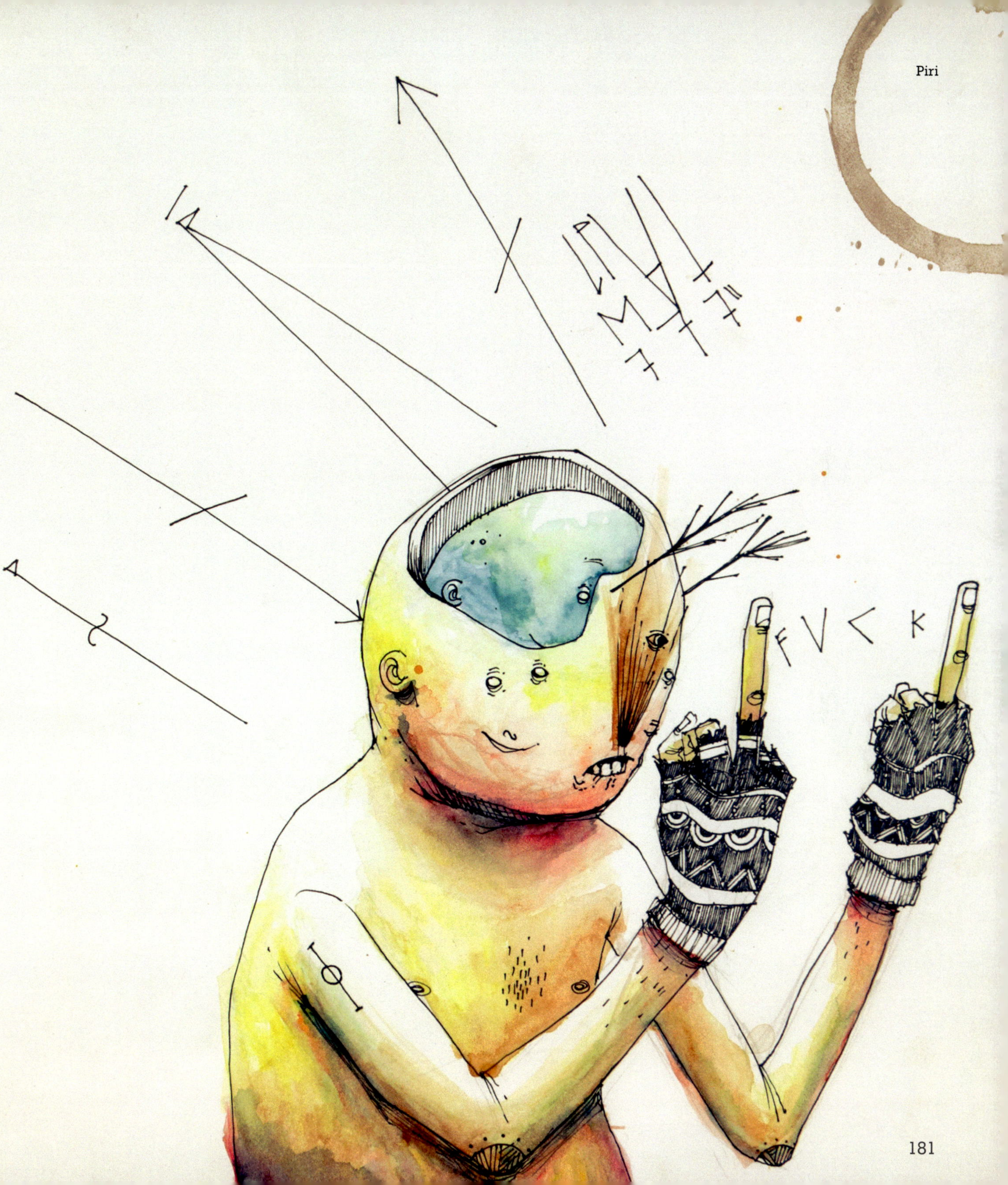
FVCK

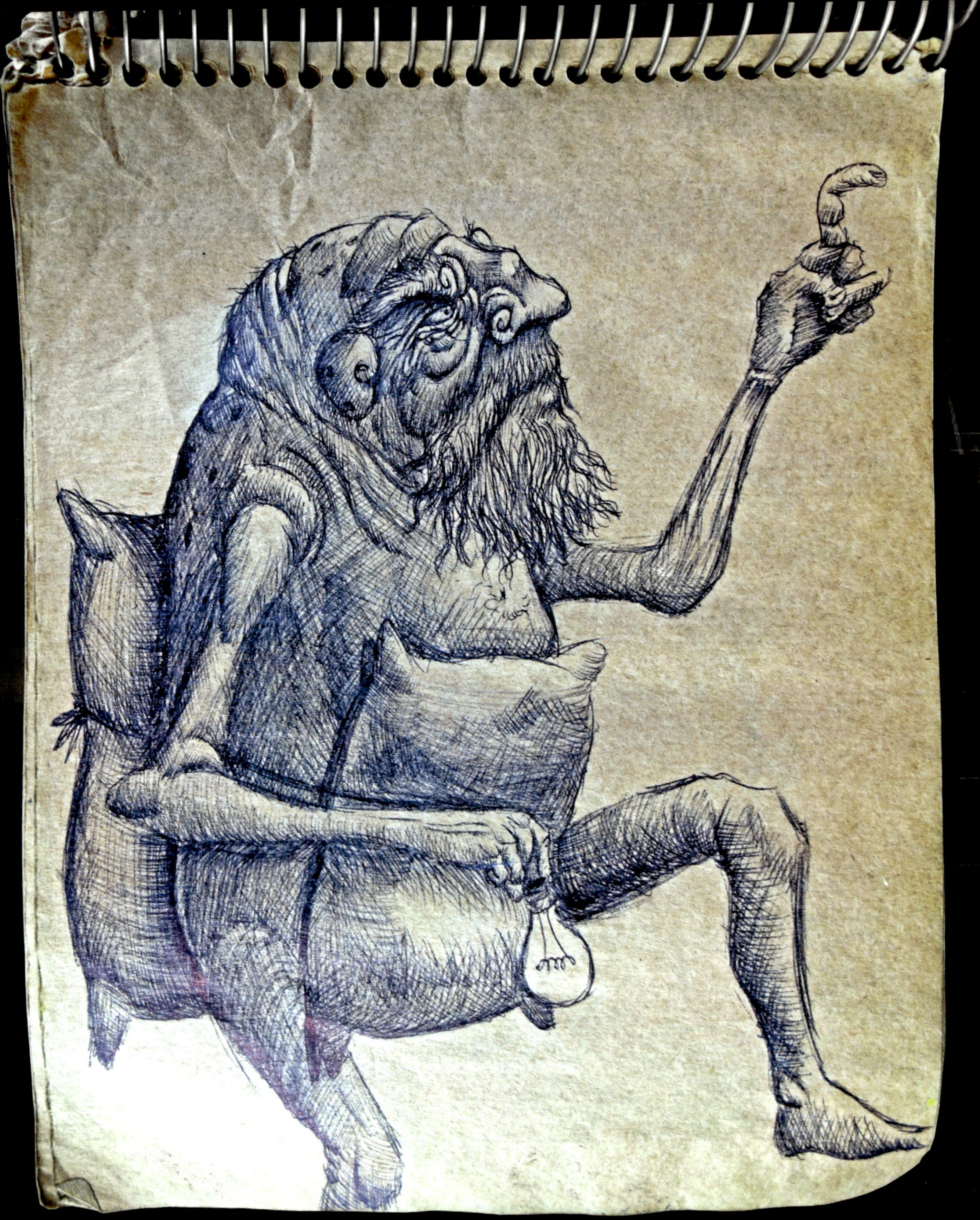

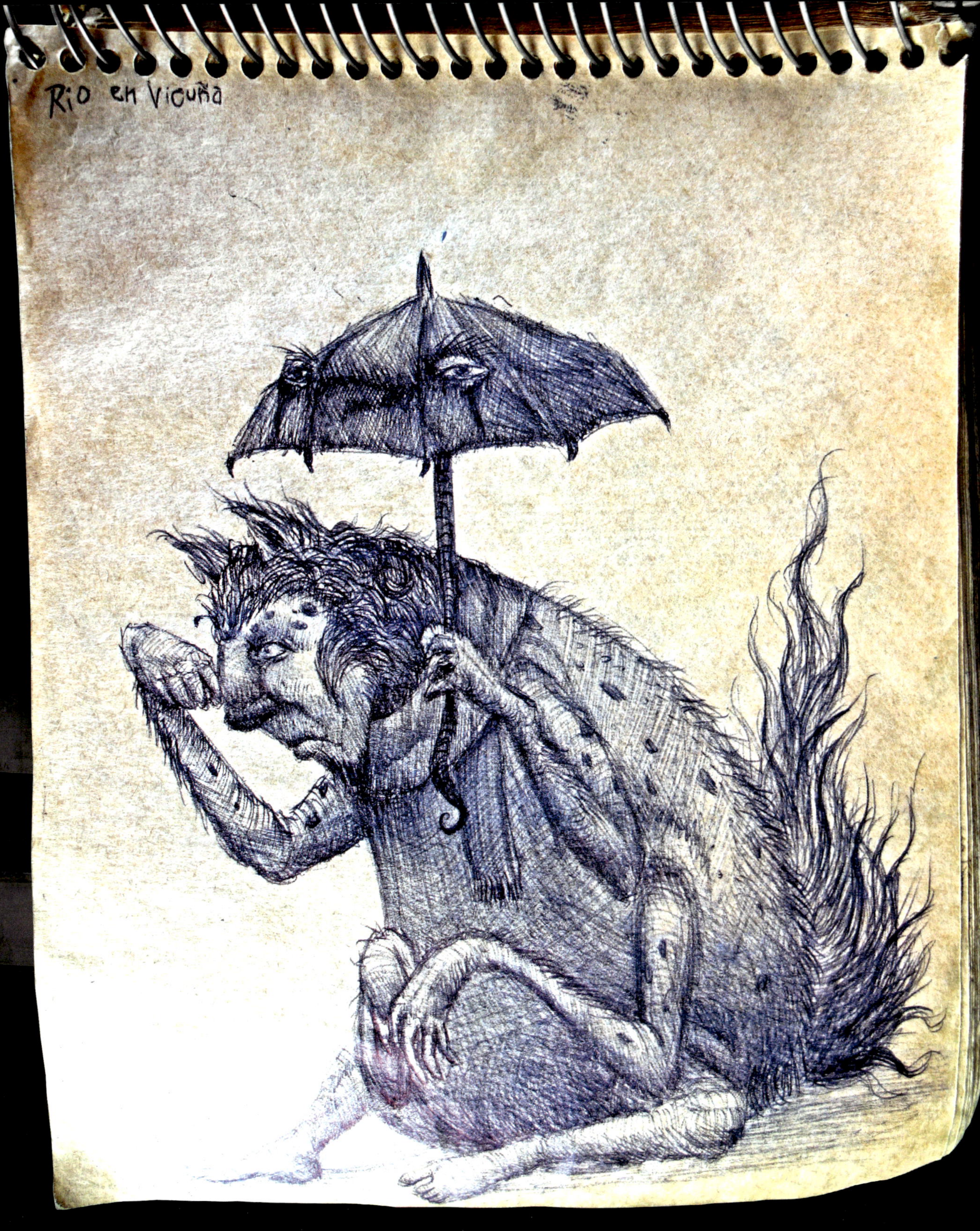

Sofrenia

Acknowledgments

Cover Design: Jorge Cordoba
Book Cover Photo: Camila Peña
Back Cover Artwork: Naira
Graphic Designer: Jorge Cordoba and his design collaborators,
Joaquín Zelaya, Julia Pérez Cassinelli and Julieta Dolinsk
Art Direction: Lord K2
Photography: Lord K2
Transcription: Alexandra Jamieson and Fernanda Alvez Macrini
Translation: Stacey Deveca
Chilean Anthropologist: Brian Gray
Assistant Interviewers: Zaines and Piguan

An expression of gratitude to the Chilean graffiti community whose passion and purpose made it easy to gather all that was necessary to build this book.

Respect to Jorge Cordoba, for his patience, expertise, and attention to detail, as well as for mentoring me throughout the book.

A big thanks to Brian Gray for his insights into the Chilean graffiti culture and for helping me assemble the text.

Last, but not least, a hug and much appreciation to Stacey Deveca for her tireless work in translating the text from Spanish so meticulously.

I dedicate this book to my colorful, fun-loving nephews Oscar and Ely, who I hope will be inspired by these art pieces to paint, spray, and continue the process of expression.

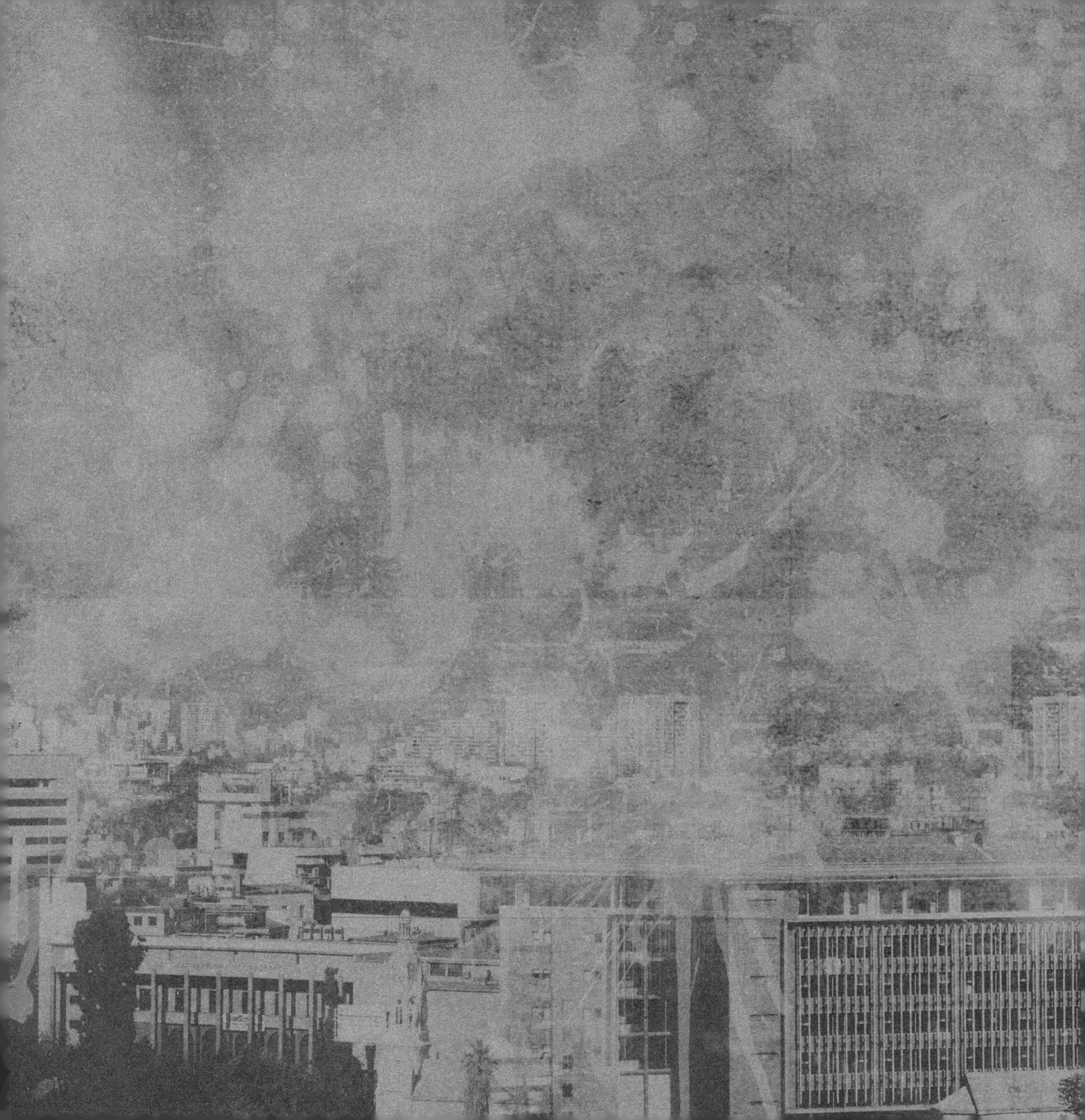